The Neighborhood

James A. Millward, Series Editor

The Silk Roads series is made possible by the generous support of the Henry Luce Foundation's Asia Program. Founded in 1936, the Luce Foundation is a not-for-profit philanthropic organization devoted to promoting innovation in academic, policy, religious, and art communities. The Asia Program aims to foster cultural and intellectual exchange between the United States and the countries of East and Southeast Asia, and to create scholarly and public resources for improved understanding of Asia in the United States.

The Neighborhood

SPACE, STATE, AND DAILY LIFE
IN A MANCHURIAN CITY

Nianshen Song

The University of Chicago Press   Chicago and London

The University of Chicago Press, Chicago 60637
The University of Chicago Press, Ltd., London
© 2025 by The University of Chicago

34 33 32 31 30 29 28 27 26 25   1 2 3 4 5

ISBN-13: 978-0-226-84328-5 (cloth)
ISBN-13: 978-0-226-84330-8 (paper)
ISBN-13: 978-0-226-84329-2 (e-book)
DOI: https://doi.org/10.7208/chicago/9780226843292.001.0001

Library of Congress Cataloging-in-Publication Data

Names: Song, Nianshen, author
Title: The neighborhood : space, state, and daily life in a Manchurian city /
    Nianshen Song.
Other titles: Silk roads (Chicago, Ill.)
Description: Chicago : The University of Chicago Press, 2025. | Series: Silk
    roads | Includes bibliographical references and index.
Identifiers: LCCN 2025006528 | ISBN 9780226843285 cloth |
    ISBN 9780226843308 paperback | ISBN 9780226843292 ebook
Subjects: LCSH: Social change—China—Shenyang (Liaoning Sheng) |
    Xita (Shenyang, Liaoning Sheng, China)—History—20th century |
    Xitas (Shenyang, Liaoning Sheng, China)—Social conditions—
    20th century | Xita (Shenyang, Liaoning Sheng, China)—Economic
    conditions—20th century
Classification: LCC DS797.62.S546 S66 2025
LC record available at https://lccn.loc.gov/2025006528

Authorized Representative for EU General Product Safety Regulation
(GPSR) queries: **Easy Access System Europe**—Mustamäe tee 50,
10621 Tallinn, Estonia, gpsr.requests@easproject.com
Any other queries: https://press.uchicago.edu/press/contact.html

To Yanling, Chuhe, and Charles

Frontispiece. "The Wretched Ruin of the West Tower," a Japanese postcard showing the West Stupa. Lafayette College Libraries, Imperial Postcard Collection.

CONTENTS

ILLUSTRATIONS

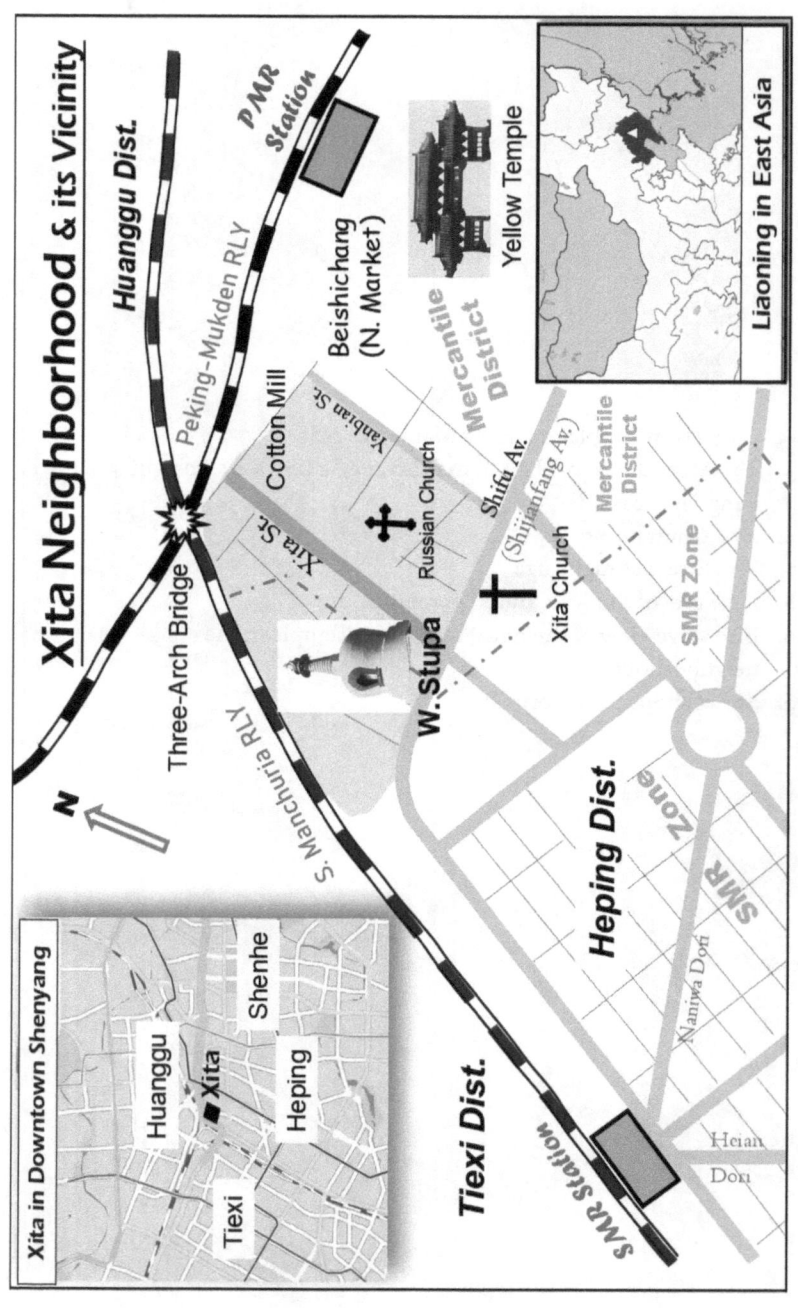

Xita Neighborhood & its Vicinity

Huanggu Dist.

PMR Station

Peking-Mukden RLY

Beishichang (N. Market)

Cotton Mill

Yanbian St.

Mercantile District

Yellow Temple

Russian Church

Shifu Av.

Xita St.

Three-Arch Bridge

(Shijianfang Av.)

W. Stupa

Xita Church

S. Manchuria RLY

Mercantile District

N

SMR Zone

Heping Dist.

SMR Zone

Naniwa Dori

Tiexi Dist.

SMR Station

Heian Dori

Xita in Downtown Shenyang

Huanggu

Shenhe

Xita

Heping

Tiexi

Liaoning in East Asia

1. Xita neighborhood and its vicinity. Map created by the author.

Introduction

A Place of Little Significance

This book tells the nearly four-centuries-old story of a small neighborhood called Xita, located in downtown Shenyang, the capital of Liaoning Province, China. But first I should clearly state that Xita is by no means a famous place. In fact, most people outside Shenyang have probably never heard of it. The word *xita* literally means "west" (xi) "tower" (ta), which refers to a Tibetan Buddhist stupa (tower) and temple once erected there. The original stupa and temple are long gone, with only a contemporary replica on the site. Compared to other tourist sites in the city, the replica is rather boring and rarely attracts any visitors. And for residents of the city, the term *xita* curiously represents something other than a historical artifact. Depending on who you ask, it could mean a famous old Korean-style cold noodle restaurant, a shiny commercial strip known as "Koreatown," a barbecue chain that incorporates the name in its brand, or an exotic red-light district that flourished in the early 2000s.

Nor was the neighborhood particularly important in any specific way. It is too small to be an independent political, economic, religious, or social unit. Geographically speaking, Xita occupies a tiny piece of land in the heart of Shenyang, the largest city in China's Northeast region (known as "Manchuria" in Western terms). In 2010, the neighborhood had a main street and several side roads leading to a few residential compounds composed of high-rise apartment buildings, with a registered population of thirty-six thousand. The total area is 1.24 square kilometers or less than half a square mile.[1] You could say it covers, to use an American expression, "just a few blocks." The main thoroughfare, called Xita Street, is nearly 700 meters long (or 0.4 miles). It takes me ten minutes to walk from the southern end of this bustling commercial street to the northern end.

Administratively, Xita used to be a subdistrict, or *jiedao*, prior to 2020. The subdistrict office (*jiedao banshichu*) is the lowest rung of government in Chinese cities, serving an area roughly comparable in size to a densely populated neighborhood in a US city. In between subdistricts and municipal governments, there is the district (*qu*) level. Xita was one of seventeen subdistricts in the Heping (meaning "peace") District, which is one of ten districts in urban Shenyang.[2] (As of 2024, metropolitan Shenyang has a total of 112 subdistricts.)[3] In December 2019, just as I started to set down my research, the Xita subdistrict office was canceled and merged into a nearby subdistrict office. But such a change, it seemed, did not bother anyone. My friends in Shenyang did not even notice since it did not impact people's daily lives in any notable way. In the book, therefore, Xita and its vicinity are treated as vague and fluid, a realm beyond the fixed boundaries of an administrative unit.

If the place has almost no significance in itself, then why write a book about it? The spatial meaning of Xita was, and still is, profoundly shaped by various political and social networks in which it served as a key knot in different historical eras. In a rather contingent way, the small neighborhood links these extraordinary spatial networks together and becomes a lens through which one can observe the composition of politics and society on a macro-spatial level. These intertwined, multilayered spatial networks are precisely some of the grand themes constituting the modern transformation of East Asia and China over the past 370 years. These themes include (but are not exclusive to) the Qing dynasty's transfrontier rule over both East Asia and Inner Asia; the mutual shaping of religion, state, and society during the Qing; the conflict and competition of modern railway capitalism in Manchuria; Japan's colonialist and imperialist enterprises in Northeast Asia; the dispersion and settlement of the Korean diaspora; the nation building and industrialization of socialist China; and the experiences with sophistication by individuals and society in the era of global neoliberalism. With that in mind, the book aims to show Xita's long and entangled metamorphosis and to depict the diverse peoples who created, reconstructed, dwelled, visited, sojourned, and left the neighborhood as well as those who are still living there.

A Place Where Core and Margin Overlapped

Xita's history began in 1643 when the founding emperor of the Qing dynasty (1636–1912) erected a Tibetan Buddhist stupa there. At the time, the place was located in the western outskirts of the old walled town. When the stupa was completed in 1644, Qing troops had just conquered Beijing. A new era unfolded in China—and East and Inner Asia. During the Qing dynasty, the West Stupa was a landmark of the political/spiritual alliance between the Manchu, Mongols, and Tibetans. It witnessed the rise and demise of the last Eurasian empire of China. In the early twentieth century, colonial powers—first Russia then Japan—and local warlords constructed competing railways that intersected in Xita, turning the place into a new urban center that manifested intensified cross-continental geopolitical struggles. Japanese colonization in the 1930s and '40s made the stupa a symbol of Japan's Pan-Asianist empire, while at the same time fueling a large wave of Korean emigration to Shenyang, which led to the formation of a Korean diasporic enclave in Xita. The daily life of the Koreans there, from the colonial period to the Mao period, illuminates the making of the ethnic Korean, or *Chaoxianzu*, identity in modern China. In the 1990s when Shenyang, socialist China's capital of heavy industry, declined to a "Rust Belt city," Xita surprisingly flourished. The (quasi-)neoliberal economic reform in post-Mao China transformed the neighborhood into a peculiar consumerist and entertainment quarter in a largely deindustrialized metropolis, albeit not without a high social cost, of course.

Over 370 years and in a nonlinear fashion, Xita developed through an intricate urbanization process. Yet a space is not merely created top-down. Multiethnic players—Tibetan, Manchu, Mongol, Han Chinese, Russian, Japanese, and Korean, and individuals across social classes—emperors, lamas, scholars, architects, colonizers, warlords, merchants, tourists, Christians, prostitutes, workers, and housewives—participated in the shaping of this urban space and left their respective legacies. The daily life of the local residents filled the neighborhood with rich and diverse artifacts and cultural meanings that could not be sanitized through official narratives. In writing a history of this neighborhood, I explore the multilayered interactions between the state, people, and urban space in imperial, colonial, nationalist, socialist, and postsocialist contexts.

But is this neighborhood truly unique, and if so, why? It goes without saying that almost every city on the globe, large or small, has experienced modernization and urbanization in the last two hundred years. Yet in terms of the extent of the diversification, Xita stands out as an extraordinary example demonstrating both global trends and local characteristics, in both premodern and modern times. Its unique historical role lies in its subtle position as simultaneously core and periphery on multiple geographical scales.

To begin with, the contemporary Xita neighborhood is located at the intersection of three districts: Heping, Huanggu, and Tiexi. This is a legacy of Shenyang's competitive urbanization in the early twentieth century, when Japanese colonizers and the local Chinese government raced one another for new city building. Since Xita sat on the border of their spheres of influence, it developed into a relatively marginal quarter in a rapidly modernized city center.

Speaking of the city, Shenyang (or Mukden), with a population of 8.3 million in the 2020s, has also exhibited a dual nature as both central and marginal. It was the largest and most flourishing metropolis in Manchuria from the Qing to the present day as well as one of the most developed industrial bases in China in the twentieth century. However, situated on the Liao River Plain and sandwiched between nomadic Mongolia, mountainous Jilin, and the Bohai Sea, Shenyang/Mukden was a frontier city that before 1900, at least in terms of commercial prosperity, could not compare with counterpart cities within the Great Wall. But since the city was situated at an intersection of multiple ecological systems, agricultural, maritime, nomadic, and hunter-gatherer cultures influenced its development.

On a regional scale, Manchuria, the imagined homeland of the ruling elites of the Qing empire, had long been a wild area and a warfront from the perspective of those in central China.[4] The internal complexity of this borderland is well illustrated by Ruth Rogaski in her recent work.[5] Manchuria, she writes, is "not one place but many" in an ecological, cultural, and spiritual sense—and, I would add, in its geopolitical complexity. In China's history, it was a unique frontier where different modes of production mingled, absorbing the direct influence of Inner China, Mongolia, Russia, Japan, and Korea as well as the indirect influence of some European and American powers. Yet precisely because of its geopolitical status as a "multilateral frontier" and "joint margin" in the Eurasian continent, twentieth-century Manchuria turned into an arena for international competition and a center for industrial development. Wars repeatedly engulfed this resource-rich borderland. Manchuria was, to a great extent, the gravitational force for East Asian power politics, and it determined the fate of the Qing empire, the Russian empire, the Republic of China, the puppet Manchukuo, the Japanese empire, and the People's Republic of China. In the late twentieth century and early twenty-first century, however, Manchuria suffered an economic downturn due to neoliberal-style economic reforms in China, receding into a marginal zone in the world capitalist system.[6]

In other words, then, being both core and marginal helped generate Xita's singular historical charm.

What This Book Is Not, and What It Is

Although this book can be read as a biography of a small urban space in the largest frontier city of a remote borderland surrounded by rival empires and states, it is also interested in the ways such a space was constructed, reshaped, and memorized by various historical forces on stage at different times. "Every place or region 'arrives' at the present moment trailing long histories," the geographer John Allen argues. 'The complex ways in which a region is constructed and read at any time is a result of these histories and of what is made of them."[7] In this vein, this book regards Xita as a place where layers of time and historical symbolism are compressed. To explore this neighborhood is to peel off these historical layers and look into the sociopolitical constructions of the Xita space-time. Methodologically, Xita is not only seen as a subject but also as a vehicle. From the perspective of this small neighborhood, an alternative story of Manchuria, China, and East Asia might be told.

Despite Xita's urban setting, the book is not an urban study per se, or at least not a conventional one. The long and wandering journey that endowed the neighborhood with rich spatial meanings does not necessarily conform to the sorts of research themes we usually see in works of urban studies, be the topic city planning, architectural design, social networking, or urban ethnography. The main focus here is space, but a space cannot be interpreted solely through its physical and material composition; its social composition in time must also be considered. What persists throughout the book is none other than the continued, fluid, and multithemed past found in a small, fixed place. History is a process in which actors and structures interact, out of which certain themes emerge. As Xita's history unfolded over the last three and half centuries, new actors constantly emerged and new structures formed so that novel themes kept being constructed. To write a *longue durée* history of Xita, therefore, is to examine the way certain large-scale themes in East Asian history found an application in a micro space or, in reverse, to see how a micro space participated in the process of creating those broader historical themes.

The Neighborhood engages with scholarly conversations in several fields of Chinese and transnational Asian histories. In different chapters, my narrative enters into multiple different scholarly dialogues. To give an example, numerous Qing scholars have talked about the Inner Asian nature of the Qing empire, partially evidenced by the Qing's patronage of Tibetan Buddhism.[8] Less clear, though, is how this patron-priest relationship was begun, built, and managed in its early period. The book contributes to this discussion by investigating the very first royal temples built by the Qing in Shenyang/Mukden. Locating the Mukden temples in the Qing's overall Buddhist network, I pay special attention to the interactions between the state, lamas, and local society. By the same token, by exploring Xita's demographic changes, spatial reconstruction, and new symbolism in the city landscape from the late Qing to the Manchukuo (1932–45) period, this study intervenes in conversations about the transition of the Manchurian frontier, including issues of geopolitical struggle, colonial modernity, state building, industrialization, and migration.[9] Finally, by documenting the life histories of Xita residents, this book expands ongoing dialogues about the making of ethnicity, religious life, daily experience, the legacy of socialism, deindustrialization, and the rise of consumerism under the People's Republic.[10] In short, my analysis of Xita integrates diverse historical themes and examines how power, symbols, and memories become entangled in a micro-level space. In highlighting the historical agency of the locals, the book rejects a single-layered narrative of Chinese history and instead embraces a more nuanced and fluid understanding of state-society relations in China.

To write a multicentury history of a small space is challenging. Luckily, developments in the fields of both microhistory and urban studies over the last few decades provided much inspiration and encouragement. If a thirteenth-century rural commune in southern France, a sixteenth-century peasant impostor in the Pyrenees, or a self-educated miller in a sixteenth-century Italian village can enrich our understanding of medieval and early modern Europe,[11] so, too, can an urban quarter in Manchuria inform us about China and Asia. Some human practices and experiences, I would argue, can only be observed from a micro perspective; they do not necessarily supplement or contradict grand narratives but manifest the latter locally in one way or another.[12] My research also incorporates the influence of numerous previous studies of Chinese cities, from Shanghai to Beijing, Yangzhou to Tianjin, Wuhan to Chengdu, and Harbin to Dalian.[13] Although not all of them focus on a small neighborhood, they tell us that the contemporary structure of an urban setting has always been created on the ruins of another. Past and present are as detached as they are connected. Not unlike what David Harvey said about Paris, the modernity that revolutionized the city landscape was all about "creative destruction."[14] Or as Madeline Yue Dong suggests in her work about Republican Beijing, modern is "created with the very fragments of the past."[15] Once we stretch the timeline to a few centuries as opposed to a few decades, we can see that creation and destruction are entangled in multiple layers. Like strata in rock, each layer contains geological information from the time, and all the layers are compressed together. There are breaks between them, for sure, but also threads that persist throughout.

One of the threads the book explores is the role that both the state and people's daily practices play in forming the meanings of a space. The importance of state, particularly, needs to be highlighted here. In some of the pioneer works of urban sociology, such as those of the Chicago School, the impact of state is either indirect or simply irrelevant. In certain other works of urban history, the state is treated as an oppressor of (naturally developed) local society. But in the Xita neighborhood, the state was essential in turning the space into a place. In various forms, the state demonstrated itself in architecture, infrastructure projects, local institutions, organized communities, official records, and public memories. One can even argue that a distinguishing characteristic of Xita's history is that states in various forms (imperial, national, colonial, imperialist, socialist, and postsocialist) are literally everywhere. Scholars are by now quite familiar with the notion that "space is constructed by social relations." In Xita, social relations were first and foremost relations with the state. On the other hand, the significance of the space was not fashioned by states only. Individuals, families, and social groups shaped the meaning of the space from the bottom up, together with the state. People from across borders and different social classes left their traces, sometimes resisting top-down efforts by the state, other times collaborating. More often than not, daily life internalized state politics. "Space has been fashioned and molded from historical and natural elements," as Henri Lefebvre once wrote, "but in a political way."[16] State and daily life, the book suggests, co-constructed the meanings of the neighborhood. The spatial politics in Xita, in turn, echoed the modern transformations of the state, peoples, and region over the last four centuries.

Xita's story is transnational and transregional, yet at the core of the story is China's stunning metamorphosis—from a multiethnic Eurasian empire into a postindustrial consumerist society. Seeing this through the lens of an urban neighborhood, I suggest that the very idea of China demands further inquiry. *The Neighborhood* views China as an entity that appears fluid and ambiguous, transcending—rather than being confined by—conventional boundaries of ethnicity, culture, nation, and state.

Plan of Chapters

To illustrate the fluidity of space and state through the transformations of daily life, it is worth introducing the contents of each chapter. My narrative follows a roughly chronological order, and each chapter deals with a historical theme of spatial politics.

Chapter 1 describes the establishment of Mukden/Shenyang as a Tibetan Buddhist center and the history of the Manchu-Mongol-Tibetan alliance. It is well-known that the Manchu emperors patronized the Gelug sect of Tibetan Buddhism in order to justify the Qing's rule over the vast Inner Asian territories. The Mukden temples were the earliest manifestations of the emperors' devotion to the religion. But why were the royal temples established? Who designed them and what did they symbolize? How were they institutionalized and mythicized? How did the Qing government support and supervise these temples? Chapter 1 answers these questions by examining the construction of the temples, inspecting their architectural contents, cultural meaning, and political symbolism, and by analyzing the multilingual texts engraved on the temples' stelae. I argue that the Manchu emperors' devotion to Tibetan Buddhism was more contingent, open, fluid, and pragmatic than usually thought. Designed by a Tibetan of the Saskya sect and combining Tibetan and Han Chinese styles, the temples create a unique case in China's urban planning history. The Qing's attitude toward Tibetan Buddhism gradually changed from patron to administrator, and the royal temple nexus in Mukden was similarly bureaucratized and embedded in the empire's expansive, institutional Tibetan Buddhism network, connecting not only Beijing but also the Inner Asian frontiers.

Mukden temples were staffed mainly by ethnic Mongol lamas. Chapter 2 takes advantage of previously underused archives to tell the stories of the local lamas. What was their connection with the state? What was their career path? How did the lamas interact with the local population? What were their internal relationships like? And importantly: How did all these relations evolve over time, especially after the collapse of the Qing? Unlike their peers in Tibet and Mongolia, the Mukden lamas were on the government payroll and accountable only to the court. They were bureaucratic lamas who enjoyed extraordinary job protection and economic privileges, which expectedly led to corruption and nepotism. Crimes and strife were not uncommon. When the Qing collapsed in 1912, the temples faced tremendous political, economic, and social turbulence from within and beyond. The state-temple relationship fundamentally changed. Without organic support from local society, Tibetan Buddhism in Mukden/Shenyang soon declined, despite the fact that the lamas skillfully bargained with the state for their economic interests and social prestige. The West Stupa Temple was ransacked during the Russian occupation of Shenyang/Mukden during the Russo-Japanese War. By the 1930s, few lamas remained there.

Chapter 3 begins in 1928 with the assassination of Zhang Zuolin, the warlord of Manchuria and the most powerful man in China. The murder happened in a place about half a mile north of the West Stupa. Two rival railway systems—the Peking-Mukden Railway (PMR), controlled by Zhang, and the South Manchuria Railway (SMR) run by the Japanese—intersected at there. The story of the railways in Manchuria started with the Russians. In 1900, Russia aggressively built a railway system to connect the Liaodong Peninsula with the Trans-Siberia Railway (TSR) and built Shenyang's first train station near Xita. After the Russo-Japanese

War, Japan inherited Russian privileges and reconstructed the station. The SMR's territory surrounded the train station. Applying European-style urban planning, the area emerged as a thriving new district of the city. To compete with Japanese railway colonialism, Zhang Zuolin extended the native PMR system, with its Shenyang train station also located not far from Xita. The competing railways accelerated the industrialization and modernization of the city, making Shenyang a hub of capitalist modernity in China. New streets, parks, public transportation, commercial districts, and factories were established. Xita was at the corner of the two competing forces. Seeing Zhang as a threat, radical officers of the Japanese Kwantung Army killed him in 1928, portending Japan's total colonization of Manchuria three years later. Chapter 3 examines the competition between two capitalist modernists, one colonialist and the other nationalist, through three spatial layers—the architectural styles of the train stations, the planning of the new urban spaces, and the expansion of the transregional railway systems.

During the Japanese colonization (1931–45), Shenyang industrialized and urbanized rapidly, becoming one of the most important heavy-industry centers for the Japanese empire. The downtown gradually shifted to what had formerly been the western edge of the city. Against this backdrop, chapter 4 probes another colonial enterprise—tourism. Tourism was a critical component of imperial Japan's ideology building. Scholars, writers, and artists traveled across Manchuria, Korea, and Japan, leaving abundant records. Many of these travels were funded or organized by the imperial government or SMR as a mean to publicize colonial achievements. Images of the historic stupas in Shenyang were mass-produced and circulated widely. More people knew about Xita through postcards, tourist guidebooks, and travel literature than before. The writings and images highlighted a Pan-Asianist "nostalgia" for a glorious ancient capital, which had been incorporated into an imperial metropolis network through modern transportation systems. Despite adjoining the SMR Territory and the Mercantile District, the Xita neighborhood remained a marginal space. It was inhabited mainly by poor laborers, opium addicts, small businessmen, and prostitutes. Brothels were the most robust business there. The prostitution industry in Xita exposed an urbanist modernity in this symbolic tourist site.

Chapter 5 features the experiences of ethnic Koreans in Xita through both archival records and the life stories of several old—particularly female—residents. In the early twentieth century, the railway brought a great number of Koreans to Shenyang, many of whom settled in Xita and established businesses. The neighborhood gradually developed into a Korean enclave where businessmen and independent activists

gathered. Xita Church was built, a tall, glowing structure situated across
the street from the ruined stupa. After the founding of the People's Republic of China (PRC) in 1949, local Koreans enjoyed certain social
benefits as ethnic minorities but also endured hardships during periods
of upheaval. Xita Church suffered due to the early PRC's hostile policy
toward religion. When it reopened in the 1980s, Korean Christians, under the leadership of Wu Ai'en, a highly respected female pastor, worked
diligently to negotiate with the government for their rights and to revive
religious activity. Xita Church grew to be one of the most reputable
churches in China. Non-Christian Koreans were also attracted to the
neighborhood by the ethnic schools, hospitals, and department stores.
During the 1980s, small, private businesses flourished. For the ethnic
Korean-Chinese community, Xita has been a symbol of their distinctive
identity.

Chapter 6 unfolds with Xita's most recent reincarnation. In the 1990s,
Northeast China suffered a dramatic downturn as the Soviet-style economic system turned into a neoliberalist one. Numerous workers in
state-owned factories were laid off. While Shenyang, like many cities in
the American Midwest, became a Rust Belt city, the Xita neighborhood
surprisingly prospered, in part due to the arrival of investors from South
Korea. Foreign and domestic capital reshaped Xita into a commercial
and entertainment quarter. It is one of the few places on earth where
North Korean and South Korean businesses operate side by side. Prostitution reemerged after being eliminated in the 1950s. Eager to have a
booming economy, however, the local government acquiesced to the
phenomenon, even promoting Xita as a "model neighborhood" and
"little Seoul" to showcase Shenyang's "ethnic solidarity" and "international attraction." New generations of ethnic Korean migrants flooded
in from the countryside, yet for the older residents, Xita was no longer
the home they recognized. In 1998, the government rebuilt the Buddhist
stupa, which had been dismantled during the Cultural Revolution. But
surrounded by tall residential buildings; commercial noise; and bright
neon signs advertising bars, restaurants, nightclubs, and saunas, the new
stupa is nothing more than a replicated cultural appendage of this increasingly consumerist city.

In the epilogue and conclusion, I continue to pursue the question of
the intricate relations between time, space, and people. As I was doing
my research and writing, the Xita neighborhood also kept changing and
transforming. Indeed, it is already not the same place described in this
book. But for the sake of completing this work, my narrative ends in the
2010s—at least for now.

CHAPTER 1

The Stupa

It was an ordinary, midsummer day. On the western outskirts of Muk-den, then the capital city of the Qing state, a grand ceremony was taking place. After more than a year of hard work, a tall, white Tibetan-style Buddhist tower known as a "stupa," or "chorten," had been erected in quiet, unspoiled land on the Manchurian Plain. The monument-like structure designed for circumambulation (where pilgrims circle clock-wise on foot while meditating) is one of the most critical components of a Tibetan Buddhist temple. A group of Manchu nobles and high-ranking officials, all dressed in their utmost formal attire, had come to honor its consecration. The delegation was headed by Jirgalang (1599–1655), Prince Zheng of the First Rank (Man. *hošoi ujen cin wang*). As a nephew of Nurhaci (1559–1626), the founder of the Manchu regime, Jirgalang was one of two coregents for Emperor Shunzhi (1638–1661), who was only six years old at the time and, therefore, too young to come. So Jirgalang attended on his behalf. Other prominent figures in the group included Abatai, a second-ranking prince, and Šose, an elder brother of the emperor. It was the twenty-eighth day of the sixth month, the first year of Shunzhi, or July 31, 1644.

A group of Mongol lamas was already waiting there. Since the monas-tery containing the stupa was still under construction, the lamas had set up a Mongol-style yurt near the stupa and were inside chanting sutras. When they finished, the head lama, recorded in Manchu as "Sibja Corji" (?–1657), came out and sat in front of the yurt. The Manchu nobles and officials took off their hats, knelt before Sibja Corji and kowtowed three times. They repeated the gesture twice more. Such a ritual performance was both extremely reverential and very rare, considering that only the emperor, the "son-of-Heaven," was honored this way (albeit with more kowtows). But that was not all. The delegation presented their gifts to

the lama one by one, with each man repeating the same kowtow ritual as they withdrew. The gifts were abundant: two horses (one with a
saddle and one without), a camel, precious animal skins, armor, a bow
and arrows, silver money, jade and silver utensils, and various silk and
satin cloth. Next, a prominent lama official, Biliktu Nangsu (?–1657),
led the group as they circled the stupa three times and then knelt and
kowtowed once more, this time to the stupa. Apparently, Biliktu Nangsu
and Sibja Corji, and not the Qing nobles, were the distinguished hosts
of the ceremony.

Then it was time for the feast. Food and drink were readied. The
royal house had contributed twenty tables, ten bottles of wine, and three
hundred meat pies. The Ministry of Rites had provided three bottles
of kumiss, a light alcohol made from fermented milk. The Ministry of
Finance had supplied one beef cattle and twenty-six lambs: their combined quantity (twenty-seven) indicated three times nine, two numbers
that symbolized one's prestigious status in Chinese texts. There were
also eight buckets of tea. Everyone, including the servants and craftsmen, had their share. The atmosphere was quite joyful.

But for Biliktu Nangsu, Sibja Corji, Jirgalang, and others, the feast
on July 31 was, perhaps, not as exciting as it sounded. After all, this was
the fourth consecration ceremony they had attended in just ten days.
Several months before his death, the late emperor, Hong Taiji, gave the
order for four Tibetan-style stupas to be built at the four cardinal points
outside the capital, each located five *li*, or one and a half miles, from the
city gates. The consecration ceremonies had begun at the stupa in the
north on July 22 and then turned clockwise to the east, south, and west,
respectively, with each ceremony held two days after the previous one.
The consecration of the West Stupa concluded the series. In all four
ceremonies, the ritual, the number of gifts, and the size of the feast were
exactly the same, just like the appearance of the four now-empowered
towers.[1]

Despite the sumptuous ceremonies, the real focus of the Qing at this
particular moment was not on Mukden. It was on another city nearly
400 miles away: Beijing, the capital of the Ming dynasty. In late April
that year, a rebel army led by Li Zicheng had taken over the city. In desperation, the Ming emperor Chongzhen (1611–1644) had hanged himself on a hill behind the Forbidden City. The news shocked Ming general
Wu Sangui (1608–1678), who was stationed with his army at the Shanhai
Pass, 195 miles east of Beijing, in defense against the Qing, a longtime
threat in the northeast frontier. After some hesitation, Wu decided to ask
for help from his enemy to expel the rebels from the capital. The Qing,
however, had another idea. Ever since its official establishment in 1636,

LAMA MONUMENT OUTSIDE MUKDEN.

2. "Lama Monument Outside Mukden," from the *Illustrated London News*, December 29, 1894, 814. This is arguably one of the first printed images of the Mukden stupa in modern media. Author's collection.

the Manchu regime had proclaimed that it was the true recipient of the Mandate of Heaven and that it should be the new ruler of China. With the sudden collapse of Ming rule, Qing leaders called on Wu Sangui to surrender and join them. He had no choice but to agree.

Led by Dorgon (1612–1650), the Qing troops entered Beijing in early June. Dorgon, Prince Rui of the First Rank (Man. *hošoi mergen cin wang*), was the other coregent for Emperor Shunzhi. But unlike Jirgalang, who was not willing to grab political power aggressively, Dorgon was autocratic, shrewd, ambitious, and cruel. He controlled a large share of the banner troops and acted as the de facto ruler of the Qing. While the princes and officials in Mukden worshipped the Buddhist stupas, Dorgon reported from Beijing that his brave cavalry, "blessed by the Heaven and Emperor," had successfully pacified a large part of northern China.[2] Finally, on October 19, Dorgon greeted young Emperor Shunzhi in Beijing.

Only three months after the consecration of the stupas, Mukden was no longer the capital of the Qing. It became an auxiliary capital. Subsequently, for many historians of Qing China, stories about Mukden were far less fascinating than those of Beijing, where the rest of the dynasty's emperors were born and where all but two died, or for that matter, those of Chengde (Jehol), where many of the Qing rulers spent their summers and two died.[3] Yet Mukden remained important. It was the capital of a critical frontier in Northeast Eurasia that was also the sacred homeland of the Manchu. The city continued to play an unparalleled role in solidifying the Qing's image as a supporter of Tibetan Buddhism, as demonstrated by the ceremonies on its outskirts in the summer of 1644. It is with this framework that I examine the spatial significance of the West Stupa (C. Xita), the main subject of this book, over the course of two centuries.

Building the City of Mukden

Today, Mukden is known by its original name of Shenyang. "Shen" refers to the Shen River, now called the Hun River, a tributary of the longest river in the Liaodong Peninsula, the Liao River. "Yang" means north (as opposed to *yin* or south). Although the history of the city can be traced to the Spring and Autumn Period (roughly 771 to 476 BC), the name Shenyang did not become official until the Yuan dynasty (1271–1368).[4] Located in the heartland of the Liaodong Peninsula, which juts out between the Bohai and Yellow Seas, the city along the north side of the Hun River has always been a geostrategic hub. It lies in the middle of the Liao River Plain, a historically agrarian zone sandwiched between the forested Changbai Mountains in southeast, the nomad zone of Mongolian steppe in northwest, and the Bohai Sea in the south. During the Ming dynasty (1368–1644), Shenyang was one of a dozen-odd garrison towns in Liaodong. Together, the garrisons comprised the Ming defense system against the Mongols in the west and the Jurchens in the east. In 1388, Ming general Min Zhong rebuilt the garrison walls in Shenyang. A square-shaped city wall was erected, each side around 1.3 kilometers, or 0.8 miles, long. Two main streets—one east to west, the other north to south—connected the four gates of the garrison and divided the city into four quadrants. The construction laid out the foundation for modern Shenyang.[5]

It was not until the seventeenth century that Shenyang transformed from a garrison town into a metropolitan center. After establishing a rebel regime in 1616 called Later Jin (Man. *aisin gurun*), Nurhaci took over the Liaodong area and proposed to move the capital to Shenyang.

Facing opposition from many princes and ministers, Nurhaci pointed out that from Shenyang, it was very easy strategically to march either to the Ming, Mongolia, or Korea. The river system would deliver wood needed for construction and fire, and there were abundant animals and fish to hunt.[6] In 1625, Shenyang became the new capital of his state. Six years later, his successor, Hong Taiji, replanned the city by increasing the height of its walls and doubling the number of gates from four to eight, two on each side. In accordance, the layout of the main streets also changed from two (like a cross) to four (like a tic-tac-toe board). The royal palace occupied a major portion of the central square and was surrounded by princes' mansions and bureaucratic buildings (fig. 3).

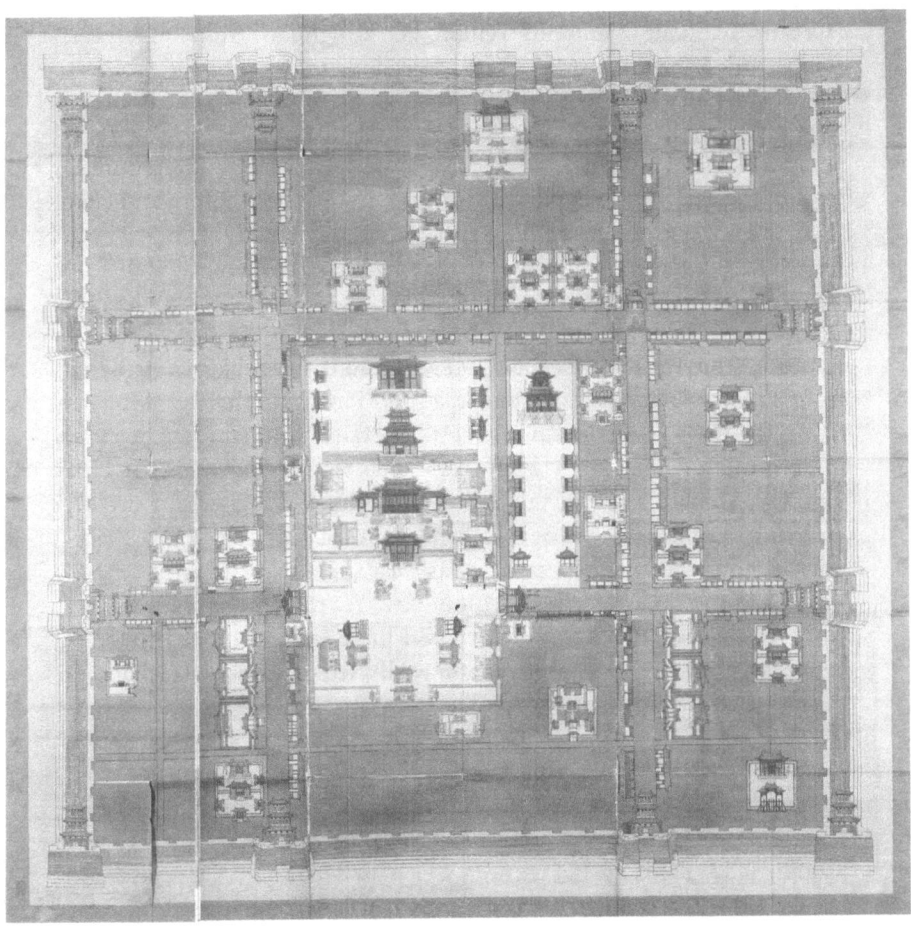

3. Shengjing cheng que tu (Map of the city of Mukden). Courtesy of First Historical Archives of China.

Markets and schools thrived. In 1634, Hong Taiji renamed the city Mukden hoton, meaning "heavenly-blessed flourishing capital." The corresponding Chinese word for the Manchu name was Shengjing. As the city gained more political and cultural gravity, it also developed into the religious center for all Manchuria.

The native religious belief of the Jurchen people was Shamanism. When Nurhaci moved the capital to Shenyang, one of his first constructions was a *tangse*, a shrine for shamanistic ceremonies, outside the east gate of the city. Nonetheless, the dominant cultural influence in the city was undoubtedly Han Chinese. Some Han rituals, such as worshipping heaven, ancestors, and Confucius, were also important rituals for the Jurchen elites. Before conquering Beijing in 1644, the Jurchen regime established the Heaven Temple (C. tiantan), Royal Ancestral Temple (C. taimiao), and Confucius Temple (C. kongmiao), respectively, either within or beyond the city walls.[7] In addition, Daoism and Chinese Buddhism had a long history in the region. Shenyang was the home of several Liao dynasty (916–1125) Buddhist pagodas. The Chang'an Temple, the oldest Han-Buddhist temple that still exists today, was rebuilt at least in the early Ming dynasty.[8] However, in the years before and after 1644, there was a foreign religious sect that fundamentally reshaped both the politics of the new state and the landscape of the new capital. That religious sect was Tibetan Buddhism.

Combining the Tantric Vajrayana tradition from India, the Mahāyāna tradition from the Chinese Central Plain, and native religious elements from Tibet, Tibetan Buddhism spread to Manchuria through Mongolia. In the early seventeenth century, Tibetan Buddhism was popular in both Ming China and Manchuria. Lamas traveled between the Han Chinese, Mongol, and Jurchen polities as both missionaries and envoys, enjoying exalted social, economic, and political status in all three societies. Among the various sects, the Saskya and Kagyu schools had made inroads in the region for quite some time. Yet they faced competition from a new sect, the Gelug, which had been expanding its influence aggressively since the sixteenth century. All tried to form a special priest-patron relationships with local rulers.

The first important lama patronized by the Jurchen state was Orlog Darhan Langsu (Mon. Örlüg Darqan Nangsu, ?–1621), a master from Tibet who had once served the Khorchin Mongols, one of Nurhaci's close allies.[9] Hearing of the lama's reputation, Nurhaci, who had just established his khanate in Hetu Ala, twice invited him to the capital and treated him with great respect. When Nurhaci defeated the Ming army in Liaoyang in 1621 and moved his capital to Shenyang, Orlog Darhan Langsu decided to leave the Khorchin and join the rising Jurchen state.

He died several months later and was buried in Liaoyang. The Later Jin/Qing regime later built a grand tomb, along with a stupa and stelae, to honor him.[10] His junior dharma brother (Man. *emu šajin i deo*) Baga ba lama (?–1637), also from Tibet, continued his mission, serving the Jurchen state until his death.[11] Together, the two masters, along with others, laid the foundation for Tibetan Buddhism in the early Qing state.

However, the new religion was not yet the dominant faith of the court, unlike the situation later, during the high Qing period in the eighteenth century. It was but one of many belief systems supported by the Jurchen khans and, later, the Manchu emperors. Both Nurhaci and his son Hong Taiji issued orders to protect lamas and their monasteries. Yet both were aware of the negative social impacts, particularly Hong Taiji. Once, he went so far as to blame the Mongol princes for "voluntarily abandoning native language and using the language of lamas in their names and titles." This, according to Hong Taiji, "caused the decline in the fortunes of the state."[12] When the regime moved its capital to Shenyang, Tibetan Buddhism did not stand out among the many state-endorsed religions—well, not until the arrival of an unusual guest in early 1635.

Welcoming Tibetan Buddhism in Mukden

On February 1, 1635, Biliktu Nangsu, the lama who later would play a prominent role in the stupa consecration in 1644 described at the beginning of this chapter, received an important order. As Hong Taiji's most trusted lama official, he was dispatched to welcome another lama who was on his way to Mukden. The next day, Biliktu Nangsu brought the guest, Mergen lama of the Chakhar Mongols, to the capital city. Unable to contain his extreme joy, Hong Taiji rewarded both lamas with a horse, precious furs, and more. He held Mergen's arrival in very high regard not because the Saskya lama was unusually distinguished but because he had come there to present a statue of Mahākāla, the most remarkable dharma protector in Tibetan Buddhism.[13]

Why was this middle-sized statue (around half a meter in height, or one and a half feet tall) so extraordinary? We need to understand its significance against the backdrop of Hong Taiji's geopolitical expansion and the symbolism of the Mahākāla statue in Tibetan-Mongol relationships.

By the early 1630s, it was clear that the Later Jin had gone from being the weakest player in continental East Asia to the most promising power. In 1627, Hong Taiji had invaded Chosŏn Korea, forcing the latter to sign a peace agreement and acknowledge an elder

4. Image of Mahākāla. Rinero/Wikimedia Commons. CC-BY-SA 3.0.

brother–younger brother relationship between the two countries. The invasion successfully eased the Jurchen regime's strategic threat in the south. Meanwhile, Hong Taiji continued his father's policy of friending various Mongol polities (Mon. *ulus*) to his north and west. This tactic enticed many Mongol nobles from smaller tribes to submit to or ally with him. But it also threatened the most influential Mongol leader at the time, Ligdan Khan (1604–1634) of Chakhar. Ever since the Yuan dynasty (1271–1368) had been expelled by the Ming and retreated to the Inner Asian Steppe, various powerful leaders had claimed to inherit the political legacy of the Yuan, the embodiment of the Great Mongol Empire (Mon. Yeke Mongyol Ulus) founded by Chinggis Khan (1162-1227). From the fourteenth to seventeenth centuries, the scattered nomad polities were loosely connected under the vague identity of Mongol. Such an identity was constructed by neither a common tongue nor a centralized administration but a shared faith that Chinggis Khan's political lineage continued, even if many so-called great khans had next to no real authority. Ligdan of Chakhar, grandson of Buyan Sechen Khan (r. 1592–1604), was the legitimate successor of the Yuan emperors, hence, the latest great khan of Mongol. However, ever since inheriting the position, he had had a difficult relationship with the Jurchen. The two regimes were constantly at war, with Ligdan allying with the Ming to attack Nurhaci and Hong Taiji. Finally in 1632, Hong Taiji, with the help of tens of thousands of Mongols who had deserted Ligdan, decisively defeated the Chakhar troops. Ligdan escaped with his family and the remnants of his force and died in Sela Tala (in today's Gansu province) in 1634.[14] Hong Taiji now controlled the entire southern portion of the Mongolian steppe. With more and more polities in the steppe now part of the Jurchen regime, the Later Jin reformed government institutions and established new ones, such as the Mongol yamen (Man. *Monggo jurgan*). Its relations with the Mongols also changed, subtly but gradually, from that of an ally to more of a ruler.[15]

It was arguably during this process that Hong Taiji realized the profound impact Tibetan Buddhism had on the Mongols.[16] The historical relations between the Mongols and Tibet Buddhism were complicated and fluid. Recent studies show that the Mongols started to adopt Tibetan Buddhism after Chinggis Khan conquered the Western Xia dynasty (1038–1227), known by the Mongols as the Tangut, in northwestern China.[17] Yet the first politically meaningful encounter between the two occurred in 1247, when Prince Köden, grandson of Chinggis Khan, met with Saskya Pandita, the head of the Saskya sect and a representative of Tibet. During their legendary meeting in Liangzhou, a former prefecture of the Western Xia, Köden agreed to not invade Tibet in exchange for Tibet's submission to the Mongol Empire. Saskya Pandita's young nephew, Phags-pa lama (1235–1280), accompanied him to Liangzhou. Later, Phags-pa served Kublai Khan (1215–1294), emperor of the Yuan dynasty and the Great Khan of the Mongols, and became one of his most important assistants. Phags-pa not only created a new set of Mongol script but also established the priest-patron relationship between a religious leader of Tibet and an emperor of China. Such a relationship, as many scholars have pointed out, was not a Mongol invention. Rather, it was established by the Tibetan lamas and Tangut kings of the Western Xia. The Mongols merely took it over and "reused it for Mongol purposes."[18]

"Priest-patron" is, of course, a simplified description for convenience. The connotation, from the perspective of state, is that a religious leader receives political benefits from the state by submitting to the latter. But from the Tibetan perspective, the relationship was often interpreted as one of "mentor-student." By performing certain secret Tantric rituals known as abhiseka, or initiation into teaching (C. *guan ding*), the lama assumed the role of spiritual instructor to the secular ruler. This was exactly what Phags-pa did for Kublai Khan. After their relationship was established, the great khan/emperor appointed Phags-pa as a "state preceptor" and later promoted him to an "imperial preceptor." In return, Phags-pa proclaimed that Kublai was a cakravartin, a universal king of Buddhism.

Between the thirteenth and the seventeenth centuries, the Han Chinese, Mongol, and Tibetan worlds all changed dramatically. In 1368, Toghon Temür, the last Yuan emperor who ruled the Central Plain, was driven out of the Great Wall by Ming troops. Subsquently, the geopolitical competition between the Ming and the Mongols lasted until the late sixteenth century. While the influence of Tibetan Buddhism in the Mongol steppe declined drastically, the Ming court inherited, and even expanded, the priest-patron relationship in an attempt to influence Tibet.[19] In Tibet, the dominance of the Saskya sect was severely challenged by the Kagyu sect. But both felt the threat of a newcomer, the thriving Gelug sect, so they tried everything to strangle it. Various sects also competed to penetrate the Chinese Central Plain and Mongolia. Despite disdain from Confucian literati, the Ming court treated Tibetan lamas with courtesy. Thousands of them went to Beijing and accepted titles like "state preceptor" or "dharma king" bestowed by the Ming government.[20] In the eyes of Tibetan lamas, Inner China or Mongolia were integrated parts of a Buddhist—hence, a Tibet-centric—world.

Then a brilliant Mongol leader, Altan Khan (1507–1582) of the Tümed, redefined Mongol relations with both the Ming and Tibet. In 1571, he negotiated a peace agreement with the Ming, making the latter open border markets with the Tümed. Accepting the Ming title "prince of shunyi" (meaning "prince who conforms to righteousness"), Altan ended long-standing military tensions between the Mongols and the Ming-Chinese. Around the same time, he was deeply drawn to Tibetan Buddhism. In 1578, he met with the Gelug leader Sonam Gyatso and granted him the title "Dalai Lama." In the Mongolian language, this newly created title meant "ocean." Sonam Gyatsho was thus known as the "Third Dalai Lama." In return, he announced that Altan was the reincarnation of Kublai Khan and, like Kublai, was a cakravartin.[21] In other words, the two leaders revived the priest-patron relationship that had occurred between Phags-pa and Kublai Khan. By supporting each other in a highly ritualized form, they aimed to overcome their own relative marginality within Tibetan and Mongolian traditions. The Gelug was facing brutal persecution in Tibet and seeking a mighty military power for protection. Altan was not born of the right lineage to be the great khan of Mongol, so he needed to demonstrate his legitimacy in another way. The significance of this alliance was more political than religious. Later, Altan's great-grandson Yonten Gyatso was chosen as the Fourth Dalai Lama. And Tibetan Buddhism was soon resurrected among the Mongols, replacing Shamanism. In many Mongol documents written after Altan, the political authority of the Mongol world came from two entangled sources: heaven (Mon. *tengri*), which blessed the lineage of Chinggis Khan, and dharma, which confirmed the power of cakravartin. Some Mongol chronologies compiled in this period even portrayed Chinggis Khan as a Buddhist ruler, which was certainly a distortion of history.[22]

Altan was not the first Mongol ruler to use the priest-patron relationship to shore up his political status, nor was he the last. Ligdan, after assuming his position as the new great khan, did the same. This is where the Mahākāla statue, which Hong Taiji received in 1635, comes into our story. From the Yuan dynasty onward, Mahākāla, the dharma protector, was widely worshipped by the Mongols as a deity of war and a guardian of the state.[23] Phags-pa himself was an enthusiastic promotor of the Mahākāla cult. Around 1256, he contributed a thousand taels of gold to make a Mahākāla statue. The statue was first enshrined in Mount Wutai in Shanxi, northern China. In Buddhist geography, Mount Wutai was identified as the Bodhimaṇḍa, or position of awakening, of Manjusri bodhisattva (C. Wenshu Pusa), one of the most popular bodhisattvas in both Tibetan and Han Chinese Buddhism. Later, Phags-pa returned to his hometown in southern Tibet, taking the statue with him. In 1617, a Saskya sect lama with the title of "sharba khutughtu" went to Chakhar and became the mentor of twenty-six-year-old Ligdan Khan. Sharba (whose real name was unknown) brought Phags-pa's Mahākāla statue to Ligdan, who knew too well the political implication of such a move. Ligdan soon built a temple in his capital for the deity. By enshrining the statue, he demonstrated again that he was the god-chosen successor of Kublai Khan.[24]

Unfortunately for Ligdan, his dream of rebuilding a unified Mongol empire failed. But it did not mean doom for a unified Mongol world. It just revealed that the gods or Heaven did not entrust Ligdan with such an enterprise. This was the belief held by many Mongols who escaped from Ligdan's authoritarian policies and went over to Hong Taiji. The coming of the Mahākāla statue to Mukden in early 1635 was nothing less than a miracle. It was a sign, at least for Hong Taiji's Mongol allies/subjects, that the gods had now chosen a Jurchen khan to be the protector of the Mongol world and the successor of Kublai Khan. No matter how he previously felt about Tibetan Buddhism, from that moment on Hong Taiji had to prove that he was a devoted patron of the religion, even if it was just for the sake of consolidating his influence over the steppe.

As if one omen was not enough, several months later Hong Taiji received another highly symbolic artifact: the Imperial Jade Seal, which was personally presented to him by Ligdan's widow. Now it seemed clear that both Heaven and dharma had decided that Hong Taiji should be the possessor of the Mandate of Heaven.[25] On May 2, 1636, forty-nine Mongol nobles from the sixteen ulus in southern Mongolia arrived in Mukden. They offered Hong Taiji the title of "bogd setsen khan" and recognized him as the Great Khan of the Mongols. At the same time, his Han Chinese ministers urged him to proclaim himself emperor. Hong Taiji gladly accepted both offers. On May 15, he changed the name of his regime to "the Great Qing" (Man. *daicing gurun*) and was enthroned as emperor.[26] Meanwhile, he adopted a new name for the Jurchen people: Manchu. The Qing emperor thus embodied a multitude of lordships at once: the holy khan of the Manchu, emperor of the Chinese and Great Khan of the Mongols.

Of course, this was far from saying that his power was accepted and admitted universally. In fact, during the enthroning ceremony, the Korean envoys refused to kneel and kowtow to Hong Taiji, because this ritual was for the Ming emperor only. Using the slight as an excuse, Hong Taiji launched his second invasion of Chosŏn Korea. Defenseless, the Chosŏn king had to surrender and publicly swear allegiance to the Qing emperor. Chosŏn was the first Confucian country to become

a subordinate state of the Qing.[27] As for the Mongols, it would take
the Qing another 120 years to successfully put the Khalkha people in
the north and the Oirat people in the west under their control.[28] Qing
reconstruction of the Mongol world was achieved through multiple
approaches, including intermarriages, military conquests, population
relocation, and bureaucratic consolidations. But no one could deny that
one of the most important tools, through which the Qing emperors
interacted with both Mongols and Tibetans, was Tibetan Buddhism.
Precisely because Tibetan Buddhism played such a critical role in the
Qing's imperial enterprise, it also occupied an irreplaceable position
in the Qing ideology and cosmology, along with Confucianism, Daoism, and Shamanism. In this sense, the arrival of the Mahākāla statue in
1635 marked a watershed moment in Qing empire building and identity
making. From then on, the Qing kept enlarging their importance in a
cross-frontier Buddhist network. Mukden, the capital of the Manchu
homeland, transformed itself into the focal point for such a network.

A Buddhist World and Its Builders

Upon receiving the Mahākāla statue, Hong Taiji had a hall built to house
it on the western outskirts of Mukden. Several months later, after he
ascended the throne, the new emperor said, "It is not appropriate to
have the Mahākāla, but no great Buddhas [Man. *amba fucihi*]. Just like
having great Buddhas, but no Mahākāla."[29] So he ordered the construction of a grand temple that would incorporate the Mahākāla hall. It was
completed in 1638. Hong Taiji named it "Shisheng" (實勝, Ma. Yargiyan
etehe), meaning "essential victory."[30] It was the Qing's very first royal
Tibetan Buddhist temple in Mukden. On September 19, the emperor
personally attended the grand opening ceremony. Many Mongol princes
came from domains far away to celebrate. The most notable persons in
the capital—the royal princes, Manchu and Chinese ministers, and two
Korean princes (who were kept in Mukden as hostages)—participated
in the ceremony. Their guards and servants carried gifts and led camels and horses. The entire party departed from the Huaiyuan Gate and
marched westward for three li (nearly one mile), until they reached
the monastery.

Upon their arrival, lamas and monks tolled bells and beat drums; mu-
sicians started to play. Banners and satins in nine colors, hanging on the
front gate and in trees, fluttered in the wind. The Essential-Victory Temple complex was the most grandiose and beautiful structure in Mukden's
western suburb at that time and remained so until the early twentieth
century. The emperor and his party passed under two adorned archways

to reach the front gate. To welcome the emperor and distinguished guests, the path between the front gate and the main hall was lined with white satin.[31] Once in, guests first crossed the Hall of Heavenly Kings (C. *tianwangdian*) and then passed through two pavilions of stelae and two side halls before finally entering the main hall (C. *zhengdian*). Grand statues of the Buddhas of the Three Times (Dipamkara, Shakyamuni, and Maitreya) and eight bodhisattvas were enshrined in the main hall. Although overall the architecture was Han Chinese in style, the internal spatial structure, decorations, and spiderweb ceiling in the main hall had all been decorated in Tibetan-Nepal style.[32] The Mahākāla hall was a separate building located to the west of the main hall. The stelae pavilions hosted two stones, 2.3 meters (7.6 feet) in height and 1 meter (3.3 feet) in width, which were engraved in four languages—Manchu, Chinese, Mongolian, and Tibetan—with an inscription that praised the greatness of Buddha, told the story of Phags-pa's Mahākāla statue, and expounded on the magnificence of the monastery.[33] It was the earliest quadrilingual literature produced in this multiethnic empire. To the average visitor, the temple's most striking feature was that all the buildings had roofs of yellow-glazed tile with a green-glazed tile border, signifying their royal identity. For this reason, the locals would later call it either "the Yellow Temple" or "the Imperial Temple" (pronounced the same as *huang si* in Mandarin). So shimmering was the complex on a bright and sunny day that over the next two hundred years writers would repeatedly describe it as "splendor like gold and jade."

The emperor and guests brought numerous gifts. The royal household alone offered 1,060 taels of silver and other precious items. Altogether, the temple received 1,260 taels of silver, 14 bolts of satins, 33 mink fur pelts, a jade flagon, a mink coat, a pair of saddles, 3,000 rolls of paper, 2 camels, and 31 horses. After the feast, Hong Taiji announced a reward for every temple worker, from supervisors to painters, blacksmiths, and carpenters. The prizes were divided into six ranks in accordance with the nature of the work. The long list of awardees, however, did not contain any architects or engineers, so it is hard to detect who actually designed this grand monastery. But the top name on the list, whose duty was recorded as "instructing the [making of] statues and paintings," was a familiar one: Biliktu Nangsu. In other words, according to the Qing court, he should take most of the credit for creating this sacred space.

Three years after being dispatched to receive the Mahākāla statue, Biliktu Nangsu experienced another highpoint. During the ceremony, he invited Hong Taiji to enter the main hall and handed him a golden mandala. The emperor took it with both hands, placed it in front of the Buddhas, and prostrated to the statues. For Biliktu Nangsu, this was no doubt a glorious moment, for it fulfilled his unusual obligation as both a Buddhist missionary and an imperial subject. Not only did he personally help the Qing emperor complete this solemn religious ritual, but his status as the emperor's right-hand man in Tibetan Buddhism–related affairs was reaffirmed by the ritual itself. It is little wonder then that several years later, he would be the host at the consecration of the four stupas around Mukden.

Biliktu Nangsu was neither Manchu nor Mongol. Like Orlog Darhan Langsu, the first lama patronized by the Manchus, he was Tibetan. The "Nangsu" (or "Langsu") in his name was a title with Tibetan roots (T. *nang so*), referring to an administrator of a Buddhist temple. In the late Ming period, the title was often given to envoys to Mongolia or Manchuria.[34] Despite his important position, we know very little about his early life. In 1652, the Fifth Dalai Lama visited the Shunzhi emperor in Beijing. Naturally, Biliktu Nangsu served as a Qing liaison and communicated frequently with this Gelug leader. In his autobiography, the Dalai Lama recorded that Biliktu Nangsu used to be an abbot of "Ngor-pa" Temple, an important Saskya sect monastery in Shigatse, southern Tibet. Apparently, the Gelug leader was very impressed by Biliktu Nangsu's intelligence, noting the latter was "very fluent in the three languages of Han Chinese, Tibetan, and Mongolian." Like many Tibetan lamas of his generation, Biliktu Nangsu left his homeland and went to preach in Mongolia. "Bilig-tü" was the name he used in Mongolia, which meant "possessed with intelligence or wisdom" in the local tongue. He came to serve the Jurchen/Manchu regime from either Kharchin or Tümed no later than 1627. It was after this transition that his recorded name was finalized in Manchu as "Biliktu Nangsu." He served the Later Jin/Qing court for almost thirty years until he died in Beijing in 1657.[35] This lama-turned-civilian official, whose original name disappeared in history, never returned to Tibet.

In 1643, Biliktu Nangsu was appointed to oversee the last Buddhist project ordered by Hong Taiji: to build stupas and temples in the eastern, southern, western, and northern outskirts of Mukden, respectively. Perhaps the emperor had accepted the suggestion of Ilaguksan Khutuktu, who was leading a Tibetan envoy mission to Mukden in an attempt to establish official relations between the Gelug sect led by the Dalai Lama and the Manchu emperor. The job was not assigned to Biliktu Nangsu alone. He supervised the project together with a colleague, Sibja Corji, later the cohost of the consecration ceremonies for the four stupas.

Sibja Corji was another Tibetan lama serving the Qing of whom we know very little. His personal background in Tibet and how he came to Mukden remain under debate, given the scarcity of reliable sources.[36] An early Qing archive records that in 1638, Hong Taiji treated him and four other lamas to a banquet after the completion of the Essential-Victory Temple.[37] From this we know that he enjoyed a privileged status. In 1646, he was appointed to Hure in eastern Mongolia and given the title "širegetü čorji" (temple master). Therefore, "čorji" (T. *chos rje*) in his name must refer to his honorary title while "Sibja" (T. Shes bya; Mo. Shibja) is his original name. While in Hure, Sibja established a grand Gelug monastery, the Xingyuan Temple. It was so prestigious that both the Fifth Dalai Lama and Emperor Shunzhi granted names to it.[38]

In contrast to the case of the Essential-Victory Temple, whose architect was unclear, we know for sure that Biliktu Nangsu and Sibja Corji directed the construction of the four stupas and temples. The temple stelae reveal that two Tibetans, commissioned by the Board of Work, were in charge of choosing the sites and supervising the project. Biliktu Nangsu also oversaw the creation of statues and paintings. In addition to the two top supervisors, the stelae record the names of the project managers, artisans, and craftsmen: Setehe and Yang Wenkui were the general supervisors; Datba Gelung and Li Daoxiu, the sculptors, Mootang, the planner of the stupas and temples; Baising, the painter; and Cui Guobao, the master plasterer. Additionally, the stelae in each temple also document, respectively, the laborers who worked on them. For example, the workers who constructed the West Stupa/temple were Shingnai (overseer of labor), Wang Xingjun (painter), Jin Shouben (carpenter), Yang Zhonghai (plasterer), Zhao Yingqian (foundry worker), and Zhang Shifu (stonemason).[39] Some of their names appeared on the stelae of other temple constructions in the early Qing. Understandably, we know nothing about these craftsmen other than their names. Were they born locally or migrants? How did they learn their trades? How were they selected, administrated, and paid? No document left a trace.

The multiethnic builders erected each temple roughly 5 li (1.5 miles) from the city wall, with each Tibetan-style stupa surrounded by a Han Chinese–style complex. Like the stupas, the structures of the monasteries were exceedingly similar; only the relative locations of the stupas within the compound varied. The Chinese names of the temples were Yongguang (永光, meaning "eternal brightness") in the east, Guangci (廣慈, "broad compassion") in the south, Yanshou (延壽, "life prolonging") in the west, and Falun (法輪, "dharma wheel") in the north.[40] But because the stupas were tall and stood out on the plain, local people nicknamed the four monasteries the East/South/West/North Stupa Temple. In Chinese, the West Stupa, the last stupa, consecrated in summer 1644, is pronounced *xita*.

When they departed from Tibet, neither Biliktu Nangsu nor Sibja Corji could have imagined that their service in the Manchu court would fundamentally reshape the landscape of a metropolitan center thousands of miles away from their home. The Mahākāla hall, the Essential-Victory Temple, and the four stupa temples constituted a comprehensive Tibetan Buddhist world in a Chinese city on the Manchurian frontier.

For historians of late imperial China, the career of Biliktu Nangsu challenged a popular image of Qing Tibetan Buddhism. For a long time, the Qing-Tibetan relationship has largely been simplified to the Qing-Gelug sect relationship. Writings on the subject were largely overshadowed by two historic summits: Emperor Shunzhi's meeting with the Fifth Dalai Lama in 1652 and Emperor Qianlong's meeting with the Sixth Panchen Lama in 1780. However, from Mergen lama to Biliktu Nangsu, we see that the Saskya lamas contributed greatly to the foundation of Tibetan Buddhism in the early Qing, even though their original names were forgotten and all the Mukden monasteries they helped construct later adopted Gelug doctrines. From the beginning, Qing Tibetan Buddhism mixed with different sects and schools, just like the hybrid architectural style of the Mukden monasteries.

Sibja Corji, on the other hand, was indeed a Gelug lama. His architectural legacies extended from Mukden to Beijing. In 1651, Emperor Shunzhi summoned him from Hure to the imperial capital to pray for the royal family. As a reward, Shunzhi bestowed on him the title "nomun han" (Mo. *nom-un qayan,* meaning "dharma king"). During his sojourn in Beijing, Sibja helped build the Yellow Temple (C. *huang si*), which later accommodated the visiting Fifth Dalai Lama and remained a core government facility for Qing Buddhism. At the same time, he suggested erecting a white stupa at a high point on a small island in the Beihai Lake next to the Forbidden City.[41] The stupa, soaring and sublime, is now regarded as an icon of Beijing, thanks in part to an extremely popular film soundtrack in the 1950s.[42] Through Sibja's religious-political enthusiasm, the Qing's old and new capitals were organically linked together. Not surprisingly at all, the white stupa in Beijing looks very much the same as the four stupas in Shenyang.

The Stupa: A Sacred World Inside Out

The stupa has its origin in a pre-Buddhist era. The mound-like or hemispherical tower was often used as a memorial or monument containing the relics of honorable monks. As this form of architecture spread to the Himalaya region, its structure and style was gradually formalized to a chorten (T. *mchod rten*). In the Chinese Buddhist tradition, another form of tower was derived from the stupa: a pagoda. Although easily distinguishable in appearance, both the stupa and pagoda are called *ta* (塔) in Chinese (or *t'ap* in Korean, *tō* in Japanese). Because of its round dome, in China a stupa is known as *fu bo ta* (覆缽塔, "a tower in the shape of an upside-down alms bowl"). The four stupas in the Mukden suburbs, the West Stupa included, were typical Tibetan style. Identical in size, shape, and color, each one of them was 26 meters (85.3 feet) high and had a footprint of 225 square meters (or 2, 422 square feet), surrounded by Han Chinese–style temple yards, pavilions, and halls. When they were first erected, the brand-new towers would have certainly seemed exotic. What did these stupas represent? And, more interestingly, why were there four of them?

The structure of a chorten stupa has three basic parts: a square base at the bottom, a hemispheric dome in the middle, and an axial pillar above the dome (fig. 5). Each section features several key design elements that bear unique religious symbolism. Using the Mukden stupas as an example, the square base was composed of a terrace three steps up, a Sumeru Throne base, and a three-tiered dome receptacle. Each represented one of Buddha's various moral and psychic powers. The dome section included the dome itself and a square-shaped enclosure, representing, respectively, the seven factors of enlightenment and the eightfold path. Last, the axial pillar was composed of thirteen discs, each representing a certain application of power, and a rain canopy that represented deep compassion. Made of bronze, the rain canopy was incorporated with shapes of a jewel, sun, moon, and pair of parasols to which twelve small bells were attached. Together, the idea of the stupa was closely associated with dharmakāya, the "reality body [kāya]" of Buddha.[43] Such a "system of overlapping symbols," as scholar Peter Harvey argues, "make the stupa as a whole into a symbol of the dharma and of the enlightened state of a Buddha."[44] This theory echoes what was recorded in one of the earliest Buddhist sutras, where Shakyamuni told a disciple that after passing away, his corpse would be burned and buried under a stupa. On the Mukden stupas, each side of the throne base was embossed with two august snow lions with a flame between them. There was a concave shrine space on the south side of the dome. On a breezy day, the bells on the parasol would ring beautifully, enhancing the solemn and mysterious atmosphere.

A stupa is usually hollow inside. According to Hindu/Buddhist customs, every stupa must contain certain items—oftentimes treasures, ritual artifacts, and sutras—to empower its sacredness. What did the engineers of the Mukden stupas, possibly Biliktu Nangsu and Sibja Corji, enclose in the towers? We would not find out until 324 years

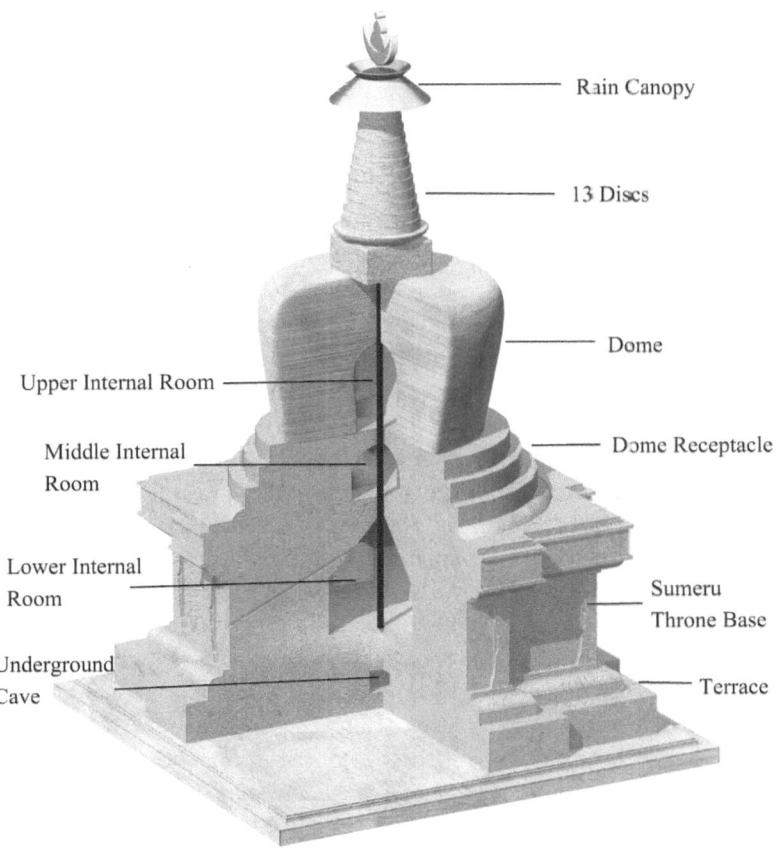

Rain Canopy

13 Discs

Dome

Upper Internal Room

Middle Internal Room

Dome Receptacle

Lower Internal Room

Sumeru Throne Base

Underground Cave

Terrace

5. External and internal structures of the West Stupa. Created by the author.

later in 1968. That year, the West Stupa was dismantled due to hazardous conditions. Thanks to the archaeologists' diligent reports, we can sneak a peek at the spiritual world of lama-officials who lived more than three centuries ago.[45]

Starting from the bottom, their excavations found that the internal structure of the West Stupa contained an underground cave and a three-story central chamber. The cave was 1 square meter large and 0.8 meter deep (about 3 feet wide and a little over 2.5 feet deep). The main item in the cave was a gilt bronze statue of yab-yum. Known in Chinese as *huanxifo* (the Buddha of joyfulness), the yab-yum depicts a male deity embracing a female deity face-to-face. This somewhat erotic figure was highly popular in Tantric Buddhism, representing the union of compassion and wisdom. The statue rested on a red copper plate in the shape

of a lotus flower that was wrapped with yellow silk. The Tibetan trans-
literation of a few Sanskrit words were engraved on the plate. In front
of the yab-yum statue were two white crystal beads, a tiny silver box,
and a jade container holding various colorful precious stones. There was
also a copper plate with pears, jujubes, peanuts, peaches, and walnuts.
Of course, only cores and nutshells remained, so fragile that they broke
apart upon gentle touch. It seems that the beads, box, container, and
fruit plate were all offerings to the yab-yum.

The lower, middle, and upper internal rooms were on the same horizontal levels of, respectively, the throne base, receptacle, and dome. The
square-shaped lower room was the largest, with each side measuring 4
meters (3.3 feet) long and 4.3 meters high. Leaning against the four walls
were thick pine or cypress branches around 2 meters high. Surprisingly,
the tree boughs were still green when the stupa was dismantled, as if
they had just been placed there. It is not hard to guess that the boughs
signified prolonged life or good health. The round middle room was
2.4 meters in diameter and 1.9 meters in high. The floor was covered
with grain, including sorghum, soybeans, wheat, and buckwheat, and
20 centimeters deep, symbolizing harmonious weather and an abundant
harvest. Resting on the grain were relics of sutra rolls written in Tibetan
and three pairs of bird skeletons. Hidden in the grain were a gold bar
(about 0.16 ounces), three pieces of silver, and many beaded necklaces
made of precious stones—likely the contribution of the social elites.
Finally, the upper room, also round, was 2.2 meters in diameter and 3.25
meters high. Along the east, west, and south sides lay altogether eighty-
odd miniature clay stupas in various sizes. They were called *tsha-tsha*
in Tibetan, probably derived from a Sanskrit or Prakrit word meaning
perfect "image" or "reproduction."[46] The practice of putting tsha-tsha in
stupas as an offering to Buddha was no longer popular in Inner China
after the Tang dynasty; therefore, scholars used to regard it as a tradition
unique only to Tibetans.[47] What puzzled archaeologists was that none of
the tsha-tsha were standing. They all lay on their sides with their spires
pointing to the east. Could it be the case that there were small stupas
inside all four towers that were pointing to the center of the city? We
can't know the answer without looking in the other three stupas.

In any case, it is clear that the West Stupa, from within and without,
constituted a sacred sphere in the western outskirts of Mukden. However, we shouldn't forget that historically the stupa also represented another system of symbolism, one that demonstrated not only its religious
meaning but also its political-geographical significance. The stupa was
often regarded by laypeople as the embodiment of Mount Meru (or
Sumeru), the sacred mountain and center of the Buddhist cosmos. This

was especially the case in Nepal and Sri Lanka, where certain kings or rulers viewed themselves as deities and their domain a manifestation of the Buddhist world. The stupa hence took on the special meaning of protecting kings and their kingdoms. French Indologist Gerard Fussman suggests that in some South Asian countries, "several kings tried to equate their kingdom with the whole world by transforming it into a replica of the cosmos, with Mount Meru at its center and a row of deities (in Hindu kingdoms) or stupas (in Buddhist countries) placed in such a way that the whole country, or at least its capital town where the king sat, was perceived as a gigantic mandala."[48] Indeed, since the four stupas changed Mukden into a holy religious sphere, many people in later generations believed that the capital had been purposefully redesigned as a mandala, a round-shaped pictogram indicating the Buddhist universe, which was often used as a spiritual map for meditation. But was this truly the case?

The mandala theory is currently the most popular iconological explanation for the spatial significance of the Qing's auxiliary capital. The Liaoning Provincial Museum, for example, demonstrated this with an impressive chart comparing a map of Shenyang with a mandala in its permanent exhibition of local history. The round shape exterior walls and square-shaped inner walls of the city coincide precisely with the outer

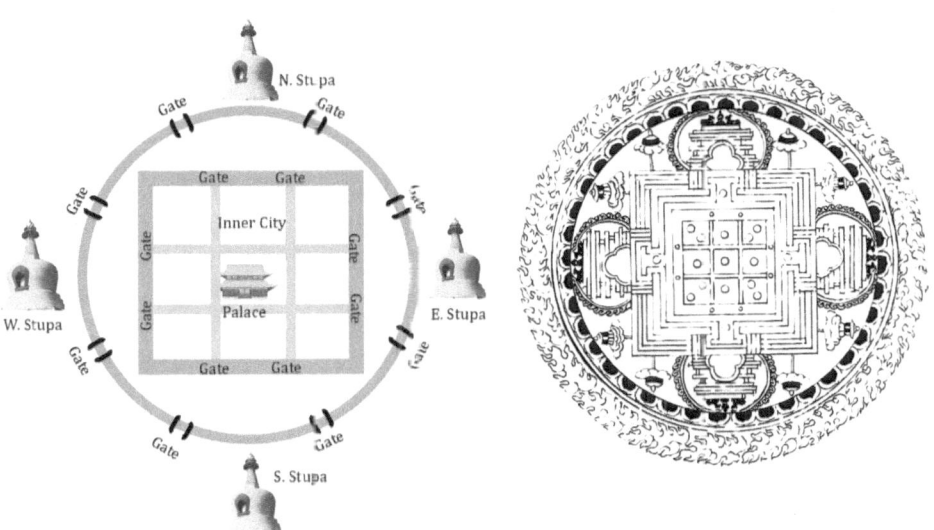

6. City plan of Qing's Mukden compared to a Buddhist mandala.
Created by the author.

and inner boundaries of a mandala, with the royal palace occupying the center and the four stupas the four ends. But this theory is problematic from both a historical and a theological perspective. To begin with, the exterior walls of Mukden were built later, in 1680, under the order of Emperor Kangxi. By that time, Biliktu Nangsu, Sibja Corji and anyone else involved in constructing the four stupa temples was long gone. Plus, this kind of defense-related construction was hardly intended to complete a Buddhist iconology. More importantly, the spatial arrangement of the deities in the city did not match the regulations of a mandala. Buddhist mandalas follow strict doctrines: a *yidam* (tutelary deity or principal deity) must occupy the center, surrounded by associated deities within its own system. The four stupa temples enshrined, respectively, Kālacakra (North), Vairocana (East), Avalokiteśvara (South), and Amitāyus (West). But who was the yidam to lead this mandala? Since the royal palace was located at the city's center, a reasonable guess might be that the Qing emperor viewed himself as the yidam. But that was anachronistic: although Shunzhi was indeed called "Manjusri Emperor" by the Dalai Lama, his father, Hong Taiji, never claimed himself as a bodhisattva. Even if he did, as Chinese historian Li Qinpu argues, in a Manjusri mandala, the associated deities in the south and north should be Ratnaketu and Amoghasiddhi rather than the two figures worshipped in the South and North Stupa Temples.[49] Could, then, the Essential-Victory Temple, where the Buddhas of the Three Times resided, be the central deities? The answer is no. It is impossible for these deities, who are not associated with each other in a coherent theological system, to construct a Tantric mandala. Moreover, geographically speaking, the Essential-Victory Temple was not even located at the center. It was in the western outskirts, quite close to the West Stupa but far away from the rest of the stupas. Even Samuel Martin Grupper, who was among the first to endorse the mandala theory, admits that "in looking for the reason why the Mukden school of iconography selected an unorthodox ensemble, I have failed to find any explanation for the distinctive array of deities chosen for the Manchu capital."[50] (He then suggests that the four stupas formed a mandala encircling the "Mahākāla temple," the palace of cakravartin, and the city. But this assertion, from the perspective of Buddhology, is even more unorthodox and less convincing).[51]

If Mukden was not a mandala, then what was it? There have been several hypotheses. Some Han Chinese authors in the Qing dynasty adopted feng shui geomantic theory and argued that the four stupas were the "four cardinal directions" (*si xiang*) and the eight city gates were the "eight trigrams" (*ba gua*).[52] In the early twentieth century, Japanese scholar Oshibuchi Hajime also supported this theory.[53] However, other than lacking document support, this Daoist interpretation was apparently too far-fetched to analyze the iconology of a Buddhist project. Li Qinpu provides an alternative theory. According to the Saskya tradition, both the stupas and the deities in the four temples bore the function of healing and prolonging life. In 1643, Hong Taiji had been severely ill for several months. It was very possible that Ilakuksan Hutuktu, the envoy of the Dalai Lama, advised him to build the stupas and temples to pray for good health. And the spatial array of the four temples, along with what was enshrined there, echoes the four enlightened activities (*'phrin las rnam bzhi*) of Tantric Buddhism: pacifying (T. *zhi-ba'i las*, east), increasing (*rgyas-pa'i las*, south), overpowering (*dbang-ba'i las*, west), and wrath (*drag-ba'i las*, north). The four activities and their embodiments constructed a Sīmābanhda (C. *jiejie*), a sacred boundary and the preparatory stage of a mandala, to protect the emperor from the intrusion of devils (in this case, disease).[54] Other scholars have also argued that at the time the project was launched, as recorded in the Manchu archives, the emperor's poor health was the biggest political concern.[55] The pine and cypress branches placed within the stupa clearly convey such a concern and wishes for his recovery. Unfortunately for Hong Taiji, he did not live long enough to witness the buildings' completion. It is especially ironic for the West Stupa Temple whose official name, Yanshou, means "prolonging life," and the principle deity enshrined there was Amitayus, the Buddha of "infinite life." Even if the emperor's recovery was indeed the initial intention, the Qing court would have been unlikely to admit it publicly.

That said, Qing sources did provide, retrospectively, a geomantic explanation. In the 1736 edition of the *General Chronicle of Shengjing* (*Shengjing tongzhi*), compiled during Yongzheng's reign (1722–35), the authors recorded that the four stupas were built "according to lama geomancy" and "it was said [the stupas] could unify [the country]" (*yun dang yi tong*).[56] Such a political interpretation was highly welcomed by an extremely ambitious Qing emperor, Qianlong (1711–99), who was also an enthusiastic patron of Tibetan Buddhism. In 1778 and in 1783, Qianlong dedicated a Chinese poem to the North Stupa (Dharma-Wheel) Temple. In both poems, he inserted footnotes to propagate the myth of geomancy and "unity." The footnote in the poem from 1783 reads, "A stupa was built in each of the four temples and they surrounded the capital. It was said that at the time there was a lama who was good at geomancy. He once said 'upon completing the four stupas, [the country] would be unified.' [What happened later] really matched his words."[57]

In this spatial interpretation, the stupas served solely as a political symbol, predicting—or more precisely, promising—the Qing's successful conquests and expansions in later generations. In the context of the late eighteenth century, the so-called unity might refer to the tortuous conquest of the Dzungar Mongols in Xinjiang. But what was the inspiration of this myth, which retrospectively linked the stupas' religious function with the empire's political endeavors, and in so doing reconstructed the stupas' spatial-ritual meaning? The answer may lie in an earlier text.

In 1645, one year after the completion of the four stupas, workers in Mukden finally finished the four temples encompassing the stupas. Like the Essential-Victory Temple, each stupa temple had two stelae that conveyed the reasons and process of the project in four languages. One stele was engraved in Manchu on the front and Han Chinese on the back; the other had Mongolian on the front and Tibetan on the back. It was the second-oldest quadrilingual literature created by the Qing, next only to the inscription on the Essential-Victory Temple stelae. The texts on the stelae were largely the same in the four temples, but there were some remarkable variations in content between the versions in different languages, especially between the Chinese and the three non-Chinese versions.[58] One important difference was that the Chinese version contained two passages absent from the Manchu, Mongolian, and Tibetan versions, both of which emphasized the virtue of the Qing ruler and the great enterprise of the Qing state. Following the beginning part of an "allegorical description" of Buddhism, the first passage reads, "The **holy king** has, by virtue of the Way, saved the dark headed people; the overwhelming [power] of **his transforming virtue** leaves none outside of it. Reflecting on **his merit and virtue**, it is proper to admire and rely on his example." The texts in all four languages then talk about both the decision-making and process of building the stupas/temples and introduce the main deities and the names of each temple one by one. After that, the Chinese version inserts a second passage, an ode to the temples:

> At each are to be erected imposing steles to last through all coming reigns. The inscription will read:
>> Auspiciously begins the **imperial plan**
>> Widely opening "precious" lands;
>> To the Buddha-sun upward looking,
>> We now ascend the altar of Spring;
>> In season follow rain and sun,
>> No calamity shall harm the **state**;
>> Not by the Three Evil Paths misled,
>> The Five Blessings to come ahead.[59]

Rarely in the other three versions could we find such direct mentions of the emperor and his state.[60] This discrepancy was certainly more than slight linguistic modifications when translating between different cultural contexts, nor was it simply a concern of literature genre. It was a careful choice to deliver different messages to the audiences of the respective versions. Other evidence can be found in the formal names of the four temples: all the Chinese names, in full, had the prefix *chi jian hu guo* (敕建護國), meaning "established under the imperial edict for protecting the state." But none of the names in the other three languages had the prefix of protecting the state. When drafting the stele inscription in 1645, the author(s) must have, as Mark Elliott puts it, "felt it was only with the Chinese audience that the imperial image needed this explicit endorsement."[61] Whereas to Inner Asian audiences, the inscription speaks only to the project's religious aspects—with the Tibetan version providing the most elaborate theological introduction of the deities. The Tibetan version also mentions the "consecrating teacher was Sibja Corji."

On top of that, the four different versions of the inscription were not equally circulated after 1645. Only the Chinese version was ever recorded and reprinted in some Qing gazetteers. None of the Inner Asian versions were reproduced in printed form until the Japanese publicized rubbings of the stelae of the North Stupa Temple in the early twentieth century. Given that each stele (with its turtle base) was as high as 4.91 meters (over 16 feet),[62] it would not be easy for a pilgrim or visitor to closely read, let alone compare, the texts when at the temples—provided that they actually had the linguistic skills to even do so. We can almost say that the Qing authority, intentionally or not, encouraged only the Chinese version concerning the "imperial plan" and "state," to be read widely, spread and eventually adopted. During the Yongzheng (1668–1735) and Qianlong's reigns, the "imperial plan" was naturally explained as the empire's successful expansion, or "unity," in Inner Asia.

An intriguing question to ask is: Who authored the inscription? The inscription records say that it was "composed" (C. *zhuan*; Man. *acabuha*; Mon. *orošiyulba*; T. *gtan tu dbab*) by Garin, Grand Secretary of the Inner State Historical Office, and then "translated" (C. *yi*; Man. *ubaliyambuha*; Mon. *orčiyulba*; T. *bsgyur ro*), respectively, by Heide into Chinese, Sidai into Mongolian, and Don bzang gu shri into Tibetan. The records suggest that the Manchu version was created first and served as a "master copy" for the rest. In this way, the narrator established a hierarchy between the different languages and highlighted the superior position of Manchu, the native language of the Qing rulers. But upon a comprehensive reading, scholars found out that the real situation was much fuzzier and ambiguous.

Among the evidence, the opening part of the inscription counters the Manchu-master-copy narrative the most. Comprised of eight sentences, it was also the opening of the Essential-Victory Temple stele inscription. It starts, "The deep valley is without prejudice; whatever sound is there will reverberate. The hollow of a great bell [only] receives, when struck it does not fail to ring." The long passage was a highly elegant and euphemistic prose on the beauty and awe of Buddha. But rather than a Manchu creation, it was a direct quote from a Chinese essay, which appeared in a sixth-century literary compendium, *Wen Xuan*, compiled by Crown Prince Zhaoming of the Liang dynasty (502–557). The essay, "The Dhūta Temple Stele Inscription" (Toutuosi beiwen), authored by Wang Che, was one of the most well-known pieces of Chinese Buddhist literature. So at least for that part, the "master copy" was in Chinese and was translated into Manchu, Mongolian, and Tibetan—not without considerable reduction and adaption. By the same token, the Tibetan version offers the most explicit description of the deities enshrined in each temple. The other three versions must have been rendered based on the Tibetan "master copy." As it turned out, each version made certain modifications to better address to their respective audiences.[63]

Therefore, "Who was the author?" or "Which version was the master copy?" are not the right questions to ask. Rather, a better question is: What was the relationship between the different languages demonstrated in this early Qing document? Certainly, the Qing authority tried to prioritize Manchu, as it would do again and again for the next two hundred years. However, it is clear that Manchu was never that prestigious in practice. (Let us not forget that the written format of Manchu was derived from Mongolian scripts, and that the Manchu vocabulary borrowed heavily from Chinese and Mongolian.) Perhaps a more reasonable assessment was that the texts in four different languages simultaneously "composed" and "translated" each other. Together, they constructed a delicate yet comprehensive intertextual interpretation of the state-church association in early Qing. Different groups of people were encouraged to understand such an association in their own ways. At the same time, the diverse understandings neither paralleled nor contradicted one aother; they were unified by a proto-narrative about Qing patronage of Tibetan Buddhism.

Tibetan Buddhist Networks: From Mukden to the Whole Empire

Throughout the Qing dynasty, there were many forms of literature—government documents, gazetteers, personal writings, and so on—that talked about the Essential-Victory Temple, including the Mahākāla hall.

There were also quite a few mentions of the four stupas and temples. But very few writings focused just on the West Stupa, or Xita. People hardly treated the Life-Prolonging Temple as an independent unit. The situation, nevertheless, reveal the precise nature of the Xita space during the Qing. Although neither a center nor a separate site with unique characteristics, the West Stupa was a key component of a larger socioreligious nexus: that of the imperial Tibetan Buddhist monasteries in Mukden. And the Mukden nexus itself, in turn, was a critical node in the much larger network of Qing Tibetan Buddhism.

The nexus of the Mukden temples was completed during Shunzhi's reign with two major developments. First, the Mahākāla hall in the Essential-Victory Temple was remodeled into a two-story pavilion on the same site. Second, in 1656, a new monastery, named Long-lasting-Peace (Changning 長寧, Man. Entehame elhe), became the latest temple to join the royal monastery nexus. Thereafter, the nexus was composed of altogether seven temples: the Essential-Victory Temple, the Mahākāla Pavilion, the Long-lasting-Peace Temple, and the four "stupa temples." The network was generally known locally as *sita qisi*, the "Four Stupas and Seven Temples." For both longtime residents and random visitors to Mukden, these monasteries were as grandiose as they were mysterious, just like the lamas dwelling there who always wore yellow hats, dressed in yellow and scarlet robes, and spoke an unknown language. As in many other places, hearsay, folk stories, and fiction mixed in memory, and the temples played a significant role in creating a legendary narrative of local history.

For example, the most noted puzzle in the monastery nexus concerned the unique statue in the Mahākāla Pavilion, the smallest "temple" among the seven, which constituted only a single structure within the Essential-Victory Temple complex. In oral tradition, the story of the renovation of the Mahākāla hall had a peculiar origin. After the Essential-Victory Temple was built, the Mahākāla statue (called "golden Buddha" in the story) snuck out of its own shrine every night. In the morning, the lamas would find the statue sitting on the roof of the main hall facing east. Initially, they thought the "golden Buddha" wanted to be enshrined in the main hall. But even after they moved the statue there, it still escaped to the roof every night. Someone realized that the deity must want to reside in a higher building. But according to regulations, no structure in the temple could be higher than the main hall. Eventually, Hong Taiji received a report and gave special approval to erect a taller pavilion for the Mahākāla statue.[64] Although fictional, the story reveals some important messages. The setting of the Mahākāla Pavilion was indeed unconventional and against both Buddhist and architectural doctrines. And it was the Qing emperor who intervened and changed the tradition. In so doing he made Mahākāla occupy an unusually high position in Qing Tibetan Buddhism.

In the first month of every year, Hong Taiji and the royal family would pilgrimage to the Essential-Victory Temple. Unlike other buildings within the compound, the Mahākāla Pavilion rarely opened to outsiders. It was more like a private shrine saved only for the emperor. During the Qing, many Korean envoys, when stopping in Mukden en route to Beijing, visited the Essential-Victory Temple, which they called "the praying hall of the (barbarian) khan" (K. *k'anji wŏntang*). While the beauty of the complex impressed them profoundly, the Mahākāla Pavilion was strictly barred from entering. Throughout the Qing dynasty, many Korean writers repeated the rumor that the building held the portraits or statues of the Qing emperors.[65]

As for the newest temple, the Long-lasting-Peace Temple, it was originally a royal garden in the northwest suburb. Some Qing documents refer to it as Hong Taiji's "refuge from smallpox" (C. *bidousuo*). Multiple times when the fatal epidemic exploded in Mukden, the emperor escaped to this garden to avoid being infected. Later the garden was converted to a Tibetan Buddhist temple by annexing another small lama temple originally located in Hong Taiji's mausoleum (Zhao Ling). Because it was directly associated with the former emperor, the Long-lasting-Peace Temple also had a prestigious role in the nexus.[66] Therefore, within the monastery nexus, there was a hierarchical structure. The Essential-Victory Temple, the largest of the seven, enjoyed the highest status. The Mahākāla Pavilion and the Long-lasting-Peace Temple were the next, followed by the four stupa temples.

Also, during Shunzhi's reign, Qing-Tibetan Buddhism relations began a critical transformation. As mentioned, ever since the Western Xia dynasty in the eleventh century, Tibetan lamas used the "priest-patron" framework to explain their relations with the rulers of China. It does not really matter whether the rulers in the east were the Tanguts, Mongols, Han Chinese, or Manchu. From the Yuan dynasty onward, Tibetan writers designated the emperor of China as the incarnation of Manjushri bodhisattva.[67] Whereas the rulers of Tibet were the embodiment of Avalokiteśvara (C. Guanyin), another highly popular bodhisattva in South and East Asia.[68] In this worldview, the Manchu emperor, who became the new ruler of China in the mid-seventeenth century, was but an inheritor of the previous rulers of China and a peer of the religious leader of Tibet. And all the realms under the glory of Buddhism were governed by the combination of two orders: that of Buddha (dharma) and that of the secular kings (politics). For that reason, Japanese scholar

Ishihama Yumiko suggests that in the early seventeenth century, the foundation of the interactions between the Manchu, Mongol, and Tibetan was a shared notion of the "two laws," or what she calls "Buddhist Government."[69] Her innovative interpretation was not without questioners.[70] But even if it was indeed the case, from the late seventeenth century onward, such a common recognition changed irreversibly. With the Qing gradually expanding and solidifying their dominance in the Mongol steppe, their role in the Tibetan Buddhist world also transformed—from that of mere patron to that of administrator.

Such a transformation was first and foremost due to the Qing's evolving geopolitical situation in the Inner Asian frontiers. After taking over Beijing, the Qing, on one hand, pacified Inner China and established its political/moral authority by endorsing Confucianism and Daoism while, on the other hand, allied with Tibetan Buddhist leaders to compete with the Khalkha and Oirat Mongols. Around the same time, the Fifth Dalai Lama successfully defeated his rivals and established Gelug sect dominance of Tibetan Buddhism. With the help of Gushri Khan (1582–1655) of the Khoshut (one of the four khanates of the Oirats), the Fifth Dalai Lama became the very first supreme leader of all Tibet since Songtsen Gampo (604–650), a great king born a thousand years before him. In 1652, the Fifth Dalai Lama visited Beijing and met with Emperor Shunzhi. The two officially formed a priest-patron association. From

7. Qing empire's Tibetan Buddhist network. Created by the author.

that moment onward, the Qing policy toward Tibetan Buddhism—and through which with the Mongol-Tibetan world—has largely been determined by its intricate relations with the Dalai Lama, the most important *tulku* (reincarnated custodian) in Tibet.[71]

Although the summit in 1652 benefited both sides significantly, the bilateral relations went sour during the Kangxi's reign. Not only did the Dalai Lama befriend the Qing's enemies—rebel Wu Sangui in the Southwest and Galdan Khan of Dzungar-Oirat—but he also handed over his political power to regent (Desi) Sanggyé Gyatso (1653–1705), who later dictated Tibetan politics by concealing the death of the Fifth Dalai Lama for as long as sixteen years. In response, Kangxi purposefully promoted the status of another Gelug tulku, the Panchen Erdeni, to balance the influence of the Dalai Lama in Tibet. During the prolonged war against Dzungar, Kangxi advocated for Jebtsundamba Khutuktu as the highest Gelug tulku in Khalkha, further diffusing the Tibetan impact in northern Mongolia. On top of that, from Kangxi to Qianlong, the Qing government entrusted many political tasks to the Changkya Khutukhtu and made the latter the most powerful Gelug tulku in Gansu, Qinghai, Inner Mongolia, and northern China. By employing a "divide and rule" policy, the Qing separated the Buddhist sphere in Tibetan Mongolia into four top tulkus' domains. The Dalai Lama and the Panchen Erdeni ruled over Tibet, and the Jebtsundamba Khutuktu and the Changkya Khutukhtu controlled, respectively, Outer and Inner Mongolia. Among the four top leaders, the Changkya lineage had the most intimate relations with the Qing emperors. Throughout the Qing dynasty, only the Changkya Khutukhtu, who had a permanent seat in Beijing, was granted the title of "state preceptor" (C. *guoshi*). Emperor Kangxi once even told the Second Changkya Khutukhtu that "All the Yellow sect [i.e., Gelug] affairs east to Tibet shall be administrated by you and you alone."[72] Such a tone, of course, revealed a sovereign-subject relationship rather than a patron-priest one.

Throughout the process, the Qing put tremendous efforts into building and financing Tibetan Buddhist temples in Beijing, Chengde, Mount Wutai, Khüree (today's Ulaanbaatar), Dolon Nor, and Guihuacheng (today's Hohhot). Beijing and Chengde especially were designed as new centers to pull the gravity of Tibetan Buddhism toward northern China. During Qianlong's reign, the government invested over ten million taels of silver in the temples in Beijing. Another five million taels were spent on temples in Chengde.[73] With the booming number of temples and lamas, beginning in the Shunzhi reign, the Qing government began to reinforce its supervision of the monasteries and personnel. The most salient move was to incorporate Tibetan Buddhist affairs into Qing bureaucratic institutions. The Lifanyuan (Man. *tulergi golo be dasara jurgan*), which was the successor to the Mongol yamen and the Qing agency for coping with affairs in the Inner Asian frontiers, was assigned as the governing body of Tibetan Buddhism. The Lifanyuan recorded detailed regulations for lamas' investiture, tributes, certifications, rewards, and punishments.[74] Judicial practices involving the Mongol lamas also grew more and more systematic and sophisticated from early to mid-Qing.[75] Finally, to prevent Mongol and Tibetan aristocrats from abusing their powers by manipulating the reincarnation of lama leaders, in 1792, Qianlong adopted the "Golden Urn" lottery institution (C. *jin ping che qian*) as the final step to determine the reincarnations of the Gelug tulku in Inner Asia.[76] That is to say, all the reincarnations of important tulkus, including the four top leaders, had to be decided through, and recognized by, the Qing government. This marked the Qing's last and the biggest institutional reform to control Tibetan Buddhism. Rather than merging politics into religion (as had the Fifth Dalai Lama), the Qing incorporated religion into politics, putting churches under government control.

In Mukden, the internal administration of the temples followed the typical structure of a Mongol-Tibetan Buddhist monastery. The difference was that the positions and rankings of the Mukden lamas were highly regulated in a bureaucratic system. In the language of *The Compiled Codes of the Qing* (*Daqing Huidian*), the certified lamas "have fixed positions and were promoted in accordance with their ranks."[77] In the early Qing, the seven monasteries altogether had 180 lama positions. By the end of the Qing, the number of the budgeted posts had increased slightly to 199. All of them, in the words of a lama leader in the early republic, "are bureaucratic monks [C. *guan seng*]" on the government payroll.[78] These numbers, of course, did not include the many intern lamas who waited for a tenured position. For example, in the late Qing period, the Essential-Victory Temple and the Mahākāla Pavilion had a total of 79 lama positions on paper. But a Korean envoy who visited the complex in 1855 recorded that the actual number of the monks there was more than 200.[79]

The head of a temple was called a Da lama and was assisted by a *demchi* (a steward of the monastery) and a *gesgui* (in charge of maintaining order in the monastery). Below these three higher-ranking posts were the *unjad* (a chanting leader), *nilba*, *gelong*, and *bandi*. The Mahākāla Pavilion, despite its smallest size, had two Da lamas. The rest of the royal monasteries, the Life-Prolonging Temple included, had just one Da lama. The Da lama of the Essential-Victory Temple was the top of the top and held the title the "Jasak Da lama who Controls the Seal."

The term Jasak (C. *zhasake*; Man. *jasak*) in the Qing dynasty referred to certain powerful Mongol princes. Adding "Jasak" before "Da lama" indicated supreme authority in the Qing's religious-bureaucratic system. When the position of Da lama was vacated in a temple, it could be filled by a senior demchi from any of the temples in the nexus. The subsequent demchi vacancy could be filled by a gesgui, and so on. But the Jasak Da lama—that is, the Da lama of the Essential-Victory Temple—could only be appointed by Beijing.

The Beijing Lama (C. *zhujing lama*) was one of the three general categories of the lama communities according to the Lifanyuan codes. The other two were the Tibetan lama (C. *zang lama*) and the Nomad lama (C. *youmu lama*) in Mongolia.[80] The domain of the Beijng Lama, headed by the Changkya Khutukhtu, was not limited to Beijing but also included Chengde, Dolon Nor, Mount Wutai, Guihuacheng, and Mukden. Being a highly politicized lama community, the Beijng Lama also included resident delegates sent by prominent monasteries in Ili, Xining, Khüree, and Lhasa.[81] Within the network of the Beijing Lama, the Qing installed a fairly sophisticated bureaucratic system. This process actually started in Mukden. Right after the seven temples were established, the Qing set up the Division of the Seal Affairs (C. *yinwuchu*) in charge of the daily administration of the Mukden nexus. The head of the Essential-Victory Temple—the Jasak Da lama—took the responsibility of director. This institution later spread to Mongolia and was eventually adopted by the entire Beijing Lama system.[82] The Jasak Da lama of Mukden, like his counterparts in other places within the system, could not be promoted locally but had to be selected and appointed from among high-ranking lamas in Beijing. On top of that, the Da lamas in the Mukden temples had to rotate to serve in Beijing for a year (a practice called *nianban*).[83]

The Mukden nexus was not only directly woven into the Beijing Lama system covering the west, north, and northeastern China but also indirectly linked to the grand Tibetan Buddhist network extending to the entire empire. The best example of this was the punishment of Damba Corji. Damba Corji was one of the high-ranking lamas in Beijing who were sent by Emperor Kangxi to visit the Fifth Dalai Lama in Lhasa. Against the emperor's order, Damba helped Sanggyé Gyatso hide the information of the Dalai Lama's death and submitted a false report to Kangxi. Outraged upon finally discovering the truth, Kangxi nevertheless remitted Damba's death sentence. Instead, Kangxi confiscated Damba Corji's personal wealth and exiled him to Mukden, ordering him to spend the rest of his life "at one of the temples upon choice."[84]

The most significant change in the Mukden nexus in the Qing dynasty occurred during Qianlong's reign. Known for his adherence to maintaining Manchu characteristics in a multiethnic empire,[85] Qianlong was also determined to highlight—or to be more precise, create—"Manchu-ness" in Tibetan Buddhism. Concerned that the Manchu-dominant empire lacked a Manchu Buddhist canon, in 1773, he commissioned the Third Changkya Khutuktu to translate Kangyur (T. *bka' 'gyur*), one of two compiled Tibetan Buddhist canons, to Manchu.[86] It took eighteen years for all 108 volumes to be translated and printed. In practice, however, a significant portion was translated from the Chinese, rather than the Mongolian, canon.[87] Meanwhile, Qianlong ordered several temples within and beyond Beijing be converted to Manchu temples, meaning temples that were staffed by Manchu and practiced exclusively Manchu sutras.

In 1778, the emperor issued an edit to the Mukden general, the highest executive in Manchuria. Since "Mukden is the place of all Manchus" (Man. *mukden serengge manjusai de ba*) and the Manchu canons "were about to be complete," he ordered the general to "choose a larger" temple, convert it to a Manchu monastery, and fill it with Manchu lamas selected from local banner men.[88] A month later, the Mukden general, Hūngšang, submitted a memorial saying, "the North Stupa Dharma-Wheel Temple, topographically higher and more open than the rest of the temples, seems to be a good choice for a Manchu lama temple." With Qianlong's permission, the Changkya Khutuktu selected two lamas in Beijing and dispatched them to the newly converted Manchu temple in Mukden.[89] The Grand Council (C. *jun ji chu*) also sent a set of Manchu Buddhist canon—one of altogether twelve sets in print—to the Dharma-Wheel Temple.[90] Thus, the North Stupa Temple was elevated in the Mukden nexus. It was headed by a Da lama and a vice Da lama. Both enjoyed similar privileges to other Da lamas. But unlike Da lamas elsewhere, the Manchu Da lamas of the Dharma-Wheel Temple were promoted only from within.[91]

Qianlong was apparently very pleased about this arrangement. As mentioned before, he dedicated two poems to the Dharma-Wheel Temple, propagating the idea that the four stupas predicted the "unity" of the empire. The two Chinese poems were composed during his third and fourth tours to Mukden in 1778 and 1783, respectively. In the first poem, he directly expressed that the reason to advocate for Tibetan Buddhism was to "cherish the Mongols,"[92] a theme later repeated in his famous essay, "The Discourse of Lama" (C. *Lama Shuo*). Qianlong's true attitude toward Tibetan Buddhism has aroused great academic interest for many years. It's debated whether he was a sincere disciple, as shown in the internal decoration of his mausoleum or a utilitarian ruler, as shown in

"The Discourse of Lama." But reading the two poems for the Dharma-Wheel Temple closely, his image becomes even more controversial.

In both poems, Qianlong associated the "dynastic language" (C. *guoyu*)—that is, the Manchu language—with his state and his extraordinary governance. In the first poem he wrote, "the dynastic language is practiced at the Dharma-Wheel Temple, so the old capital is protected forever." In the 1783 poem, he further provided a theological connection between the "dynastic language" and himself as a cakravartin, the universal king:

> The Sanskrit term "cakravartin" is also called Dishitian [heavenly
>   emperor]
> It refers to the secular ruler, whom we call the emperor
> Buddhist Dharma and secular laws are mutually needed and
>   interpreted
> The four stupas surround the capital, and this one is in the north
> The unity really realized, matching the good omen predicted
> Therefore [We] ordered [this temple] to use dynastic language to
>   convey the three vehicles [of Buddhism]
> [So to remind us] not to forget the past, and demonstrate my
>   devotion in front of the two mausoleums.[93]

Qianlong's notion of cakravartin came from the Han Chinese name for the temple, Dharma-Wheel (Falun). In Tantric Buddhist tradition, the Wheel of Dharma (Dharmacakra in Sanskrit) was a symbol of cakravartin, so Qianlong naturally took the name of the temple as a reference to himself.

However, it was here that the emperor made a stunning mistake. The Chinese name, it turns out, did not correspond with the Manchu, Mongolian, and Tibetan names for the temple, and it failed to reflect the principal deity enshrined there: Kālacakra. Kālacakra, meaning the "Wheel of Time," is a Buddha who controls time and symbolizes the union of passion and wisdom. The image of Kālacakra, as the statue erected at the North Stupa Temple, is a yab-yum. All the non-Chinese names convey this theological message accurately: it was called the Temple of the Wheel of Time in Tibetan (Dus kyi 'khor-lo'i lha khang) and Mongolian (Caɣ-un kürdün-ü süm-e), and the Temple of the Buddha of Mastered Time in Manchu (Forgon be ejelehe fucihi). The non-Chinese versions of the quadrilingual stele inscriptions also made it clear that the aim of this temple was "bringing perpetual strength to the Imperial Throne" or "making the imperial rule firm with the power of time." Therefore, the principal deity was Kālachakra, the Master of Time. The Han Chinese version, in contrast, omits specific information about the deities in the four temples (only vaguely saying that "each temple has a big Buddha statue"). It also interprets the aim of the North Stupa Temple as "the promulgation of the True Law." Hence, the temple was named Falun, the Wheel of Dharma (Law).[94]

The perplexing question here is not so much why the Chinese version was different from the others, but why Emperor Qianlong was misguided by the "wrong" Chinese text. If he, who proudly presented his image as a "Manjushri Emperor," was indeed a devoted believer and a highly accomplished expert in Tibetan Buddhism, there was no way he could have missed the gigantic yab-yum statue in the temple or failed to recognized that it was Kālachakra. Indeed, it was strikingly different from the rest of the Buddhist statues in Mukden. Or if he, the holy Manchu khan, was indeed an enthusiastic advocator of the Manchu language, it is unthinkable that he completely ignored the Manchu name of the temple and the Manchu version of the stele inscription. Not only that, it seems that Qianlong, who claimed to have had studied Mongolian and Tibetan sutras for decades, did not consult any Inner Asian sources when composing the Chinese poems to brag about the Manchu-ness of the temple. Was he misguided by ignorant lamas in the temple? Highly unlikely. The Changkya Khutuktu would not pick some junior students to lead this important royal monastery. A 1930s pamphlet from the Dharma-Wheel Temple shows that the local lamas never confused the "Wheel of Time" with the "Wheel of Dharma."[95] But if Qianlong was aware of the discrepancy, why rather than correcting the wrong did he promote the mistake? Was it because the emperor was so obsessed with the political symbolism of cakravartin and "dynastic language" that he did not even care about the discrepancy between his personal interpretation and Buddhist doctrines? Just as Pamala Crossley says, Qianlong was an "internally satisfied and externally omnicompetent mien of the transcendent, universal ruler."[96] Or alternatively, Qianlong's poetic compositions themselves were shaped by the specific courtly culture and intended audience, meaning that his politically didactic poetry inevitably operated within the constraints of this system.[97] His poem on the North Stupa Temple begins with the Chinese name of a Tibetan Buddhist monastery, moves through praise for "unity" and the "dynastic language," and ultimately culminates in a consolatory gesture toward the "two mausoleums" (i.e., his ancestors). In doing so, it intertwines Tibetan Buddhism, the Mongol world, the Manchu way, and Confucian values, thus asserting sovereignty over all the key components of the empire. Within this context, whether it is the "Wheel of Dharma" or the "Wheel of Time," it seems, is merely a trivial detail.

More embarrassingly, the emperor's plan to recruit lamas from local banner men encountered difficulty because no Manchu at the time "was willing to become a lama." Hūngšang had to recruit altogether thirty Sibe banner boys as the "Manchu lamas." The ethnic Sibe (C. Xibo), after being transferred from eastern and northeast Manchuria to Mukden around 1699, had adopted Manchu as their native tongue. In 1764, more than four thousand Sibe banner soldiers, along with their families and relatives, were once again transferred to Ili in modern day Xinjiang after the Qing conquest of this westmost frontier. But Mukden remained an important home for the Sibe, which is one of the officially recognized ethnic minorities in contemporary China.[98] Hūngšang hoped that, with some religious training, the Sibe lamas could easily chant Manchu sutras. Subsequently, all the lamas in the North Stupa Temple have been Sibe.[99] That is to say, the only "Manchu" temple in the Manchu capital was staffed by people who never consider themselves as ethnic Manchu.[100]

Mukden: A Transfrontier and International City

The best-known folktale about the Tibetan Buddhist temples in Shenyang is about a white camel. The original story can be found in the 1736 version of the *Shengjing Tong Zhi* (the *General Chronicle of Shengjing*). It was said that a white camel carried the Mahākāla statue down from the steppe to Hong Taiji. When it arrived, the exhausted animal laid down and died. Therefore, the Essential-Victory Temple was set up at the point where it died.[101] In another version of the story, Mergen lama did not know where to go when Ligdan was defeated. A white camel appeared carrying the statue and led the lama all the way to Mukden. Mergen lama thought this was an oracle from Mahākāla that the deity had chosen this place as his home.[102] Today, the white camel is one of the most popular icons of the city. In 2003, a giant camel statue made of white marble was erected in front of the entrance to the Essential-Victory Temple. Every tour guide will tell you the legend while adding her/his own details to the myth.

Camels are not a native animal of the Liaodong Peninsula, nor of Manchuria. They were from steppe or desert regions. As in the ritual ceremonies described earlier, in the Qing period, camels were often presented as precious gifts, tribute items, or rewards, especially on occasions related to Inner Asian affairs.[103] Like the stupa, the coming of the camel indicated a growing trans-ecological communication between the agrarian zone of Liaodong and the nomad zone of Inner Asia. During the Qing period, a large part of Manchuria was preserved as a "reservoir" and banned from development.[104] Yet Mukden transformed from a military garrison to a political, religious, cultural, and commercial metropolis—one of the largest outside the Great Wall. This was partially because the old capital had retained a fairly complete bureaucratic system, which was used to govern entire Manchuria. But equally important was the fact that the Qing kept strengthening their tie with the Mongol steppe—and Tibetan Buddhism played a significant role in this, creating a transportation hub connecting all places in the empire.

From the early Qing onward, many Mongols started to live permanently in Mukden. There were the members of the Mongol Eight Banners (Man. Monggo gūsa), the offspring of Mongol princes or princesses, and, of course, the Mongol lamas and their relatives. Because the Essential-Victory Temple was a huge attraction for the Mongol nobles, many merchants drove their caravans, horses and camels all the way from Hure in Inner Mongolia, passed Zhangwu and Xinmin, to Mukden. They stayed in the area surrounding the Essential-Victory Temple, forming a commercial street and Mongol enclave in the west suburb.[105] But the most thriving commercial district was still found in the city center, especially Siping Street between the Drum Tower and Bell Tower. Military and civilian officials, immigrants, merchants, and political exiles from Inner China transformed the city into an economically prosperous and culturally vigorous metropolis. From the perspective of ecology, these people were very much what Peter Purdue would call "transfrontiersmen," who made Mukden a transfrontiers city.[106]

Moreover, as the Qing developed into one of the world empires in the early modern period, Mukden simultaneously gained international fame. In 1644, around the same time the Qing moved the capital to Beijing, fifteen Japanese were escorted to Mukden and stayed there for more than twenty days. They were the only survivors of a group of fifty-eight boatmen from the Fukui Domain who drifted to Manchuria and were attacked by the local Warka tribe. The survivors were treated well by Manchu officials, who later sent them to Beijing and arranged for them to return to Japan via Korea. They later reported to Japanese authorities what they witnessed. "The Tartar capital," as they called Mukden, "was the size of approximately two square Japanese *ri*." There were big buildings as magnificent as the Buddhist temples in Japan, with round pillars and glazed tiles, colorful and dazzling.[107] Nearly three hundred years later when Shenyang was under Japanese colonial rule, Oshibuchi Hajime published a study on the history of the city. In his narrative, the accidental meeting between these "ignorant merchants" and this "spectacular city rising in the vast Liaodong Plain" was nothing less than a romantic encounter.[108]

Intellectuals in early modern Europe also learned about Mukden through Jesuits missionaries serving in the Qing court. Ferdinand Verbiest (1623–1688), a Flemish father, accompanied Emperor Kangxi on a tour to Manchuria (called "East Tartary" by Verbiest) in 1682. In a letter, he reported that the capital of "the province of Leauton (Liaodong)" is "of considerable size and beauty, and no contemptible specimen of a royal residence." While he carefully measured the longitude and latitude of the city, Verbiest nevertheless spelled its name inconsistently, either as "Xynyam," "Xinyam," or "Y[X]im-yam."[109] The next year, he once again escorted the emperor on an imperial tour. This time they went to the Mongolian region, which Verbiest called "West Tartary." He went to great lengths to report what he observed was Kangxi's attitude toward Tibetan Buddhism: "It is known that the first Tartar emperor subjected the West Tartars by policy and subtlety; for among other means which he employed were the priests, named lamas, whom he lured to his service by good offices and presents. . . . For the same reason the emperor, who now rules both China and the two Tartaries, looks with an eye of favor on the lamas, and uses them to hold the Tartars in obedience, though he abhors them in his heart as men unclean and destitute of arts and sciences."[110]

In 1710, Kangxi commissioned some French Jesuits to map Manchuria, a project later extended to the entire empire. The result of this unprecedented geographical survey was the so-called *Kangxi Atlas* (*Huangyu quanlan tu*), one of the most accurate cartographic works in the contemporary world created by using cutting-edge technologies. Reproduced by French cartographer Jean Baptiste Bourguignon d'Anville (1697–1782), the *Kangxi Atlas* was widely circulated in Europe.[111] The location of Mukden was clearly marked, with its name spelled as either "Chinyan/Mougden" or "Chin-Yang/Moucden."[112] Apparently, nearly a hundred years after the city was renamed, its old name was still popular. The city received fervent attention in Europe when Emperor Qianlong's *Ode to Mukden* (1724) was translated and published in France. In this piece, Qianlong used the most extravagant rhetoric to praise his ancestors' great enterprise in creating the foundation of the empire.[113] Voltaire (1694–1778), an enlightenment thinker and a harsh critic of the Roman Catholic Church, highly praised *Ode to Mukden* as it further justified his admiration for Qianlong and the virtuous way the Chinese emperor governed his country.

During the Qing dynasty, the most detailed and consistent foreign records about the city came from Koreans. Korean diplomatic envoys to Beijing (K. *yŏnhaengsa*) were perhaps the most important channel for the Chosŏn dynasty to communicate with the outside world. Between

1637 and 1874, the Chosŏn court dispatched a total of 664 missions to the Qing, an average of 2.73 times per year.[114] Beginning in the early Shunzhi period, the envoys were required to stop in Mukden before heading to Beijing. The diplomats and secretaries made numerous observations in their travel writings, generally known as the *Yŏnhaengnok*, "Travelogues to Beijing." In the early Qing period, the overall Korean attitude toward the Manchu capital was quite negative. "A camel team came with a foul wind," one author documented in his poem, "and the barbarians on the camel backs wore skirt made by brocade."[115] Some expressed criticism that the city wasted too much money on the Buddhist temples.[116] Visiting the Simgwan (house of Shenyang), where the Korean princes had been kept hostage after Hong Taiji's second invasion, many authors couldn't help but lament the ill fate of their country and people.

Starting in the late seventeenth century, however, the tone of the Korean observers gradually softened. A great number of their writings openly praised the grandiosity of the architecture and the bustling market. Many asserted that Shenyang was the biggest city outside the Great Wall whose prosperity was next only to Beijing. Kim Ch'ang-ŏp wrote in 1712, "Hundreds of goods are shining in the stores across the street. Within a hundred steps' realm, countless musk deer, deer, and rabbits are piled up. All kinds of craftsmen—from carpenter, cartwright, blacksmith to tailor—can be found. Their tools are so convenient that one person could do ten persons' work in our country."[117] Yi Ch'ŏl-pu admitted in 1737 that "what is most impressive is that the inner and outer city walls are neatly designed and firmly built. Seeing this, I know that city-buildings in our country are almost like a joke."[118]

While no Korean observer made mention of the Life-Prolonging (West Stupa) Temple, most of all them visited the Essential-Victory Temple with great interest. Some dropped by the South Stupa and North Stupa temples. Tibetan Buddhism was something a neo-Confucian writer was neither familiar with nor willing to learn in detail. Except for Pak Chi-won, a renowned scholar who introduced the Gelug sect and the Panchen lama in length in his writings, most authors simply recorded what they saw as "ridiculous" about these Mongol "monks": They had a fearsome appearance, wore yellow kasaya, drank butter tea, and ate meat. They claimed they came six thousand li afar from the west and were the "teacher of the Emperor," but most of them didn't read or speak Chinese. Printed on their sutras were strange characters (Tibetan), so that some Korean visitors could not tell what they were.[119] What they could tell, from the splendid buildings and luxurious settings of the temples, was that the Qing emperor had invested endless money in this belief. As a writer in the Qianlong period commented:

"the barbarian [i.e., the Manchu] devotion of Buddhism had its long tradition."[120]

Although they were keenly aware that the temples were unusual, none of the Korean writers seemed to notice a unique feature of these royal monasteries: they were semibureaucratic institutions fully supported by the state. Yes, the lamas enjoyed economic privileges from the government. But their privileges were monetary only. Unlike temples in Tibet or Mongolia, the temples in Mukden did not, and were strictly forbidden to, intervene in local governance or social structure.[121] Their main function was to serve the emperor and the state, nothing more. The bureaucratic nature of the monastery nexus, thus, foresaw the fate of Tibetan Buddhism in Mukden. Was it a blessing or a curse?

CHAPTER 2

The Lama

After it was erected, the tall white West Stupa stood there rather lonely for over two centuries. Aside from the lamas of the Life-Prolonging Temple, civilians rarely paid it a visit except, perhaps, during Buddhist holidays. Until the late nineteenth century, the area around the West Stupa was largely an undeveloped, wild space. Though the Life-Prolonging Temple was only about 1.6 kilometers or a mile to the northeast of the popular Essential-Victory Temple, the smaller monastery did not garner much attention. It never received an imperial visit, unlike the Essential-Victory, Long-lasting-Peace, and Dharma-Wheel Temples. Emperor Qianlong once bestowed the Life-Prolonging Temple (along with the other three stupa temples) with a plaque engraved with his calligraphy, but nothing else ever warranted another sentence in official gazetteers. Nor did the Korean emissaries, who left numerous observations about the Essential-Victory Temple, make mention the West Stupa, partly because the highway to Beijing turned north immediately after the Essential-Victory Temple, rather than extending a little farther west to the Life-Prolonging Temple. Despite that the temple complex was regularly maintained by the government, the stupa had gradually become dilapidated and discolored. Grass and other plants thrived on the top of the Sumeru Throne base and the dome receptacle.

However, even in a marginal location like the West Stupa, human experiences filled the space with meaning. During Qianlong's reign, the government established twenty tenured lama positions at the Life-Prolonging Temple.[1] Some of the lamas were fortunate enough to get promoted and rotate to the other six temples within the Mukden nexus. Only the luckiest few, not just in the Life-Prolonging Temple but in all the temples, could rise to head of a monastery, the Da lama. Therefore, to better understand the West Stupa as a human created social space, it makes much more sense to investigate the main actors, the lamas, in the entire Mukden nexus rather than seeing such a space as independent and isolated.

How many lamas were there in Mukden? Where did they come from? No archive provides an accurate account. The only concrete figure, calculated from various versions of the *Da Qing Huidian* (*The Comprehensive Codes of the Great Qing*), is that there were 199 assigned positions in the seven temples by the end of the dynasty. We know that the actual number is much higher. The official job posts did not include the young disciples in training and the Sula (leisured) lamas, both waiting for a vacancy. In a report submitted in 1912, the Jasak Da lama claimed that he "rules over more than 400 lamas," which gives us a rough idea of the total headcount in the seven temples.[2] In addition, there were many more nonroyal temples established in the city that had little or no affiliation with the government. Varying in size and sources of patronage, they were attracted to Mukden precisely because the "Big Seven" had shaped the city into a Tibetan Buddhist center. The temples were numerous, to the extent that they were packed, one after another, near the suburb between the Huaiyuan Gate and the Essential-Victory Temple. In terms of the origin of the lamas, aside from the Dharma-Wheel Temple, which was staffed by local Sibe, most lamas were Mongols either born locally or arrived from

8. Lama priests in Mukden (1904). Photo by Douglas Story; published by Charles Voisey.

the steppe. The aforementioned 1912 report states that most lamas "came from the Mongol banners of the East Three Leagues." The so-called East Three Leagues refers to the Leagues of Jirem, Juu Uda, and Josutu, which ruled over the eastern part of today's Inner Mongolia. When the Qing regime rose in the early seventeenth century, the Mongol ulus in this region—for instance, the Khorchin, Dörbet, Aohan, and Kharchin—were the earliest and most stalwart allies of the Manchu state.

The West Stupa space, along with the rest of the Mukden nexus, had been created and maintained by both state and religion. At the same time, it was unavoidably integrated into local society in one way or another. The Mongol lamas, as individuals and as a group, manifested the intertwined relations between the church, state, and society. "Speaking Mongolian, men of an alien race and an alien religion," as a British journalist described them in the early twentieth century, "the Lamas were strangers in a strange land."[3] What did a lama's life look like? What were the lamas' connections with the state? How did they interact with the local population? How did they interact together? Official documents only scratch the surface, providing details about a lucky handful from their résumés. Take for example, this résumé submitted for review in 1907:

> The Da lama of the East Stupa (Temple), Ishi Sangbo (C. Yexisangbu), was a Mongol of the Tümed banner. He took the tonsure as a kid and lived in a temple at age eight, received the ordination and became a bandi at age nine, and became a gelong at age 25. He had taken the position of nirba for four years, then shangjodba for eight years, then gesgui for one year. In the fourteenth year of Guangxu (1888) he was a secondary nominee for Da lama. He had been a demchi for 11 years. In the sixteenth year of Guangxu (1890), he was a secondary nominee for Da lama. In the sixth month of the twenty-fourth year (1898), he was appointed as the Da lama of the East Stupa. In the thirty-first year (1904) he went to Beijing for a year on rotation. He has been on the payroll for 34 years and taken the duty of Da lama for 10 years. He is now 53 and practices sutras very well.[4]

To a certain extent, a résumé like this one reveals the social structure of the Mukden lamas. That year, the Da lama position at the Long-lasting-Peace Temple, one of the seven temples, was vacated. Since the Long-lasting-Peace was a prestigious monastery, next only to the Essential-Victory, its Da lama should be promoted from the Da lamas of the Mahākāla Pavilion or the West, South, and East Stupa Temples (the North Stupa, being an equally prestigious Manchu temple, did not participate in the selection). Ranked by seniority, the résumés of all the Da lamas are exceedingly similar in both format and content. Although straightfoward and succinct, the résumés nevertheless reveal the life trajectories of these elite lamas. For starters, all lamas serving in the seven royal temples had to "take the tonsure as a kid" (*naidi chujia*, 奶的出家). That is to say, they had to start their lifelong careers from early childhood, normally between ages of six and ten. Second, they had to acquire certain degrees in Buddhist study (bandi and gelong) before officially enrolling in the royal monasteries. For example, in the case of Ishi Sangbo, he entered a temple at the age of eight but was not listed on the "government payroll" (*shi qianliang*, 食錢糧) until he was nineteen. Third, the lamas had to climb an inflexible bureaucratic ladder to become elite. The hierarchy mimicked the temples in Tibet and Mongolia, though it was not exactly the same.[5] The bottom rung was held by the *nirba*, who assumed the role of temple accountant or rent collector, followed by the *shangjodba*, a butler (or in other cases, the umjia, a chanting leader). The gesgui was the third-ranking administrator responsible for maintaining discipline. The demchi (the steward) ranked second and could, after serving as a secondary nominee (*ni pei*, 拟陪) at least once, later become a primary nominee (*ni zheng*, 拟正) and be promoted to Da lama upon government approval. For the Mukden lamas, Da lama was their ceiling. They could not become the Jasak Da lama—that is, the Da lama of the Essential-Victory Temple; the lama in this role had to be selected in, appointed by, and transferred from Beijing.

But there is a more important enigma that a résumé cannot solve. How did the triangular relations of church, state, and society evolve over time, both during the Qing dynasty and after the collapse of the Qing? The answer is not easy to ascertain because the available historical records are scarce and scattered. That said, we can piece together a picture, using patchy information gathered from government codes and archives as well as lawsuit and trial documents. As narrative is a more effective approach than abstract analysis in this context, chapter 2 will convey the picture through stories about the lamas. Some of the stories are simple, some more intricate. Take Ishi Sangbo, whose résumé we just read. In 1907, his résumé was at the bottom of the pile. As the most junior of all the qualified candidates, he was not nominated for the position. However, two decades later, he had moved to the top and become a central figure in an intriguing and dramatic conflict. We will get back to him later.

The Wallet of Lama

Not many stories focus exclusively on the Life-Prolonging (West Stupa)
Temple in the Qing dynasty. I have found just two episodes in different
genres: the first is a folktale; the other, a criminal case. Both of them
involve the killing of a Da lama, but one is understandably more fictional and the other historical. The folktale was told by Chang Haifeng
(born around 1910), one of the last Mongol lamas who once served at
the Life-Prolonging. Thanks to a national effort to collect folktales and
literature in 1980s China, we are able to learn the story that was passed
on to Chang orally.[6] It goes like this:

> Hong Taiji believed in Lamaism [*sic*], and Lamaism was brought
> by the Mongols. The Life-Prolonging Temple was a lama temple, so
> only ethnic Mongols could be lamas. There are 11 lamas at the Life-
> Prolonging Temple. The Da lama is called *Makhadorji* (C. *Mahadu-
> erji*). The emperor invests him with the rank of a second-rank official.
> He can go directly to the palace to meet the emperor without being
> stopped by the banner guards. The emperor invites Makhadorji from
> Inner Mongolia. He practiced [Tibetan Buddhism] for many years
> before coming here to teach. [He recites sutras for local people who
> come to worship the Long-Life Buddha.] Makhadorji is very strict
> with the junior lamas. He establishes hundreds of regulations. Of
> course, doing that is for the good of Buddhism. According to tradi-
> tion, [the temple] distributes salaries to the lamas only on the last
> day of the year, not on normal days. One year, on the twenty-third
> day of the twelve month, the junior lamas requested to get paid in
> advance so they could purchase goods to celebrate the "minor new
> year."[7] Makhadorji rejected them. They are so angry that they kill the
> Da lama. . . . [Later, the deified Makhadorji turned himself to a Lord
> of Soil and received offers from local people.]

The second episode, a criminal case, happened in 1863. At midnight
on November 8, two thieves climbed over the wall and snuck into the
bedroom of Baldan (C. Baladan), the Da lama of the Life-Prolonging
Temple. When Baldan woke up, shocked by the intruders, they stabbed
him and ran away. The Da lama lost some money and cloth, worth about
106 taels of silver. Worse still, he died from the injury a month later. After
four months of "extensive investigation," the local authorities closed the
case because the thieves had left no trace. "No civilians," according to
their report, "live near the temple." Regarding Baldan, the report only

says that he was born to the Beizi Banner of Tümed and had come to the Essential-Victory Temple as a child. It does not even reveal the deceased's age.[8]

Despite the differences in genres, both stories confirm the origin of the elite lamas in Mukden: many, if not most, came from Inner Mongolia. They had had years of training before being stationed at the Life-Prolonging Temple. Unlike what people would usually imagine of a religious space, life in the temple was far from tranquil. Rather, there were tensions, sometimes as radical as manslaughter. In the folktale, the conflict was due to internal stratification: either the Da lama treated his juniors too harshly, or the juniors were too worldly. In contrast, in the criminal case, the violence came from outside the temple walls. One striking difference is how the two stories viewed the temple's social connections. In their oral tradition, the lamas did not regard the temple as a separate space from the local environment. Makhadorji later reincarnated to a Lord of Soil, who, in Han Chinese tradition, is a popular Daoist deity in charge of local affairs. This episode reveals the merging of Tibetan culture and local Han Chinese culture. And the folktale also suggests that the temple had quite intimate interactions with both the state (with obvious exaggeration) and local believers. In contrast, the officials in the criminal case provide a different image: the lama leader was the target of thieves who coveted his wealth. The temple was geographically and socially marginal. Even if a felony had been committed, the authorities dropped the case due to a lack of information, if not a lack of interest. The stories were told from very different perspectives—one from the lamas, the other from local officials—and in very different tones. Therefore, both are revealing but neither necessarily more so than the other.

Nevertheless, the stories share a common theme—the cause of the fatal conflicts was money. It begs the following questions: What was the Mukden lamas' economic status? What were their sources of income? How fat were their wallets? First, let's first probe into these questions through the lens of the Korean literati. As mentioned in chapter 1, Korean envoys visited the Essential-Victory Temple quite often. Many were amazed by the beauty of the temple architecturally and the luxurious interiors. Take the account by Sŏ U-jŭng, who visited the temple in 1818. "My eyes were dazzled by the crafted beams and painted rafters." There was a "Mongol monk"—obviously he is referring to the Jasak Da lama—wearing yellow:

> He invited the three envoys to his bed-table and presented us with fragrant tea, bobo (a kind of cake, which is about the size of an egg with wax-like stuff painted on the outside and sugar stuffed inside. Made

with barley, it would be as big as a crab apple if sold in the market. The taste is not good), and milk (*tarak*). They were said to be bestowed by the emperor. The artifacts on the bed-table, all of them—chiming clocks and the like—were extremely exquisite. There were four or five peacock feathers more than several *ch'ŏk* high. On the right of the bed was a place covered with red carpet: this was where the emperor had sat. On top of the table, there is a seal that belonged to the monk. When asked about it, he said (the seal) indicated that he was in charge of all the temples beyond the Shanhai Pass.[9]

Sŏ followed his description with a satirical poem: "Wearing royal color, the old Mongol monk rarely moves from his yellow-felt-bed (it is said that the Imperial Preceptor does not even bow to the emperor)." Elaborating on the affluence of the temple, Sŏ, like many Korean observers, lamented that Confucianism was not honored in China: "It turns out that Buddha himself favors riches and glory, and our teaching has completely declined." Of course, the account is full of misinformation; for example, the Da lama was never an imperial preceptor, and dressing in yellow was just a Gelug tradition. But nevertheless, it reveals a Korean official's first impressions of the lamas' lives.

The artifacts mentioned by Sŏ—snacks, chiming clocks, and peacock feathers, not to mention the fascinating ornaments inside the room—all indicated a privileged status. They reminded visitors that the seven temples were royal institutions. Being royal meant that all the religious supplies—facilities, offerings, instruments, treasures, and sutras—came from the state. It also meant that all expenses related to religious activities, including ritual materials and temple maintenance, were paid for or provided by the government, either Beijing or Mukden. As recorded in the Qianlong version of the *Da Qing Huidian*, for example, each year the Mukden Board of Finance supplied the monasteries with grain, flour, salt, vegetables, fruit, geese, chicken, and papers used in ritual ceremonies. Aside from this, the board also provided the Essential-Victory Temple with nearly 80 taels of silver for "incense and candle money," 310 taels for "sutra chanting money," and 200 *jin* of tea. The Mahākāla Pavilion received nearly 50 taels of "incense and candle money," 210 taels of "sutra chanting money," and 60 jin of tea. The four stupa temples altogether acquired nearly 200 taels of "incense and candle money" and 600 jin of tea.[10] But the largest expenditure item, it seems, was maintenance. In the archives related to the Mukden temples, there were maintenance projects requests almost every year. The costs spanned from dozens to thousands of taels of silver. Some estimate that in the Qing era, the seven temples were repaired more than a thousand times.[11] In the First

Historical Archive of China, I found nearly twenty repair requests from the Life-Prolonging (West Stupa) Temple from 1755 to 1893, all of which were major projects that needed the central government's approval.[12]

What about benefits for the lamas? Imagine a young boy born in the early nineteenth century, whom we shall call L.[13] Upon entering a temple, L follows a master and serves him. The master provides L with basic religious training and pays for his food and clothing. The training is a decade-long process during which L is required to study "the Tibetan theology, the literature of Tibet and Mongolia, Tibetan medicine, astronomy, astrology, and Buddhist philosophy."[14] After years of service, there is a vacancy and the master successfully arranges for L to get the position. From that moment, L is enrolled on the government payroll and receives benefits. He starts at the lowest rank, a bandi. As a teenager, he can earn a salary, called a *kuoliangyin* (口糧銀, food money), of 7.7 taels of silver a year. Aside from that, every other year he receives a bundle of red cotton cloth and a hat made of fox fur, all provided by the Mukden Board of Finance. Eventually, L passes the gelong degree and earns himself the official title of "lama." Since he is already an adult, from now on he receives a new bundle of cloth and a hat every three years. The cloth color is no longer limited to red, instead it now comes in three shades: red, light yellow, and gold. After perhaps another decade of service and some luck, L gets the position of gesgui. Now he earns nearly 8.8 taels a year, roughly the income of a tenant peasant in the secular world. The salary may seem humble, but being a gesgui guarantees L entrance to the club of the highest elites. If nothing goes wrong, in his thirties or forties, L is promoted to demchi, earning a salary of 10.5 taels—still not a big income increase. But more significant than money, he is now qualified to be a Da lama candidate—provided there is a vacancy. The rest is about waiting and getting a nomination. Sometimes a demchi has to wait another twenty years for the chance, sometimes just a year. Finally, L succeeds in getting the dream position all lamas covet. Now his salary takes a huge leap: the Da lamas of the West, East, and South Stupa Temples earn more than 116 taels a year. That is an elevenfold increase. The Da lamas of the Dharma-Wheel, Long-lasting-Peace, and Essential-Victory Temples earn an even higher income, 166.2 taels. The two Da lamas of the Mahākāla Pavilion, however, share the salary of one, getting 81 taels each. How does the financial status of Da lamas compare with that of normal people? According to one estimate, in Qianlong's reign, the household income of a midlevel rural family was roughly 35 taels a year.[15] Of course, salary is just what's on the books. The total benefits L gets, based on his current distinguished social and religious status, are much more, for sure.

During Jiaqing's reign (1796–1820), the salaries of the Mukden lamas cost the government more than 2,300 taels of silver per year. Over the next several decades, the total payment varied from 2,100 odd to 2,500 odd taels reflecting changes in the lama population.[16] The financial burden was on the treasury of the local government. How did the authorities pay the lamas? The term *salary* or *payroll* is used more as equivalence or metaphor for convenience, in light of the complexity of the situation. The real scenario was tricky: the Mukden government patronized the royal lamas in the form of agricultural rent by assigning certain manors to the temples. The lands were called *yangzhandi* (养瞻地, dependency land). During the Qing, yangzhandi usually referred to the lands rewarded to the heads of government manors (*zhuangtou*, who organized and supervised farming on the manors) to sustain their own livelihood.[17] Dependency lands were inheritable yet not salable on the market. Initially, the lamas were paid with agricultural products (hence, their compensation was called "food money"). After 1811, the material taxes were converted to cash and paid on schedule and in a fixed amount Therefore, on the surface, it looked exactly like the state was paying "salaries" to the lamas. However, there were still problems with this arrangement. One came from the nature of the state-temple relations: Were the two institutions, in terms of their relation to the lands, essentially the same? Even more problematic was the nature of these dependency lands. Prior to 1811, the temples directly taxed the lands without any interference from the state. If the lands were rewarded—as a source of income—to the temples, were they the property of the temples or of the state? The confusion caused a major dispute between the lamas, the state, and local society in the early nineteenth century, and exposed serious problems with the Qing's land system.

The Death of Manor Heads

On October 21, 1806, Zheng Guotai hung himself. Zheng was a manor head (C. *zhuangtou*; Man. *tokso i jangturi*) who supervised the farming and taxation of a government manor (C. *guanzhuang*). His younger brother, Zheng Wu, another manor head, committed suicide the same way a little over a month afterward on November 25. Three days later, the widows of the Zheng brothers filed a lawsuit with the Mukden authority. They accused the Da lama of the East Stupa (Eternal-Brightness) Temple, Lobdzang Teliyei, of being responsible for the deaths. They alleged that the Da lama had violently pressed the Zhengs to submit offerings in an unreasonably high volume, leading to the brothers' suicides. Worse than that, after learning of the tragedies, the Da lama induced a nephew of the Zheng brothers to falsely testify that the incidents had nothing to do with the Da lama but instead were due to a domestic conflict.[18] In Qing dynasty Manchuria as well as in North China, the government manor was a critical component of banner farmland (Man. *tokso*).[19] Nurhaci established the manor system along with the Eight-Banner system, and the two systems were closely associated with each other.[20] During the expansion of the Later Jin and the Qing, more and more laborers— most of them Han Chinese—were organized to work on government manors. In Shunzhi's period, Han Chinese from North China flooded to the Liaodong region and were registered, forcefully or voluntarily, to these manors. The government appointed manor heads from among them as administrators. Although the manor heads had tremendous hereditary powers in the community, neither did they possess the land nor were they free laborers. As "banner people" who enjoyed certain social-political privileges, they and their offspring were actually more like permanent servants bound to the manors. One of their most important jobs was to submit rents in various forms on time. Failure to do so led to severe punishments, from being physically beaten to degraded as slaves.[21]

Land and labor, along with the social relations created by the land-holding system, determined basic social economic ecology in Manchuria. A component of that ecology was that Tibetan Buddhist monasteries attained unusual access to farmland and labor. Historian Christopher Mills Isett, who studies the agricultural economy in Qing Manchuria, suggests that social and political arrangements to access basic elements of production, or what he calls "social property relations," are the key to understanding the Manchurian economy. Correctly pointing out that social property relations "are politically determined," he argues that the economic actors "must . . . pursue to the best of their abilities those ends that secure their individual reproduction within the prevailing property system."[22] This observation is useful in analyzing the actions of both the manor heads and the lamas in our case. Therefore, the case, in turn, reveals enough for us to recognize some critical features of the Manchurian economy in general and the temple economy in particular.

Like many manor heads, the Zheng brothers inherited the title from their forefathers. The manor they ran was under the administration of the Mukden Board of Finance, the department responsible for funding the seven temples. Later, the board reassigned Zheng's manor to the East Stupa Temple, meaning the taxes extracted would directly go to the temple to support the livelihood of the lamas. The taxes included various materials: grain, flour, oil, meat, firewood, and other miscellany. Half went directly to the Da lama, the other half was shared by the rest. As in many other places, the Qing state authorized the temples to collect the taxes by themselves and rarely recorded the amount. The only exception was in 1778, when the Dharma-Wheel Temple was converted to a Manchu temple. The local government registered the incomes of the seven temples to use as a reference for funding the newly installed "Manchu" lamas. It was this record, in the early nineteenth century, that disclosed the fact that the temples had significantly increased taxes in the past twenty-five years. Yet from the early Qing onward, the amount of land under the Zhengs' supervision had shrunk from 540 *mu* to less than 400 mu due to soil erosion. According to the two widows, the previous Da lama had been kind enough to tolerate late or lower submissions. But since Lobdzang Teliyei had assumed the position in 1800, not only did he show no sympathy, but he also requested that one-tenth of the supplies be converted to a fixed cash payment of 110 *qian* (one *qian* is one thousand cooper coins) and the rest of the materials paid in full. Twice, in 1804 and 1805, Lobdzang Teliyei beat Zheng Guotai because the latter failed to provide the right quantity of firewood. In the summer of 1806, a flood destroyed Zheng's manor and the harvest was merely 30 percent of that of normal years. Zheng repeatedly pleaded to reduce the grain submission. But though Lobdzang Teliyei forgave some of the burden, the amount he requested was still much higher than what Zheng had. The deadline for submission was October 21, the exact day Zheng Guotai killed himself. His brother Zheng Wu went to the temple seven or eight times to continue to beg for a reduction in the tax, but the Da lama declined to meet with him. In desperation, Zheng Wu, too, ended his life.

After receiving the report on the matter from Mukdengge, the director of the Mukden Board of Justice, Emperor Jiaqing commented furiously that Lobdzang Teliyei had not only compelled the manor heads to death by raising taxes but also abetted perjury, declaring, "This was truly detestable." The emperor ordered him be deprived of his lama status (a punishment called *bohuang*). Following Qing codes, Lobdzang Teliyei was sentenced to exile. The tragedy made the local officials, particularly Mukdengge, realize there was a more serious problem. As he wrote in the report, "the manor heads are doing the tasks assigned by the government—they are not servants of the lamas. How could they suffer bullying like this?" In a subsequent report, the Mukden Board of Rites decided to thoroughly examine the taxes the temples imposed on the manors and to send supervisors every autumn to make sure that the lamas did not secretly raise taxes. Furthermore, Mukdengge requested that starting in 1807, the material taxes in each category be reduced by one-tenth.[23] His suggestion was adopted as a new government guideline. The state used this case to clarify an important point: Government manors were not temple properties and the manor heads were responsible only to the state, not to the temple.

The story was far from over. Two years later, a manor worker filed a lawsuit against another Da lama. This time the plaintiff, You Jun, took his complaint all the way to the Grand Council (*junjichu*) in Beijing, the highest decision-making body of the Qing.[24] Like the Zheng brothers, You was registered and bonded to the Mukden Board of Finance as a permanent servant. Unlike the Zhengs, he was just a laborer (*zhuangding*)[25] who provided corvée services to the temples, rather than harvests from the land. A corvée labor in the Qing did not have to actually work for the master. Instead, he could pay a sum of money as a poll tax, known as *dingying* (丁銀). This was exactly what You and other families had always done. During Kangxi's reign, You's forefathers, along with several other families, were transferred from the South Stupa to the Mahākāla Pavilion. They paid two taels of silver per household per year to fulfill their financial obligation. In 1786, however, the then Da lama not only requested payments from each laborer (instead of from each household) but also changed the poll tax to a grain tax. The grain tax, which could be converted to cash, was much costlier and beyond their ability to pay. When the families attempted to use their private lands as collateral to raise funds, the Da lama accused them of stealing and selling temple farmlands (*xianghuodi*, 香火地). Both sides appeared in the court, but there was no resolution.

In 1801, the new Da lama of the Mahākāla Pavilion, Lobdzang Rabtan, sued You and the other laborers for not submitting the grain tax and illegally selling temple farms. The lawsuit concluded in 1804. Disappointingly, the Mukden Board of Finance accepted the false claims of the lamas and arbitrarily declared the laborers' private lands property of the temple. During the process, You Jun and several others were put in prison. Some died from illness, others committed suicide. After he was released, You had to rent land from the temple in order to survive. After the Zheng case, the Mukden authority had ordered all the temples to reduce taxes by one-tenth. However, Lobdzang Rabtan ignored the order and still urged You to submit in the full amount. On top of that, the Da lama forced You to compensate for outstanding debts in previous years, threatening to stop renting him land if he refused. Once again, the poor laborer was backed into a corner. He decided to go to Beijing.

Beijing was so shocked by the complaint that it appointed two high-ranking officials, Inghe and Chu Pengling, as imperial commissioners to investigate the case, together with their local colleagues. You and the others provided solid evidence to prove that their only obligation should be the poll tax and that the lands they held were indeed private property inherited from their forefathers. The lamas, on the other hand, failed to present a strong counterargument. They said that since all taxpayers, regardless of what they submitted, had farmlands, the temples just assumed that the lands were one and the same (i.e., belonged to the temple). It was for this reason that they had mistakenly changed the poll tax to a grain tax.

The final verdict came out in late 1810. The laborers got their justice: Their private lands were not temple farms. Lobdzang Rabtan, who was born to a banner family, was deprived of his lama status (bohuang) and sent to the army after taking a bludgeon penalty (beaten by heavy sticks). Other lamas who had given false testimony in the previous trials—including the Da lamas of the South and West Stupas, Lobdzang Gendün and Lobdzang Awangdüchen—were fired and sentenced to the bludgeon penalty as well. Lobdzang Teliyei, the former Da lama of the East Stupa, should have received the same penalty, but he had already been punished in the Zheng brothers' case. Along with them, all the remaining civil officials responsible for the previous wrong verdicts were demoted by a level.

The Zhang and You cases rocked the Mukden nexus like an earthquake. Half of the Da lamas, as well as some of their disciples, were removed from their posts. The origin of the conflict was the question of who ultimately owned the dependency lands. And the difficulty came from the ambiguity of Qing policy. Seeing it from the temples' perspective, since the lands were "assigned" to them, the lamas should have full rights regarding the lands. Even if ultimate ownership belonged to the state, were they not the agent of the state? However, from the state's perspective, the people working on the farms—manor heads and laborers—determined the nature of the lands. The lands were indeed assigned to the temples, but the people attached to the lands answered only to the state. The problem, according to government officials, was that the lamas were too greedy and did not know how to properly manage the land and the people assigned to them. Therefore, major reform was necessary and urgent.

In early 1811, Sabintu, the new director of the Mukden Board of Finance, submitted a memorial to Emperor Jiaqing.[26] After a comprehensive survey of the temples' incomes—the first ever since their establishments—the local official suggested taking back taxation privileges from the temples. "The lamas at the seven Mukden temples," he said, "have their assigned government lands and labors respectively. The lands provide grains and the labors submitted poll monies to fund the lamas." Yet there was no regulation about how much the taxes should be, which made the greedy Da lamas keep elevating their rates. From now on, Sabintu proposed, the various taxes should be combined and converted to a fixed monetary payment. The payment would be collected by the local government first and then redistributed to the temples. That way, the lamas were guaranteed a sufficient salary regardless of whether it was a good year or a bad one, and the laborers and manor heads would only pay the government a fixed fee, their burdens could not be arbitrarily increased. Then in another memorial several months later,[27] Sabintu offered a complex calculation and concluded that the total lama salary cost 2,325 odd taels of silver. The tax money subtracted from the lands affiliated with the seven temples should cover the cost.

This was a major intervention by the state. The policy to monetarize the material and corvée taxes corresponded with tax reform in other Mukden manors beginning in the late Qianlong period.[28] The simplified tax payment not only further bound the seven temples financially but also demonstrated that the state almost completely controlled the temple economy. However, Sabintu's plan was somewhat capricious. When he calculated the amount of lands, he took into account not only the lands assigned by the government—about 26,578 mu—but also the lands separately owned by the temples. He argued that these lands, about 12,598 mu in total, had been owned by corvée families initially. Because some families did not have heirs to inherit the deeds, the temples took advantage of them and rented the lands out. It was only fair, Sabintu believed, to annex these temple lands.

The backlash was swift. The following year, the local government began to receive complains from the lamas saying the income was not enough. The negotiation process must have been tedious because it took the government several years to finally agree on a compromise. In 1818, Fujun, the Mukden general, reported to the throne that his predecessor had gotten the approval to return the temple lands to the lamas. These lands—now 13,820 mu—were "private properties," according to Fujun, which the temples had either purchased or received as donations. Fujun initially requested that the lamas impose a fixed tax on the lands, mirroring what the government did with the state-owned manors. But the lamas pushed back, arguing that a fixed tax would hurt both the temples and the tenants when there was a poor harvest. They insisted on a floating rate and promised not to enforce a harsh rent. The general backed down and said the request was reasonable in that the situation was different from the assigned government lands. Since these lands were private properties, the temples, like landlords, should be allowed to recruit tenants and collect rent on their own. Besides, the tenants, unlike the manor laborers, were free laborers who had certain bargaining power. There was no need for the government to interfere with their business.[29] So, six years after the state punished the lamas and withdrew their taxation autonomy, the lamas had negotiated part of their economic rights back. They now had two sources of income. The majority still came from the fixed salary distributed by the Mukden Board of Finance. A smaller amount (or at least smaller on the books) came from temple-owned lands that were beyond state audit. The land dispute was settled, however temporarily, until a century later in the early Republican period.

Crime, Punishment, and Ritual Dance

The Qing's enthusiastic endorsement of Tibetan Buddhism was no doubt a critical part of its Inner Asia politics. Here emperors' personal faith and their political concern were not necessarily two separate things. Remember that a significant portion of the financial support for temple construction and maintenance came from the Imperial Household Department, which could be regarded as the royal family's fund. But while the emperors' passion for the faith was one thing, their personal attitude toward the lamas—especially those with less prestigious status—was quite another. Even the biggest supporters—Hong Taiji, Kangxi, and Qianlong—had all expressed criticism in one way or another. Emperor Yongzheng, Kangxi's son and Qianlong's father, was no different. After taking the throne, he converted his former residence to a monastery, which later became the Yonghe Temple, the imperial center of the Qing's Tibetan Buddhist administration.

Once, however, Yongzheng pointed his finger at a group of lamas, none other than the ones at the Mukden temples. In an edict in 1728, Yongzheng started out by praising the newly appointed Da lama of the Long-lasting-Peace Temple, Lobdzang Baljor Gabchu, as "a good lama." Then he changed his tone and criticized the Mukden lamas: "[Their] custom is very bad" (Man. *tacin umesi ehe*; C. *xiqi shenshu buhao*). He enjoined the new Da lama to supervise them and "do not make it a pattern" (Man. *erebe kooli obuci ojorkū*; C. *buke yi ci wei li*).[30] The background for the emperor's accusation is not known. But apparently, as early as the early eighteenth century, the Mukden lamas had already earned themselves a negative reputation. According to the archive, this "bad custom," it seems, did not change much in later years. Perhaps the following three criminal cases can provide an annotation to Yongzheng's foresighted comments.

The first case occurred in the winter of 1780, when a lama accidently killed his disciple.[31] The murderer, Be Danjin, had come to the Essential-Victory Temple at age ten and was still a bandi at age forty-seven. One day he went to the city to purchase cloth, but ended up drinking at an alcohol shop instead. Arriving home late and drunk, he saw his disciple, a ten-year-old named Doyod, playing with a knife. He took the knife, scolded the boy, and accidently stabbed him as he tried to stop the child from running away. It turned out that Doyod was the grandson of Be Danjin's brother. Be Danjin had brought him to the temple two years prior as his disciple. He was escorted to the local government authorities and later sentenced to death by hanging.

The main actor in the second case, a true rogue, was recorded as Guan San lama (his Mongol name was Sangjay).[32] Born to a Manchu banner family, Guan San lama first came to the Life-Prolonging Temple as a young boy. Later he was fired for calling a prostitute. After being forced to return home, he married another woman. But soon after, he shaved his head again and, along with his wife, moved to a small (nongovernment) temple as a lama manager. It was there he became addicted to opium. In 1854, he intervened in an affair: The child bride of a banner family had run away with her lover, and her father-in-law asked Guan San lama to find her. He did but then refused to return the girl. At first, he requested a large ransom from the family, and then he coerced the poor girl to have sex with him. He was sentence to death by hanging.

The third case involved two separate bribery incidents around 1832.[33] In both, the Da lama of the Mahākāla Pavilion, Shirab Jamsu (C. Sela Jiamucuo), was asked to lobby his good friend Rongzhi, a clerk in charge of Mongol-related affairs at the Mukden Board of Justice. In the first incident, a Han Chinese man came to Shirab Jamsu, begging him to persuade Rongzhi to judge a kidnap marriage case in favor of his brother. The Da lama asked for 100 taels of silver in return. But Rongzhi was not able to help because the disputed interethnic marriage—the couple consisted of a Han civilian and a Mongol banner woman—was against Qing law. The second incident was more complex. Several Mongol nobles (taiji) escaped to Mukden after committing crimes and were captured by the Mukden Board of Justice. To shield them, a Khorchin prince hoped the board would extradite the suspects instead of trying them in Mukden. He sought help from Ishi (C. Yishi), the Jasak Da lama of the Essential-Victory Temple. It was actually unnecessary. Since both the suspects and victims were Mongol, the board would hand the case over to a Mongol court anyway. When Rongzhi gave the information to Shirab Jamsu, who passed it on to Ishi, the Jasak Da lama sought to profit from it. Claiming he had paid a bribe of 250 taels of silver to get the result, Ishi demanded that the prince compensate him. Although in both cases, no bribe was actually delivered, all the lamas involved were fired and sentenced to take the bludgeon penalty, and Ishi was exiled.

None of these cases were historically significant, nor do I suggest they represent the general behavior of all Mukden lamas. Nonetheless, they reveal some interesting information about their habits, relationships, and social connections. Many Mukden lamas did not follow the Buddhist commandments strictly. They drank alcohol, ate meat, and got married. As we will see later in the chapter, it was not uncommon for the Mukden lamas to have another life outside the monasteries. Since the Mukden nexus was a rather small and closed circle, and since being a royal lama was considered a prestigious and profitable career, many lamas recruited their family members to join this circle. At the same time, the highly hierarchical structure of the nexus determined that the superior/inferior and master/disciple relationships were the basic personal relations within the nexus. In the late Qing period, the origins of the lamas became concentrated in just two or three places, namely, Mukden city, Fuxin, and Zhangwu—the latter two were towns near the Mukden–Inner Mongolian border. This situation almost certainly led to nepotism and factionalism. Understandably, corruption was rampant. Given the royal temples' close connection with the state, local society— Mongol and Han alike—regarded the lamas as a means to communicate with the local government. Some lamas did take advantage of their roles as mediators. As we can see from the third case, the financial reward was tempting. Of course, the state strictly forbade the lamas from being involved in governmental business. But whether severe punishments were effective enough to stop the practices is unknown.

A temple is first and foremost a religious space. Its role in a local society, therefore, should first and foremost be religious. Yet the seven temples' role in Mukden society, it seems, was less so. Reading local gazetteers and the Korean travelers' notes, one does not get the strong impression that local residents—especially commoners—passionately patronized these temples, if the temples indeed welcomed the local population. In fact, in their travelogues, the Korean literati detailed the architecture and lamas in the temples but surprisingly did not mention any pilgrims.

Due to their neo-Confucian ideology, the Korean literati generally despised the Mukden lamas. Yet despite their discriminatory rhetoric, their writings do reveal some parts of the lamas' everyday lives. "Living in there are all Mongol monks as many as fifty to sixty," Han Tae-dung observed in his description of the Essential-Victory Temple. "They wear yellow cloth, ride horses and eat meat, no different than common people . . . When we entered (the temple), they treated us with butter tea and cheese."[34] After visiting the Essential-Victory, Yi Hap wrote about the lamas, "their hats and cloths were all yellow. During the night they slept in the niche of Buddha statues, often set up tents in open wilds when traveling. It is their custom. Every one of them was ferocious and I felt quite disgusting when looking at them."[35] Han Dok-hu also claimed that the look of the master of the Essential-Victory "was hideous and strong."[36] Nevertheless, during their meetings, the lamas and the literati treated each other with courtesy. Most of time, the heads of the temples came out to greet the Korean guests and offered them butter tea and cheese. The guests would return with ch'onsŏmhwan (清心丸), a popular medicine, and folding fans. The conversations between the Koreans and lamas were generally relaxed. The lamas resolved some questions the Koreans had: Whether lamas could do sorcery, and why they dressed in yellow—a color supposedly reserved only for the royal family.[37]

Although the Korean envoys provided a vivid picture of their interactions with the lamas, it was not always easy for them to get into the temple in the first place. Several noted that they entered through a side door because the front gate was closed. A few—but not many—even had to bribe the lamas to tour the Essential-Victory Temple. For example, Hong Dae-yon, a prominent scholar who joined a mission in 1765, was stopped at the main hall of the Essential-Victory by some "monks in yellow" with keys in their hands. They asked Hong for ch'onsŏmhwan. Only after he bribed them with a hundred pieces of copper money was he allowed to enter the main hall.[38]

That being said, we should not jump to conclude that interactions between the temples and local society did not occur. Local people did go to the temples, but most went to attend fairs on certain holidays. The fairs were related to religion (e.g., celebrating the birthday of Buddha) but not all about religion. The local population was attracted by the Buddhist rituals as well as various entertainment and commercial activities. In the Qing dynasty, each temple had its own fairs. Among them the most important and celebrated was the one that the seven temples jointly presented: tiaobuzha (跳布扎), or the "Dance to Expel Demons."

The term tiaobuzha combines the Chinese verb for "dance" (tiao) and a Mongolian noun for "dance" (büjig). The masquerade ritual dance, derived from the Tibetan 'cham (which also means dance), was widely performed in Tibetan Buddhist monasteries across the country, and each region had its own variation.[39] The main theme was expelling the enemies of Buddhism and protecting the world from demons. The dance had a mythological origin linked to the legendary anti-Buddhism campaign of Langdarma in ninth century Tibet. It is said that Langdarma, the last ruler of the unified Tibetan Empire, brutally persecuted Buddhists in order to promote Bon, the native religion. Later, he was assassinated by a hero, who disguised himself while escaping. In the Tibetan historical narrative, this period marked the "dark age" of Buddhism. Oral traditions added more details to the myth. For example, the Mukden lamas, in two interviews (one in the 1930s and one in the 1980s), indicated that the Tibetan tyrant was an ox in his previous life. He resented Buddha because his hard work building a stupa/temple was not rewarded.[40] Interestingly, this episode echoes the portrait of Langdarma as an ox demon in Tibetan folktales. But as many historians have pointed out, the legend was very much a fabrication, a "collective memory" after the eleventh century, that was constructed to memorize a declining era of Buddhism in both Tibet and India.[41] Nevertheless, the story was key to establishing the core status of the religion in a three-phase narrative of Tibetan history. The so-called dark age ended the "first dissemination period" when Buddhism was first introduced to Tibet and introduced the "second dissemination period" when Buddhism was revived in Tibet by Tibetan monks. Moreover, memory of the dark age, via tiaobuzha, was localized and reincarnated in folk festivals in all the societies influenced by Tibetan Buddhism.[42] Mukden, Manchuria, was not an exception.

Twice a year—in the first and fourth lunar month—the Mukden lamas performed this highly florid ritual dance.[43] The one in the first month coincided with the Chinese New Year, and therefore was more opulent and prolonged. The atmosphere was bustling. "Each lama played a role as ghost or god," according to a local gazetteer, "They played instruments and chanted sutras to expel demons. The audiences crowded in like walls."[44] The Mukden general would participate in the ceremony and present gifts on behalf of the emperor. A unique custom in Mukden was to transfer—or "greet"—a statue of Maitreya from the (North Stupa) Dharma-Wheel Temple to the Essential-Victory Temple. As Chang Haifeng recalled, on the seventh day of the first month, the demchis and gesguis of all the temples gathered at the Essential-Victory. At dawn, they marched to the North Stupa, dressing in their showiest clothes. The lamas at the Dharma-Wheel had already settled the statue on a festooned vehicle. When the music started, the parade began. Women among the onlookers struggled for a chance to push the vehicle, believing it would bring them good fortune. Along the road people set up altars, lit firecrackers, and threw money at the vehicle. The journey was slow, it took about five to six hours before the vehicle arrived at the Essential-Victory Temple, where the Jasak Da Lama and Da lamas waited and welcomed the Maitreya statue in. From the eighth day to the thirteenth, the lamas chanted sutras and conducted consecration ceremonies within the main hall.

Finally, on the fourteenth day of the first month, the climax of the event occured. Around 1:00 p.m., conches sounded, percussionists roared, and the ritual dance was staged. The entire performance required around 180 lamas, so almost every lama had a role to play. Taking turns, they walked into the circle to dance, all wearing helmet masks. Some played dharma protectors, some bodhisattvas, and some demons. Four lama boys kept order by throwing flour on the audiences when they pushed too close to the stage. The next day, the Maitreya statue was escorted back to the Dharma-Wheel Temple.[45] What did the performance look (and sound) like? Douglas Story, a British journalist who came to Mukden to cover the Russo-Japanese War in 1904, recorded his experience:

> The great day came, when the Dai Lama, magnificent in silken robes two hundred and fifty years old emblazoned with precious stones, and wearing the hat of his mandarinate, presided over the devotions of his fellows. Here again the ritual was strangely familiar. The shaven heads of the monks, the vestments, the altars, and the chanting of the choristers might, but for the surroundings of pagoda roofs and pig-tailed worshippers, have belonged to some old-time priory of Italy or Spain. The music was sad and plaintive, a miserere chanted in deepest bass by the singers of the abbey. To me it sounded as the music I had heard in St John Lateran's in Rome on Good Friday afternoon.[46]

In the Qing dynasty, it seemed, these popular fairs created the most intimate connections between the seven temples and local society. The ceremony continued, although with much difficulty, into the early twentieth century. Residents in Shenyang now remembered tiaobuzha, which they abbreviated as *tiaota*, as a local folk tradition, despite the fact that those who have actually witnessed it are fewer and fewer. In 2018, an online news media published an oral history about *tiaota*. Mr. Yang Kuibin, the interviewee, recalls:

> When there was a tiaota, we children would love to join and watch. The peddlers went there as well. The scenery was bustling and grand.... When the time was up, someone informed: "Tiaota is here, tiaota is here," we would say, "Let's go to watch tiaota!" ... The whole crew [of performers] was more than a hundred, who were mostly Mongols but a few Tibetans too. It was crowded and policemen came to keep the order. The lamas in tiaota had ranks. The highest was the great lama, also called the first lord [Da lama], followed by the second [demchi] and the third lord [gesgui]. I don't know whether there was

9. The lamas at the Shisheng Temple wearing *tiaobuzha* costumes.
Photo taken by Naitō Konan. Source: Naitō Torajirō. *Manshū shashinchō*,
image no. 64, 1908.

a fourth lord or not. I knew an Uncle Jin, who was initially a third lord
later promoted to a first lord. Lord Jin was our landlord. He wore a
jacket during performance. Most lamas had to wear masks but he did
not. I also knew a Mr. Guo who wore a deer mask and a boy named
Nanhai who wore a white mask. Everyone had a fixed role to play so
they wore whatever they should wear. The costumes used in the tiaota
were stored on the upper floor of my home. We children would go
upstairs, put them on, and dance a little. The costumes were made of
linen and satin instead of ordinary fabrics.[47]

This is one of the most affectionate and humanistic accounts of the
Mukden temples by a local resident. Yang does not know the theological origin of the performance, that the seemingly joyful dance actually
delivered a hidden memory of a dark age in Tibet. Yes, the memory
was constructed. But it was a necessary construction. The collective
creation solidified the legitimacy of Buddhism in a Tibetan time. The
memory then spread from Tibet to Mongolia, the Central Plain, and
finally Manchuria, transforming into a folk festival integrated in daily
life. Yet the dance became something of an omen; in the late nineteenth

century, when the Mukden lamas danced on the stage, they could not
have realized that a real dark age was approaching.

The Decline of the Mukden Nexus

During the entire Qing dynasty, Mukden, as the auxiliary capital, received ten imperial tours. Compared to the imperial tours to the Jiangnan region (known as Southern Touring), tours to Manchuria (known
as East Touring) carried greater ritual and political symbolism.[48] Touring reinforced the roots of Manchu legitimacy and memorialized the
imperial ancestors. Making offerings to the Mukden temples, especially
the Essential-Victory, was a must-do for emperors. However, since the
last tour by Emperor Daoguang in 1829, no other monarch had ever paid
special attention to the temples.[49]

The mid- and late nineteenth century marked a watershed moment
in modern Chinese, and East Asian history. The two Opium Wars (1839
and 1859), the Taiping Rebellion (1851–64), the Nian Rebellion (1851–
68), the Dungan Revolt (1862–77), the Sino-French War (1884–85),
the First Sino-Japanese War (1894), along with other significant unrest,
fundamentally destabilized Qing's ruling bases and changed China's sociopolitical landscapes. While the affluent coastal regions of South and
Southeast China faced devastating peasant rebellions and endured capitalist and imperialist pressures from Western powers, Qing dominance
over the frontier regions significantly weakened. Mukden was hardly
immune to the chaos. It witnessed major warfare twice in the late Qing
period. In 1900, Russia invaded and occupied Manchuria in the name
of suppressing the Boxer Rebellion (1899–1900). This partially led to
the fierce Russo-Japanese War (1904–5), in which Mukden was one of
the battlegrounds.

In both wars, the Mukden monasteries were ransacked.[50] The Life-
Prolonging Temple suffered greatly, multiple buildings in the complex—
the front gate, Hall of Heavenly Kings, drum tower, bell tower, and sutra
tower—were all burned down. And the flames of war wiped out the
South Stupa Temple almost completely, with only the stupa left stand-
ing.[51] Burning and looting by foreign soldiers were not the only damage
done. The theft of the temple treasures also aggravated the destruction.
In the Dharma-Wheel Temple, nearly 70 percent of the gold and silver-
ware was either stolen by the lamas or robbed by local bandits.[52] Douglas
Story had some brief conversations with the Da lama of the Essential-
Victory Temple during the Russo-Japanese War. "From the old Dai [sic]
Lama," he said, "I learned his fears of the War, his dread of the Russians,
and his admiration of the little Japanese."[53]

In the last decade of the Qing dynasty, the government found it more and more difficult to support the Mukden temples financially. Zengqi, the Mukden general during the Russian occupation, reported in 1902 that the lamas "were living bitterly and poorly" after the invasion. He had to transfer 140 silver dollars to them in emergency assistance.[54] Regular support was hard to sustain. In 1910, the Jasak Da lama, Shirab Jamsu (C. Shilebu Zhamusu), complained to the authorities that the lamas had not received any new cloth for five years. The accounting bureau acknowledged the arrears but said "the inventory is not enough" to clear the debts. It could only supply cloth for the current year and try to make up the rest "when the situation improved." But in the following year, the government fell short again.[55] Maintenance was another problem. In 1911 and 1912, Shirab Jamsu submitted several requests to repair the damaged temple walls and houses originally built for the emperor's tour. Finally, in April 1912, Zhao Erxun, the top ruling official in Manchuria, approved the requests but asked the temple to pay first. Of course, the project was suspended.[56]

When Zhao Erxun issued his reply, his official title had just changed: He was no longer the "Viceroy of the East Three Provinces" of the Qing but now the "Military Governor of the East Three Provinces, the Republic of China." On February 12, the last emperor of the Qing, Xuantong (Puyi), issued the Edict of the Abdication under pressure from Yuan Shikai (1859–1916), the military strongman who mediated negotiations between the Qing and the revolutionaries. But in the northeast frontier, nothing else seemed to change dramatically. The transition from monarchy to republic, for the most part at least, was gradual and peaceful. The bureaucratic institutions and established elites remained largely unaffected. A more significant reform had already happened several years before in 1906 when the Mukden general officially became a "province," along with Jilin and Heilongjiang. The capital city and the province now shared the same new name, Fengtian, meaning "mandate for Heaven." However, for the Mukden nexus of Tibetan Buddhism, the 1912 transition was devastating.

The new state had a very different relationship with Tibetan Buddhism than the Qing had. In theory, the republic inherited all territories from the Qing—including provinces in China proper as well as the frontiers in Inner Asia. But in practice, the new government failed to solidify its control over the vast realm. Not only Tibet but also Xinjiang and Outer Mongolia fell into the spheres of influence of various imperialist powers; even China proper was divided and ruled by competing warlords. From 1912 to 1928, Manchuria was essentially an independent kingdom of Zhang Zuolin (1875–1928), who was promoted by both

Zhao Erxun and Yuan Shikai. Despite that, the new state made efforts to demonstrate its authority over the frontiers, for example, by setting up special institutions to oversee Mongolian and Tibetan affairs. The previous intimacy between Inner Asia and Beijing—nourished by personal ties like kinship, bloodline, and shared belief—hardly continued in the new era. Against this backdrop, the role of Tibetan Buddhism became increasingly awkward. Sure, the state vowed to continue supporting the religion, but that support did not follow the logic of "priest-patron" in an empire. Instead, the relationship was more in the spirit of state-church separation in a modern republic. In other words, the royal temples were no longer royal. Under state supervision, they were not any different from other temples.

Meanwhile, the lamas strove for favorable status in the new state, both for the religion and themselves. For example, when the Zasagtu prince of Khorchin proclaimed independence in May 1912, Shirab Jamsu soon dispatched several lamas to various banners in eastern Mongolia and persuaded the local leaders not to follow the rebel. The Jasak Da lama also paid a visit to Beijing, expressing his loyalty to the republic in front of President Yuan Shikai.[57] Over the subsequent decades, the lamas argued for continued state investment, on one hand, and took advantage of the new state's ignorance of temple affairs, on the other. It was a game of survival and, whenever possible, of maximizing personal interests. For them, the biggest impacts of the new temple-state relations were twofold. First, the temples had lost their prior economic privilege. Second, ties with Beijing were cut off and the Mukden nexus became an isolated circle. How did the lamas respond to these changes? Moreover, how did state and local society, in turn, react to their responses?

In June 1915, the Da lamas of the seven temples, led by Shirab Jamsu, submitted a petition to the Fengtian provincial government.[58] Their request: sell the "dependency lands." Their petition stated, "the lamas had altogether 26,532 mu of dependency lands" which had initially been managed by the temples on their own. Then, starting in 1816, "the government managed the business on our behalf" (guanfu daiwei jingli) and continued entrusting the manor heads and tenants to farm and pay tax. "Ever since the establishment of the Republic," they said, "things are expensive, our income cannot cover the spending, and the lamas in the temples are suffering." Therefore, after some discussion, they proposed selling the dependency lands in accordance with the policy of "measuring and opening royal farms." According to the government policy, 20 percent of the earnings would go to the state, and the state would also acquire all the extra lands (fuduo) previously not under registration. The rest of the earnings "should be given to the lamas to purchase other properties as permanent sources of income." On the bottom of the petition, they signed their names and listed all the farms they claimed ownership of.

After Puyi's abdication, how to deal with the banner farmlands—including government manors, royal manors, and banner men's farms—became yet another conundrum. The new republic allowed the royal family and banner men to sell the lands as private property. It was a win-win. In Fengtian and other places, many manor heads were privatizing farms, on which families had lived and worked for hundreds of years. Lacking the ability to stop them, the royal family was willing to cash out of the farms to gain income. The new government, which desperately needed money to fund various state-building projects, also welcomed the sales because it was guaranteed 20 percent of the selling price and land tax in the future. Plus, when surveying the royal farms, the local government could confiscate all unregistered extra lands.[59] This was the backdrop for the lamas' petition.

The lamas concealed a key fact. As the Zheng brothers' case in 1806 demonstrated, the lands were the property of the Qing state assigned to the temples. The temples relied on the revenue extracted from these lands, but they did not technically own them. By saying the lands had been managed solely by the temples, their petition deliberately blurred the boundary between temple farms and state farms. It also portrayed the state as the agent of the temple, not the other way around. The lamas raised their request at the precise moment when the government of the republic was busy surveying the pervious royal farms. It was really the last opportunity to fish in troubled waters, if only they could successfully convince the new authority that the phrasing "lands assigned to the temple" was equivalent to the "lands of the temple."

However, the plan encountered fierce resistance. A month later, thirty-two manor heads co-filed a protest letter and provided their version of the story. "Our forefathers moved to Fengtian from Shangdong in the early Qing to reclaim wildlands," the letter said, "but they were not able to claim these lands without joining the banner system." Therefore, their forefathers "brought their own lands to take part in [the system]" (*daidi touru*). Although the revenue generated from the lands was later used to fund the temples, the lands had nothing to do with the temples. Denouncing the idea that they were the "dependency lands" of the temples, the manor heads rebuked the lamas. "How dare they attempt to sell our lands and hurt ten thousand people's lives? They are evil in the extreme!" The manor heads further raised four points: First, all lands had been registered under someone's name, where were the lamas' names in the books? Second, they had submitted their tax money to the treasury (of the Mukden Board of Finance), not the temples. Third, there had been no such thing as "the government managed the business" on the lamas' behalf. Last but not least, they had heard that the lamas had sold all the temple farms. They had never informed the government before, why now?

The manor heads made some good arguments. But they, too, muddied the water. They established a theory that the lands had initially been their ancestors' properties, which indicated that they had rights to the lands under the new circumstances. At the time, it was a common excuse used by manor heads to justify their privatization of Qing farmlands. Like the lamas, they also concealed an inconvenient fact: the Qing state had assigned the lands to the temples and their ancestors had paid to the temples directly prior to 1806. Nor were the four points they raised equally convincing. For example, in the Qing context it was unnecessary to register lands under a lama's name because, as the temples later countered, "all temples in Fengtian (city) were bureaucratic temples and all lamas were bureaucratic monks. The dependency lands assigned to us were seen as the same as those assigned to the princes."

Eventually, after several rounds of exchanges, the lamas failed to get what they wanted. As "a gesture of solicitude," the government offered the temples half of the selling price of 2,794 mu of extra lands discovered during the survey. Of course, the sum was utterly inadequate to solve the financial crisis the temples were facing. Note that land disputes such as this were countless at the time. After the collapse of the Qing, the banner farmlands suddenly emerged as a legal gray zone. Every party took advantage of the ambiguity of the property rights to benefit themselves. The lamas were the most disadvantaged when it came to seeking clarification.

A second factor, that the Mukden nexus was now independent, further corrupted the system from within. In the Qing dynasty, Beijing supervised the internal affairs of all royal temples. It controlled the Mukden nexus by appointing/transferring the Jasak Da lama and requested that the Da lamas take turns serving in Beijing. After 1912, the vertical, religious-administrative system ceased to exist. Any temple affair was now local business. The Jasak Da lama and the Da lamas, the supreme leaders in their respective temples, acted like sovereigns. With the declining financial privilege of the Da lamas, temple power was increasingly centralized. Internal strife, already a severe problem before the collapse of the Qing, became a daily phenomenon. In theory, the Fengtian provincial government oversaw local religious issues and had final decision-making power. But the secular institution, in the best scenario, was not helping and perhaps even aggravating the conflict. The republic bureaucrats had next to zero knowledge about temple affairs.

They could not care less about "trivial" matters, such as which demchi should become the Da lama (and why should they?)

In 1918, Shirab Jamsa, the last Jasak Da lama appointed by the Qing, passed away. In the years that followed, the Da lama of the East Stupa Temple supervised the Mukden nexus as the acting Jasak Da lama, until his title became official in 1930.[60] In other words, he was the very first Jasak Da lama promoted from inside the nexus in nearly 300 years. The man was Ishi Sangbo, whom I introduced at the beginning of this chapter. The most junior Da lama in 1906 had eventually become the most powerful leader in the Mukden nexus. It is time tell his story.[61]

In June 1926, Ishi Sangbo, the then acting Jasak Da lama, fired the Da lama of the East Stupa, Rinchen Nyima (C. Linqin Nima), because Rinchen Nyima was involved in a civil lawsuit with a widow, Li Qu. A year before, Li accused Rinchen Nyima of occupying her homestead. The court ruled in Li's favor. Yet Rinchen Nyima repeatedly appealed and insisted the land he occupied was not Li's homestead. Tired of waiting, Li Qu sued him again, compounding the accusation by accusing him of breaking the monk's code by marrying a woman. The Da lama, she claimed, used a Han Chinese alias, Liu Huanchen, and had four daughters and a son. Local police confirmed the information and requested the Essential-Victory Temple—that is, Ishi Sangbo—to "discipline" Rinchen Nyima "seriously." A month after he expelled Rinchen Nyima, Ishi Sangbo recommended that the demchi of the East Stupa, Ganjurjab (C. Gazhouchibu), become the new Da lama.[62]

Rinchen Nyima quickly fought back. He dismissed Li Qu's new accusation as a pure vendetta, saying, "Whether I married or not is not her business." He protested that the rush decision to fire him was groundless and alleged that Li was instigated by his rival, Ganjurjab. It was Ganjurjab, Ishi Sangbo's younger brother, who had abetted Li in suing him again, which had given Ishi Sangbo the absurd excuse to let him go. As a result, Ganjurjab had successfully seized his position. "But this lama," Rinchen Nyima contended, "not only has a wife but also smokes opium. He is much worse and should not have the position." In the same complaint, he implored the provincial government to help. "Most lamas entered the Essential-Victory Temple as kids. Being a lama was just another way of saying doing hard labor. . . . I came to the temple when I was seven and now more than thirty years have passed. I worked diligently, never avoided hardship, suffered half of my life, and finally became a Da lama. As I was just about to take charge of the temple, I was fired for an ambiguous reason." Firing a lama, he lamented, was tantamount to sentencing him to death. Not only was he not able to get his former position back, but he was also forbidden to take other positions.

The provincial government rejected his request as well as his allega-
tions. The government's logic was that since the local police had confirmed his unethical behaviors, his counteraccusation against Ganjurjab
"must be a randomly made false charge and won't be accepted." Rinchen
Nyima was removed, but the lawsuit between Liu Huanchen (his alias)
and Li Qu continued. After several rounds in court between the two, the
provincial government determined that both Liu and Li were occupying
public space. That is to say, the land under dispute was not Li's homestead. Rinchen Nyima might look like just another lama being punished
for his misbehavior. But his discharge was the prelude to a huge power
struggle four years later, which turned the seven temples upside down.

Before the battle brewing on the horizon, there had been some disturbing harbingers. In 1929, a lower-ranking lama filed a complaint with
the provincial government, accusing Ishi Sangbo of being too old to
manage temple affairs. Instead, he was entrusting all business to his four
henchmen who monopolized power, illegally sold temple properties,
altered rent prices, and embezzled temple incomes. Other lamas dared
not speak out. Anyone who refused to bribe them was fired for trivial
faults. "Ever since they took control, more than twenty to thirty people
were fired." Those who fawned over the henchmen could do whatever
they wanted without punishment. But this complaint did not create a
big splash. The lamas mediated the dispute internally before the government intervened.[63]

Then in early 1930, Ganjurjab, the Da lama of the East Stupa, was
reported to the authorities by one of his subordinates for selling temple
properties and other illegal acts. Ganjurjab rejected the charge by filing a
counterclaim against his accuser. This time, the government responded
that it would investigate. However, Ganjurjab died on April 15, some
said he was terrified of the coming investigation.[64]

The Da lama position for the East Stupa was now open. A month
later, Ishi Sangbo submitted a list of all the "qualified candidates" to
the provincial government. According to regulations and tradition, the
government would decide the successor from among the candidates.
But to anyone familiar with the standard procedure, the list looks irreg-
ular and suspicious in many ways. For starters, there were no nominees
recommended. A list of all qualified candidates was not considered an
official recommendation. It was simply a reference for the Jasak Da lama
to pick among his nominees—normally the top two seniors. The Jasagh
Da lama should have put his first and second choices at the start of the
list, and the governor would choose the top one as the final appointee.
But this time, Ishi Sangbo put forward a list without recommending
any nominees. Second, the list was too long, with altogether fourteen

candidates. Strikingly, not all of the nominees were demchi—the only qualified category in theory. There were also six gesguis, with the youngest one, Bürintusa (C. Boluntuse), being only thirty-three years old. But Ishi Sangbo claimed, "All of them had the right status for promotion." Most surprising of all, the provincial government "picked" Bürintusa, the youngest gesgui, to be the new Da lama. The reason the government selected him is not known. In any case, his letter of appointment was issued on June 14.

On June 23, all eight of the higher-ranking demchis on the candidate list co-filed a complaint with the provincial government. The selection process, they protested, was utterly unconventional and against regulations. It turned out that Bürintusa was none other than Ishi Sangbo's own grandson. As we know, this was not the first time Ishi Sangbo had broken the rules. When the late Da lama of East Stupa, Ganjurjab, took the position, the brother of Ishi Sangbo was ranked only third in terms of seniority. But this time Ishi Sangbo had crossed the line. Not only had he recommended a family member once again, but also a gesgui never had been promoted directly to Da lama.

Before the government could respond, on July 14, altogether fifteen young lamas (mostly in their thirties) also filed a complaint against Ishi Sangbo and his clique. In addition to his cronyism, they alleged that his henchmen ruled the seven temples with autocratic methods and arbitrarily trampled long-term regulations. "The situation was even worse than when Ganjurjab was alive," they declared. Also around this time, Ishi Sangbo had not only willfully created a new demchi position at the Essential-Victory Temple (already a violation of the rules) but had also promoted a low-ranking nirba to fill it. The young lamas harshly criticized Ishi Sangbo, saying he "was old and muddleheaded. The so-called Jasak Da lama was surrounded by a few villains. The seven temples are almost his private assets. . . . For the sake of the general good, we cannot be silent. All the facts are here, we dare not to conjecture. The episodes we advise about here are merely a few of the most serious ones. . . . We asked you to investigate and select a person with merit and virtue to take over the temple affairs."

All the accumulated grievances, it seems, broke out at the same moment. Earlier that day, Ulimbu (C. Wulinbu), a demchi and an opponent of the Ishi Sangbo clique, entered the Jasak Da lama's bedroom uninvited, along with four other lamas, and urged him to withdraw the recent appointment. Shocked, Ishi Sangbo fell into a coma and died in less than a month. His disciples filed an accusation with the provincial government. They charged Ulimbu and others with deliberately humiliating their mentor, causing Ishi Sangbo to die from fright and anger.

How did the government react to this mess? On July 21, the government replied to the demchis' complaint submitted nearly a month before. "The government picked and promoted [Bürintusa] from the list presented [by the Jasak Da lama]," the letter read, "What is wrong with that?" It criticized the demchis for making trouble. "If a gesgui doesn't have the qualifications to fill a Da lama position, why did the Jasak Da lama list him? Why did he confirm that gesguis could be recommended?" The government requested that the Essential-Victory Temple clarify the matter.

The demchis sent another letter to the government to explain. Yes, they wrote, there was one precedent where gesguis had been listed as candidates for Da lama. It was in 1888, when four Da lama positions were vacated simultaneously. At the time, there were seven demchis, but two of them had been punished and lost their candidacies. Since each vacant position had to have two nominees (a primary and a secondary), the temples had no choice but to put forth three gesguis as secondary nominees in order to have the required numbers. Regardless, a Da lama vacancy must be filled by a demchi, and a demchi vacancy by a gesgui. "In our two hundred-odd years' history, not a single gesgui turned himself to a Da lama directly," the letter asserted. In the present situation, although the fourteen candidates were ranked according to their seniority, their résumés were vague, without detailed description. Bürintusa, who absolutely did not meet the criteria of a candidate, had been promoted only because he was the grandson of Ishi Sangbo. Therefore, the eight demchis begged the government to withdraw his appointment.

But the government refused to admit its ignorance and error. It drafted a note on August 13 saying, "the decision . . . was made in accordance with the recommended list submitted by the late Ishi Sangbo. The case has been confirmed and cannot be easily changed. . . . No further discussion in future." The handwriting is sloppy, with many cross outs and revisions, showing someone was not satisfied with the draft. Several days later, a new note, written by the chairman of the Liaoning Provincial Government (presumably Zang Shiyi), was attached to the first draft. "This case has been repeatedly presented and replied to. What the demchis presented this time has no real evidence. They even went so far as to cite examples from the former Qing dynasty and argue endlessly. This is extremely absurd!" The chair then threatened to punish the troublemakers. "Many lamas are reasonable, but there are also many who do not obey Buddhist principles. This government was tolerant enough not to be too serious about (their behaviors). But if they still don't follow the government order and make further false accusations, I will surely punish [them] harshly to correct this unruly behavior!"

In late August, the investigation of the late Ganjurjab concluded. The government confirmed that all accusations against him were true. The old Jasak Da lama had entrusted many temple affairs to his younger brother. Ganjurjab, possibly under the instruction of Ishi Sangbo, had secretly sold many temple properties. And the promotion of Ganjurjab to the Da lama of the East Stupa Temple indeed violated the rules. "(They) should have been severely punished," the provincial government noted, "But both Ishi Sangbo and Ganjurjab have died." Shortly before, following the death of Ishi Sangbo, the government had swiftly appointed the Da lama of the Life-Prolonging Temple, Delegjab (C. Delizejiabu), as the acting Jasak Da lama. As for Bürintusa, there was no further action against him. The new Da lama of the East Stupa conveniently attributed every crime and misconduct to his late grandfather, Ishi Sangbo.

Opportunists took advantage of a messy situation. In August and September, the government received several reports with deliberate misinformation about standard bureaucratic procedures. For example, a gesgui stated falsely that his rank was actually higher than that of a demchi, and therefore should be considered for the Da lama position. The same letter also impugned a demchi, who was about to succeed Delegjab as the Da lama of the Life-Prolonging Temple, for colluding with the Japanese (though there was no evidence). The Dharma-Wheel Temple also submitted a statement to the provincial government arguing that both the Da lama and vice Da lama of the temple should be the candidates for the Jasak Da lama. This, it turned out, was a groundless statement because the vice Da lama, a position that existed uniquely at the North Stupa, did not meet the criteria until he became a full Da lama first.

For the lamas, the state gradually drifting away from temple affairs was an opportunity. But for the republic, a temple nexus which had gradually detached from a larger religious network had less and less value. In the republic era, the only highlight of the former Mukden nexus was the arrival of the ninth Panchen Erdeni (1883–1937). Suppressed by the thirteenth Dalai Lama and welcomed by Zhang Zuolin, Panchen spent several years in Fengtian (1926–31) and resided at the Essential-Victory Temple. But Zhang was not a religious person. He embraced the Panchen lama for purely political reasons. In 1916, the Jasak Da lama invited Zhang to participate in the tiaobuzha (as he did all previous top governors). Zhang refused on the grounds that he did not believe in the gods. Instead, he offered twenty silver dollars and asked his deputy to attend on his behalf.[65] This developed into a routine where the provincial government donated twenty silver dollars to the ceremony. But in 1931, when the Jasak Da lama petitioned to increase the amount of financial assistance for the highly popular ritual dance, the provincial government rejected the request, saying, "This is a vulgar custom. From now on [the government] will stop providing any subsidies or incense money."[66] The attitude of the state went from pragmatic, to indifferent, unsympathetic, and even hostile.

In the ensuing decades, the state-temple relationship changed little. In June 1931, the Executive Yuan of the Republic of China issued *The Supervising Regulations on the Mongol Lama Temples*.[67] All Tibetan Buddhist temples outside Tibet, including Mongolia, Beiping (Beijing), Shenyang, Chengde, Mount Wutai, Guisui, Gansu, and Qinghai, were subject to the new code. The regulations empowered the Mongolian and Tibetan Affairs Commission (Mengzang weiyuanhui, a continuation of the Lifanyuan during the Qing), established in 1928, as the administrative organ of the temple affairs. Local governments would not intervene in the selection of temple heads. Only three months later, however, the Mukden Incident occurred. Japan colonized Manchuria and installed a puppet state, the Manchukuo (1932–45). In August 1940, the General Affairs State Council (Guowuyuan) of the Manchukuo issued the *Outline of Lamaism Organization*, deciding to set up an institution to "promote Dharma and protect the nation." In December, the Order of Lamaism of the Manchukuo Empire (Manzhou diguo lamajiao zongtuan) was established. The principles of the order were "to promote the state-building spirit and friendship among East Asian lamaist believers. To expel the thoughts of communism, so that to revive Dharma and protect the nation." The Fengtian branch of the order was set up at the Essential-Victory Temple.[68]

But the former Mukden nexus was hardly a Tibetan Buddhist center anymore. During the Qing dynasty, all lamas (except the Sibe lamas at the North Stupa Dharma-Wheel Temple) had to learn to read and chant Tibetan sutra. By 1921, however, the Essential-Victory Temple had to recruit a lama from Fuxin to teach them Tibetan.[69] By 1936, the total number of lamas was less than a hundred and sixty-five of them had official positions.[70] According to the temples' financial report, the main sources of income were derived from renting or selling land, whereas donations from believers accounted for less than 1.3 percent of the income.[71] After the establishment of the People's Republic in 1949, the seven temples were supervised by the Division of Religious Affairs, Shenyang municipal government. A survey in 1950 shows that there were only thirty-two lamas remaining, with seventeen either too old or ill to work. The Essential-Victory Temple was the only one barely functional. When a new abbot was transferred to the temple in 1961, only twenty-odd lamas were there, all very old.[72]

The abrupt change in state-temple relations caused the rapid decline of the Mukden nexus. Why didn't they, like many other Tibetan Buddhist temples, survive the change? Their vulnerability came precisely from having exceedingly strong support from the former imperial state. In Mongolia, the Buddhist temples were self-sufficient sociopolitical units. Yes, many created strong bonds with the Qing state and acquired imperial patronage. But they also had their own feudal or quasi-feudal societal ecology. Most of the big temples had their own *tulku* (reincarnated leader), farmlands, herds, and dependent population (Mon. *shabi*) who answered directly to the temples.[73] They received patronage from the entire local society, rather than the government only. Some even held certain political and judicial powers. When state supports (some substantial, some symbolic) were curtailed, these temples suffered considerably less than the Mukden nexus, which had none of these securities. After all, the Tibetan Buddhist world in that city was artificially created and arbitrarily maintained for the political needs of the Qing throne. Once the state supports ended, this network could no longer sustain itself and soon withered due to poverty, corruption, strife, and social indifference.

The Mahākāla Statue Disappeared

The Mukden nexus of Tibetan Buddhism collapsed the same way it was created. In 1946, the golden Mahākāla statue, which had been enshrined in the city since 1635, disappeared mysteriously. Made by Phags-pa for Kublai Khan and presented by Mergen lama to Hong Taiji, the Mahākāla statue marked the miraculous rise of Qing Tibetan Buddhism. And now it had vanished without a trace. Everyone believed it had been stolen. But how was it stolen, by whom, for what purpose, and where did it go? No one knows. What we do know comes from the recollections of the lamas.[74]

It was March 31. Around 5:00 a.m., a lama named Ürgün Dalai got up to check the Mahākāla Pavilion. An important guest was scheduled to visit the Mahākāla statue that day, so the lama wanted to make sure everything was in order. Appallingly, he found all the locks—which prevented people from, respectively, entering the pavilion, climbing to the second floor, and going into the shrine—destroyed. Gone was the Mahākāla statue, along with the offerings the guest had sent someone to deliver the day before. Everyone in the Essential-Victory Temple panicked. Lamas cried and shouted, punching the walls and stomping on the floor. After searching in vain, they reported the theft to the police at noon. At 2:00 p.m., the guest showed up. He was Xu Zhen, chairman of the Liaoning Provincial Government.

Xu, the representative of the ruling Nationalist Party (KMT), had arrived in Shenyang only two days before. When Japan surrendered the previous August, the Soviet Red Army occupied the city. The Chinese Communist Party (CCP) arrived first to take over but then withdrew in January under pressure from both the Soviets and the KMT. On the second day after he arrived in Shenyang, Xu Zhen sent his secretary, Mr. Lan, and his friend Li Panxi, a local layman, to the Essential-Victory Temple to announce that he would pay a visit to the Mahākāla statue the next day. At the behest of the messengers, the lamas hesitantly made an exception, unlocking the doors and allowing Mr. Lan and Li inside to see the statue. Ürgün Dalai recalled that Mr. Li worshipped the statue seriously, but Mr. Lan, who toured around with no particular interest, did not. They were the last outsiders to see the Mahākāla statue at the temple.

Upon learning about the incident, Chairman Xu ordered the police to solve the case as soon as possible. The police suspected the lamas—after all, they had a reputation for stealing and selling temple treasures. All but three were detained: One was left there to guard the temple, the other two were too old or sick to move. The rest were interrogated, some were soon released, some bitterly tortured. But no one confessed. After a month, all the lamas returned to the temple. Chairman Xu came to the temple again to comfort them. "He said to us," a lama recollected, "'Since the golden Buddha is hard to find, you don't have to worry about it. Do not mention it in the future.'" The case, therefore, was dropped. Although people continued to talk about it and shared various conspiracy theories (with Xu being a major suspect), none of the rumors could be confirmed. Xu died in 1949, in the famous Taiping shipwreck en route to Taiwan to seek refuge after the KMT lost the civil war.

With the waning of the Mukden nexus, the religious significance of the West Stupa space diminished. Its role as a key component of a Buddhist network, itself a node in an imperial web tying Manchuria, China proper, Mongolia, and Tibet together, ended. However, thanks to the decline of the nexus, the place acquired a brand-new, and independent, spatial meaning. Only then did the space transform, from "the stupa in the west" to "Xita." What transformed it was the railway.

CHAPTER 3

The Railway

At the cockcrow on June 4, 1928, the young lamas at the Life-Prolonging Temple rose to sweep the yard and begin their morning study like every other day.[1] The sunglow had already spread all over the stupa, casting a long shadow of it on the ground. At 5:23 a.m., however, a huge blast very close by interrupted their morning chant.

At a spot only 700 meters, or 765 yards, north of the ancient Tibetan Buddhist tower, thirty bags of TNT, weighing 150 kilograms had blown up a small railway bridge called Three-Arch Bridge (Sandongqiao). The explosion hit its target: a passing train. Black smoke created by the bomb unfurled as high as 200 meters into the morning sky.[2] No doubt everyone living in the Xita neighborhood was startled from sleep. The explosion rocked not only the temple but the city of Fengtian (Mukden). What happened that early morning soon stunned the world.

The target of the attack was Marshal Zhang Zuolin (1875–1928), China's most powerful warlord and the de facto head of the Beiyang Military Government of the Republic of China. Zhang controlled Manchuria and North China and had prolonged military clashes with other Chinese warlords. His army had recently suffered a series of defeats in northern China, south of the Shanhai Pass. Zhang's private train had departed from Beijing the day before, in retreat to his home base of Fengtian. The explosion precisely and completely blew up Zhang's personal carriage, the tenth car in a twenty-carriage train. Many others were injured and seventeen killed, including the governor of Heilongjiang province, Wu Junsheng, who died instantly when a nail struck his head. Though mortally wounded, Zhang Zuolin did not die immediately. He was transferred to his downtown residence in a hurry. Waking temporarily from a coma, the marshal asked in a quavering voice:

"Caught [the assassins]?"
"Caught," replied one of his assistants, comforting him with a false claim.
"Where [are they] from?"
"Still interrogating."

Several hours later, the fifty-three-year-old warlord stopped breathing.[3]

Rumors about who had plotted and executed the murder soon spread. Over the next two months, the evidence pointed increasingly at the Japanese Kwantung Army, despite the latter trying hard to mislead the investigation. Generally known as the "Huanggutun Incident" (named after the train station nearby), the notorious assassination was widely regarded as the prelude to the Mukden Incident and the Japanese invasion of Manchuria three years later, which itself was defined by many historians as the starting point of World War II in East Asia.[4] Most narratives highlight, correctly, the imperialist impulse of radical

10. The blast at the Three-Arch Bridge. Image courtesy of P. A. Crush Chinese Railway Collection and Special Collections, University of Bristol Library (www.hpcbristol.net).

officers of the Japanese army, who provoked Chinese nationalism in the years to come.[5]

In this chapter, however, we will consider the context through a different lens, a lens of spatial politics and economics. Particularly, I focus on the railways, train stations, and new urban spaces that emerged around the stations. The assassination, I argue, was not merely another dark moment in China's century-long national humiliation, nor was it just an early indication of the pending horrific international war. Rather, it was the result of an intense conflict between two types of capitalist modernity in aggressive expansion in Manchuria. Both types of capitalist modernity—one colonialist and the other nationalist—depended heavily on the railway, a newly imported, powerful form of transportation that fundamentally changed mankind's sense of space and time. Thus, the railway was not only the dramatic arena for geopolitical competition but also the most striking sign of modern transformation in Manchuria. The Xita neighborhood, despite its tiny size, was a critical point in the railway network in the vast Eurasian frontier of Manchuria. It occupied a peculiar position in the modern transition of East Asia and Inner Asia.

The story of the railway in Xita, where Zhang was killed, began in the late nineteenth century. The people who first extended the "iron road" into this space were neither Chinese nor Japanese, but Russian.

The Railways Come to Town

For Dr. Dugald Christie (1855–1936), a medical missionary for the United Presbyterian Church of Scotland, who had lived in Mukden since 1882, the winter of 1895 warranted a special place in his memoir. For the first time in thirteen years, he had a strong feeling that, "the great world outside was stretching its covetous fingers into the plains and valleys of Manchuria." What brought about this impression was an unexpected encounter with a Russian colonel and lieutenant, "attended by four Cossacks, the first we had ever seen." The soldiers had traveled through Korea and northern Manchuria before visiting the city. After spending a pleasant evening with them, the forty-year-old doctor watched the pair get on their horses and leave "by the light of the brilliant winter stars." "Manchuria," he later remarked, "was to be left to her isolation no longer."[6]

The year witnessed the conclusion of the First Sino-Japanese War. China had suffered by far the most devastating military and political defeat. The Qing government's representative, Li Hongzhang (1823–1901), was coerced by his Japanese counterparts into signing the humiliating Treaty of Shimonoseki in Japan. According to the treaty, Chosŏn Korea, a longtime subordinate ally of the Qing, was now formally "independent," marking the official end of a China-centered world system. In addition to from a huge indemnity (300 million taels of silver), the Qing was forced to cede both Taiwan and the Liaodong Peninsula to Japan. However, czarist Russia, along with Germany and France, protested the Liaodong concession on the grounds that it would severely undermine its special interests in China. Although outraged by the so-called Triple Intervention, Japan had no choice but to return the Liaodong (in exchange for another 30 million taels of silver from China), only to be more vigilant about Russian expansion.

Russia, on the other hand, was pushing hard on an extremely ambitious transportation project: building a cross-Eurasian railway connecting Vladivostok, the strategic, warmwater port in the Far East, and St. Petersburg in the west, passing through the frozen steppe and forests of Siberia. The idea of such a grand railway was not particularly novel; people had been talking and debating about it for decades. But the project only seriously materialized in the 1890s, facilitated greatly by His Majesty's Finance Minister—known as the "Father of the Trans-Siberian Railway"—Sergei Yulyevich Witte (1849–1915).[7] For Witte, the Trans-Siberian Railway (TSR) was more than just a railway. Rather, Russia's national economy, industrialization, geostrategic privileges in the Eurasian continent, global power position, and even its sacred mission of spreading civilization to barbaric lands were all interwoven in this grand project.[8]

While Dr. Christie in Mukden enjoyed his dinner with the Russian soldiers, Minister Witte in St. Petersburg, thousands of miles away, was deeply troubled by a conundrum: How to extend the last section of the TSR from the Transbaikal, a region bordering northwestern Manchuria, to the Primorye (Maritime Province), a region bordering southeastern Manchuria. It would be a great hassle to take a long, winding route around the Chinese border, not to mention that the harsh weather and geological conditions would significantly increase the cost and delay the construction. A better option was to build a shortcut, a straight-line connecting Chita in the Transbaikal and Vladivostok in the Primorye directly through Manchuria. In the summer of 1895, the Russian government sent secret survey missions to explore the possibility—the team Dr. Christie ran into was likely one of them. A section of the railway would trespass on Chinese territory. Would the Qing government agree to such a violation of its sovereignty? Witte decided to give it a try. He thought of Li Hongzhang.

In the summer of 1896, Li led a Qing diplomatic mission to Russia to attend the coronation ceremony of Czar Nicolas II in the first step of a global tour in the Western world. Witte saw his visit as the best opportunity to persuade this prestigious Chinese politician to agree with his plan. He gave Li a warm welcome in St. Petersburg during Li's three-week sojourn there. Taking credit for the Triple Intervention and the financial aid Russia provided to China, Witte argued that the new railway would strengthen Russo-Chinese military cooperation against Japanese intrusion. At the same time, he promised that Japan would not oppose the project either because it provided the Japanese with a convenient means to travel to Europe.[9] After several rounds of negotiations, and possibly with a fat bribe to Li,[10] the two parties agreed in June to a secret pact, known as the "Li–Lobanov Treaty." China allowed Russia to construct the China Eastern Railway (CER) connecting Vladivostok and Chita through Jilin and Heilongjiang. Moreover, a strip of land along the railway was also ceded for the purpose of construction and operation. On the surface, the Russian government neither conducted nor financed the project directly: it was run by the "private" Chinese Eastern Railway Company and financed by the joint venture Russo-Chinese Bank. But both institutions were essentially controlled by the Russians. Furthermore, in December, Russia secured more privileges along the CER with a new treaty, *The Statutes of the Chinese Eastern Railway*, which promised Russia's monopoly of mining, commerce, industry, and telegraph businesses in the railway zone.[11]

Colonial imperialism was always competitive. In the same month, Germany, another actor in the Triple Intervention, asked Beijing if it could lease the Jiaozhou Bay of the Shandong Peninsula as a German naval base. The request was turned down. The following year, using the murder of two German missionaries (known as the Juye Incident) as an excuse, the German Imperial Navy occupied Jiaozhou and forced the Qing to cede the bay area as a leased territory. With German influence now penetrating into the hinterland province of Shandong, Russia, which had also coveted Jiaozhou, responded in 1898 by taking over two adjacent ports on the tip of the Liaodong Peninsula: the military port of Lüshun (Port Arthur) and the commercial port of Dalian (R. Dalniy; J. Dairen). Along with Vladivostok, Russia had now secured two warm-water naval bases in the Pacific.

In his memoir written after the Russo-Japanese War, Witte claimed that he had resolutely opposed the occupation of Port Arthur and Dalian. "The proposed measure would be extremely dangerous even from the standpoint of our own self-interest," he said. "We were engaged in building a rail-road in Chinese territory and that step would arouse the country against us, thus endangering the railroad construction." Moreover, he raised a critical point of objection: "Besides, the occupied ports . . . *would have to be connected by rail with the trunk line,* such a circumstance would drag us into complications likely to have disastrous results."[12] It would seem that ironically, Witte, the chief architect of the TSR, was against the plan to build a southward extension of the CER. However, historical records show a different scenario. Rather than an opponent of a southern branch, he was the first one to promote it. As early as 1896, Witte had already demanded such a branch when negotiating with Li Hongzhang. He also instructed Prince Esper E. Ukhtomsky (1861–1921), the special ambassador to Beijing and the chairman of the Russo-Chinese Bank, to sell the plan to the Qing government in 1897.[13] But such an extension should be long-term and gradual, and he hoped could eventually reach Beijing or even a port in Shandong. The seizure of Port Arthur and Dalian, for him, was too sudden and too aggressive, and would only invite the immediate hostility of the other powers. As he later commented, the policy was "a fatal step, which eventually brought about the unhappy Japanese War and the subsequent revolution."[14]

Nevertheless, the construction of the southern Manchurian branch soon started. The railway, using broad-gauge track (the Russian standard), began in Port Arthur and extended northeast, connecting Dalian,

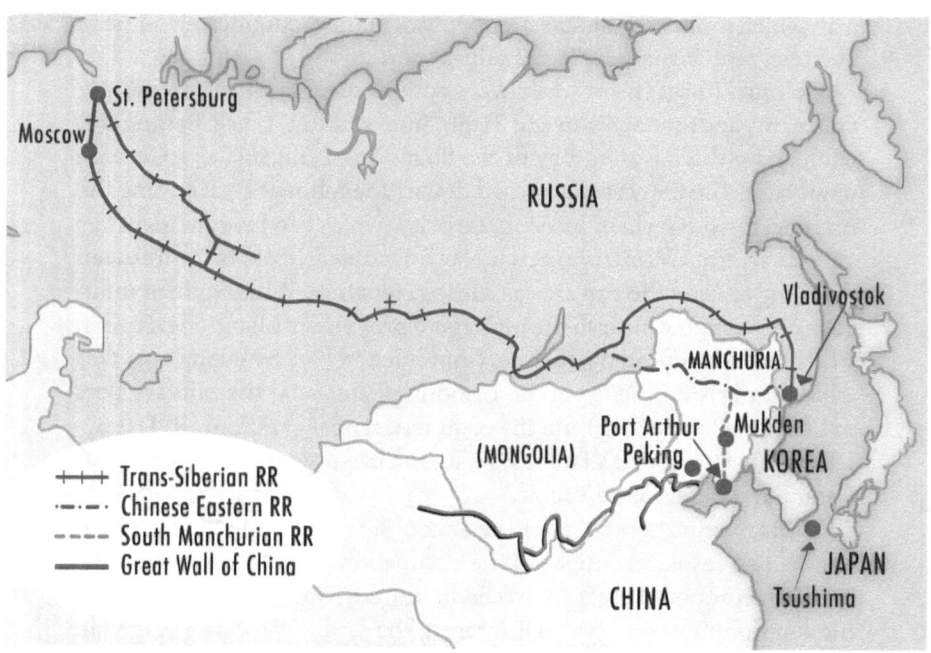

11. The Trans-Siberian Railway and the Chinese Eastern Railway (circa 1905). MIT Visualizing Cultures, offered by Creative Commons (with adaption by the author).

Mukden, Changchun, and finally joining the CER trunk line in Harbin. Thus, a T-shaped railway network gripped Manchuria in the hands of the Russians (fig. 11). The southern branch of the CER ran about 940 kilometers (584 miles), compared to the CER trunk line, which was about 1,480 kilometers (920 miles). The whole TSR, was about 9,288 kilometers (5,770 miles), dwarfing the Transcontinental Railroad that spans the United States and measures 3,069 kilometers (1,907 miles).

Dr. Christie, the Scottish missionary, keenly observed the change occurring in his daily life. "In Moukden [*sic*] little was heard of it for some time," he recorded, "Russian engineers surveyed and made maps and went away again, and it was reported that they were making a railway over the desert mountains in the far north. Gradually people grew accustomed to Russian visits."[15]

But Christie also realized that Mukden presented a problem for railway construction. As the railway "had gradually taken shape," he remarked, "Superstitious prejudices had prevented its coming closer to Moukden than about ten miles, lest the Imperial Tombs be disturbed and the prosperity of the dynasty destroyed."[16] In fact, when the southern branch was still in blueprint, the Qing had made it very clear that Mukden, where several imperial mausoleums and old palaces were located, must be strictly protected from intrusion by the railway. Any construction should be distanced from the mausoleums by at least thirty Chinese li (about fifteen kilometers) so that the "Dragon Vein" was carefully protected. Li Hongzhang even went so far as to arbitrarily assign the railway to turn west and go around the city, adding more than one hundred kilometers extra to the route. However, a Russian engineer, recorded in the Chinese archive as "Jilishiman," found the plan not only inconvenient but also unsafe because the Juliu River flowed nearby and could easily erode the rail base. After several exchanges, the Russian decided to ignore Li's request and moved that section of the track significantly eastward. Still avoiding the city walls and the mausoleums, the railway passed the auxiliary capital through its western outskirts.[17]

In 1899, a train station was established at a place about 2.5 kilometers (1.6 miles) west of the city walls, the very first in the sacred capital. Staffed by nineteen employees, fifteen army soldiers, and twenty-four Cossack cavalrymen, the Russian Mukden Station (recorded as "Maogudian" in Chinese documents) was one of the CER's smaller outposts.[18] The terminal building was very simple, nothing more than a single-story brick house of no particular style, erected in a wide and empty area. There was, however, another building nearby: The West Stupa Life-Prolonging Temple.

While the lamas at the West Stupa watched curiously as the iron tracks were laid beside their monastery, disturbing news was coming from south of the Shanhai Pass. Trigged in part by German colonial infiltration, in the Shangdong province, a spiritual-martial organization known as the Boxers had mobilized local peasants and was calling for expelling and killing all foreigners.[19] Within months, the riot spread to the whole of northern China and, finally, Manchuria: 1900, the Year of the Rat, was full of unrest and chaos. In Mukden and elsewhere, peasants who had lost their lands to the railway construction joined the uprising and vented their anger at the CER. On July 1, the Boxers set the CER Company office in Mukden on fire. Many tracks, telegraph wires, and trains were also destroyed, forcing the construction to stop.[20] Russia quickly responded with an invasion of terror, brutally massacring tens of thousands of Chinese civilians living in the border region and, in just three months, occupying all of Manchuria. In the next five years, Russia became the de facto ruler of this frontier. It was under this colonized circumstance that, in 1903, the CER opened for operation.

Although the Russians brought the railway to Manchuria first, they were not the only ones. The Qing, in a bid to protect its holy, imperial frontier, proactively responded by extending its own railway into Manchuria.[21] As early as 1890, Li Hongzhang proposed building the Trans-Shanhai Pass Railway (TSPR, also known as the Imperial Railways of North China) to connect Tianjin and Mukden, with a vision that it might later extend further east to Jilin and Ningguta. The plan was financially and technologically supported by Great Britain, Russia's major rival in Europe. The construction, however, was much slower and often curtailed due to war (the Sino-Japanese War), rioting (the Boxer Rebellion), or a shortage of funds. After the Boxer Rebellion was suppressed, building of the TSPR finally resumed with the starting point now modified to Beijing. When the CER was completed in 1903, the Chinese-owned railway had reached Xinmin, less than sixty kilometers west of Mukden city. However, construction was halted there for two years due to Russian protest.[22]

"Nothing else in the nineteenth century," remarked Alan Trachtenberg, "seemed as vivid and dramatic a sign of modernity as the railroad."[23] Only three years into the twentieth century, railway modernity came to Manchuria. Wherever the tracks stretched to, they compressed time and space and completely altered local people's understanding of the physical world surrounding them. Take the Scottish missionary Dr. Christie as an example. When he first journeyed to China in the 1880s, the voyage from London to Shanghai normally took six weeks. After waiting for as long as ten days, a steamboat carried him to Niuzhuang (nowadays Yingkou), a port in the Bohai Bay, a journey that took another three days. Then the doctor had to wait a few more days before hiring a cart to travel north to Mukden. Even Li Hongzhang, when he visited Russia in summer 1896, had to cross almost half the globe via the maritime route before arriving at Odessa after thirty days. But by the early twentieth century, as Dr. Christie noted, "one can now leave London at nine o'clock on a Monday morning, and after a comfortable sleeping-car journey drive through the Moukden [*sic*] streets in the afternoon of Friday, eleven days later." Personally experiencing this dramatic transition, he claimed in his writing that "there are few parts of the world where the modern change in ease of access has been more marked than in Manchuria."[24]

The most salient change the new transportation brought were immigrants. Due to a long-term ban to exploit in the previous centuries, population density in Manchuria was among the lowest in the entire Qing empire. Since the mid-nineteenth century, the Qing had gradually eased the ban and endorsed a new policy of "strengthening the frontier by migration" (*yi min shi bian*). Immigrants, mostly peasants, soon flooded in from overpopulated provinces, notably Shandong and Zhili. Beyond the conventional maritime route, the construction of the CER and the TSPR opened new channels of entry. The CER alone, from 1898 to 1900, recruited and employed about 200,000 laborers from Inner China,[25] many of them later resettled in the new towns and villages along the railway. Following the extension of the TSPR, more people moved to the Northeast, either by train or by walking along the tracks. In the early twentieth century, the Fengtian Province (Liaoning) absorbed more immigrants than Jilin and Heilongjiang. From 1897 to 1908, the population of the Fengtian Province more than doubled, increasing from 4.96 million people to over 11 million, or 56 percent of the entirety of Manchuria.[26]

Fengtian city (Mukden), the capital of the Fengtian Province, registered approximately 100,000 urban residents and 470,000 rural residents in 1910.[27] Other than native Manchu, Mongol, Han Chinese, and Hui Muslim, there were also 2,500 Japanese living in the Fengtian-Yingkou area.[28] But noticeably, over 10,000 Russians (including Cossacks) were stationed in the city before the Russo-Japanese War in 1904–5. Russian flags and signboards hung in the most bustling streets. A small episode recorded by Douglas Story shows an intimate interaction between Russians and the Tibetan Buddhist monasteries. During the tiaobuzha ceremony in 1904, a "Cossack soldier" with a rifle on his shoulder suddenly went into the Essential-Victory Temple. Throwing himself in front of the Buddha statue, the soldier kowtowed three times and received a blessing from the Da lama. It turned out that he was a Buryat, an ethnic Mongol originating from southeastern Siberia. "His devotions done, the Buriat [sic] became a soldier again, clattered heavily back to the service of the Czar."[29]

The railways changed not only local demography but also the native ecologies of production, communication, and living. They broke down the barriers between the agricultural, nomad, and forest zones and, in so doing, integrated—gradually but irreversibly—separate and diverse human societies into a homogeneous economic circle. The CER outcompeted traditional caravan trade and river transport, at the same time delivering tens of thousands of peasants to the scarcely populated steppe and forest regions. Historian Owen Lattimore, who witnessed what he called "the Chinese colonization" of Manchuria and Mongolia in the early twentieth century, argued that with the railways it "became possible for the first time in Chinese history to link an extensive frontier agriculture closely with an intensive domestic agriculture." Thanks to the new transportation, "the age-old gap between China and the steppe" was now closing.[30]

Lattimore's perspective is not without problems, but it can still be used to explain the impact and transformation the railway brought to a mini local space: Xita, where the Mongol lamas were the main dwellers. In the summer of 1902, the Da lama of the West Stupa Temple, Tegshi Bayan, submitted a petition to the Mukden Board of Rite through Balji, the Jasak Da lama. The topic was the wasteland surrounding the temple. Some temple-owned lands, Tegshi Bayan said, had been enfolded into the railway zone by the Russians. Aside from that, there were also sixty mu of wildlands and eight houses near the stupa. A shop called Fu Qing Tang, mediated by an interpreter, wanted to rent it for potential residential, commercial, or industrial developments. After consulting with the demchis of the temple, Tegshi Bayan was inclined to take the offer. The Da lama reasoned, "Had all the temple lands been enclosed by the Russian, the compensation—supposing there is some—would not be sufficient to sustain us for long. Besides, these lands are close to the railway, neither merchant nor farmer dare live there." He then begged for permission to lease the properties for 180 taels of silver per year to Fu Qing Tang. If a contract was signed, he suggested that the money be used for a public fund for the temple.[31]

The document reveals an intriguing case of the "production of space," borrowing Henri Lefevre's phrase, in the wake of railway capitalism. The Qing West Stupa, as explained in the prior chapters, had been a component of a religious-bureaucratic nexus that symbolized the transfrontier, spiritual-political link between Mukden and the Mongolian-Tibetan

region. As a Tibetan Buddhist space physically isolated in the underde-
veloped western edge of the city, it did not have an independent and
unique spatial meaning of its own. The railway changed that. The steam
engines crushed the conventional spiritual, political, and economic links
to the Inner Asian frontiers. The barren lands surrounding the temple,
previously of little use, were now open to the opportunity for commerce,
industry, and new dwellers. The sacred, empty, religious space was ready
to be divided, measured, calculated, and cashed out. In a way, the West
Stupa/Xita space mirrored a contracted Manchuria: a previously ritualized margin area soon to be centralized and capitalized.

On February 8, 1904, the Japanese Imperial Navy launched a surprise
attack against the Russian battleships at Port Arthur, igniting the Russo-
Japanese War. The Liaodong Peninsula was a major battlefield. A year
later, the flames of war spread to Mukden/Fengtian. Both sides suffered
greatly. A Japanese source indicates that the number of deaths in the
Battle of Fengtian accounted for one-third of the total Japanese deaths
in the war.[32] Under the mediation of US President Theodore Roosevelt,
the two empires signed the Treaty of Portsmouth on September 5, end-
ing by far "the first modern, technological conflict" in East Asia.[33] Japan
took over all the Russian privileges in southern Manchuria, including
the Kwantung Leased Territory (Lüshun and Dalian), the CER branch
from Lüshun/Dalian all the way to Changchun, and the railway concessions along the line. Although withdrawing from southern Manchuria,
Russia still controlled the CER trunk line and the Changchun-Harbin
section of the branch.

Japan knew only too well the importance of the railway. During the
war, Japan built a narrow-gauge railroad from Andong, a border town
on the Qing-Korean Yalu River boundary, to Fengtian. The Andong-
Fengtian Railway (AFR), built without Chinese permission, was supposed to be a temporary project for war purposes only. After the war,
however, Japan converted it to a standard gauge railway and kept it as
a permanent subbranch of the southern CER branch.[34] The Japanese
also took over the TSPR project and arbitrarily extended it from Xinmin farther east to Huanggutun, a place just 3.9 kilometers (2.4 miles)
northwest of Fengtian city. Like the AFR, when this project started, the
Qing government did not know anything about it.[35]

The year 1906 marked the beginning of Japanese railway colonialism in China. The south CER branch, now controlled by Japan, was
officially renamed the South Manchuria Railway (SMR), which also
incorporated the AFR and other smaller branches. In December, the
South Manchuria Railway Company, popularly known by its Japanese
abbreviation, Mantetsu, was established as the managerial authority of

the SMR.[36] Gotō Shinpei (1857–1929), the former head of civilian affairs in Japanese Taiwan, was inaugurated as its first director. The initial capital investment of the company was 200 million yen, half of which came from the Japanese government. Over the next four decades, Mantetsu developed into a gigantic and almighty colonial agency in Manchuria, parallel to the British East India Company in nineteenth-century South Asia. From time to time, its huge political, economic, and cultural influences penetrated Korea, North China, and even East China. Immediately after the founding of Mantetsu, Japan started expanding its railway empire. In 1907, it converted all the SMR tracks from wide gauge to standard gauge. In 1909, a year before the Japanese annexation of Korea, construction began on the cross–Yalu River railway bridge, which linked Andong in China and Sinŭiju in Korea. Upon its completion two years later, a train from Korea could smoothly enter the AFR-SMR system via the bridge (and vice versa). To build coherent, transcolonial railway capitalism, Mantetsu acquired the rights to manage the Korean railways on behave of the Korean agency until 1925.[37]

Meanwhile, the Qing government negotiated with Japan to buy back the newly extended Xinmin-Huanggutun section of the TSPR, converted it to standard gauge like the rest of the line, and built a new terminal in Huanggutun. In 1907, the whole line was renamed the Peking-Mukden Railway (PMR). The city now had another station, aside from the Russian Mukden Station built in 1899. Although technically, it was still 3.9 kilometers distance from the city, the Huanggutun Station was used as the Fengtian terminal of the PMR over the next four years.

This was an encouraging development for the Chinese. At that moment—only 3.9 kilometers of track were left in order to accomplish Li Hongzhang's ambition of building a railway to Mukden/Fengtian. Understandably, the Qing government was eager to complete this last section. But Japan opposed the plan fiercely. The reason was obvious. To accomplish it, the Chinese-controlled PMR (running east to west) would have to cut through the Japanese-controlled SMR (running southwest to northeast) since the SMR line lay between Huanggutun and the city. This was unacceptable because the intersection would challenge Japan's absolute control of the SMR and the railway territory (concession), causing legal and administrative headaches.[38] As a matter of fact, from 1905, when the Russo-Japanese War ended to 1909, right before the Japanese annexation of Korea, China and Japan were trapped in a series of conflicts in Manchuria. They involved railway rights and mining rights as well as a prolonged territorial dispute regarding the Sino-Korean Tumen River boundary.[39] Finally in 1909, the two sides reached a package deal to solve all the conflicts. According to the agreement, Japan no longer objected to the Chinese plan to stretch the PMR track to the city walls. In return, China had to yield significant economic privileges to Japan.[40]

In accordance with the bilateral agreement, on September 2, 1911, negotiator Xu Dinglin from the Qing dynasty's Fengtian Foreign Office, together with the specially dispatched engineer Sun Duoyu from the Ministry of Posts and Communications, signed the "Agreement on the Extension of the PMR" with the Japanese consul general in Fengtian, Koike Chozo, and Hori Sannosuke, chief of the Mantetsu Construction Department. The accord specified that at the intersection of the two railway lines, the SMR would build a bridge so that the PMR rail could pass underneath. The project was slated for completion within three months. The agreement also included a "Construction Method Book," detailing that at the intersection, the PMR would dig seven feet lower while the SMR would be elevated by fourteen feet. Furthermore, "At the point where the PMR intersects with the SMR, a new inclined bridge with an angle of approximately forty-five degrees shall be constructed. This bridge comprises three tunnels, each with a diameter of thirty feet. The two northern tunnels serve the railway, while the southern one is designed for road passage. The height from the railway track surface to the lower end of the bridge girder must be sixteen feet six inches or more."[41] As one may guess, this bridge is none other than the Three-Arch Bridge, where Zhang Zuolin met his tragic fate seventeen years later.

Approaching the end of 1911, the entire PMR project was completed at last. Another train station was erected at a site a mile north of the Smaller West Side Gate (*xiao xi bian men*), close to the Essential-Victory Temple. It replaced Huanggutun as the new (but temporary) Fengtian Terminal of the PMR. On New Year's Day 1912, after overcoming two decades of misfortune and difficulties, the whole PMR line opened for traffic. Only forty-three days later, however, the Qing dynasty collapsed.

Railway Modernity

How to depict the extraordinary changes in Muken/Fengtian after the coming of the railway? If you allow me to borrow, mimic, even "plagiarize" what geographer David Harvey described about Paris after the 1848 revolution, it would go like this:

> *Something very dramatic happened in* Manchuria *in general, and in* Mukden/Fengtian *in particular, with the arrival of the railways. The argument for some radical break in the city's political economy, life, and culture around the railway is, on the surface at least, entirely plausible.... Before, there was an urban vision that at best could only tinker with the*

problems of a medieval urban infrastructure; then came the railways—
not one but two—*which bludgeoned the city into modernity. Before
there were* horses and camels lining the streets single file in caravans;
and after, there were steam engines, telegraph wires, and asphalt roads
which delivered materials, passengers, and messages instantly. *Before
there were dispersed manufacturing industries organized along artisanal
lines; much of that then gave way to machinery and modern industry.
Before, there were small stores along narrow streets within the city walls
or in the open markets; and after came the vast sprawling department
stores that spilled out onto the boulevards. Before, there was* Buddhism,
Daoism, Shamanism, and Confucianism; *and after there was hard-
headed managerialism and scientific capitalism.*[42]

All italics are Harvey's original words. This is, of course, not a frivolous,
teleological suggestion that what Fengtian experienced in the 1920s and
'30s followed what Paris had had in the 1850s and '60s. Rather, the message is that the "radical break" of modernity is a hegemonic power engulfing urban spaces all around the world. Different events and agencies
triggered the modern transformation of the two cities. In Paris, the 1848
revolution unveiled the Second French Empire and Georges-Eugène
Haussmann's massive urban project, which completely renewed the sociopolitical landscape of the imperial capital. Harvey believes that this
was the "decisive moment of creative destruction." But in Fengtian, there
wasn't a Haussmann, or at least not just one Haussmann. The "creative
destruction" in this imperial capital cannot be understood as plotted
by one individual, one company, or one state. If there was a "decisive
moment," it was the moment when the SMR and the PMR crossed each
other at its western outskirts.

From 1912 to 1931, the western part of Fengtian—the Xita neighborhood included—was completely renovated. The railways pulled the
gravity of the city westward, changing the barren suburb into a bustling urban center. Unlike Paris, there was not just one authoritative
power who designed and implemented the expansion plan from the top
down. Instead, the city was reshaped by two powers in competition: the
Japanese colonial agencies, represented by Mantetsu, and the Chinese
warlord regime, headed by Zhang Zuolin. Zhang, who had gradually
solidified his power in Manchuria after the collapse of the Qing, maintained a subtle relationship with Japan until his death. Initially seeking Japanese collaboration, beginning in the 1920s, he became more
confident and ambitious enough to establish his own control over the
abundant resources and capitalist potential in Manchuria. The focus of
their conflict was railway power. For this reason, at least before 1931, the

framework of "colonial modernity" alone might not be sufficient enough to explain the dramatic urban transition in Fengtian.[43] I hereby propose a lens of "dual modernity," referring to the two sets of contested ideas and practices rebuilding Fengtian and Manchuria.[44] Although often in direct conflict, the colonial and nationalist impulses of capitalism inspired each other and jointly pushed the modern transition of the city and the frontier.

The two forces competed in three spatial layers. Going from microlevel to macrolevel, we begin with the two railway stations (the SMR Fengtian Station versus the PMR Liaoning General Station), then pan out to the new urban environments surrounding the stations (namely, the SMR zone versus the Mercantile District), and last, zoom further out to the vast territories the two railway systems stretched across. Using the analogy of the human blood system, we can see how the spatial power struggles between colonial modernity and nationalist modernity permeated both the arteries and capillaries, with the former being comparable to the main lines and the latter their branches. The three spatial layers require different lenses to be properly observed—a microscope, a magnifying glass, and a telescope. Let's first look through a microscope.

Under the Microscope: The Two Train Stations

In July 1910, the SMR had a brand-new Fengtian Station. Known in Japanese as Hōten-eki (奉天驛), it was one of the largest terminals of the SMR, not only replacing the much smaller Russian station but also developing into something much more than a train station. The construction started in 1908, right after Russia handed over the railway rights to Japan. The original plan was ambitious. Realizing that Fengtian was the political and economic center of southern Manchuria, Mantetsu initially proposed to establish it as the shared station for both the SMR and PMR. Of course, the Chinese did not approve such a bold suggestion. Nonetheless, Mantetsu still envisaged the terminal building and its front square as the pivot of Japanese-controlled railway territory in Fengtian. A large space was dedicated to the station, initially around 27 acres (331,706 *tsubo*, about 109,480 square meters); then an additional 18 acres (22,333 tsubo, or 73,670 square meters) was added. Mantetsu invested 300,000 to 340,000 yen into the project. Upon completion, the terminal building occupied 19,205 square feet (541 tsubo, or 1,785 square meters), easily the largest building on the western edge of the city. It was a two-story masonry structure. The second floor contained a hotel. Of course, such a grand construction had to be situated a little farther from the West Stupa. The new terminal was located 1.7 kilometers

(1 mile) south of the temple; still a close distance, yet not as close as the demolished Russian station.

Much more breathtaking than the size itself was the building's architectural style (fig. 12). The station was made of red brick with concrete ornaments along the roof line and windows on the facade. Two wings extended symmetrically from the main entrance. A green-colored dome adorned with twelve small windows rose above the central hall—perhaps the most eye-catching part of the building. There were two white towers on the two wings, each with its own green dome, albeit smaller and lower than the central dome. The entire facade, including the rectangular shape, structure, and ornamentations, was neither Chinese nor Japanese in style, but instead typical of nineteenth-century European style. More specifically, it was somewhat a mixture of neo-Renaissance and Gothic Revival.[45] Aside from being exotic, the highly symmetric and sublime masonry broadcast modernity's unquestionable power. In Japan as well as the Japanese colonies—Taiwan, Korea, and Manchuria—similar designs were highly popular at the time. They were often called the "Tatsuno style" buildings, named after the pioneering Japanese architect Tatsuno Kingo (1854–1919).[46]

The architect of the SMR Fengtian Station was not Tatsuno but his student Ōta Takeshi (1876–1911). Like most Japanese architects working in the colonies, Ōta graduated from the department of architecture at

12. Mukden train station of the SMR (Hōten-eki). Inufuusen/Wikimedia Commons.

Tokyo Imperial University (Tōdai). Starting in 1901, he worked as an architect for the Ministry of Justice and the Ministry of Finance before joining the Architectural Section of Mantetsu in 1907.[47] The Japanese colonies provided young architects like Ōta not only job opportunities but also testing grounds to freely practice what they had learned in school. In 1910, about 13 percent of the members of the Japan Association of Architects were living in Korea, Taiwan, or China, up from 4 percent in 1899. They were what Japanese historian Nishizawa Yasuhiko called "architect adventurers."[48] During his short tenure at Mantetsu, Ōta also designed or codesigned several landmarks in Dalian, including the Yamato Hotel (a chain hotel with the Mantetsu brand), the Mantetsu headquarters, and the Dalian branch of the Yokohama Specie Bank. The buildings were critical components of Mantetsu architecture in railway cities like Lüshun, Dalian, Fengtian, Andong, and Changchun—all in various European styles with a "Tatsuno" trademark.

"[A] consistency of styles was apparent in many of the Mantetsu railway towns," argues Bill Sewell in his study on Japanese Changchun, "that [was] unsurprising given the similar training of most Japanese architects."[49] The Tōdai architecture department was the breeding ground of modern Japanese architecture. Formerly the architecture department of the Imperial College of Engineering (ICE), its founding faculty was British, notably Josiah Conder (1852–1920). Coming to Japan during the heyday of the Meiji Restoration, Conder not only designed numerous monumental public and private structures in Tokyo (e.g., the Rokumeikan and Tokyo National Museum) but also laid the foundation of modern architectural education in Japan. One of his first graduated disciples was Tatsuno Kingo, who later succeeded Conder in 1884 after further pursuing studies at the University of London. Like his teacher, Tatsuno had his own practice. While Ōta Takeshi was designing the SMR Fengtian Station, Tatsuno, who left Tōdai in 1902, was entrusted to design the Tokyo Station of the Japanese Government Railway, completed in 1914.

No evidence shows that Ōta ever consulted with Tatsuno when designing the Fengtian Station (or vice versa). But anyone can tell the obvious similarities between the two buildings: the general shape, use of red brick, concrete ornamentation, windows, and European-style decorations. In fact, if a tourist in the 1930s or early '40s departed from Tokyo on a trip to Korea and Manchuria—a journey quite popular at the time—she would probably find that all the big stations en route (Tokyo, Pusan, Seoul [Keijō], Dalian, all the way to Fengtian) looked a lot like each other.[50] Unlike many British architects in India who adopted the Indo-Saracenic style, which incorporated Mughal architectural elements so as to soften the alienation of British Raj,[51] their Japanese counterparts preferred nonnative, Western-style buildings in their empire. Aside from temples or Shinto shrines, Japanese symbols, if any, were displayed only modestly in the interior, not the exterior. This was not because they were asked to do so. Nishizawa explains that "few Japanese architects were competent in the traditional Japanese style because their training was based on the British system."[52] Indeed, more enthusiastic endorsements of "Oriental" architectural traditions came later, largely due to the endless efforts of another ICE graduate, Itō Chūta. But more importantly, for many of the first generation of Japanese designers, the European styles represented fashion and power. They transplanted diverse European styles to East Asia: neoclassicism, historical eclecticism, and art nouveau, among others. The choice was always associated with a vision of world civilization and Japan's position in it. Here again, Haussmann's new Paris proves relevant. As Sewell points out, "the Second [French] Empire became popular among graduates of Tōdai's College of Engineering, understandable given that the Second Empire's neo-baroque was then becoming a preferred means of expressing state power around the world. . . . in taming foreign architectural idioms and mastering new methods of construction, they succeeded in making a statement about modern civilization and articulating it as an aspect of Japanese identity."[53] Considering the "Tatsuno style" was pervasive in Japan as well as its colonies, these imperial architects created a cross-border connection that bound the suzerain and colonies tightly together with a coherent visual exhibition of architectural modernity.

The Fengtian Station was one of Ōta Takeshi's last works—he died one year after its completion. Likely due to the architect's poor health, the latter half of the project was carried out by a junior, Yoshida Sōtarō (1885–1959), a graduate of the ICE-affiliated Koshu Gakko (technician school). Upon finishing, Yoshida, who later became a foster son of the Ōta family,[54] went to study at Columbia University. After spending eleven years in the US and another eight years in Japan, Ōta Sōtarō returned to Mantetsu in 1929 and was appointed the director of the Architectural Section several years later. His most important architectural legacy in Fengtian, other than the train station, is the famous Yamato Hotel (1929, now the Liaoning Hotel), the most luxurious hotel in the SMR zone and indeed the entire city. The hotel was a completely different world from the rest of the city. A single drink here was nearly enough to pay for one and a half dozen rickshaw drivers to have a feast at a small restaurant in the old town.[55] It was in this hotel that radical Kwantung Army officers Itagaki Seishirō, Ishiwara Kanji, and Doihara Kenji plotted the 1931 Mukden Incident.

A year and a half before the incident, in March 1930, the Chinese PMR also established a brand-new terminal. Since the province of Fengtian had just been renamed "Liaoning" (as it is now known),[56] the station was officially titled the "General Station of Liaoning" (C. Liaoning zong zhan). Located between the Smaller West Side Gate and the Essential-Victory Temple, it was about 1.6 kilometers (1 mile) east of the West Stupa and only 3 kilometers (1.86 miles) northeast of the SMR station. The grand terminal building demonstrated Zhang Zuolin's last efforts to confront Japan's railway colonialism in Manchuria. While the SMR station was one of its architects' last works, the PMR station, initiated in 1927, was its designer's very first. The architect was Yang Tingbao (1901–1982), a recent graduate of the University of Pennsylvania.

Among the many prestigious universities in the US, the University of Pennsylvania (UPenn) was particularly attractive to young Chinese students who wanted to study architecture. Partially due to the kindness of the chair of the Department of Architecture, Paul Phillippe Cret (1876–1945), "Penn became for the young Chinese architects of the 1920s and 1930s a haven not unlike what the Bauhaus was becoming at the same time in Germany for aspiring architects of many nations."[57] Several of the greatest architects of twentieth-century China graduated from UPenn, including Liang Sicheng (1927), Chen Zhi (1927), Tong Jun (1928), and Yang himself. Yang went there in 1921 after completing preparatory study at Tsinghua College, funded by the Boxer Indemnity, which aimed to support young Chinese to attend American universities. His cohorts included Louis Kahn (1901–1974), one of the greatest architects of the twentieth century, who praised Yang as a genius his entire life. Studying under John Harbeson and Cret, Yang won several awards as a student and was widely regarded as a rising star. When Yang got his master's degree in 1925, Cret invited the young man to join his architectural firm in Philadelphia. Yang spent only a year there before returning to China.[58]

In 1926, Yang joined Kwan, Chu, and Yang Architects (C. Jitai gongcheng si) as a partner. The founder of the firm, Guan Songsheng (Kwan Sung-sing), maintained a good personal relationship with Zhang Xueliang (1901–2001), son and hire of Zhang Zuolin. Through this connection, Kwan, Chu, and Yang Architects was contracted for nine buildings in Fengtian from 1927 to 1930, all designed by Yang.[59] The very first was the PMR Liaoning station. Heavily influenced by Cret's Beaux-Arts style, Yang initially submitted a plan for a building with a modernist, West European appearance. But both railway officials and his colleagues requested modifications. They said the new terminal should look like the station in Beijing, the other end of the PMR.[60]

The PMR Beijing station, in the heart of the Qing capital, was completed in 1906. Like the railway itself, the train terminal was built by the British. Although the architect's name is hard to determine, the scheme had to have been approved by Chief Engineer and Manager Claud W. Kinder (1852–1936). Trained in St. Petersburg as a technician, Kinder first served the Japanese Imperial Railway and then the Chinese Engineering & Mining Company. Before retiring in 1909, Kinder was the chief engineer for the PMR for over twenty years. From 1902 to 1909, he also held the concurrent position of PMR chief manager.[61] The Beijing terminal was in a classical European style, with a tall bell tower on the right side, making the two-story building asymmetrical. The facade included native ornaments such as Chinese dragons. But the most prominent feature of the red-and-white building was the huge vault in the middle. Yang decided to transplant this key element. He designed the Liaoning station as a three-story, symmetrical building with a high—almost exaggerated—vault also in the middle, demonstrating the architectural affiliation between Fengtian and Beijing (fig. 13). But Yang's design was undoubtedly more modern. Most of the windows on facade were rectangular, and all lines were straight, forming a strong visual contrast to the semicircular vault.

13. Liaoning General Station of the PMR. Tonyxy1992/Wikimedia Commons.

Upon completion, the General Station of Liaoning was the largest train station in China, measuring nearly 7,000 square meters (75,347 square feet). "The integrity of this building showcased the twenty-six-year-old Yang's extraordinary confidence as an architect," architecture scholar Xing Ruan commented. "But above all, the skillful fit of the railway station into both its content and context evoked a building character that, rather than being regional, catered to China's voracious appetite for things Western in the early twentieth century."[62] On the other hand, Yang's compromise brings a meaningful comparison: While his Japanese counterparts enjoyed the freedom to express their understanding of modern, Yang's pursuit of modernity was more or less constrained. His impulse to depart from classicism was arrested by his employers' requirement to echo it. Yet such a requirement could not be seen as purely stylistic. Not unlike the coherent Tatsuno style along the Japanese railways, which demanded recognition of colonial modernity, the two PMR train stations also attempted to create a strong, if not stronger, connection with the modern in a nationalist space.

In practice, the PMR Liaoning station was constrained not only in design but also in construction. Remember that the station was close to the Essential-Victory Temple, the center point of the Tibetan Buddhism nexus in the city. Unavoidably, the religious space faced encroachment by the railway space. The "creative destruction" of the Essential-Victory Temple space was quite similar to what had happened to the West Stupa when the Russian station was built, only on a larger scale. For the city planning around the station, the PMR bureau designated an area of the Essential-Victory Temple for future development. The temple complained several times to the provincial government, attempting to negotiate a more favorable solution. In October 1929, the Da lama of the Mahākāla Pavilion, Wang Xi, submitted a petition requesting to preserve the rear building of the Essential-Victory Temple. Skillfully employing the political rhetoric of "modern" and "civilization," the Da lama made his argument both powerfully and smartly. Saying all lamas welcomed railway development wholeheartedly, the petition went on to say, "But if half of the temple was dismantled, it would also impact [our pursuit of] modern trends (*jindai chaoliu*)." According to the Da lama, there were three reasons why the building must be saved. First, many Mongol princes went there on pilgrimages and stayed in the rear building. Tearing down the building would hurt "their admiration of civilization." Second, the building was the residence of the Panchen lama during his visits. If his temporary home was preserved, "our Eastern land would be shone under Buddha's light—it sounds superstitious but could cherish the Mongols." Third, a "civilized state," no matter what industry it develops, should protect everything with historical value. Not to mention that financially, "a hundred-odd lamas depend on it to receive the Mongol princes," who were a large source of their income. The petition requested the provincial chairman, who "oversees the frontier and treats the five ethnic groups as one family," to instruct the railway bureau to "slightly move the boundary marks." The Da lama eloquently employed au courant terms like *modern, civilization*, and the *Five Nationalities Republic*. He minimized the influence of religious factors, going so far as to admit that it was somewhat "superstitious." By emphasizing the importance of ethnic minorities in the frontiers and highlighting the modern state's commitment to preserving cultural heritage, he successfully transformed the special significance of the Essential-Victory Temple. His strategy worked. The government approved the petition. As a matter of fact, from August 1929 to April 1930, the authority altered its plan several times to accommodate the Essential-Victory, saving not only the rear building and backyard, but also an archway. One exception was a screen wall, which was located right in the middle of a planned street.[63]

Both the SMR and the PMR stations "modernized" and subjugated suburban Fengtian. Despite that one was to colonize the space and the other to resist that colonization, the source of their modernity was the same: Western architectural style. The architects were all very young when they designed the buildings: Ōta Takeshi was in his early thirties, Yoshida Sōtarō was twenty-four, and Yang Tingbao was twenty-six. The difference was that Ōta and his peers were trained in Japan by a fairly established domestic education system. But when Yang returned to China, architectural education in Chinese universities was still rare. In Fengtian, Zhang Xueliang–funded Northeastern University decided to create one of the first architecture departments in China. The school invited Yang to chair it. Committed to his firm, Yang turned down the offer but recommended his friend Liang Sicheng (1901–1972), a fellow UPenn graduate. Sicheng's father, the great thinker Liang Qichao (1873–1929), gladly accepted the offer on his son's behalf. In 1928, Liang Sicheng returned home via the TSR after a tour of Europe. He became one of the two founding faculty members of the department.[64] The other was his wife, Lin Huiyin (1904–1955), a talented architect who graduated from UPenn's School of Fine Arts because the School of Architecture did not accept female students at the time. They further recruited more alumni, including Tong Jun and Chen Zhi, to Northeastern. The young professors transplanted the UPenn curriculum to the capital of Manchuria. Although short-lived due to the Mukden Incident in 1931, the department graduated several students who later became the second generation of modern Chinese architects.[65] From this perspective, the city presented itself not only a testing ground for both Japanese and Chinese architects but also one of the cradles of modern architectural education in China.

Magnifying Glass: The Urban Districts

We now switch to a magnifying glass to investigate the middle-layer space—the city and its districts.

"Railroad stations altered cityscapes," observes historian Jürgen Osterhammel, "They could sometimes revolutionize the whole character of a city."[66] This statement applies to Fengtian perfectly. Since the arrival of the railways, the urban circles in this ancient city numbered not one, not even two, but three in total. Aside from the walled, old inner city, each of the two railway terminals helped construct their own urban space. The Japanese SMR station was the pivot point of the "Railway Concession." The Chinese PMR station was located in the Mercantile District (C. *Shang bu di*), which had been established a short while before. The two new urban areas adjoined each other, with the Xita neighborhood right across their invisible boundary. Therefore, before 1931, Fengtian demonstrated exactly what Wolfgang Schivelbusch comments about European cities, "The railroad made its most immediate and visible impression on those parts of the city with which it interacted physically, i.e., the districts immediately adjoining the tracks and the stations. Here, the railroad changed the physiognomy of the old cities with bold strokes."[67] In Fengtian, new streets were paved and European-style buildings erected, transforming the city's outlook fundamentally. Both the SMR zone and the Mercantile District developed into thriving business and entertainment areas with, of course, different characteristics. Also established there were certain factories that later helped turn the western end of Fengtian into one of the key centers of Chinese industrialization.

The official term for the SMR zone (J. *Mantetsu fuzokuchi*) was the "railway concession," which was coined by the Russians (*kontsessiya zheleznoy dorogi*). As mentioned before, Russia not only acquired the right to build part of the TSR on Chinese soil but also seized a strip of land "attached to," or "affiliated with," the tracks. But the concession was never limited only to the lands used for laying tracks or building stations. A large portion of it was intended to transform to the new urban spaces surrounding the train stations. The cities of Harbin and Changchun were examples of this kind of railway metropolis created almost from scratch. After the Russo-Japanese War, Japan not only inherited but also largely expanded the Russian concessions in southern Manchuria. By definition, a railway concession was not a colony. Sovereignty over these lands still belonged to China. Nor was it a "leased territory" like the Japanese Kwantung Territory (Lüshun-Dalian), where a foreign administration was installed to rule local affairs. But Chinese sovereignty existed only in theory. The possessors of the concessions, first the Russians and then Mantetsu, had full right to explore the space, develop businesses, and set up their own rule without Chinese interference.[68] Therefore, as one volume suggests, "railway power created 'gray areas' of sovereignty in which territorial rule was continually contested and where the often problematic term 'quasi-colonial' fits quite well."[69] Or, a railway concession could simply be understood as a colony without the colony's name; an independent kingdom within a sovereign state. That is why Japanese railway imperialism in Manchuria is sometimes deemed "informal."[70] Among all the SMR zones, the Fengtian zone was not the largest but definitely the most critical in terms of its geostrategic importance. When Japan took it over from Russia, the Fengtian SMR zone was about 5.95 square kilometers (about 2.3 square miles). A decade later, in 1926, the area had more than doubled, to nearly 12.8 square kilometers (nearly 5 square miles), through either occupation, purchase, or forced lease.[71]

After the conclusion of the Russo-Japanese War, the Qing government finally got the chance to implement a revolutionary policy initially planned before the war: to create Mercantile Districts (MDs henceforth) in several Manchurian cities. An MD was a zone open to all merchants, Chinese and non-Chinese alike, to lease land and conduct business. Such a reform was in accordance with two trade treaties China signed in 1903 with, respectively, the US and Japan. On the surface, the practice of MDs followed that of "treaty ports" on the coastline as well as some transportation hubs. But unlike the forcefully opened treaty ports, where foreign powers enjoyed certain extraterritorialities, MDs were initiated by the Chinese authorities and solely under Chinese jurisdiction. In Manchuria, the Qing government proactively established MDs in order to counter the intrusions of both Russia and Japan. In 1908, the establishment of the Fengtian MD was officially announced.[72] Located outside the Small West Side Gate, the MD was gradually opened in three phases with the obvious intention to contain the SMR zone. The first phase was to set up a primary domain—called "zheng jie"—that encompassed the north and northeast sides of the SMR zone. It was followed by a secondary domain (*fu jie*) in the middle and a preparatory domain (*yu bei jie*) in the south and southeast. The whole MD was about 12 square kilometers. The primary domain, roughly 5.3 square kilometers, included the area from the city wall to the West Stupa, with the Life-Prolonging Temple sitting right on the Chinese side of the unmarked border.

（永清真写館製） ARRAY COMPANY OF SOLDIERS BARRACKS AT MOUKDEN 奉天守備兵隊営

14. "Array Company of Soldiers Barracks at Moukuden." A postcard photo
providing a view of the Japanese garrison at Xita, with the West Stupa
in the background.

In the same year, Fengtian saw its very first modern avenue, which
connected the SMR station with the west city gate through the division
of the two contested zones. The avenue was called Shijianfang, meaning
"ten houses," so named because there used to be several shabby houses in
a sorghum field between the Life-Prolonging and the Essential-Victory
Temples. Opposite to the stupa, just across the avenue, was first the
railway military garrison (fig. 14), and then, after 1936, the grand building
of the Mantetsu Railway General Bureau.

Along with the avenue came the first public transportation in the
city, a horse-drawn streetcar run by a Sino-Japanese joint venture company. In December 1907, as soon as the streetcar tracks were laid, it was
considered a significant event by many foreigners. The US consulate
general in Mukden, closely monitoring the economic developments
in Manchuria, promptly submitted a lengthy report to the State Department in Washington. The report specifically introduced the share-
holding situation and operational prospects of this streetcar company,
emphasizing its "chief value" as "providing a direct rail communication between the Southern Manchuria Railway and the city of Mukden."[73] From 1908, when it was installed, to 1925, when it was replaced

by trollies, the horse streetcar operated 160 round trips per day on a three-mile-long route, delivering on average seven thousand passengers.[74] A one-way trip cost thirteen Fengtian dollars (*Feng xiao yang*), seven dollars cheaper than another popular way of commuting: human-pulled rickshaws.[75] There was a landmark in the middle of the journey that no passenger could miss: the ancient West Stupa. As described in the 1910 edition of *Cook's Handbook for Tourists* (the equivalent of today's *Lonely Planet*):

> On leaving the South Manchuria (Japanese) station, the main road on which the tram-cars run bears to the left. This road for a considerable part of the distance is almost straight, and a few hundred yards ahead will be seen within a walled enclosure a sort of monument or dagoba having a circular base supported on arches about twenty feet high. On this base rests a very solid-looking dome, from the peak of which is built a spiral structure somewhat resembling a miniature pagoda.
> This is the Mukden Western Pagoda, the design pure Manchurian.[76]

What was described by the author as a "pure Manchurian" tower, 1.7 kilometers from the SMR station, marked roughly the northern end of the SMR zone. With the station as the center, the zone also extended southward about the same distance. A narrow strip of land west of the railway was assigned as an industrial zone for factories. A much larger area east of the railway—as wide as 1.5 kilometers, or 0.93 mile—was planned as a commercial, residential, and cultural entertainment neighborhood. This was the facade of the Japanese-directed urbanization enterprise. Because the rail track was a slanting line from southwest to northeast on the map, the SMR zone, which stretched along the rail track, roughly took the shape of a tilted rectangle on most maps. Within the rectangle, streets, alleys, public squares, and parks carved the urban setting into small, neat blocks, with most streets or alleys either parallel to or vertical with the rail track. There were, however, two main avenues that radiated from the terminal square to, respectively, the northeastern and southeastern corners of the zone. They were the two most famous and flourishing commercial streets of the SMR zone, Naniwa Dori (north) and Heian Dori (south). Apparently, their names echoed the historic Japanese cities, Osaka (formerly Naniwa) and Kyoto (formerly Heian). By 1931, the SMR zone had fifty-three streets with Japanese names.[77] German journalist and sinologist Ernst Cordes, in the mid-1930s, described "a main street in the Japanese district of Fengtian" as follows:

Yellow and gray buses rumbled past from time to time, while horse-drawn carriages rattled noisily over the road. If it weren't for the cries of the cart drivers, rickshaws would be the quietest means of transportation on the street. . . . On the street, there were Japanese, Koreans, Chinese, impoverished White Russians, Japanese women dressed in European-style or traditional Japanese attire, Chinese women in elegant blue cheongsams, as well as Europeans and Americans. Both European and Asian ethnic groups could be seen here.[78]

In between the SMR zone (called "new town" on the map) and the round-shaped, walled city ("old town") was the irregular-shaped Mercantile District. Together, the three spheres composed the central area of modern Fengtian. In the MD, city planners also divided the area into geometric blocks. Streets and roads were given numerical names, with the vertical streets called *jing* (longitude) and horizontal roads *wei* (latitude). This method for place-naming was very popular in many newly created urban spaces in China. In the Fengtian MD, the numbers ascended from east to west and north to south, with the 1-Wei Road merging with the Shijianfang Avenue, the 5-Wei Road running through the Naniwa dori, and the 7-Jing Street serving as the eastern end of the SMR zone. But because of the district's awkward configuration, the horizontal or vertical streets hardly cut the space into coherent or even regular shapes. On a map, the SMR zone and the MD look like two grids with quite different patterns being forcefully woven together. This spatial situation remains today.

Like the train stations, city planning manifested two powers' contested pursuit of modernity. The Fengtian SMR zone was the place where Mantetsu "put its utmost efforts to extend our country's influence."[79] From the very beginning, Gotō Shinpei, assisted by city planner Katō Yonokichi (1867–1933), envisaged the SMR zones not as temporarily occupied spaces but as permanent Japanese enclaves. Therefore, the main task of the urban planners was to attract more settlers and provide them a whole set of urban experiences: department stores, schools, hospitals, parks, restaurants, hotels, and entertainment and religious facilities as well as banking and postal services—all aimed at creating modern living conditions and promising business opportunities.[80] Needless to say, Euro-American cities, designed with a novel sense of science and rationality, were the model. By 1911, Mantetsu had invested 5.38 million yen in urban infrastructure in Manchuria, 1.22 million spent on the Fengtian zone.[81] After the SMR station in 1908, Mantetsu built its Fengtian branch office building in 1910, which was followed by the Haruhi-chō Park (1910), the police station building (1913), the main campus of the South Manchuria Medical School (1914), the Post Office (1915), the Hōten Shinto Shrine (1916), the Haruhi-chō Market (1917), and the Naniwa Square (1921). The decade after World War I was the golden age of construction in the zone. During this period, Mantetsu not only continued urban building—especially residential houses—but civil construction was also booming. European- and Japanese-style architectural structures were erected one after another, including the Hōten theater (1919), the Nishi Hongan-ji Temple (1919), the Fengtian branch of the Oriental Development Company (1920), the new Esturai-san Hotel (1920), and the Shengjing Daily building (1921). Along with them were new sewer and electric systems.[82] It is worth mentioning that Fengtian's first power station, with an installed capacity of 120 kilowatts, was built in the Xita neighborhood in 1908. Although in operation for only two years, the station was responsible for generating electric power for the SMR zone until it was replaced by more powerful stations.[83]

"By the Second World War, no other foreign power had embarked on such an ambitious programme of urban planning overseas before and, outside of wartime, none has tried since."[84] In less than three decades, the number of Japanese settlers in the Fengtian SMR zone increased nearly fifty times over, from 1,330 persons (451 households) in 1906 to 65,565 (15,202 households) in 1936.[85] Japanese companies and residents also extended extensively into the Mercantile District and the old town. Many of them settled along Shijianfang Avenue. The urban planning practices in Manchuria were later implemented in other parts of the empire. Leaving Mantetsu in 1908, Gotō Shinpei returned to Japan and served in multiple positions, including as the head of the Railway Bureau (1908–11) and the mayor of Tokyo (1920–23). After the devastating Kantō earthquake in 1923, Gotō shepherded the Resurrection Plan for the Imperial City. The reconstruction fundamentally reshaped Tokyo, the historic capital since the Edo period, in accordance with modern European cities and with Haussmann's Paris a source of inspiration.[86]

On the Chinese side, city planners sought to modernize the urban space to counter the Japanese colonial space. In 1919, the Fengtian provincial government issued a revised regulation for the Mercantile District that stated frankly the purpose of opening MDs was "expanding commercial activities and solidifying sovereignty."[87] In 1923, Fengtian established its municipal government (*shizheng gongshu*), with Zeng Youyi (1870–1936) as the first mayor. But the one who changed the city more profoundly was his assistant, later the second mayor, Li Dexin (1892–1945). A graduate of Tokyo Imperial University, Li took the right job at the right time. He had the unusual opportunity to systematically implement his urban reform scheme. "Reforming urban districts," he

said in a report in 1927, "is the primary task of a municipal administration. In the civilized states of both the East (*dong yang*) and West
(*xi yang*), all the great metropolis have neat urban streets and grand
architecture, which can be said as utmost good and beauty."[88] During
his tenure, Li installed a sewer system, paved gravel or asphalt roads,
and established public parks. One major reform was to divide the old
town into six districts and set up three new industrial and commercial
districts in the outskirts. In the northwestern suburb, the Huigong
Industrial District connected with the MD. It borrowed the city planning of the SMR zone and included factories and a market. Another
major project was to transform the Zhao Mausoleum (Hong Taiji's
tomb), one of the most popular tourist sites, into a large public park,
Beiling Park.[89]

As for the Mercantile District, Zhang Zuolin's plan to use the advantage of the PMR station to attract commercial and financial investments
partially worked. Colonial powers hungry to explore potential business
in Manchuria established their general consulates in the MD. The British, American, Japanese, French, Soviet, Austrian, German, and Italian
consulates were concentrated in the core of the "primary domain," south
of the Shijianfang Avenue, forming the diplomatic quarter of the city.
The US consulate general constantly received requests from American
businessmen at home, either inquiring about commercial opportunities
in Manchuria or asking to advertise their products to the locals.[90] Big
companies and banks, such as British American Tobacco, Banque de
l'Indochine, Bank of Korea, Mitsui Company, and Andersen, Meyer &
Company, set up their Fengtian branches in the MD, along with many
others. But the problem was that most of these big companies were
foreign, in particular, Japanese. By 1919, the Japanese owned eighty-four
companies in Fengtian with a total capital of 124 million yen. Japanese
commodities almost monopolized the market. In contrast, Chinese
businesses, with an average capital of just 200 Fengtian dollars each,
were largely small restaurants, family shops, drugstores, and groceries.[91]
The situation was described in a petition submitted to the provincial
government in 1923 by thirty-five Chinese merchants, "Now the Chinese and foreigners mix together, the foreign merchants concentrated
here . . . they suck our blood, grab our profit, and are powerful enough
to put us to death." The Fengtian General Chamber of Commerce also
pointed out, "Businesses in the MD just started. In Shijianfang, outside
the Small West Side Gate, the majority of the merchants are foreigners. In the newly established north market, most [Chinese] traders are
small businessmen. A rich merchant is rare. In the Xita area, only a few
are equipped with better funds because they have run businesses for

longer. But nearly no one has more than 5,000 [Fengtian] dollars, not to mention the rest."[92]

There was, however, one exception: the Fengtian Cotton Mill (Fengtian fangsha chang). In 1921, Zhang Zuolin approved Provincial Governor Wang Yongjiang's proposal to establish a public-private joint venture mill factory. The government contributed initial funding of 4.5 million Fengtian dollars. This was to counter Japan's industrial expansion in the SMR zone, particularly on the west side of the railway. Located at the northern end of the MD's primary domain—less than a ten-minute walk from the West Stupa—the factory was the largest domestic cotton mill factory in Manchuria. With spinning machines imported from the US and cotton purchased from local famers, it employed more than 1,000 male workers and 300 female workers when it opened in 1923. Due to the high quality of its products, the factory soon earned a considerable profit and challenged the Japanese textile monopoly in Manchuria. By 1928, it employed more than 4,700 male workers, 400 female workers, and 250 administrative staff.[93] The growth in domestic manufacturing in the MD came along with the growing working class in the city. In the 1920s, workers at the Fengtian Cotton Mill launched several strikes demanding salary increases.[94] It is worth noting that the Communist leader Liu Shaoqi (1898–1969), later chairman of the PRC, came to the factory to lead the worker's movement in 1929. He was arrested and bailed out a month later. During the Cultural Revolution (1966–76), however, his experience there was framed as evidence of him being a traitor, which led to Liu's persecution and death.[95]

The Fengtian Cotton Mill was a part of Zhang Zuolin's overall industrialization project in the capital city. The project was very much driven by war. As historian Rana Mitter observes, "Since the early 1920s a military-industrial complex of a sort had built up, centered on Zhang Zuolin's need for modern armaments. The Shenyang arsenal, founded in 1919, produced rifles and ammunition, and its 20,000 well-trained employees worked at high capacity throughout the Zhili-Fengtian wars, producing 400,000 rounds a day at its peak in 1924–25."[96] Needless to say, Japan was increasingly watchful of Zhang's growing military and industrial capacity, which eventually led to his assassination.

From the perspective of spatial politics, the SMR zone and the MD were like two city-states confronting each other face-to-face. Although the Xita area sat in between the two railway stations (roughly 1.6 kilometers, or 1 mile from either), it was not at the core of either newly emerged urban space. Rather, this small neighborhood was relatively marginal, lying on the two zones' borderless borderland. Still, alongside rapid capitalization of the western suburb, competition over this small

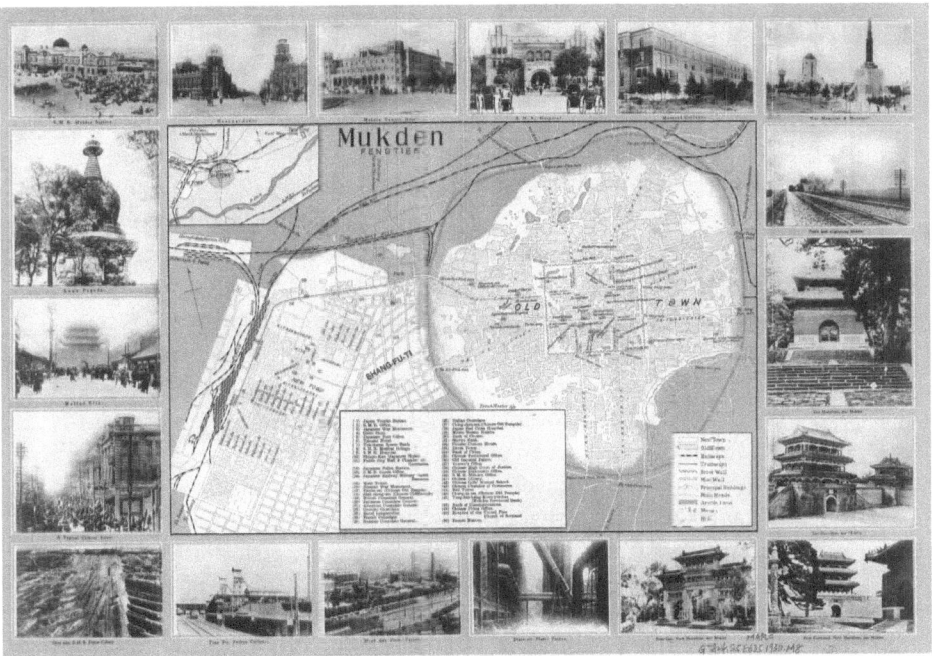

15. A tourist map of Mukden/Fengtian showing the spatial relations between the old town (the round-shaped zone on the right), the SMR zone (the square-shaped zone on the left), and the MD (in between). Author's collection.

area was both intense and subtle. Mantetsu separated the SMR zone into many "machi" (neighborhoods or blocks). The one right next to the West Stupa Temple was known as Yanagi-machi. In 1910, Japanese residents erected a small Shinto shrine there, called Seitō Jinja, which was later incorporated into an external miniature shrine of the Hōten (Fengtian) Shrine at the heart of the SMR zone.[97] *Seitō* was the Japanese pronunciation of Xita, West Stupa. Of course, the name had lost its original meaning in Tibetan Buddhism and instead referred to a local place in an abstract sense. The shrine, serving the Japanese households nearby, instilled a new religious atmosphere in this space. The most thriving business in Yanagi-machi was entertainment—that is, escort girls or prostitutes serving in Japanese restaurants. Japanese prostitutes arrived in Fengtian before the Russo-Japanese War. In the SMR zone, there were a few blocks where high-end brothels were concentrated. Although Yanagi-machi was not among them, it was one of the earliest in the neighborhood—as early as 1906.[98]

On the Chinese side, in 1913, Zhang Zuolin ordered the opening of two entertainment/consumerist neighborhoods, called Nanshichang (the southern market) and Beishichang (the northern market), in the MD to attract local businessmen and tourists. Beishichang, originally a small quarter containing just one or two blocks at the northern end of the MD, gradually expanded to a fairly large area between the West Stupa and Essential-Victory Temples. Partially because the area surrounding the Essential-Victory Temple had already developed into a bustling marketplace, in the 1920s and '30s, Beishichang soon grew to be a district famous for small businesses, folk performances, and entertainment. Known as *zabadir* (雜巴地兒), and similar to the Tianqiao area in Beijing,[99] Beishichang was composed of tea houses, theaters, opium dens, fortune-teller shops, street acrobats, gambling houses, drugstores, pawnshops, restaurants, bathhouses, and, last but not least, brothels. *Pingkang-li*, a term for a brothel area, referred to the most popular red-light district in the new urban setting. It was a place full of grassroots culture and people with lower-class occupations coruled by local police and gangsters. The district was set up largely to compete with its Japanese counterparts.[100] Spurred by the urban contest, the Xita space completed its first transformation. By the 1920s, the toll of the bell from the Buddhist tower and the sounds of camel caravans had faded away. They were easily overwhelmed by the noise of trains, streetcars, factories, peddlers, and brothels.

Telescope: Manchuria on a Global Scale

Finally, let us use a telescope to examine the macro-spatial layer.

On January 9, 1911, the US consulate in Mukden received a letter from the chief of the Seventh District Police Station. The document stated that a highly contagious disease has arrived in Fengtian. Four or five days before, two Chinese individuals who "had been to Shijianfang and Xita got infected separately. They soon died." Since the US consulate was in the same district, it needed extra protection. Along with the letter, the officer delivered a bottle of disinfectant "to be used in disinfecting the consular premises against the plague." As a matter of fact, Han Guojun, the commissioner of the (Provincial) Foreign Office, had sent another letter as early as January 5 informing the foreign consulates that a suspicious case of illness had been discovered in the city two days before. The patient died after being sent to a hospital. This letter started with the following sentence: "Plague has been prevalent in Harbin lately. Since communication by railroad is so convenient, this disease spreads easily."[101]

Indeed, railway modernity brought not only new urban spaces, European style architectures, streetlights, factories, and department stores but also disease. In 1910–11, Manchuria was severely hit by a pneumonic plague that eventually took sixty thousand lives.[102] The pandemic started in the Russo-Chinese border area and then spread rapidly along the rail in CER towns and cities. The mortality rate was nearly 100 percent. Wu Lien-teh, a Cambridge-trained doctor, led Chinese government work to contain the disease. He adopted the practice of wearing masks and quarantine to successfully prevent more infections in populated Harbin. In Fengtian, Dr. Christie and other foreign doctors joined local efforts to stop the pandemic. Christie noticed that all the early victims in the city came by rail from the north. "It was evident that the railways were the most urgent source of danger, and that if the traffic continued, not only would Moukden be infected, but the disease would be carried by the Chinese line to Tientsin (Tianjin) and Peking (Beijing), and introduced among the closely packed millions of the provinces of China." Despite approaching Chinese New Year, for which thousands of migrant workers would have planned to return home via railway, the Qing government resolutely stopped the flow of people from Fengtian to Beijing. Several days later, the Japanese authority also curtailed traffic on the Japanese-controlled SMR. "Owing to the effective measures taken." remarked Christie, "the mortality in Moukden from Plague did not actually rise high." But it seemed that the western suburb, where the train stations were located, was the worst-hit area. "Most of the deaths were in the western slums of the city where the migratory coolie class congregate, for the bacilli seem to thrive in darkness, dirt, and overcrowded rooms." Unfortunately, a young British doctor, Arthur Jackson, who volunteered to take care of patients at the Chinese train station, contracted the plague and died.[103]

The episode also revealed the fact that, despite being separately controlled by three contested authorities (Russia, Japan, and China), overall, the rail system in Manchuria was relatively well-integrated at the time. Chinese laborers traveled back and forth from Inner China to northern Manchuria, switching freely between the PMR, SMR, and CER. Between 1905, when the Russo-Japanese War concluded, to the mid-1930s, when Japan finally monopolized all the railways in Manchuria, a dominant theme in this newly developed geopolitical arena was the trilateral struggle over railway power, a power so critical that it could determine the economic and military fate of each player in this frontier. After the Mukden Incident in September 1931, Japan was the obvious winner of the competition. But up until that moment, the result had been far from clear. This was especially the case in southern Manchuria, where the contest between Mantetsu and the Zhang regime escalated year by year.

It was Russia who constructed the SMR, but it was Japan who made the SMR an artery of the Manchurian economy. With the rapid increase in immigration, the fertile Manchurian plains were soon agricultural-ized. Soybeans were the driving force of the agrarian transformation. At the turn of the twentieth century, China was the world's largest soybean producer with most of the soybeans grown in Manchuria. In international markets, demand for Manchurian soybeans and soy prod-ucts (soybean oil and soybean meal) boomed at the same time as the oil and farming industries flourished in both Japan and Europe. There-fore, soybean exports soon became a strategic trading commodity that connected the frontier's development with the global capitalist system. Before the establishment of Mantetsu, Manchurian peasants delivered soybean products by either horse or boat to Yingkou, the largest seaport in Manchuria. In 1907, the year Mantetsu was found, nearly two-thirds of Manchurian exports went through Yingkou. But Mantetsu quickly changed the situation. The company adopted a geo-economic strategy of "Dalian centralism" and, with the convenience of railway freight, made Dalian the transportation hub. From 1910 onward, although the volume of soybeans and the crop's products took up only about 20 percent of the SMR cargo, the profits generated were about 40 to 50 percent of total Mantetsu earnings.[104] With this development, by 1914, Dalian "had garnered nearly half of Manchuria's exports, at 46.8 percent, while Ying-kow (Yingkou) languished with 18.2 percent."[105] The outbreak of World War I in Europe in 1914 further stimulated cargo freight in Manchuria, which included not only agricultural products but also coal, timber, and other commodities. In 1917, SMR cargo tonnage hit 6.6 million, a fivefold increase from 1907. Ten years later, in 1927, the number climbed to 18.4 million, a more than twofold increase from 1917.[106] Noted that Mantetsu businesses interests were not limited to railway: It operated multiple enterprises, with harbors, warehouses, automobile, hotel, mining and financial investments, and research. But rail transportation remained the biggest source of income for the company. In 1931, income from cargo freight was 82 percent of its total revenue and passenger transportation another 12 percent.[107]

The SMR was an integrated railway system. By 1931, it had expanded beyond the trunk line between Dalian and Changchun. A main branch, the AFR, which joined the SMR trunk line at the Sujiatun station in southern suburb of Fengtian, connected with the Korean Railway via the Yalu River bridge. In 1913, Japan acquired the privileges to finance five extended lines of the SMR. These lines, although owned by the Chinese government in name, would essentially expand the SMR sphere of in-fluence to Jilin and eastern Mongolia. Construction began on one of the lines, the Sipingjie-Taonan Railway in 1917 and was completed in 1923. In 1927, this line was extended farther north and cut through the CER at Ang'angxi, approaching the capital of Heilongjiang province, Qiqihar. On top of that, Mantetsu also built several shorter spurs to link strategic mining towns, such as Anshan (coal) and Benxihu (iron), to either the trunk or the main branch. In this way the SMR successfully strung multiple spaces of capitalist production together—from resources to manufacture to shipping, trade, and consumption. In other words, the SMR was not merely a transportation line, but a relatively comprehensive capitalist system.

But the SMR itself, in turn, was only one component of an ambitious global transportation system schemed up by the Japanese empire. In Gotō Shimpei's eyes, Japan served as a pivot of this global network, with the SMR as the "intermediary" between Europe and Asia, and the Japanese Government Railway as the center of the Pacific corridor connecting East Asia and North America. As historian Kate McDonald demonstrates, such a "global transportation network was in many ways an entity unto itself, composed of local, international, and imperialist railways yet taking on political and geographical dimensions that exceeded any one railway."[108] In practice, the trans-Eurasian route was soon implemented. A Japanese traveler could board a ferry from Shimonoseki or Yokohama, get off in either Pusan or Dalian, take a train (either the Korean Railway or the SMR) to Changchun, and transfer to the CER and the TSR to Europe. In 1913, a one-way trip from Berlin to Tokyo via the land route took only thirteen days and at half the price of a maritime route through the Suez Canal.[109] Needless to say, the SMR played a central role in forming this global network. Geographically, in the east and south, the SMR linked the Korean Railway, the Japan–continent maritime route, and the Japanese Government Railway, while in the west and north, it connected the PMR and TSR respectively. The transregional integration signified not just the convenience of travelers, but mainly the penetration of Japanese capitalist influence. In the mid-1910s, the imperial government, pushed by the domestic textile industry, introduced the "triple line intermodal transportation" policy. It allowed Japanese commodities, mainly textiles, to have a reduced tariff and freight fee when being shipped to Manchuria via the Shimonoseki-Pusan ferry, the Korean Rail, and the AFR, creating a significant advantage for Japanese goods to monopolize the market. However, Mantetsu fiercely opposed the plan as it would move the economic center of Manchuria to Fengtian, hence jeopardizing the strategic status of Dalian.[110]

The debate between "Dalian centralism" and "Fengtian centralism" was a minor dispute among empire builders over the principles of capitalist integration in East Asia. Yet there was a major threat gradually taking shape in the 1920s that went beyond Japanese domination of the intermodal transportation system. In order to break the SMR monopoly, Zhang Zuolin decided to aggressively expand the Chinese railway network in Manchuria. From Zhang's point of view, the existence of the SMR sabotaged his independent military, economic, and political control of Manchuria. Plus, Chinese merchants and producers were also tired of being exploited by Mantetsu. There was popular demand to create an autonomous nationalist transportation system so that the benefits of frontier development no longer fell in the hands of the Japanese. In 1924, Zhang established the Transportation Commission of the Three Eastern Provinces, an institution in charge of planning, facilitating, and supervising the Chinese transportation system in Manchuria.

One of the commission's priority tasks was to construct two "arterial routes," both extending from the PMR trunk, to encircle the SMR from two directions.[111] In the east, the PMR stretched from Fengtian to Hailong, and farther from Hailong to Jilin city, the capital of Jilin Province (i.e., the Fengtian-Hailong line and the Jilin-Hailong line). In the west, the PMR lay new track from Dahushan to Tongliao, which would later merge into the Sipingjie-Taonan and Taonan-Ang'angxi lines, and extended even farther north from Qiqihar to Keshan. Aside from two lines funded with a Japanese loan (the Sipingjie-Taonan, and Taonan-Ang'angxi), the rest of the railways were either solely funded by provincial governments, or jointly funded by governments and local merchants. In 1928 alone, the Zhang regime bought about 21,000 tons of rail and 244 steel bridges from the US, "all of which were shipped from Baltimore to Dalian to build the Jilin-Hailong line with the purpose of bypassing the SMR."[112] When the new railroads were under construction, Japan immediately sensed danger. The Japanese diplomats repeatedly protested the projects on the grounds that Beijing and Tokyo had agreed in 1905 that no parallel lines to the SMR could be built by China. Nevertheless, Zhang Zuolin was not willing to be set back by the Japanese warnings. In a meeting with Japanese General Consular Yoshizawa Kenkichi in October 1927, Zhang rebuked the Japanese complaints about the Chinese railway construction. "The operation and profits of the railway in the East Provinces were all grabbed by the SMR. Your country acquired huge interests from it. But when China wanted to modestly develop the railways, your country immediately stood up and opposed. This is truly unreasonable," he stated.[113]

Even Zhang's sudden death did not stop the Chinese government's determination to compete with the Japanese rail system. On the contrary, construction of the SMR parallel lines continued under his heir, Zhang

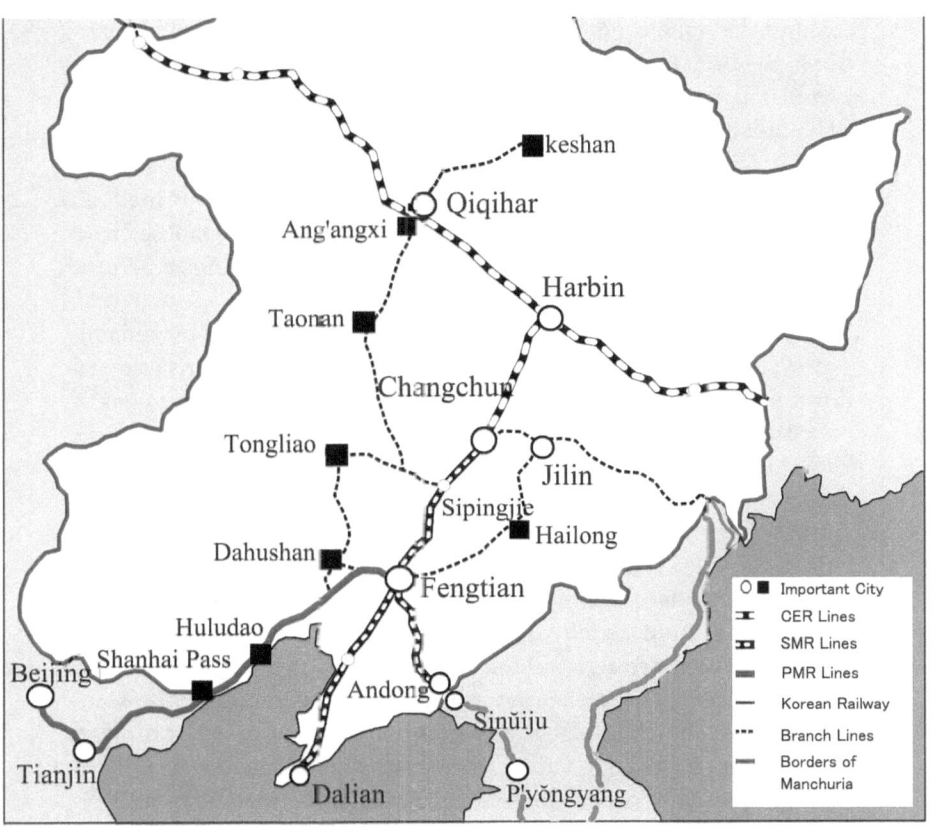

16. Zhang Zuolin's railway construction versus South Manchurian Railways.
Created by the author.

Xueliang. By the late 1920s, the Fengtian-Hailong and Jilin-Hailong Railways were completed. The Chinese authority soon integrated the two lines and promoted an express service from Jilin to Fengtian via Hailong. A comic advertisement (fig. 17) depicts a youth striding forward with one foot in Shenyang (Fengtian) and the other in Jilin. The caption reads, "It really is breaking the world records of affordability, rapidity, and safety." It goes on to specifically criticize its competitor, the SMR, which had a route connecting the same two cities via Changchun. "If you took *the other route*, the price for a one-way ticket can buy a round-trip ticket [on our route] with extra money to spare. Therefore [taking our train], you would earn not only a sense of patriotism but also a benefit."[114] In December 1929, the four rails composing the western parallel—the Qiqihar-Keshan, Taonan-Ang'angxi, Sipingjie-Taonan, and Dahushan-Tongliao Railways—began coordinated operation.

Around the same time, Zhang Xueliang was investing in another harbor in the Bohai Bay, the port of Huludao, as an alternative to Dalian. If completed, cargo from northern Manchuria could go all the way south to Huludao through the PMR trunk, connecting with the world market without Mantetsu's intermediation. By 1931, Manchuria had 44 percent of the railway networks on Chinese soil. Within it, Chinese-owned rail took the largest share with 37 percent, surpassing the Japanese share (both owned and controlled) at 36 percent. The remaining 27 percent was jointly owned by China and the Soviet Union.[115]

From the mid-1920s to the early 1930s, while the Chinese-owned railway system accelerated construction, Mantetsu's rail enterprise slowed down due to constant protests by local Chinese, waves of campaigns to boycott Japanese goods, and last but not least, a global financial crisis. Unlike China, whose currency followed the silver standard, the Japanese financial system, which Mantetsu was a part of, adopted the gold standard. A steep fall in the price of silver in the late 1920s made Mantetsu vulnerable when facing its Chinese competitors' price reduction strategy. In 1930, Mantetsu's two-decade-long period of growth finally ended. Cargo freight tonnage fell 3.36 million compared to the previous year and income dropped 21.35 million yen. The following year, the situation did not improve. Turbulence in the world market destabilized the Manchurian economy. Although the volume of freight increased by 260,000 tons, Mantetsu's revenue suffered a decrease of more than seven million yen. The company "was immersed in pessimism for the whole year."[116]

The capitalist competition between the SMR and the PMR was nothing less than a total war between two sovereign countries. As a Japanese official commented about the Chinese railway projects, "Had all these schemes been successfully consummated, they would not only have destroyed the value of the SMR and Dalian harbor but would have wiped out Japan's special interests in Manchuria from the very foundation. . . . Japan was finally forced to the position where she had to make the momentous decision either to stand by her rights and remain in Manchuria or to renounce them and get out."[117] It was against this backdrop that Japan fabricated the Mukden Incident and colonized the whole of Manchuria.

The railways compressed national interest and power into thin, long spaces composed of tracks and hubs. In the case of early twentieth century Manchuria, it was the railway, rather than the boundary, that defined the reach of state influences. The rival states were not divided by horizontal, linear borders marked on maps. Rather, their de facto territories overlapped in this new frontier, forming an intricate cross-spatial intersection. The situation urges us to rethink the shape of the state in

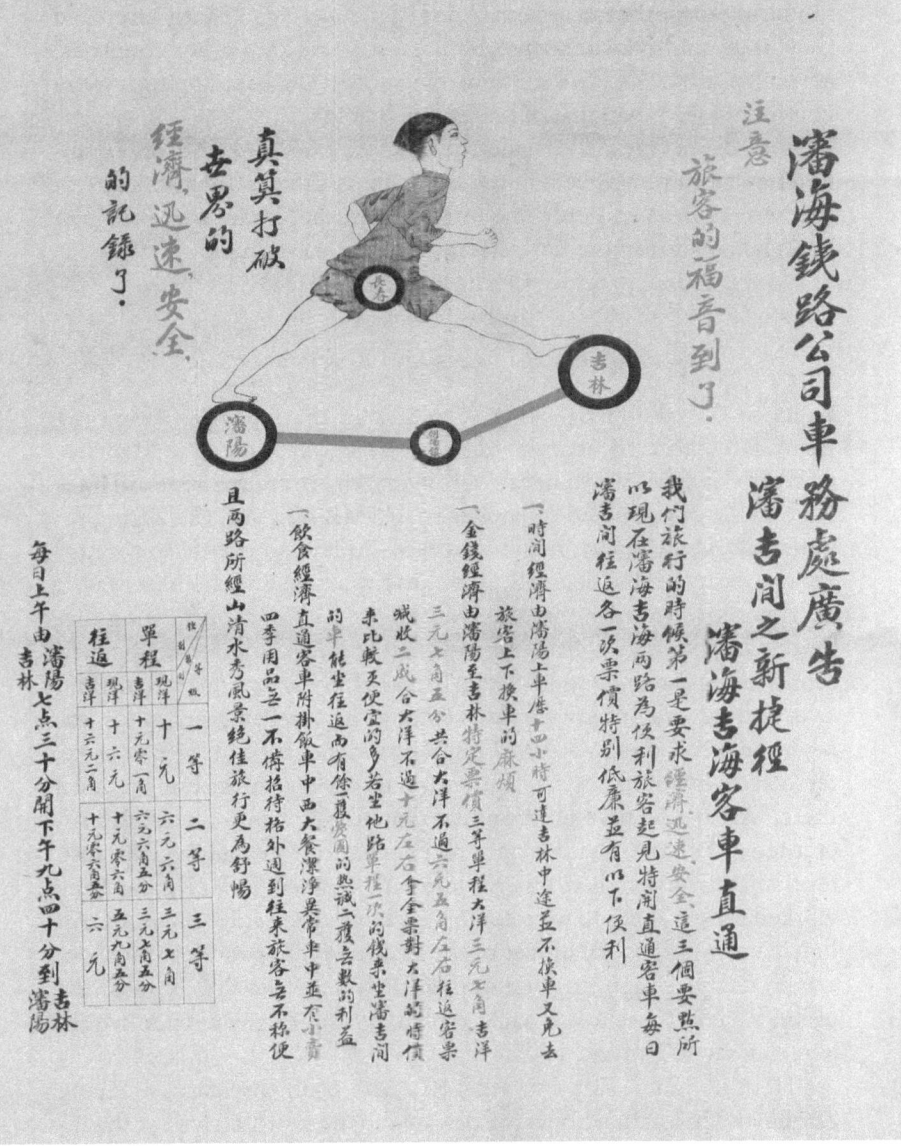

17. Comic advertisement promoting the Shenyang-Hailong-Jilin Line.
Image courtesy of Liaoning Provincial Archive.

colonial and imperialist contexts. In most places, a territorial state, im-
aged as a "geobody," exists only in concept. With the penetration of the
modern transportation system, colonial powers significantly stretched
their state space beyond their borders, dipping into other countries'
sovereign space. Hence, a status of intersection and overlapping is more
commonly seen than that of linear demarcation.

Both the Japanese SMR and the Chinese PMR linked to an expansive transportation system in the Eurasian continent. The trunk line of
the two rail lines had only one intersection: the Three-Arch Bridge in
Fengtian, seven hundred meters north of the West Stupa.

Now, it is time to return to Xita and the year 1928.

The Incidents, Railways, and Russian Legacies

Kōmoto Daisaku (1883–1955), a colonel in the Japanese Kwantung
Army, felt extremely angry about what he saw happening in Manchuria: Anti-Japanese movements were everywhere, competitive rail lines
were being constructed to squeeze the SMR out, and the Zhang regime had intentionally introduced Euro-American capital to counter
Japanese capital. He decided, "The head must be killed. There wasn't
an alternative to solve the Manchurian problem." Upon hearing that
Zhang Zuolin might return to Fengtian from Beijing, he dispatched
scouts along the route to detect possible locations for an assassination.
Everywhere was under strict surveillance by the Fengtian police, except one place: the SMR-PMR intersection. Because the two lines intersected, "it would not catch attention if some Japanese hung around
there." All the details were carefully plotted out. Upon receiving a secret telegraph that Zhang's train had departed from Beijing, Kōmoto
immediately dispatched several combat engineers from Korea. They
worked for six hours to wire explosives under the bridge. Senior Cap-
itan Tōmiya Kaneo, an officer of the Fengtian Independent Garrison,
was in charge of igniting the dynamite. In case the first blow failed
to kill Zhang, there was a backup plan: a team of swordsman would
launch a second attack.

"Here it came," Kōmoto recalled, "The train that carried Zhang
Zuolin and his staff, who were unaware of [the plot], arrived at the intersection. With the sound of a loud of blast, black smoke rose to the
sky, as high as two hundred meters. I could only imagine: did Zhang
Zuolin's bones also fly up to the sky? But the horrifying black smoke and
blast even shocked me and made me nervous. The powder was really
that powerful."[118]

Contrary to Japanese expectations, however, Zhang's son, Xueliang, did not yield. The day of his father's assassination, it turned out, was his birthday (in the lunar calendar), which he swore thereafter not to celebrate any more. Later the same year, he announced he was joining Chiang Kai-shek's nationalist government, so to officially integrate Manchuria into the Republic of China (Nanjing). Mindful of the enmity, the junior marshal accelerated his father's endeavor to establish an independent transportation system in Manchuria. After solidifying his power, he even went so far as to revoke Soviet interests in northern Manchuria and to try to take back the CER in 1929. This attempt, however, failed due to Joseph Stalin's strong counteraction. Meanwhile, Japan could no longer tolerate Xueliang's nationalist economic policies or the aggressive development of the Chinese railways. Action had to be taken before it was too late.

On the night of September 18, 1931, a small team from the Kwantung Army blew up a section of the SMR railway at Liutiaohu, north of Fengtian city. The Japanese immediately asserted that the railway had been attacked by Chinese troops. In "response," the local Japanese army bombarded Beidaying, a Chinese military camp on the north outskirts of the city. This was the infamous Mukden Incident. The artillery was fired from Xita, where the Japanese Fengtian Independent Garrison was stationed. According to a newspaper report, "The Japanese soldiers had set up several cannons in Xita for quite some time. They had targeted at Beidaying, measured and prepared." When the Xita residents heard the cannons, they thought it was nothing but a normal drill.[119] Within months, Japan occupied entire Manchuria.

The following year, a puppet state, the Manchukuo, was established under Japanese manipulation. Headed by the abdicated Qing emperor, Puyi, Manchukuo entrusted all its railway rights to Mantetsu. In 1935, the Soviet government sold the CER rights to Japan, thereby withdrawing from the railway competition in Manchuria. Mantetsu gradually annexed the SMR system (called "company lines") and non-SMR system (called "state lines"), completing the total integration of the Manchurian railway networks. Its economic vigor soon returned. Meanwhile in Fengtian, the largest metropolis in Manchukuo, colonial bureaucrats implemented new city planning. They canceled the SMR zone, the Mercantile District, and the old town, replacing them with new and amalgamated urban districts. In 1938, the Fengtian municipal government combined the SMR zone and the MD into a new urban district: Yamato (C. Dahe) District. Further in 1941, the Yamato District was divided into three districts: the former SMR zone inherited the title

of Yamato while the other two were Shikishima (C. Fudao) District in
the north and Asahi (C. Zhaori) District in the south. Aside from this
trio, all the other districts in the city were given Chinese names. For
example, the expanded industrial zone west of the SMR railway was
called Tiexi District, meaning "west of iron [road]." It later became the
cradle of heavy industry in China. North of Tiexi was Huanggu District,
which had the Three-Arch Bridge in its southeast section. The West
Stupa Temple was in the southwest corner of the Shikishima District,
but the Xita neighborhood referred to the area covered by the western
part of Shikishima, which was adjacent to Yamato, Tiexi, and Huanggu.
During the Japanese colonization, Fengtian grew to be one of the most
robust urban centers in Manchukuo, and Manchukuo into a model of
Japanese colonial modernity in East Asia.[120]

The railway reshaped the city, especially its former western outskirts.
However, the role of Russia, which first introduced the railway to the
city, left few traces. Talking about the modern transition of Fengtian/
Mukden, most narratives focus on Japan, or in the case of the pre-1931
period, the Zhang regime. In today's Shenyang, Russian relics are
hardly found anywhere—anywhere but Xita. After the Russo-Japanese
War, a modest-sized square between the Life-Prolonging Temple and
Beishichang was designated as a Russian cemetery to commemorate
the war dead. In 1912, Russian merchants in Harbin, led by a business-
man named I. F. Chistyakov, donated money to build a small Orthodox
church in the middle of the cemetery. The church, called the "Military
Temple-Monument in the Name of Christ the Savior" (Voinskiy Khram-
Pamyatnik vo imya Khrista Spasitelya), is arguably the only Orthodox
architecture that survived in Shenyang (fig. 18).[121] About ten meters
(thirty-three feet) in height, the main section of this octagonal masonry
building features a scale-like bronze roof and a helmet-shaped dome.
The Japanese called it the "Russian Monument to the Loyal Dead," echoing the name for a much larger Japanese war monument at the core of
the SMR zone. In the 1990s, the local government removed the cemetery
and converted the space into a residential and office area. The church
remained, preserved by the municipality as an "unremovable cultural
heritage."[122] Today, the Russian building stands alone in a parking lot,
falling into disrepair, and almost completely ignored by the locals. That
said, when standing in front of it for the first time in 2017, I couldn't help
but be amazed by its elegant design and solemn beauty. It reminds us of
the once-existed Russian space in the neighborhood.

There is yet another kind of Russian legacy. Thanks to an anonymous photographer, we have perhaps the earliest, real-life photo of the
West Stupa. A Russian photo-postcard depicting the tower can be easily

18. Military Temple-Monument in the Name of Christ the Savior, Shenyang.
Photo taken by the author, 2017.

purchased online at an affordable price more than a hundred years later
(fig. 19). Never had the stupa been so vividly visualized before. From this
printed material, we know that it had not been maintained well. It was
shabby and decaying, the outer bricks had fallen down, and grass and
bushes were growing on the dome as well as at the base. Only four or five
of the original twelve copper bells were still hanging under the parasol.
The color in both the axial pillar and the dome had faded away. But

Мукденъ. № 5.

19. Russian postcard showing the West Stupa (circa 1904). Author's collection.

despite its ruined shape (or maybe precisely because of it), the tall Buddhist stupa caught the eye and interest of a Russian photographer and his publisher. They decided to capture this *exotic* architecture and introduce it—along with images of the royal palace, imperial mausoleums, and old city gates—as a visual representation of Mukden, Manchuria, and China. In the process, they brought a new kind of gaze—through the camera lens rather than the naked eye—and created a new kind of relationship between the old stupa being watched and the people who were watching it. With the help of recently imported photographic technology, collotype printing, and the transnational postal system—all of them associated with the railways—the stupa acquired new meanings and interpretations. Its image was introduced to a wide range of audiences and consumers to fuel their imaginations about the Orient. Later, the Japanese continued the Russian initiative and massively produced images, texts, and films about Manchuria.

Speaking of the Japanese production of Manchurian space, let's return again to the early morning of June 4, 1928. When the dynamite exploded at the Three-Arch Bridge, renowned Japanese feminist poet Yosano Akiko (1878–1942) was drafting letters to her children in her room at the Yamato Hotel in the SMR Station, 1.7 kilometers (1 mile) south of the West Stupa. She recorded in her travelogue that she and her husband heard a "faint strange sound." Less than twenty minutes later, they noticed that suddenly "people were rushing about in the station below, but we just thought that it was due to the crowds of passengers."[123] An hour later, they learned that there had been an "unexpected incident."

The fact that she and her husband happened to be in the neighborhood at that precise moment in the high point of the Sino-Japanese railway competition was not so much a coincidence. With the rise of the tourist industry in early twentieth-century Japan, many middle-class Japanese, such as the Yosanos, came to this new frontier of the empire, consuming the spatial meanings introduced by these products on the one hand while reproducing more on the other. The transborder and cross-cultural production, reproduction, circulation, and consumption of new spatial meanings in the colonial period is a major theme of the next chapter.

CHAPTER 4

The Visitor

On September 26, 1917, the West Stupa received a distinguished visitor. Leading Japanese journalist and public intellectual, Tokutomi Sohō (1863–1957) was touring China for the second time. The fifty-four-year-old writer had a photo taken of himself and his family standing in front of the half-ruined stupa (fig. 20) and dedicated a poem to it. Caught up in the moment, Tokutomi perceived the Buddhist tower as a symbol that embodied his high emotions. Composed in elegant, classical Chinese, the poem goes

> The white stupa gracefully touches the azure sky
> The sorghum paves the land, waving in the golden wind.
> So bright and so vast are heaven and earth
> I am immersed in the autumn colors of Shenyang.

It was the most beautiful season in Manchuria. Tokutomi had a full itinerary that day: First he went to Beiling (Hongtaiji's mausoleum) and then to the old Mukden Palace and the Essential-Victory Temple. The West Stupa was perhaps his last stop. In his travelogue, a short comment followed the poem, "The white stupa is the west tower in the Life-Prolonging Temple. The original bricks were painted in white. The gigantic lions engraved on the bricks are particularly worth seeing."[1]

Standing beneath the stupa in 1917, Tokutomi thought about the Japanese empire, which was in a watershed moment in its history. "Since I came to Manchuria," he remarked that same day, "I increasingly believed in the Gospel of Might [J. Chikara no fukuin]. What I mean by 'might' is not 'violence' but the might to implement our policies of national governance comprehensively." The policies of national governance, in this context, referred to the colonial development of

20. Tokutomi Sohō and his family standing in front of the West Stupa.
Courtesy of the Tokutomi Sohō Museum.

Manchuria. "The world powers have acknowledged our status in Manchuria," he wrote. "But our infrastructure has not yet met the expectation of other countries."

Ever since the late nineteenth century, Tokutomi had proactively participated in almost every important political movement in Japan through his extensive writing, publications, and social networking. He was the rare individual whose thoughts and voice profoundly shaped Japanese public opinion from the late Meiji period all the way to the end of World War II. Tokutomi was arrested as a Class A war criminal in 1945 by the International Military Tribunal for the Far East, because of his role as a top propagandist for the war. But he was not brought to trial in the end.

Between 1905, when Japan defeated Russia in the Russo-Japanese War, and 1945, when Japan was crushed in World War II, numerous Japanese tourists came to Manchuria. Most of them visited Fengtian (Mukden or Shenyang), the largest metropolis, which they called "Hōten." Although not everyone spent time touring the West Stupa like Tokutomi, most would have passed by the temple or at least sojourned in the Xita (J. Nishitō) neighborhood. This was because, as we now know, Xita was adjacent to the South Manchurian Railway (SMR) station and on the edge of the Japanese-dominated SMR zone. It was the place where the tourists had their first glimpse of the city and where they stayed during their visits. Arriving by train, they checked into the hotels run by Mantetsu and set out every morning to sightsee. From this vantage, the city of Fengtian unfolded in front of them.

In many tourist books or pamphlets, the Tibetan Buddhist temples (the West Stupa included), the mausoleums, and the Qing royal palace were listed as must-sees. Tourists patronized these places and, in so doing, produced more text or visual materials about them. However, during the colonial period in the twentieth century, the arresting tower and its neighborhood took on a completely different meaning. The historical relics, along with many other sites of the city, became subjects of the lens through which Japanese tourists created, or adopted, an understanding of Manchuria, China, and Asia in relation to world civilization. Over time, the understanding became not about China/Asia but about Japan—Japan's place in both the world and in history, that was, in both space and time.

To borrow Mary Louise Pratt's concepts, Xita and Fengtian were seen as a "contact zone" through "imperial eyes."[2] Japanese tourists, many of whom were supported by various colonial agencies, came to this "colonial frontier" in the hopes of realizing an image of the political and historical bonds between Japan and the non-Japanese world. As many studies on tourism have pointed out, such a place was where the guests and hosts encountered, conflicted, negotiated, and mutually created.[3] However, interactions through diverse tourist activities in twentieth-century Fengtian were much more sophisticated and nuanced than a simple dualism of guests (Japanese) versus hosts (Other). For one, Japan viewed Fengtian (and Manchuria) as a place that was neither purely "us" nor simply "them" but a curious combination of both. The city had been an ancient capital with a gloried history; now it was a modern metropolis with significant Japanese inputs, and it was going to become a global, industrial-commercial center presaging a flourishing, Pan-Asian empire. It simultaneously manifested the imperial ideals of the past, present and future. More importantly, when inventing a unique national identity for Japan via traveling through its colonies, Japanese visitors conceived Others in multiple layers. An obvious one was the colonized peoples, through whom Japan portrayed itself as a more "civilized" superior. But there was also a hidden one: the Western colonial powers that dominated the narrative of human civilization. To distinguish and compete with this Other, the Japanese promoted an abstract identity of Asia enthusiastically, of which both Japan and its colonies were an integral part. Such a controversial approach makes it impossible to describe the spatial meaning of colonial Fengtian through a single perspective.

Chapter 4 unveils the significance of Xita and its surroundings as a multilayered "contact zone" in the first half of the twentieth century. The narrative encompasses five interlocking themes. First, the focus is on a group of pioneer scholars whose career trajectories intersected in the fall of 1905 at the Mukden/Fengtian temples. They were the first people who conducted academic research on these ancient relics and, in so doing, positioned their subjects in the broader historical, geographical, and political context of Japan's imperial ideology. Next, several renowned Japanese writers who visited the city and the neighborhood from 1906 to the 1920s. The writers, despite possessing different views on China, Manchuria, and the local peoples, represented Japanese elites' general attitude toward colonial relations during the interwar period. The narrative then moves to the third theme, mass tourism as an imperial industry from the 1920s to 1945. The fourth part investigates Xita as a host place and pays special attention to the formation of an entertainment quarter or red-light district. The last section briefly introduces some writings by Chinese and Korean visitors to examine how the colonized projected their anxieties and concerns on this newly thriving, urban space.

Reorienting Japan in the Mukden Temples

Twelve years before the aforementioned trip by writer Tokutomi, a good friend of his had approached him to discuss a planned trip to Fengtian. It was spring 1905, and the friend was Naitō Konan (1866–1934), another influential journalist who would later become one of the greatest Japanese sinologists.[4] Like Tokutomi, Naitō had been trained in Chinese classics since childhood and remained an active scholar of Chinese history. Three years before, in 1902, Naitō visited Mukden for the first time as a correspondent for the *Osaka Asahi News*. Something that deeply amazed him were the precious textual materials preserved in the royal institutions, especially the Buddhist sutras in Mongolian and Manchu scripts in the Mukden temples and the books collection at in the Wensuge, the royal library. But due to the Russian occupation, he had not been able to access the materials or conduct a thorough investigation. The recent Japanese military victory against Russia, however, provided an opportunity to continue this endeavor. On March 30, he published an opinion piece in the *Osaka Asahi News* calling Mukden/Fengtian a "treasure house of Oriental Studies (Tōyō gaku)." He continued: "Occupying Fengtian means we now control the political pivot of the East Three Provinces [of China]. At the same time, it also means we open a treasure house of Oriental Studies, which deserves the great attention of scholars in our country. . . . With the opening of the Fengtian treasure house, the most meaningful and intriguing enterprise is to explore Manchurian historical resources. For scholars, this is a career that is comparable to the brilliant achievements of our army and is something that our generation must put great effort on."[5]

Immediately after, he started seeking financial support for his own Fengtian trip. He thought of the Imperial General Headquarters (of the Supreme War Council) and the Ministry of Education and for that matter, consulted with Tokutomi. Telling Naitō that funds from the Ministry of Education might not be enough, Tokutomi kindly offered to put in a word with Prince Yamagata Aritomo (1838–1922), one of the top leaders of the Japanese Imperial Army. In addition, Naitō reached out to the Ministry of Foreign Affairs, from which he successfully secured some funding in the name of conducting research on "local civil affairs." A month later, Tokutomi brought even better news: the Imperial General Headquarters agreed to lend its help.[6]

Accompanied by his hometown colleague, a law major named Ōsato Buhachirō, Naitō departed Japan in early July. The pair arrived at Fengtian on July 29 and spent the next four months in Manchuria. For Naitō, the most fruitful period was from late July to early September, when he combed the city for precious Qing documents and visited its historical sites. The support from the Japanese military proved to be decisive. He met with Commander-in-Chief Fukushima Yasumasa frequently, got to see whatever he wanted without any obstacle, and even lived in the military garrison near the Essential-Victory Temple. The treasure house was wide open to him. At the royal palace, Naitō was given access to multilingual Qing archives and books previously unknown to the world. With the help of the Jasak Da lama Shirab Jamsu he visited all the Mukden temples and saw invaluable sutras in Tibetan, Mongolian, and Manchu scripts.[7] He indexed all the materials, made copies of some, and took many photos. For the burgeoning field of Japanese oriental studies, this was one of the most exciting journeys of the early twentieth century.

Naitō visited the West Stupa Temple on August 18. Although no sutra was found there, he was impressed by the Buddhist statues in the monastery and commented that they 'are even better than [the statues] of the Yellow [i.e., Essential-Victory] Temple."[8] The photo of the statues he took arguably remains the only one showing the original interior of the temple.[9]

Thanks to Naitō's journal, we know about his activities in Fengtian day by day: where he went, what he did, how he did it, and who he met.[10] One of the most intriguing discoveries to come from this record is that Naitō was just one of many prominent scholars of Japanese oriental studies who happened to be in the city in the fall of 1905. Although most of them, like Naitō, were still in the early phase of their careers, the trip left its mark on their later splendid professional trajectories. For that matter, Fengtian and its temples served as peculiar junction for Japanese oriental studies in the twentieth century.

On August 29, at the royal palace, Naitō met with Ichimura Sanjirō (1864–1947), a history professor at Tokyo Imperial University. Ichimura was in fact one of the first persons Naitō had contacted when planning his trip back in April. Fascinated by the royal library collection that Naitō described, Ichimura had applied for and received a research fund from the Ministry of Education. Like Naitō, Ichimura was trained in Chinese classics at an early age. But unlike Naitō, who never got a college degree, Ichimura enrolled at Tōdai in 1884 and acquired a teaching position there in 1898.[11] Hence, he became one of the first professional historians with a focus on Chinese history at the most prestigious university in Japan. Together with Shiratori Kurakichi (1865–1942), Ichimura laid the foundation for oriental studies at Tōdai, from which emerged numerous outstanding scholars.[12] The significance of such a development should be understood in the context that Japan, while absorbing as much modern Western scholarship as possible, was also eager to promote its own way to study the Orient. In Fengtian, according to Naitō's journal, Ichimura mostly engaged in a survey of the Qing documents in the royal palace but not those in the temples. This was partly because Naitō had already completed his investigation of Buddhist sutras when Ichimura arrived. That said, Naitō did take him to visit the Essential-Victory, Long-lasting-Peace, and North Stupa Temples.

Ichimura did not come alone. Accompanying him was another Tōdai professor, Itō Chūta (1367–1954), a distinguished architect and architectural historian. In the field of Japanese architectural studies, Itō's star shone as brightly as Tatsuno Kingo (see chap. 3). Commencing in the

1890s, Itō was dedicated to challenging the Eurocentric narrative of the history of architecture. Through the study of Japanese native buildings, especially the Hōryūji temple, he began to rethink the position of the oriental tradition and saw architecture in both East and West as a part of the universal development of the human spirit. To prove this thesis, Itō spent three years, from 1902 to 1905, traveling through the Eurasian continent—from China, Southeast Asia, and South Asia all the way to Turkey and Greece. As Sebastian Conrad remarks, the long journey was "a quest for the origin (*hekitō*) of Japanese architecture" which resulted in a fundamental reinterpretation of Japan's—and Asia's—position in the world.[13] The Fengtian trip followed his groundbreaking Eurasian tour by a mere two months. Itō was commissioned by the Ministry of Education to investigate architecture in Manchuria. Like Naitō, Itō recorded in painstaking detail what he saw, not so much in text, but mainly in hand-drawn sketches or photos.[14] From these materials, we can see that Itō was particularly interested in the structures, spatial arrays, statues, vessels, and ornaments of Buddhist temples. This was a persistent theme in his career, from his PhD thesis on the Hōryūji to his earlier tours to various Buddhist grottos in China and his extensive studies of the temples in Manchuria. The West Stupa Temple took up one page of his field notes, on which he drew the layout of the monastery buildings, an ornament, and the design of a Buddhist staff (danda) (fig. 21). The images would later appear in his paper on Manchurian architecture.[15]

A few days later, another scholar, who was newly appointed as a Tōdai lecturer, joined the group. Naitō recorded on September 7, "Torii Ryūzō came from Liaoyang and stayed in the same house as Ichimura etc." A legendary anthropologist and archaeologist, Torii Ryūzō (1870–1953) was famous for his extensive ethnographical surveys in Southwest China, Taiwan, Manchuria, Mongolia, Korea, the Russian Far East, and Hokkaido. Anthropology was introduced to Japan from Western Europe in the Meiji period, along with many other modern disciplines. The founding father, Tsuboi Shōgorō (1863–1913), brought his training in Britain back to Japan and established the earliest anthropology workshop at Tōdai. As one of his most distinguished students, Torii was initially nourished by the British school of physical and cultural anthropology.[16] Torii's fieldwork, at least in the early stages, followed the path of the Japanese expansion.[17] His first survey took place in 1895 in the Liaodong Peninsula just a few months after the Sino-Japanese War. It was followed by several ethnographic investigations of aboriginals in Taiwan, which was ceded to Japan as a result of the Sino-Japanese War (1894–95). After a trip to the Kuril Islands in 1899, Torii continued his work on the continent. From 1902 to 1903, he conducted a seminal

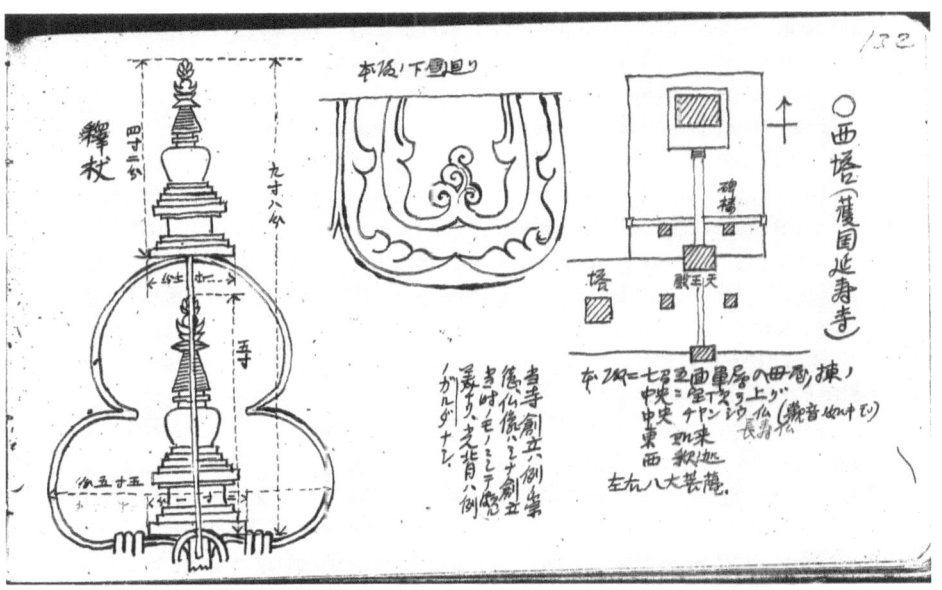

21. Itō Chūta's sketch of the West Stupa Temple. *Nochō* (Itō Chūta Shiryō), vol. 14, "Shinkoku Manshū," Architectural Institute of Japan.

survey on the ethnic Miao (Hmong) in Southwest China. Through these early surveys—all of which were aided by the government—Torii gradually formed his own subject of inquiry in Japanese anthropology: the racial origin of the Japanese and their relation to other Asian peoples. Torii was first involved in this discussion during his 1899 trip to the Kuril Islands, and his study on the Miao was partially triggered by the question of whether the aboriginals in Taiwan and Southwest China shared origins.[18] After the Russo-Japanese War, Torii went to Manchuria once again. The purpose of this trip was to measure the physical features of ethnic Manchu and Mongols, as well as to conduct archaeological and custom surveys.[19] In Fengtian, according to Naitō's diary, Torii visited some temples and palaces, took photos of Manchu women, and (with the help of Naitō and others) "measured the shape of Mongol lamas' skulls at the Yellow Temple."[20]

Last but not least, during Naitō's sojourn, he was constantly either assisted or accompanied by members of a semiacademic Buddhist organization, the Nishi Honganji Temple of Kyoto. In the first half of the twentieth century, the Nishi Honganji was one of the largest and most proactive civil organizations in Japan, whose religious, scholarly and political influence extended way beyond the archipelago. The twenty-second abbot, Count Ōtani Kōzui (1876–1948), was a talented yet

controversial leader who used his prestigious religious-political status
to connect Buddhist modernization in Japan with the empire's military
expansion and archaeological exploration in Asia. Japanese Buddhism
in the early Meiji period was under tremendous pressure from within
and without. Internally, the new government promoted native Shinto
as the state religion and persecuted Buddhism.[21] Externally, Japanese
Buddhism faced the aggressive spread of Catholicism and Christianity on one hand and the pressure of European oriental studies on the
other. The latter, based on the extensive use of the Pali and Sanskrit texts,
dominated the interpretation of the "original" Buddhist canons, hence
shaking the foundation of Japanese Buddhism, which relied solely on
the Chinese translation.[22]

Ōtani confronted these challenges in three ways. First, as a brother-in-
law of Crown Prince Yoshihito (and later Emperor Taishō), he enthusiastically promoted the idea that Japanese Buddhism was an integral part of
the empire and his sect a close ally of the government. During the Sino-
Japanese and Russo-Japanese Wars, the Nishi Honganji dispatched acolytes to provide religious and intelligence services to the imperial army.[23]
Second, as a fellow of the Royal Geographical Society (Britain), he maintained a close relationship with European academia, sending students to
study ancient South Asian languages and organizing his own archaeological explorations of the Buddhist relics in Central Asia.[24] Known as the
Ōtani Expeditions, these travels followed in the footsteps of prominent
European explorers such as Sven Hedin, Paul Pelliot, and Marc Aurel Stein
with an aim to examine the historical trajectory of Japanese Buddhism.
Last, Ōtani sent missionaries overseas and expanded the Nishi Honganji's
influence aggressively in the world. Imitating Christian missions, these
forays by the Nishi Honganji were a way to redefine Japanese Buddhism
as a Pan-Asian or even world religion.[25] As a result, the oversea activities
of the temple often combined religious, military, and scholarly ends.

The year 1905 was an important one for the Nishi Honganji's oversea
enterprises. Right after its first expedition to Central Asia (1902–4), the
sect pivoted its focus to serve the Japanese army in the war against Russia.
Ōtani had already sent 105 staff to the Manchurian front the year before.
When the war approached an end, he dispatched his younger brother,
Ōtani Sonju (1886–1939) to establish a branch temple in Dalian, a major leap in the sect's expansion in Manchuria. When Naitō Konan and
others arrived at Fengtian, Ōtani Sonju and some followers had already
been there for a while. They lived in the Essential-Victory Temple and
set up a temporary service tent at the West Stupa Temple.[26] Although
their main purpose was hardly academic, the Nishi Honganji acolytes,
who apparently had formed a good relationship with the Mongol lamas,

generously rendered the scholars their time and help. The names that appeared in Naitō's diary, aside from Ōtani Sonju, included Watanabe Tetsusuke (whose brother, Watanabe Tesshin, was a key member of the first Ōtani Expedition), Kawakami Sadanobu (a Tibetan language teacher and Buddhist scholar), Honda Eryū (another key member of the first Ōtani Expedition), and Tasue Yoshinobu (an anthropologist who had surveyed Australian islanders).[27]

This was perhaps one of the most fascinating encounters in the history of modern Japanese scholarship. Some of the future leaders in the fields of history, architecture, anthropology, religion, and archaeology met in Fengtian, a foreign city far from their homes, all lured by the Tibetan Buddhist temples there.[28] But the fact that their career paths happened to intersect at this specific location was hardly a coincidence. Rather, it was the result of a multifaceted "resonance"—both a resonance between politics and scholarship and between multiple disciplines within modern oriental studies.

The resonance between politics and scholarship came from the recent victory over Russia. For the Japanese, defeating a "Western" power proved that Japan, an oriental power, was not inferior on the battlefield. It boosted national pride in late Meiji Japan, so much so that most of the Japanese elite believed their country had successfully established itself as one of the most civilized nations in the world. As Naitō pointed out in his article, scholars should be making efforts to match such an extraordinary achievement. It was time to stimulate Japanese scholarship and prove that Japan was not academically inferior either. Such an endeavor, simultaneously nationalistic and imperialistic, was well supported by the Japanese government. As we saw, most scholars traveled to Fengtian thanks to financial aid from either the Ministry of Education or the Ministry of Foreign Affairs, and all of them received assistance from the imperial army.

More importantly, with Manchuria (and Korea) becoming Japan's new frontier, scholars had the chance to reimagine and remap Japan's position within world civilization. More scholars began to explore the authentic origins and unique path of Japanese civilization rather than perceiving Japan as primitive or semimature in the Eurocentric lineage of human development. Such ambition resettled Japan in a vast spatial context, much larger and more open than that of China, which was previously regarded as the most important external source of Japanese culture. The new spatial imagination incorporated East Asia, Inner Asia, South Asia, Southeast Asia, Pacific Islands, and more. Against this backdrop, Fengtian—particularly its Tibetan Buddhist temples—emerged as a critical link connecting Japan with not only Inner China but also

Manchuria, Mongolia, Central Asia, and even India. This was how the temples, with their rich historical components, created resonance between the different fields in oriental studies. All the scholars found valuable sources in the temples despite being engaged in different disciplines. For Naitō Konan and Ichimura Sanjirō, it was the multilingual Qing documents and Buddhist sutras; for Itō Chūta, the art styles of the architecture, ornaments, and instruments; for Torii Ryūzō, the physical features of the Mongol lamas; and for the Nishi Honganji missionaries, the indication of a Pan-Asian Buddhist community.

The 1905 Fengtian trip had a significant impact on their respective careers thereafter. When Naitō Konan returned to Japan, he was commissioned by the imperial government to write a report on a contemporary dispute between the Qing and Korea over the Tumen River boundary.[29] Employing historical materials collected in Fengtian, he submitted his first thesis on the so-called Jiandao/Kantō issue. Satisfied with his work, the Ministry of Foreign Affairs entrusted him to investigate the dispute further with the purpose of intervening in favor of Japanese interests. Naitō quit his journalist job and devoted himself to the mission. Funded by the ministry, he took two more trips to Manchuria in 1906 and 1908. Each time he revisited Fengtian to collect more materials.[30] Beyond providing his own reports and opinions, he arguably also lent his help to Shinoda Jisaku, a jurist and colonial official in charge of the negotiations with China, whom he became acquainted with during the 1905 trip through his friend Ōsato Buhachirō.[31] His service to the imperial government paid off. In 1907, Naitō used his new thesis on the history of the Sino-Korean border to successfully secure a faculty position at Kyoto Imperial University. He founded the Kyoto School of Oriental Studies, a competitor of the Tokyo School, to which Ichimura Sanjirō belonged. Naitō viewed Japan not just as a member of a China-centered, Pan-Asian cultural sphere but also as a newly emerged leader in this sphere. His extensive use of Manchu, Mongolian, and Korean materials constructed a novel trend in Japanese oriental studies that highlighted the dynamic connections between Japan and Northeast Asia. This approach in a subtle way echoed the national expansion policy of the imperial government. The precious multilingual materials that Naitō had viewed in Fengtian were later acquired by the Japanese army and sent to Tokyo Imperial University. Unfortunately, they were lost to fire in the Great Japan Earthquake of 1923. Among them were Buddhist canons in Mongolian and Manchu previously preserved in the Essential-Victory and North Stupa Temples.[32]

The trip to Manchuria further solidified Itō Chūta's belief that various local architecture shared a common source of influence, which he defined as "Greece." But this concept of Greece, as Conrad comments, cannot be reduced to the West. Rather, it represented a universal beauty and spirit that nourished both oriental and occidental traditions.[33] Arts in East and West resonated with each other, he later said, just as the waves washing up on the shore in Tokyo Bay and London, or the New York coast and Osaka Bay, are all linked together.[34] Through his extensive survey in Manchuria, Itō generated a genealogy of Buddhist towers in Asia. In his paper "The Buddhist Architecture in Manchuria" ("Manshū no butsuji kenchiku"), published in 1909, he traced the different styles of the towers and determined, correctly, that all of them derived from the Indian-style stupa. Interestingly, however, he argued that the Indian stupa had developed three major branches: (1) the Manchurian-style pagoda, (2) the Tibetan-style chorten, and (3) the Gandhāra/Shina (Chinese)–style pagoda. In other words, he saw Manchuria as an independent realm in terms of the evolution of Buddhist architecture, separate from both Tibet and China. Such a categorization implied, no matter how indirectly, a new geocultural vision emerging from Japan's geopolitical expansion.

Around the same time, Itō was commissioned to design a Buddhist monument in the historic Kasuisai Temple, Shizuoka Prefecture in Japan. The project, called Gokokutō (meaning "the nation-protecting tower"), was to commemorate the dead in the Russo-Japanese War. During a planning meeting, Itō claimed that the "Chinese style of pagoda, so prevalent in Japan, did not clearly express Buddhism's Indian origins." Since Gandhāra was the "mother country" of Japanese Buddhism, he suggested adopting the Gandharan Indian–style stupa to better reflect the project's name.[35] Nevertheless, when completed in 1911, the memorial reflected neither Chinese nor Gandharan style. The axial pillar on the top was unmistakably Tibetan in style, exactly like that of the stupas of the four "state-protecting" temples in Fengtian (which Itō had carefully observed during his trip). Moreover, the dome and the rounded main body of the structure did not mimic a stupa at all. They were more likely borrowed from a Roman-style Pantheon (fig. 22). Indeed, if that was his intention, then Itō's tower combined two sources: one Indian-Tibetan and the other Greek-Roman. Integrated into one construction, the different styles demonstrated what Itō believed to be the "origins" of Japanese architecture and, in so doing, highlighted the theme of "protecting nation." In the subsequent decades, Itō's architectural practices were associated even more closely with Japan's empire building in Asia. His designs included the Shinto shrines in Seoul and Taipei, and multiple constructions of the Yasukuni Shrine in Tokyo. In 1934, Itō completed one of his most representative works, a (mostly) Indian-style complex for the Nishi Hongaji, generally known as the Tsukiji Honganji.

Meanwhile, fellow archaeologist and anthropologist Torii Ryūzō commented about his 1905 trip, "Upon completing my second survey [in Manchuria], I consider it extremely fruitful for my scholarship." And he acknowledged that "the survey got tremendous assistance from the army, whom I sincerely appreciate."[36]

The trip greatly triggered his interest in studying the Mongols. Shortly after, Ichimura Sanjirō provided him with him an opportunity, the prince of the Right Banner of the Kharchin Mongols, Gungsang-norbu, was looking for a Japanese teacher. Seizing the opportunity, Torii and his wife spent the next two years in Kharchin studying the Mongolian language and conducting ethnographic surveys.[37] He was also commissioned by the Ministry of Foreign Affairs to investigate the local situation and submit a report.[38] Over the next three decades, Torii further conducted about seven more surveys in Manchuria and three more in Mongolia. These extensive trips shaped the characteristics of not only Torii's scholarship but also Japanese anthropology in general. As David Askew pointed out, one major distinction between anthropology in Japan and that in the West was that the former was much closer to the subjects of their study. It was a study of the "closely related Other."[39] Torii later developed a theory on the origin of the Japanese people; the majority, the Yamato race, came from the Tungus/Mongol people who

22. Gokokutō at Kasuisai, designed by Itō Chūtai. Courtesy of the Kasuisai Temple.

migrated through Manchuria and Korea. The political implication of this theory could not be clearer. Since Japan had been a melting-pot of Asian races in the past it was not unreasonable that Japan continue to be so by taking over the continent today. Unsurprisingly, he supported the annexation of Korea and promoted the theory that Japanese and Koreans shared common ancestors.

While Itō and Torii searched for the Asian roots of a "modernized" Japan via architecture and anthropology, the Nishi Honganji was devoted to the same job via Buddhism. When the war with Russia ended, Ōtani Kōzui resumed his interest in ancient Buddhist relics in Western China, particularly Xinjiang. From 1908 to 1912, he dispatched two more expeditions there, both led by a young monk named Tachibana Zuichō (1890–1968). In the Lob Desert and the Dunhuang Grotto, the explorers discovered or purchased precious documents, including a manuscript from the fourth century. Despite the fact that the Ōtani Expeditions were curtailed in 1914 due to a financial scandal, the ancient materials they took out of China aroused great interest in Europe and Japan.[40] Taking advantage of these materials, the Kyoto School of Oriental Studies, headed by Naitō Konan, significantly advanced Japan's study of Central Asia and Dunhuang. Meanwhile, the Nishi Honganji continued to expand its branch monasteries in various Asian cities, such as Shanghai, Vladivostok, Hankou, and Taipei. In Fengtian, they established a branch in Yamato-machi, a small neighborhood diagonally opposite the West Stupa across Shijianfang Avenue.

All the elite scholars traveled to the city with their respective research agendas. Far from randomly intersecting in this place, they were brought there by a shared vision of a Pan-Asian network in which Japan played a leading role. Through their travels, the Japanese scholars also tried to position Japan as a cradle of civilization, representing Asia on a global scale. All of them found what they needed to co-construct this vision. From this perspective, the West Stupa presented one small component affirming this grand geocultural and geopolitical idea. At a time when the temple had gradually lost its original significance due to the decline of one empire, it was gaining a new meaning due to the rise of another.

Fengtian in Prose

In the nineteenth and twentieth centuries, tourism developed into a new, even ritual way for colonial powers to establish their identity among "less civilized" others Travel writing and travel books helped reassure tourists of a spiritual hierarchy between guests and hosts. "Travel books," as Mary Louise Pratt argues, "created a sense of curiosity, excitement, adventure, and even moral fervor about European expansionism."[41]

Soon after the extension of the railway, which made travel to Manchuria and Inner China much easier and cheaper, the new destinations were advertised to European tourists. The biggest selling point was that these places had not been changed by "modern civilization." In the 1910 edition of *Cook's Handbook for Tourists* for northern China and Manchuria, the author set the tone. "Fortunately . . . to-day the Chinese people are as simple and primitive in their habits and customs as they have been for ages past. Industrial methods, food, habitations, monasteries, temples, religions, veneration for family ties (ancestral worship) remain exactly the same as when Europe was in a state of semi-barbarism and the great continents of the Western Hemisphere were unknown."[42]

Compared to some European writers who sought to find oriental backwardness, the Japanese writers demonstrated diverse and complicated attitudes when traveling to the new frontier. "For Japanese travelers," Joshua Fogel once remarked, "China occupied the area of overlap between the 'other' and the 'self.'"[43] This was especially true for those who toured Manchuria. Just like the scholars analyzed in this chapter, these writers used the city, the temples, and the local people to construct a vision of an ideal world and, in so doing, to interpret history and the future. In their mind, Fengtian was like a vessel containing not only China's antiquities, but also Japan's prospects. Colonial expectations created new geographic understanding and tourism acted as a productive tool to implement this "imagined geography" that legitimized imperial Japan's territorial ambition.[44] From this viewpoint, Manchuria was tightly linked with Korea and Mongolia. Tourists had easy access to all these domains via the aggressively expanded modern transportation systems. For Japan in the period after the Russo-Japanese War, the railway and tourism were a matter of not only colonial capitalist development but also imperial ideology building. Japanese writers' different views of the city reflected, essentially, their views about the imperial enterprise.

In October 1909, the literary giant Natsume Sōseki (1867–1916) began publishing a travelogue series in the *Asahi News*. Titled "Here and There in Manchuria and Korea" ("Mankan tokorodokoro"), it was arguably the first newspaper serial about touring Manchuria written by a nationally renowned writer. His visit, which had taken place a little over a month prior, was intended as a public relations campaign for Mantetsu. Nakamura Zekō, president of the company and a friend of the writer, invited him to witness "what the overseas Japanese were doing." But Natsume was reluctant at first. Poor health dimmed his enthusiasm, if there was any in the first place, to explore remote and strange frontiers. Even though he got on board eventually, his writing does not express any particular interest in either the ancient civilization or the recent development of Manchuria. He randomly recorded what he saw and heard on the trip, without providing any historical background or political interpretation. The writing style was highly individualized, full of anecdotes, personal feelings, and delicate sarcasm.[45]

Natsume had nothing positive to say about the city of Fengtian. He barely mentioned any places specifically, except the train station, the Mantetsu office in the city, the Beiling Park, and the horse-drawn streetcar (which bypassed Xita). During his four-day visit, he went through a city gate (presumably the Huaiyuan Gate) several times yet still forgot its name. That said, Natsume's personal sensitivities reveal a domineering, disdainful perspective. He remarked several times about the "stinky smell" of the Chinese houses and the "strange smell" of the water, not even trying to hide his disgust. "A strange, stinky smell diffused in the room. It is the stinky smell deliberately kept by the Chinese. So, no matter how hard the cleanliness-loving Japanese tried to eradicate it, it is still very smelly." A fellow traveler spread a rumor that for hundreds of years, Fengtian had not had a sewer system to wash away human urine and feces, which affected the quality of the drinking water. Although Natsume thought the story was doubtful, he later commented, "It is said that the hotel will move to a place near the train station after being rebuilt there. In this case, the stinky smell will be removed. However, be prepared: as long as the hotel is still in Fengtian, the sour water will continue affecting humans and animals."

Natsume's writing, intentionally or unintentionally, betrayed his deep contempt toward the Chinese and the Koreans. In Fengtian, he constantly complained about his coachmen or rickshaw pullers for either driving too fast or not steadily. He condemned the Chinese who showed no sympathy to an old man hit by traffic, despite that he himself did nothing either. "When I got off [the coach] at the front gate of the hotel," he recorded, "I came up with the mood that I finally break off ties with the cruel Chinese, which cheered me up." On another occasion, he observed that although "the rickshaw was invented by the Japanese, we must be cautious if the pullers are Chinese or Korean. They think since it was not invented by them anyway, they pull it in a way that has no respect for the rickshaw at all." Because the road was bumpy, the writer reported scornfully, "we were treated brutally. In the end, I almost want to hang the head of the Korean puller in public." To be fair, Natsume's contempt did not target the colonized only. The last piece in the series recorded his visit to the Fushun coal mine, where he met with the British consulate. Though a scholar of English literature, Natsume did not exchange a word with him in English. He even felt pity that the British gentleman, who had been living in China for many years, could not use chopsticks and did not eat rice.

By the end of the year, Natsume decided to stop publishing his travelogue. This was partly because the assassination of Itō Hirobumi (1841–1909) by Korean independent activist An Chung-gŭn (1879–1910) in October created a tense public mood in Japan. The politicized environment made his highly personalized narrative unattractive, if not inappropriate. *Here and There in Manchuria and Korea* ended up only having accounts of Manchuria not Korea.

Contrary to Natsume, in the travelogue for his second China tour (*Shina man'yūki*, or *Journey to China*) in 1917, Tokutomi Sohō depicted Fengtian as a dynamic city with both a rich history and a promising future. His entire journey lasted two and a half months from September to December. During the trip, he visited Manchuria and northern and eastern China. In Dalian, he also met an old friend who had taken up residence there in seclusion: Ōtani Kōzui, who had resigned from his position as the abbot of Nishi Honganji. *Journey to China* was then dedicated to Ōtani, who was then facing adversity. Fengtian took him two full days, where Tokutomi not only revisited historical ruins but also met with Zhang Zuolin.[46] As we saw in his poem at the beginning of this chapter, he always associated the landscapes or historical sites with his political ideals. Witnessing the mausoleum of Hong Taiji being overtaken by wilderness, he imagined the glorious military achievements of the Qing empire and "could not help bursting into tears." Standing at the Phoenix Pavilion of the royal palace, he lamented about the destiny of China, citing a Tang dynasty poem, "The setting sun looks glorious indeed, only it is so close to night." But taking the train to the city, he also expressed his joy that "Fengtian is finally becoming the center of the development in southern Manchuria . . . it turned out to be so energetic after this spring." What was most interesting, however, was a comment he wrote on the same day he composed the West Stupa poem, "Since I came to Manchuria, I increasingly believed in the Gospel of Might."

A Christian intellectual, Tokutomi Sohō had gone from being a supporter of the Freedom and People's Rights Movement to a firm promoter of imperial authority and Japanese expansionism since 1894, the eve of the Sino-Japanese War.[47] The Triple Intervention further aggravated his resentment toward the Western powers. In the 1910s, he enthusiastically endorsed the idea of "Japan's Gospel of Might," which called for resistance against the Euro-American colonization in Asia by, ironically, promoting Japanese colonization in Asia. Several months before his trip to China in 1917, *The Japan Chronicle* published a selected translation of his famous article "The Rising Generation in the Taishō Era and the

Future of the Japanese Empire." The title, "Japan's Mighty Mission," highlighted his concept of the "Asiatic Monroe Doctrine" based on the racial competition theory:

> What . . . is the mission of the Japanese Empire? In my opinion, it is of more urgent importance for Japan to try to restore the equilibrium between the White and Yellow races than to indulge in the chimerical theory of accomplishing the unification of the world. . . .
>
> By the Asiatic Monroe Doctrine, we mean the principle that Asiatic affairs should be dealt with by the Asiatics. As, however, there is no Asiatic nation except the Japanese capable of under taking these duties, the Asiatic Monroe Doctrine is virtually the principle of the Japanese dealing with Asiatic Affairs.[48]

Only by cross-referencing this writing can we understand why, witnessing the rapid transformation of a historical Asian frontier, Tokutomi would further solidify his belief in the "Gospel of Might," on one hand, yet urge infrastructure building to "meet the expectation of other countries," on the other. Standing amid the relics of Fengtian, his nostalgia for a glorious Asian past was unambiguously reiterated. But his narrative was also a clear statement that only Japan could revive this great Asian civilization.

Tokutomi's attitude toward the Chinese was complex. Like Natsume, he often ridiculed some "national characteristics" of the Chinese, saying the Chinese "in many respects are the most enlightened race but are also the world champion in terms of not cleaning their urine and feces." He criticized the Chinese for having no foresight and for taking advantage of every possible opportunity. But he also praised the social progress made in recent years and did not hesitate to express his sincere admiration for China's ancient civilization. Of course, he wrote, the Chinese today "lack the qualifications to represent this civilization." He believed the shortcoming of the Chinese was not that "they are ignorant or barbaric but that they are over-civilized" to the extent that "China is a country poisoned by its civilization."

At the end of the travelogue, Tokutomi offered high hopes for Japanese-Chinese collaboration. He viewed China not just as a place for nostalgia or a museum preserving "living samples" of an ancient civilization but also as a "great country playing a role on the world stage." Although the Chinese had many flaws, they are "a great race in East Asia. We won't achieve anything without China if we want to change the overall situation of East Asia." Claiming that a great nation like the Chinese would not see themselves enslaved by the White race, Tokutomi ended his piece by saying, "The key to Japanese-Chinese intimacy is to mutually recognize that we are Asian."

Tokutomi's Pan-Asian ideal turned out to be nothing but an illusion. While he was touring in China, the Japanese government coerced the Chinese Beiyang government to yield more national interests, which culminated in a huge patriotic protest—the May Fourth Movement—in 1919, less than two years after his visit there. Chinese nationalism in the early twentieth century was ignited, to a large extent, by Japanese colonialism in Manchuria and other places. By the 1920s, it was clear that Japanese imperialism was a major menace to China, as dangerous as—if not more than—Western imperialism.

This was the context for the China visit by Akutagawa Ryūnosuke (1892–1927), perhaps the most celebrated modern Japanese short story author, in 1921. Akutagawa's *Shina Yū-ki* (*Travels in China*), somewhat neglected travel literature in Taishō Japan, painstakingly recorded the author's experiences in Shanghai, the lower and mid-Yangtze River regions and Beijing. Only in the very last section does it briefly mention Manchuria. There are just two subheadings and both texts are very succinct—one sentence each. Under the subheading "Fengtian," the sentence reads:

When I saw forty or fifty Japanese passing by the train station in the sunset, I almost want to agree with the theory of the Yellow Peril.

Under the subheading "The South Manchurian Railway," it reads:

A centipede with a hundred-feet crawling on the root of sorghum.[49]

Throughout his nearly four-month journey, Akutagawa acquired first-hand observations of China in the early 1920s. He indulged himself in the richness of Chinese culture and social life, which he enjoyed so much, while at the same time witnessing the chaos and decay of a semicolonial society. Unlike Tokutomi, Akutagawa rarely made political comments directly. He used a subtle narrative to express his sympathy and criticism. His self-identity, along with the journey, also changed subtly—from more or less seeing the Chinese as "one of them" to more or less embracing himself as one of the Chinese.[50] This was partly because his criticism of modern China (what he referred to as "the deprivation of the nation") was often overwhelmed by his disgust of Westerners' behavior in China. In Beijing, he dressed in Chinese attire and was obsessed with local culture, even expressing nostalgia when leaving the city. "No, I don't want to return to Japan. I want to return to Beijing."[51]

This strong identification with Chinese culture explained his acute satire of the Japanese expansion in Manchuria. Located in the core of the SMR zone, the railway station demonstrated the colonial nature of Fengtian. Analogizing the SMR tracks to a centipede—a ferocious and predatory arthropod—Akutagawa painted a dreadful and desperate picture of Japanese railway colonialism in the new frontier. Despite the brevity, his writing revealed a surprisingly vivid recognition of the significance of the railway space.

The political tension caused by the railway continued to foment in the 1920s, culminating in the assassination of Zhang Zuolin in 1928. As we learned in chapter 3, the famous feminist poet Yosano Akiko (1878–1942) personally heard the bomb blast. She and her husband Yosano Tekkan, also a poet, were traveling through Manchuria and Mongolia. The tour, arranged by Mantetsu, resulted in the book *Manmō Yū-ki* (*Travelogue of Manchuria and Mongolia*), which attracted heated discussion after World War II. Some scholars believed that the tour was a turning point for Akiko's career, changing her from one of the strongest antiwar voices in Japan to a war supporter.[52] Other scholars reject such a trajectory, arguing that her attitude toward war was always fluid, and beneath the fluidity was her solid embracement of the Japanese throne.[53] In any case, her travelogue was an intricate text demonstrating the close collaboration between the powerful colonial agency and cultural celebrities, a relationship that began with Natsume Sōseki's tour in 1909.

A great number of studies have talked about the Yosanos' Manchurian-Mongolian trip, so it is not necessary to give a comprehensive analysis here. But one detail deserves mentioning. On June 6, two days after Zhang's assassination, the couple, at the advice of a Japanese general, took a car to go sightseeing, visiting Hong Taiji's mausoleum in the northern suburb. Akiko wrote, "When we crossed the South Manchurian Railway tracks en route, far off to the right we could see a famous lama tower, and to the left closer at hand was a Chinese college. This college was said to be the base of operations for the local anti-Japanese students."[54]

The lama tower she saw would have been the North Stupa, and the college was most likely Northeastern University. Throughout their entire trip, Akiko and Tekkan followed Mantetsu's itinerary, honoring Russo-Japanese War remains, visiting the Mantetsu enterprises, and participating in various social or literary events. All of these activities aimed to boost the positive image of Japanese colonization in general and Mantetsu in particular. However, she also encountered the high tide of anti-Japanese sentiment in Chinese society and, unmistakably, felt the danger of a Sino-Japanese clash. The messages received during the trip, when switching between the colonial environment and the colonized environment, were certainly controversial. The sentence cited in the previous paragraph depicts such an intricate spatial-political array. The tourist attraction (the lama tower) was far, but the political tension (the anti-Japanese college students) was near. Linking the two images were the SMR tracks— symbol of the colonial regime and its aggression. As tourists, the writers were caught in between the two. During the trip, the couple, in writings and public speeches, kept promoting the theme of "peace" and the "brotherhood" of the Japanese and Chinese. Yet both Akiko and Tekkan cautiously avoided the key issue: exactly who and what was instigating the conflict.

In the imperialist era, travel literature almost always mirrored colonial ideology. But how Japan's literary society imagined Manchuria differed from how the Europeans, who tended to see the frontier merely as a museum of antiquities, did. For Japan, Manchuria was not just a (semi)colony, but also a land of promise. It was a subject of conquest, yet the conquest carried the peculiar intention of resistance. The railways, relics, and cities comprised an imperial frontier that was both functional and symbolic, material and spiritual. Such a frontier had to be differentiated and assimilated at the same time. A racial-civilizational hierarchy existing in the present had to be accompanied by nostalgia for the past and anticipation for the future. The space, therefore, was resignified in light of nostalgia for the future.

Imperial War and Mass Tourism

Images of the Fengtian stupas, particularly the West Stupa, spread widely. They can be seen in old postcards, magazines, photo albums, maps, tourist guidebooks, advertisements, propaganda pamphlets, yearbooks, even documentary films—any visual media that was employed in the first half of the twentieth century (figs. 23 and 24). The illustrations were written in Japanese, Chinese, Russian, or English, welcoming tourists from all over the world. The sudden profusion of images was no doubt due to the popularity of new media technology, novel means of transport, and the booming tourist industry. But far from a pure product of techno-commercial development, the prevalence of images of the ancient Buddhist stupa were first and foremost a result of the new spatial order. The stupa space, along with all the other sites in Manchuria, Korea and North China that were carefully promoted by Japanese tourist agencies, mosaicked an overall identity of the Japanese empire. Tourism not only showcased but also constructed the empire. A phenomenon Kate McDonald calls "spatial politics of empire," imperial tourism justified and praised colonialism and aggression. "In this sense, tourism and the places it sold were an argument about the global social and geopolitical

（行發局務畫亞東）　WEST TOWER, MUKDEN.　　　塔　西　天　奉

23. Japanese postcard of the West Stupa. Author's collection.

order."[55] The thriving tourism in Fengtian, especially after the Mukden Incident in 1931, has to be understood against this backdrop.

The colonial elites made no effort to hide the connection between tourism (J. *kankō*) and empire building. In 1939, the Manchurian Branch of the Japan Tourist Bureau (JTB) issued *The Tourist Yearbook of Manchuria and China* (*Man-Shi ryokō nenkan*), which featured an editorial titled "The Significance of Tourist Industry." In it, the author argued that tourism should not be regarded as just a business about amusement and leisure but as an enterprise that "decisively mobilizes both materials (*mono*) and the mind (*kokoro*)." Tourism helped investigate local material resources, develop infrastructure, transportation and facilities, and stimulate propaganda and PR campaigns, all of which encouraged systematic collaboration. Promoting tourism would strengthen one's consciousness of membership in the state and society all while encouraging international friendship on the other. Under the "coordination" of the JTB, the Manchukuo government established the Manchuria Tourist Commission and its executive organ, the Manchuria Tourism Alliance. One of the major aims of the two organizations was to advance the "re-recognition of Manchuria." But the geopolitical vision of the editorial went beyond Manchuria. "Today," the author concluded, "the Far East has become the center of two tourist axis. One is Tokyo-Shinkyō

24. A tourist pamphlet made by Mantetsu, with the image of a stupa on its cover. Author's collection.

(Changchun)-Beijing tourist axis, the other is the greater tourist axis of Tokyo-Rome-Berlin."[56]

The sneak attack on Pearl Harbor in 1941 marked the start of the Pacific War, or what Japan called the Great East Asia War. Japan soon entered a stage of total mobilization in which tourism was a critical component. The following year, the former vice mayor of Fengtian and right-wing activist Yamaguchi Jūji (1892–1979) published a short essay in the magazine *Manchuria Tourism* (*Kankō Manchū*) titled "The Great

East Asia War and the New Mission of Tourism." In it, he debunked the view that tourism was an "inappropriate mistake." Instead, he argued, the current war was a perpetual war that would not be decided by military force only. It was also an economic war and a thought war that relied on the exploitation of resources in Japan, Manchuria, China, and Southeast Asia and winning the minds of "alien nations." Tourism, therefore, had a new mission of fighting on the economic and thought fronts of the Great East Asia War.[57]

Systematic efforts were made to construct a new sociopolitical order, one that reorganized time and space to meet the needs of tourists. Time became the schedule and space turned into the sites to see, all arranged in advance so that nothing was unpredictable. Various agencies, Mantetsu and the JTB being the most prominent, supported imperial tourism, which dynamically linked Japan with its continental colonies, not unlike the war machine that integrated all parts of the empire. When we view the legacies of such efforts, old postcards, cartoons, guidebooks, maps, and so on, bear in mind that these were not merely souvenirs sold for their commercial value but also pedagogical tools that had specific political and ideological functions. To produce and promote these materials required cutting-edge technology, a rational arrangement of money, a strict sense of time, and a clear goal regarding discipline and education.

The best representatives of the cutting-edge technology were new trains and cameras. In 1933, a super express train, Asia Express (Aji'a), began operating between Dalian and Changchun, then the capital of Manchukuo. With a high speed of 110 kilometers per hour, the Asia Express was the fastest steam locomotive in Asia, and possibly the world, at the time. The journey took only eight and half hours from start to end, beating the previous fast train by more than two hours.[58] Of all the stations en route, Fengtian was arguably the most important one. Situated at the intersection of the four major trunk lines in Manchuria (connecting Dalian, Changchun, Andong, and Beijing), it was often called "Manchuria's entrance" in tourist literature. Twenty thousand passengers passed through the Fengtian train stations daily. In 1940, a Japanese visitor could depart Dalian in the late morning and arrive at the SMR Fengtian Station at 3:44 p.m., just four hours and forty-nine minutes later.[59] When people measured such a distance (around 350 kilometers) in such a short time, their spatial sense was largely compressed. The experience was no longer a wandering journey but a leap from one point to another. Upon arriving in Fengtian, most visitors had only one day (or two at best) to tour the city before jumping on the next train. What to see and how to record it when in such a hurry?

The camera offered an easy solution. The Japanese scholars and writers previously discussed in this chapter—Naitō Konan, Itō Chūta, Torii Ryūzō, Tokutomi Sohō, and Yosano Akiko—all used cameras extensively during their visits. Since the 1910s, photographs had become an indispensable part of tourism, so much so that all printed tourist materials, from guidebooks and maps to magazines and advertisements, featured photos to spur local tourism. What photography brought was a new relationship between people and space. Subjects were carefully selected and pictures conscientiously composed. The images not only presented the space but also interpreted, sometimes with the help of textual illustrations, the meaning of the space.

In photos, the West Stupa usually occupied the center of the frame, against an empty sky. A shabby bungalow and an old tree stood beside it. In this way, the photographers made viewers focus on the stupa's solemn and historical appearance. Most captions, if there were any, simply described the stupa as Buddhist architecture built in the early Qing dynasty. Rarely was the tower depicted in its real surroundings—Western-style buildings, a bustling avenue, and a red-light district.[60] Together, rail transportation and photography greatly extended a tourist's reach on her trip. Yet at the same time, they regulated what was seen, how it was seen, and how it was understood.

Tourism is a luxury that requires making the best use of your money. This was especially true for the emerging middle-class in Japan in the first half of the twentieth century. "Japanese are not pleasant when living in Japan," Naitō Konan once said, "but what if we took the humble money we earned and spent it in the colonies? I cannot say it is good or bad. But in any case, I feel that Fengtian is indeed a very good place."[61] In every tourist guidebook, cost was one of the most important subjects covered in the contents. The authors listed in detail the prices for transportation, meals, lodging, and sightseeing, along with other essential information like currency exchange rates and discounts. Prices varied, depending on the class of the ticket (first class to third class), the number of travelers (individual or group), the duration of the trip, or the style of cuisine (e.g., Japanese or Western). Prices were reduced by as much as 30 percent for groups, especially teachers and young students.[62] To encourage far-reaching tour of the continental colonies, specially priced tickets were issued for those who visited both Korea and Manchuria or Korea, Manchuria, and North China. A guidebook published in 1939 revealed that the cost of visiting Manchuria with a tourist group (twenty members or more) was within the range of 100 to 190 yen, depending on the chosen routes and the type of train ticket. It was significantly lower than the reverse tour from Manchuria to Japan, which usually cost between 150 to 400 yen.[63]

In addition to financing, taking a vacation to tour Manchuria was also a challenging job in terms of time management. Visitors had to create a comprehensive schedule, paying attention to the different calendars and time zones. For the Japanese, the best season to travel to Manchuria was late spring or early summer. A tourist almanac in 1939 recorded the number of incoming tourist groups between October 1937 and August 1938. May was the busiest month of the year, with 92 groups visiting out of a total of 247 for the entire period. The groups ranged in size from as few as nine members to as many as 296. A large number of them were student groups (184).[64] The tourists had very tight schedules; the arrival and departure times had to be precise in order to connect from one transportation system to another. For example, a typical thirteen-day trip to Korea and Manchuria included a day trip to each of the major cities (Seoul, Fengtian, Changchun, Harbin, Dalian, and Port Author) and a half-day trip to Pyongyang and Fushun. Tourists only slept in hotels six of the nights. The rest were spent on the move, either on a train, bus, or ferry.[65]

As if this was not tiresome enough, different calendars and time zones created more confusion. Since the railways in Manchuria were once owned by contested regimes, railway schedules were printed in different calendar systems. Hence, the year 1934 was simultaneously "the Ninth Year of Shōwa (Japan)" on the SMR lines, "the first year of Kangde (Manchukuo)" on non-SMR lines, and "the Twenty-Third Year of the Republic of China" on other lines connecting to Inner China. This persisted until 1940 when all the lines were unified under the Japanese system. As for time zones, picture a traveler in 1931 taking the train to Fengtian from Korea. She would need to set her watch one hour backward when crossing the border because southern Manchuria, unlike Korea, had adopted a different time zone than Japan. Moreover, if the trip went farther north to Changchun and Harbin, she would need to set her watch forward by twenty-three minutes. This was Harbin Time used in the CER domain and the Far East of Soviet Russia. Eventually, the Manchukuo government did away with the discrepancies, abolishing Harbin Time in 1932 and, later, accepting Japan Standard Time in 1937.[66] After that, Japanese tourists did not have to worry about the time differences between home and the colonies. The empire had mastered time too.

When the time was dictated by modern transportation, so was space. Since most tourists had only a limited time to experience the colonies, sightseeing had to be planned in advance and just for cities along the railways. Furthermore, because only hours, if not minutes, could be spent at a destination, tourists relied on guidebooks, maps, and tourist pamphlets for an introduction and background information. These materials, mostly provided by Mantetsu or the JTB, became pedagogical tools for the empire to complete a circle of education. The colonies were presented in accordance with the imperial curriculum and tourists were the students, literally and figuratively. They were supposed to learn about the famous battlefields of the Sino-Japanese and Russo-Japanese Wars, pay their respect at the war monuments and local Shinto shrines, be amazed by the modern enterprises installed by the colonizers, enjoy the urban parks and local markets, and, last but not least, visit the splendid ancient cultural ruins.[67] All of these sites formed a spatial order that was set up to serve the imperial ideology of building a Pan-Asian "paradise of Kingly way."

The effectiveness of this pedagogy can be seen in *Tsuzurikata Manshū* (*Composing about Manchuria*), the collective writings of ten Japanese primary school students who toured Manchuria in August 1939.[68] Funded by Mantetsu, the group, called the Tsuzurikata envoy, departed from Tokyo and visited Fengtian, Fushun, Changchun, Harbin, Dalian, and Port Arthur in twenty days. Wherever they went, the group were given a special reception by local authorities and celebrated by local students. When they returned home, each student submitted a written piece detailing their experiences and feelings, along with photos. The writing revealed their pride and joyfulness. One student wrote, "Fengtian . . . the Fengtian of the ancient battlefield of the Japan-Russian War . . . the Fengtian where my father used to live more than 10 years ago . . . the Fengtian that I was so eager to see by any means ever since I attended the school until today. . . . Now I came, at 16:55 on August 12."

The lama tower, interestingly, appeared in her story. When her father lived and worked in Tiexi, the student's narrative goes, the place was empty and wild. Every evening, her father took the horse streetcar at the station "under the West Stupa" to a language school to study Russian and Chinese. Since the Mukden Incident, the city had witnessed huge development, to the extent that, "Tiexi is now an industrial area not inferior to Osaka or Kitakyushu."[69] In a personal and touching tone, the essay reaffirmed the message that it was Japanese sacrifice that brought prosperity to the city.

This kind of education went two-ways. The following year, ten students from Manchukuo—five boys and five girls, each pair chosen from one of the five major ethnic groups (Japanese, Chinese, Mongolian, Korean, and Russian)—set out on a trip to Japan. Needless to say, the purpose of the outbound trip, like the inbound one, was to cultivate a sense of community between the colony and the suzerain. Echoing the *Tsuzurikata Manshū*, their travel writings were published in a similar book, *Tsuzurikata Nihon* (*Composing about Japan*).[70] Among the Manchukuo envoys, two were from the new urban areas of Fengtian, one was a Japanese girl enrolled at the Shikishima Primary School and the other a Korean boy enrolled at the Xita (West Stupa) Primary School.[71]

Many guidebooks, though not all, recommended that tourists stop by the West Stupa when visiting Fengtian. Compared with other highlighted sites, such as those associated with the war efforts, the Beidaying Garrison (where the Mukden Incident started) and the Monument of the Loyal Dead, or the much more famous historical structures, the Beiling Park (Hong Taiji's mausoleum) and the royal palace, the West Stupa was smaller in scale and did not require a lot of time to visit. However, because of its convenient location, it attracted quite a lot of tourists, most of whom stayed near the SMR station. Travel literature, more frequently than not, mentioned the West Stupa. In an English guidebook for Fengtian (published by Mantetsu), "The West Tower" was introduced as "the representative" of the four stupas. "The embossed carving of a lion is seen on a side of the Tower, so fascinating as to remind tourists of the period when the Lamaism prevailed over the land."[72] Guidebooks in Japanese interpreted the structure in a similar way. A 1930 guidebook stated that on one side of Xita Avenue stood the West Stupa of the Life-Prolonging Temple, which was the "representative of the lama towers."[73] It also described the stupa as *koshoku sōzen* (古色蒼然), which can only be loosely translated as when one is infused with a sense of history and the sublime when viewing an old relic. Interestingly, a lot of Japanese travel literature would later on employ the exact same words to describe sightseeing at the West Stupa. It was not a coincidence. More than likely, tourists would have referred to guidebooks before or after their visits, internalized what they read, and adopted the descriptions. In this way, the significance of subject and space, which had been primed for them by imperial agencies, was further solidified.

The spatial meaning of the stupa was not an independent thing. It could not be isolated from interpretations of other tourist sites in Fengtian. As a city with multilayered facets, Fengtian mingled history and modernity, past and future. Tourists recognized and appreciated the koshoku sōzen sensation of the West Stupa precisely because it stood in contrast to a rapidly urbanizing environment. By the same token, Fengtian could not be separated from all the other cities connected by imperial tourism. Together with Dalian, Changchun, Harbin, Seoul, Pusan, and many others, it wove a web of significance. The images and illustrations of the West Stupa in Fengtian, though numerous in quantity, were almost identical. But the landmark was not supposed to be interpreted by itself. Popular in media, the massively reproduced space was but a node embedded in the vast network of the imperial landscape created by colonialism.

Needless to say, the more complex dimensions of this space, especially its darker aspects, are absent in the tourism literature crafted by the empire. In the mid-1930s, the German sinologist and journalist Ernst Cordes traveled from Siberia through Manchuria, visiting several cities, including Harbin, Changchun, Fengtian, and Beijing. In his travelogue, *The Youngest Empire: Sleeping and Awakening Manchukuo* (*Das jüngste kaiserreich: schlafendes-wachendes Mandschukuo*), we frequently encounter the tremendous conflicts brought about by the expansion of colonial modernity. In a chapter on Fengtian, he devotes significant attention to describing a dying laborer lying in a trash heap at the corner of a wall. This scene unfolds right in front of the Yamato Hotel, the most luxurious hotel in the city, and not far from Xita:

> I look over: there lies a corpse, dressed in rags, in the middle of the garbage, among peels, rotting fruit, stones, shards of pottery, and cardboard boxes, crushed into powder, as I can tell from the green label. The person is dirty and gray from head to toe, barefoot, and thin to the bone; there is a large open wound on their arm. An open wound runs from the ankle of the left leg up to the calf, which is already completely eaten away. One hand of the man claws at the damp, dirty ground in pain, while the other tightly grips an indescribably filthy old sackcloth placed over his head.

When Cordes tried to express his shock at this horrifying scene to the hotel owner, the owner was more concerned about the pomegranates in the garden that were about to ripen. He suggested they have a drink and chat about "a more funny story." "Nothing here in this garden reminds one of danger, of war, or of China's misery," Cordes lamented, "unless, of course, one has impossible associations with the word 'pomegranates,' which glow so beautifully gold and red here among the thick green leaves."[74]

Xita: As a Host Neighborhood

Travel literature or guidebooks viewed the city via an outsider's lens. They rarely touched on local life. On the other hand, tourism, both foreign and domestic, changed local life in a profound way. "As a host community adapts to tourism, in its facilitation to tourists' needs, attitudes, and values, the host community must become more like the tourists' culture."[75] This comment, at least partially, applied to Fengtian, particularly the new urban center of the SMR zone and the Mercantile District. The rapid urbanization of the former western outskirts of the city brought modern transportation, hotels, banks, department stores, restaurants, theaters, and religious facilities, mimicking what Japanese or European cities had. While foreigners—settlers and tourists alike—were consuming the colonial space, native residents also adapted to the changes. Domestic tours and consumption, not unlike the foreign ones, filled the space with new meanings.

The Xita neighborhood was such an example. Located on the edge of the SMR zone and the MD, the previously sacred religious space was gradually surrounded by an entertainment area. The most thriving businesses in the area were various forms of the sex industry.[76] But unlike places of prostitution in other Chinese cities, such as Suzhou,[77] the rise of the red-light district in Xita had a notably colonial origin. "Sex workers," as Marc Driscoll argues, were one of the "most important constituent forces in consolidating Japan's imperialism in its biopolitical phase."[78] In colonies like Manchuria, prostitution was not simply allowed by the imperial authority but actively promoted. Modern transportations facilitated the commodification of women and helped create a transboundary prostitution network. One estimation calculated that over one hundred thousand Japanese women were either forced or cajoled by human traffickers into various forms of the sex trade throughout the Asia-Pacific region from the 1870s to the 1930s.[79]

Prostitution emerged and expanded along the path of Japanese capitalism and imperialism. According to *Hōten nijūnenshi* (Twenty years' history of Fengtian), Japanese sex workers first came to Mukden during the Sino-Japanese War and reemerged after the Russo-Japanese War. Most worked in so-called restaurants (*ryōriya*), so popular that sex-hungry Japanese soldiers and immigrants lined up in front of their doors.[80] They were known as *jōshigun* (娘子軍), or the "army of women." The term emerged first in the nineteenth century, referring to Japanese sex workers in Southeast Asia. Because a lot of them came from poor fishing families in the Amakusa Islands (off the west coast of Kyushu), they were also sometimes called "Amakusa girls." In 1909, more than 130 Japanese ryōriya restaurants were established in the western suburb, hosting 636 geisha or prostitutes.[81] In the SMR zone alone, there were 220 geisha or escorts (out of a total of 5,000 Japanese residents) in early 1912, accounting for one-seventh of all Japanese women in the enclave.[82] During the Manchukuo period, along with the rapid increase in immigration and the tourism fever, female entertainment or prostitution in

Japanese Fengtian became one of the most thriving local businesses. A 1934 survey showed that Japanese- and Korean-run service facilities—hotels, restaurants, bars, cafés, and performing houses—employed 205 taxi dancers, 996 geishas, and 450 prostitutes.[83]

Most of the facilities were concentrated along Shijianfang Avenue and Yanagi-machi. Both were in the border area between the SMR zone and the MD, with the former being located southeast of Xita and the latter right beside the Life-Prolonging Temple in the west. In a 1928 Japanese tourist map (fig. 25), Yanagi-machi was marked as a *yūkaku* (遊廓), meaning a red-light district.[84] Business was directly connected with tourism. One statistic on sales at Japanese and Korean *ryōriya* restaurants in the Shijianfang area showed a 30 percent decrease in late 1928 due to a significant drop in the number of tourists. Upon analysis, what caused the decrease was a large drop in expenditures for geisha or escorts, which were two to six times that from dining on normal days.[85] In the days after the Mukden Incident, sales at Japanese restaurants in Yanagi-machi experienced major slumps, dropping 15 percent that September. But the next month, they went up by 38 percent, followed by a further 76 percent jump in November. In Shijianfang, about half of the restaurant income came from escort services, whereas in Yanagi-machi the portion was even higher: about 70 percent.[86] Meanwhile, the Korean restaurants also experienced a major rise in sales, about 20 percent more than the same period the previous year. As one report explained, "now [after the Incident] 15 more staff were added, and the Korean restaurants were so bustling that they were full all day and all night. Under the red lights, drunk men of various kinds were pursuing beautiful Korean prostitutes."[87]

Indeed, the war boosted the sex business. Japanese writer Usui Kameo recorded that after the Mukden Incident, the imperial army and observers flooded in. Business owners had to recruit entertainers from Dalian and Seoul to cope with the rising demand. Meanwhile, new girls were imported from Japan's Kantō and Tohoku regions (east and northeast of Honshu Island), many of them farm girls with no training. "But after a year they knew how to read and [the business] was so flourishing that there was no sleep and no rest." In just one year after the incident, the number of female entertainers doubled.[88] By 1941, Yanagi-machi alone was home to over thirty Japanese and Korean restaurants. A Japanese tourist guidebook described it as a *karyūgai* (花柳街)—another name for red-light district. Because the West Stupa was erected in the neighborhood, the same guidebook stated, "local Chinese also called it Baita-jie" (白塔街, the white tower street).[89]

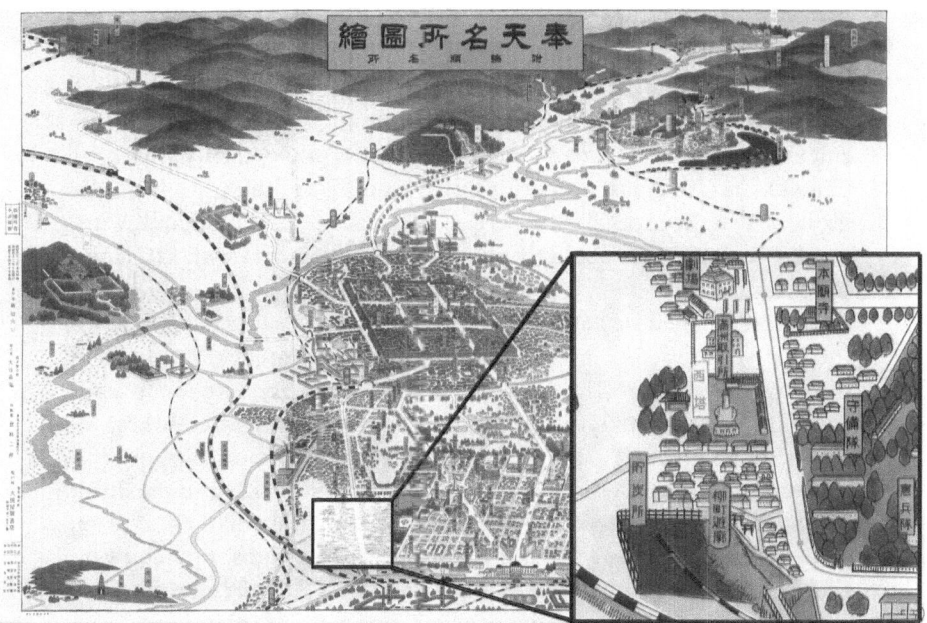

25. The Xita section of "Hōten meisho zue," a bird's-eye map of Fengtian,
where "Yanagi-machi" is marked as a *yūkaku* (red-light district).
Author's collection.

As mentioned in chapter 3, Zhang Zuolin, who intended to compete
with the Japanese in urban development, moved the Chinese brothels in
the old town to the Mercantile District. This led to the prosperity of the
sex industry in the MD, mainly in the Beishichang (northern market)
area, which was located northeast of the Xita neighborhood. At its peak,
Beishichang had about 130 brothels with over one thousand registered
or unregistered prostitutes. The high-end Chinese prostitutes worked
in brothels called *shuguan* (书馆), literally meaning "book house." But
many others worked in opium dens, hotels, and even their homes. The
business had its own guild, called the shuihui or "water association,"
which was originally set up for firefighters. The heads of the shuihui
maintained internal order while nourishing a mutually beneficial relationship with the local police. Most of the heads were brothel owners
or gangsters themselves.[90]

Foreign opposition ensued when the Chinese government introduced the sex industry there. In 1921, the British Consul General F. E.
Wilkinson and his American counterpart A. W. Pontius issued diplomatic notes urging local authorities to relocate the brothel buildings
in planning. They objected to the project with concerns about security,

hygiene, and morality. Separately, an American pastor also protested that the brothel area was opposite a planned church school, hence corrupting future students. "Our church firmly believes that there are more methods to develop the commercial district than making humans sacrifice, coercing women to do such a shameless job, and harming other people's life." The local authority, however, refused their request on the grounds that the brothel area was quite a distance from the church. Plus, similar projects were perfectly fine in other open ports such as Tianjin or Shanghai.[91]

As in the Japanese case, where geisha, dancers, escorts, and prostitutes satisfied different levels of consumption, a hierarchy existed within the Chinese brothels. The prostitutes were categorized into four classes according to age, looks, education, and artistic talents. But few first- or second-class brothels—the high-end and most expensive categories—were established in Beishichang. Many brothels there fell into the third-class category, serving lower-middle-class customers like policemen, civil services, officers, and small businessmen. The most popular were the fourth-class brothels located in the northwest part of the area, whose clientele were workers, rickshaw pullers, peddlers, or other lower-class men.[92] Although Chinese brothels might not rely on foreign tourists as much as their Japanese counterparts, they too were sensitive to changes in urban development. In 1925, representatives of the brothel business in Beishichang petitioned to convert the third-class brothels to fourth-class. One of the major reasons, according to the petitioners, was that workers at the nearby Fengtian Cotton Mill and at British American Tobacco had become important sources of revenue. These single males only looked for fourth-class prostitutes, rarely paying for third-class ones.[93]

Women in brothels were consumed not only by men but also by the media. In local newspapers, prostitutes were the favorite subjects of the social gossip section. Most of the stories were short anecdotes or advertisements: the arrival of a new girl, the officials who were infected with a sex disease after visiting a brothel, or an aging prostitute downgraded from third class to fourth, and similar. In 1906, the *Shengjing shibao* (*Shengjing Times*), a Japanese-owned Chinese newspaper, published the article "Beautiful Spring in Shenyang." Employing flowery language, it reviewed the charms of the prostitutes who had recently been transferred to the city from Tianjin, Tanggu, and Shanghai.[94] This stimulated similar contributions evaluating local prostitutes. In November, the newspaper even published a comprehensive ranking of famous prostitutes, following the ranking of the civil service examination.[95] Ironically, the author borrowed feminist rhetoric to justify the subjectification of women.

"China emphasizes the male but ignores the female so that women's education was not established and women's study is not flourishing."

Likewise, Japanese travel agencies also encouraged, however implicitly, visitors to find girl entertainers during their trips to Korea and Manchuria. In a pamphlet issued by the Japan Tourist Bureau in 1937, *Touring Chosen & Manchoukuo,* a section dedicated to "amusements" explained, "in Chosen, Keisang, the charming entertainers who resemble somewhat the Geisha girl of Japan, attend the guests in restaurants and tea-houses." Whereas, "the singing girls of Manchoukuo, unlike their sisters, the Japanese Geisha and Corean Keisang, are not responsible for entertaining guests with anything other than singing, and as a rule will stay for only half an hour or so at a party."[96] Perhaps the most surprising fact about this pamphlet was not so much its content but that it was printed in English, targeting a specific group of customers.

In his 1936 travelogue, Ernst Cordes, the German journalist, documented his encounters with both Japanese and Chinese entertainers or sex workers. At a Japanese dance hall called "Broadway," the taxi dancers were dressed in bright and colorful attire. They worked from 9 p.m. to 3:30 a.m. daily, and men could freely choose their dance partners. Each dance lasted 4 to 5 minutes, after which the men would give the girls "dance tickets," each worth 0.25 yen. One of the dancers, named Cilly, was a superstar at the time. However, due to the toll of long and grueling work hours, she developed a nearly incurable case of tuberculosis and had to return to Tokyo.[97] In a bar, a "delicate and small" Japanese military geisha named Sussuka poured drinks for Cordes while showing him photos of herself fighting alongside Japanese soldiers in Rehe (Jehol) with excitement. Cordes recorded: "Sussuka earns about 150 yen (approximately 130 marks) per month. She is one of many little geshas that the soldiers love."[98]

In a Chinese brothel, Cordes chose a girl named "Tssuee-Lan," who was no more than seventeen or eighteen years old. They cracked sunflower seeds and chatted, while Cordes learned prostitutes' life stories. Typically, human traffickers would buy young girls from impoverished parents for 10–20 yuan, then sell them to brothels for 50 to 300 Chinese dollars when the girls reached the ages of 12 to 14. Virgins, referred to as "green fruits," could command prices of 200 to 800 dollars for their first night. The greatest hope for these sex workers was for a man to buy their freedom and take them as concubines. By the time they reached the age of 30–35, prostitutes might have the chance to buy their own freedom, usually at an assessed value of no more than 500 dollars. The girl can pay off through her earnings after deducting expenses for clothing, food, and pocket money. But the truly difficult part was life after leaving the brothels—the environment they knew best. "They realize too late that their freedom only begins once it has already ended."[99]

At Tssuee-Lan's place, Cordes smoked opium for the first time, documenting the entire process with highly detailed and literary flair. Smoking opium is an art that requires patience and practice, with just the preparation taking 10 to 15 minutes. "Tsusee-Lan is practiced at this, as she has to do it daily. It is part of her profession." After four attempts, Cordes finally managed to indulge like a seasoned opium smoker, describing the experience as "My joints loosen as though in somnambulism or under hypnotic influence . . . as if I lay on the North Sea beach while my soul sailed away with an eternal cloud."[100]

The sex industry was always tightly connected with drugs, in not only this part of the city but also the entire empire. As many scholars have pointed out, prostitution and opium not merely were the products of the Japanese colonial empire but also helped create it. Opium greatly financed Japanese expansion in East Asia, even contributing to one-sixth of the total revenues of Manchukuo, the Japanese puppet regime.[101] The state tried to monopolize opium production and circulation, yet its efforts were never really successful. In December 1932, altogether six hundred opium retailers were authorized to have establishments across Manchukuo, but Fengtian alone had about one thousand opium shops operating.[102] The Japanese were not alone in their involvement with the drug business; the Chinese and Koreans also trafficked their fair share. Most Chinese hotels or brothels held licenses to operate opium businesses.

In the spring of 1935, a fire engulfed several brothels in Beishichang and took the lives of five or six prostitutes. It started in the kitchen of a brothel and ignited the raw opium secretly hidden there. The deadly fire wiped out the Pingkangli brothel area almost entirely, until the sex industry quarter was rebuilt later.[103] Data collected before the crackdown on brothels by the Communist government in 1952 showed that 64 percent of prostitutes were drug addicts. Indeed, drugs were the most common reason for a woman to sell her body (61.1 percent). Other reasons included poverty (25.2 percent), human trafficking (9.7 percent), and spousal abandonment (2.4 percent). Sixty-five percent of the prostitutes were between the ages of twenty-one and thirty-one, and 65.1 percent were illiterate.[104] No doubt they easily fell victim to the owners, pimps, and gangsters.

As in many cities around the world, the sex industry contributed to the prosperity of the local economy, although the space was often reviled as a hotbed of crime, corruption, deprivation, and immorality or simply as "a tumor of the city." The Japanese/Korean restaurants and the Chinese brothels ensured that Xita and its surroundings were bus-tling while creating serious social problems. Together, they transformed Xita into a place with a prominent gender mark. In Fengtian, an in-dustrial and commercial metropolis, Xita featured as an entertainment-commercial space where the female body was the major commodity to lure foreign and domestic visitors.

Seeing Like a Colonized: Chinese and Korean Visitors

So far, this chapter has focused on Japanese literature and images about the West Stupa, the Xita neighborhood, and the new urban space in Fengtian. However, this is not to suggest that other people, especially those who endured Japanese aggression, left no record. This last section serves as a brief introduction to how a few Chinese and Korean writers made sense of this place. Although their numbers were not as great as the Japanese, they provided more layers of emotion and meaning to the colonial space.

In the spring of 1913, Ning Xiewan (1881–1946) departed from the Huangpu pier in Shanghai, heading to Dalian. From there he traveled first along with the SMR and then switched to the TSR to Russia. His ultimate destination included several European countries: Germany, Belgium, France, and Britain. Born in Hunan Province and a veteran anti-Qing revolutionary, Ning participated in the Wuchang Uprising in 1911 but was utterly disappointed when Yuan Shikai seized power. He quit his appointment as the minister to Portugal and embarked on a journey to observe world politics. In his travelogue, *Xizheng jishi* (*Travel to the West*), he extensively recorded the geographical, historical, social, economic, and political situations observed en route. As he stated in the preface, Ning believed that the contemporary world was "a world of industry and commerce," "a world of civilization," and "a world of armed peace and international competition."[105] Therefore, his journey was a sociopolitical study of the world situation, aiming at resolving the crises in China.

In Fengtian, Ning toured several historical sites. At Hong Taiji's mau-soleum, he was impressed by the exaltedness of the place while still accusing the Qing of "losing the virtue." At the royal palace, he remarked in praise that the "culture in Fengtian was the best in Manchuria." Then he introduced the four 'lama towers at the four cardinal directions of the city":

Each tower belongs to its temple. The west one belongs to the Life-Prolonging Temple. . . . The four temples are generally called the state-protecting temples whereas the towers the state-protecting towers. All buildings were erected several hundred years ago. During the sunset with evening clouds, they stand among fog and wild grass. People who passed by could not help expressing their sorrow.[106]

Just like an old-style scholar-official standing and lamenting in front of the remains of previous dynasties, Ning saw the Buddhist buildings as an abstract existence fading away in a long-wandering history. These "state-protecting" temples and towers revealed the irresistible power of time. Viewing them not as landmarks of an alien culture, he instead smoothly incorporated these exotic symbols into the Han Chinese literary tradition. "Sorrow" was the only emotion he felt when visiting these sites. Despite that *Travel to the West* was an immediate success, Ning failed to solve China's crises through politics. Feeling tired of the endless strife of the Beiyang government, he quit all political positions and dedicated himself to education. In the 1920s and 1930s, Ning taught international law at universities in Beijing until the Japanese army occupied the city in 1937.

In the same year, a young poet from Jilin published a new collection, *Liuwangzhe zhige* (*Songs of the Exiles*). Mu Mutian (1900–1971), who had embraced French symbolism during his studies at Tokyo Imperial University, now turned to realism in this volume.[107] Witnessing his homeland being brutally exploited by Japanese imperialism, Mu no longer indulged himself in individual moroseness and depression. Instead, his writing style was sharper, more robust, and energetic, focusing on the suffering of the people and calling for national resistance. Leaving Manchuria in 1931, he went to Shanghai and joined Zuolian, the League of Left-Wing Writers. *Songs of the Exiles* was a collection of poems composed during his self-exile. One, titled "At the Fengtian Train Station" ("Fengtian yi zhong"), depicted the image of the SMR zone in the writer's eyes:

This is my homeland,
But my homeland changed unexpectedly in the past decade.
Yesterday it was simple farmland,
Today it filled with the smoke of the factories.
Now, lights in yellow, lights in yellow,
Now, the sound of cars, sounds of cars,
Everywhere, we can see the Chinese in hunger,
Everywhere, Japanese imperialism is so happy.
. . . Looking at the dust in gray and yellow,

I think about the places far away, think about people, think quietly
  with sadness,
Alas, the whistles of the train, is there any one of them that did not
  take over endless blood and sweat,
Alas, is there any one of them that did not bring countless guns and
  swords?[108]

Making the train station an icon of contrast and conflict, Mu stressed the
colonialist tension embedded in his innocent homeland space. Modern
developments—industrialization and urbanization—were overshadowed by the binary between the colonial and the colonized. In a way,
the theme echoed Akutagawa Ryūnosuke's writings on the same subject.

Twenty-seven years before, in August 1910, Japan annexed Korea.
In the years that followed, numerous Koreans left their homeland for
China, either temporarily or permanently. Some travelers provided
a glimpse of Xita in their writings. Among them were Yi Sŭng-hŭi
(1841–1916) and An Hyo-jin (1855–1943), who visited Fengtian in the
1910s. The two men shared a similar background: both were traditional
Confucian scholars who were dedicated to saving Korea by reviving
Confucianism—not just as moral teaching but as the national religion.

Yi, a distinguished independent activist, organized the Korean Confucian Church in the East Three Provinces (Tongsamsŏn Hanin Kong-
gyohoe) in Manchuria. In early 1914, he traveled to Beijing to acquire an
endorsement from the Chinese Confucian Church (Kongjiaohui) led
by Kang Youwei.[109] A poem he wrote en route, titled "Fengtian Province" (Ponch'ŏnsŏn), depicted the West Stupa. Like Ning Xiewan, he
set the scene at dusk. "I watch the horizon far away in a haze / Erected
along with the sunset was Fengtian's West Stupa." The poem then used
many classic allusions to lament ill-fated Confucian Korea and China,
first being conquered by the Qing and then by Japan. Now, the author
noted, with the country of Korea no more and the Qing overthrown
by the revolution, "I have no one to tell my grievance after crossing the
border."[110] Yi never returned to his home country. He died in 1916 in
Fengtian.

Different from Yi's sorrowful mood, An Hyo-jin felt quite joyful when
visiting Fengtian in 1917. He took a train from Seoul—just a few months
before Tokutomi Sohō. Like Tokutomi, he was very impressed by the
West Stupa. "The images of lions and Buddhas were in various forms.
Their strangeness is beyond my words. It was built by the first emperor
of the Qing . . . And this one is called the West Stupa."[111] An was on
his way to Qufu in East China's Shandong Province to meet with the

descendants of Confucius. One of the purposes of his visit was to get the latter's permission to establish a branch of the Confucian Church in his hometown, Jinju in South Kyŏngsang Province. It was said to be the first Confucian Church in Korea.[112] Unlike Yi, who refused to return to colonial Korea, An devoted his whole life to preserving Confucianism—one of the most important sources of Korean tradition—under Japanese rule.

The tone of An's writing is reminiscent of the Korean envoys during the mid-Qing period. He was dazzled by the busy market and the prosperity of the city. But the fact that both scholars, unlike the envoys before them, undeniably paid attention to the historic stupa is itself revealing. The reason was that along with the coming of the railway and new urban development, the Xita area attracted many Korean immigrants in the early twentieth century. A Korean enclave had formed here. When Koreans arrived in Fengtian, Xita was usually the first place they settled. As a result, a new identity, for both the Korean settlers and the space, was gradually taking shape. The subsequent chapters tell the stories.

CHAPTER 5

The Enclave

In 1914, the West Stupa was depicted in a poem by Yi Sŭng-hŭi's poem. Nearly a century later, the structure inspired another ethnic Korean poet. Jin Changyong (K. Kim Ch'ang-yŏng) published a book of poetry titled *Sŏt'ap* (the Korean pronunciation of the West Stupa or Xita). Yi's poem was written in classical Chinese, whereas Kim's was in Korean. The key theme of *Sŏt'ap*, as a literary critic points out, is "the self-recognition of a national and ethnic identity." Such an identity, "obviously distinct from North or South Korean culture," refers to a "new ethnic cultural community: the Korean-Chinese (zhongguo chaoxianzu)."[1] The poems in the collection are a comprehensive reflection on the meaning of being an ethnic Korean, or *Chaoxianzu*, in China, both in the present and in the past. The first poem in the volume, in which the author encounters his grandfather in a dream, seems to echo the bygone era of Yi Sŭng-hŭi:

> Thinking about grandpa
> who appeared in my dream last night
> I came to the West Stupa at dawn
> At the foot of the tower, I listened carefully to its words
> I drank a bowl of soup at Grandma Hyŏnpun's bone soup
>   restaurant
> and bypassed Myohyangsan, Moranbong, and Hallasan
> Grandpa, whom I never met
> was beckoning to me in front, or following me behind
> Suddenly, I turned around and found myself standing beneath the
>   tower
> from the faraway sky, I heard grandpa's voice:
> "Hey son, you have to keep Sŏt'ap in your heart!"[2]

The names Myohyangsan, Moranbong, and Hallasan mentioned in the poem refer both to Korean restaurants in the neighborhood and famous mountains on the Korean Peninsula. In this way, the poet draws a parallel between his morning walk to the West Stupa and his ancestors' migrant journey to Xita/Sŏt'ap. For those who eventually settled in the area, Xita/Sŏt'ap was no longer the name of a Buddhist tower but a symbol of their unique identity. Therefore, the author imagines that his grandfather urges him to remember the West Stupa, their shared identity, forever.

In the first half of the twentieth century, the former western outskirts of Mukden transformed into the center of the new Shenyang (Fengtian) city. A foreign enclave formed in this area. To be clear: Koreans were not the first to settle there but were the ones who became natives. Before 1945, Japanese immigrants occupied the SMR zone and made up the largest share of the local population.[3] Residential buildings, companies, stores, restaurants, schools, parks, shrines, hotels, and other facilities filled the Japanese quarter in a Chinese city. World-renowned conductor Ozawa Seiji was born there in 1935. His father Ozawa Kaisau, a dentist and nationalist, came to serve in the colony and befriended Itagaki Seishirō and Ishiwara Kanji, the two officers who plotted the Mukden Incident in 1931. Picking one character from each of their names, he named his third son Seiji, revealing his deep admiration for their ideals. After the war, most Japanese were repatriated, leaving only empty houses waiting to be occupied by new owners. Some Koreans also went back to the peninsula. Some stayed. Still, a great number moved from other parts of the province—especially from the countryside—to the Xita neighborhood. Hence, an urban ethnic community persisted and a new generation of the Korean diaspora in China took shape.

At the turn of the twentieth century, a few Korean peddlers had moved to the Xita area and made a living selling straw rope and rice sugar. By 1910, according to local memories, there were approximately fifty Korean households in the area.[4] But what caused a surge in the Korean population, as mentioned in the previous chapter, was the arrival of the railways, especially the SMR. The Japanese colonization of Korea pushed Koreans, mainly poor peasants, out of the peninsula to Manchuria. Many took the train and got off in Fengtian. Since Xita was adjacent to the train station while at the same time on the margin of the SMR zone, it provided an opportunity for the new immigrants, who longed both for jobs and an affordable place to live. Prior to 1931, Koreans had already established some small businesses in Xita, such as restaurants and lodges. The Mukden Incident and the creation of Manchukuo further stimulated incoming migration. From 1931 to 1942, while the Chinese and Japanese populations in Fengtian increased about 4.2 times and 8.5 times, respectively, the Korean population had a stunning rise of 11.8 times, to about sixty-six thousand.[5] The majority lived in rural areas and were farmers. Those in urban areas were concentrated mainly in the Yamato District (where Xita was located) and the Tiexi industrial district. Xita and Shijianfang Avenue, with over six thousand Korean residents in 1936, accounted for nearly half the Koreans living in the downtown area.[6]

In his autobiography, literature scholar Zheng Panlong (K. Chŏng P'al-lyong) recorded his arrival in Xita as a five-year-old.[7] It was mid-March 1937 and the weather bitterly cold. The whole family—his parents and six children—left their home in Damyang, Chŏllanam-do on the southern part of the peninsula, journey to Fengtian by train. A Chinese person wearing a padded cotton jacket pointed the way to Xita. "At the time, Xita accommodated nearly a thousand Korean households. Most Koreans were either running small grocery stores or working as laborers." In Zheng's eyes, Xita was nothing but a ghetto:

> Although Xita was located in metropolitan Shenyang, it was remote and marginal. Local residents were either drug addicts, beggars, prostitutes, or coolies, the poorest and lowest class. In late March, dead bodies from either starvation or freezing appeared in the dark corners of the streets. Local people told us that when someone spent all his money on opium, this was the result. During our several days staying in Xita, we saw three or four bodies. My father used to think that those who snuck out of their hometowns were unwilling to return home[because they were unsuccessful] so they had to try all methods to survive. But for those who took the whole family running away from huge debts, how could they return home whenever they want? However, Manchuria did not provide any support for them. . . . Many Koreans were so hopeless that they had to sell their daughters to the Chinese.

Zheng's father, a bamboo craftsman, barely found work in Fengtian. Following the advice of another Korean, the family left the city for a farm in Yingkou. Decades later, Zheng, who had the rare opportunity to study in both China and Russia, became a professor and vice president of Yanbian University. Thanks to his writing, we have a short but vivid account of Xita in the 1930s from the perspective of a new immigrant.

Of course, not all Koreans turned into intellectuals like Zheng. Statistics show that by the mid-1930s, in terms of size the Korean population in Fengtian matched that of the Hui Muslims, one of the largest ethnic minorities there, who had been settled in the city for several centuries. But in terms of those who engaged in elite jobs such as teachers, civil servants, managers, and doctors, the number of Koreans was much lower than that of the Hui Muslims.[8] Understandably, most Koreans, unlike Professor Zheng, did not leave any trace in historical documents, neither in the archives nor in other written sources. While there is much new scholarship dedicated to urban development in the PRC, especially Manchuria, most focuses on the top-down dynamics of city planning and the bottom-up responses of local society. Yet for a micro-level social space like Xita, peoples' daily lives was one of the most valuable (if not the most valuable) aspects of its history. Such a history has its own logic and does not necessarily fit into the state-society dichotomy.

To remedy this, I conducted extensive interviews with local residents—men and women—and cross-examined the oral sources with written ones. With full acknowledgment that memory alone cannot and should not be treated simply as reliable material, I endeavor to lay out a personal reflection of the past, or, as anthropologist Wang Mingke said, a "social memory" that reveals the relationship between individual identity and social structure.[9] All the stories I collected cannot be condensed into one chapter. Instead, my strategy is to highlight the accounts of three or four individuals while adding other voices to supplement the narrative. The individuals were chosen mainly because their stories were relatively constant, spanning Japanese colonization, the early People's Republic, and the post-Mao era. From their shared but diverse experiences, a rich, humanistic layer to the neighborhood space unfolds.[10]

The Ghetto, the Church, and the Korean Network

Che Renxi (K. Ch'a In-sŏk) ran away from home when she was sixteen. Born and raised in Sinŭiju, a border town in P'yŏng'anbuk-do in northern Korea, she used to go to Andong, a Chinese city opposite Sinŭiju across the Yalu River. At the time, crossing the border was not difficult: no passport was needed, let alone a visa. As a girl living in Korea, Che was well educated: she attended both primary and middle school. Her Japanese was even better than her Korean. One day, Japanese recruiters appeared looking for healthy girls. She heard that some girls were being forced to join the "advanced team" and sent to the frontline to serve as "comfort women." Feeling scared about the future, she ran away to Fengtian. It was February 1943; she remembered the point in time clearly.[11]

"That was in the Manchukuo period," Che talked to me at her home in Xita. "I saw a job advertisement in a local newspaper. So, I started my first job as a (document) keeper in a Japanese company." She was very lucky. At the time, a similar staff position in Korea earned about ten to twenty yen per month. In Fengtian, Che earned a monthly salary of fifty yen, enough to feed her whole family. After six months, she wrote home asking them to come to Fengtian. Because her grandfather was reluctant to move, only after he passed away in 1944 did the family—grandma, parents, two younger brothers, and a younger sister—take a train from Andong to join her there in November that year.

In 1944, Song Jishu (K. Song Hŭi-suk) was nine. Unlike Che, Song was born and raised in Xita. Her grandmother brought her dad, two uncles, and an aunt to Fengtian in the 1920s. She remembers that their *kohyang*, or hometown, was in P'yŏng'annam-do, a place thirty ri away from Pyongyang. Her mom died not long after she was born. Her dad, who had only a modest education, ran a small business in Xita. Her uncles and aunt graduated from Xita Elementary, a primary school established for and attended by Korean immigrants. Life in Fengtian had been "OK" (*hai xing*) according to Song, "We were not rich but not too poor either." When she began school, however, the family encountered financial difficulties and had to temporarily leave Fengtian for the countryside in Fushun. A relative there provided humble shelter and the family started to farm, something they had never done before. This kind of situation was quite common for early Korean immigrants. By the time Che Renxin welcomed her family to Xita, Song's family had been gone for a year.[12] The following year, in 1945, Japan was defeated in World War II and most of the Japanese left Fengtian. The Chinese Civil War between Nationalist and Communist forces ensued. After losing her job and struggling to purchase enough grain in the city, Che and her family also moved to the countryside. They went to Manrong, a rural village not far from downtown Shenyang, where many Korean peasants worked and lived. They rented a portion of a field and grew rice for a living.

While criticizing colonialism for depriving the colonized of their rights, many studies also acknowledge that colonizers brought "modernization" to colonies, though not necessarily for the benefit of the natives. Japanese Fengtian could be described as a center of colonial modernity. However, while this urban quarter thrived, many other neighborhoods in the city paid the price. In Xita, Korean memories and documents testify to the poor condition of both the infrastructure and living standards. For example, the *Chosŏn Shinbun* reported in 1936 that roads in Xita were under renovation because there was no sewer system, resulting in years of "stench and unhygienic" conditions there.[13] This echoes Professor Zheng's impression of the neighborhood in 1937 as previously referenced. Che, despite having a relatively good job, had to live in a low, thatched house that required major repair every year. She had to bend halfway to get through the door. "The most difficult thing was going to the restroom," she said. "There was only one public restroom on the entire street. Every time I went in, my eyes stung."[14]

The situation seemed not to improve much. In July 1938, the *Sahae-gongnon*, a Korean literary magazine in Kyŏngsŏng (today's Seoul), published an essay titled "The Memory of Xita in Fengtian." The author lamented the dirtiness of the area. The air was so dry that when the wind blew, it became so dusty that one couldn't move around with his mouth open. Because the neighborhood lacked a sewage system, when it rained the road got muddy and filled with filthy water up to the knee. "When a wagon passed by," the author complained, "it spread dirt all over, and so anyone squeamish would be too disgusted to live there." The tone of the essay, nevertheless, suddenly turned nostalgic when talking about the people. The ladies in Xita wore Korean clothes and local residents shared a sense of community. After living in Xita for a while, the author felt, the place was not that different from "our Korea." He worked very hard and hoped to get some money from home to invest in this place, despite that few Korean actually earned a fortune.[15]

During the Manchukuo period, Koreans enjoyed certain privileges as secondary Japanese subjects. Within the community, people's living standards reflected a hierarchy based on nationality. For example, food was supplied under a ration system. Song explained that residents were divided into three categories. "Those [Koreans] who were naturalized as Japanese citizens got green-colored certificate books. The Koreans received white books and the Chinese got yellow." One of her relatives had a green certificate book and was given white sugar, cookies, and rice every month. "They ran a small factory and lived well. The hierarchy was very strict. The Koreans with white books [got] much inferior [staples], let alone the Chinese with only yellow books. They were even worse off." This was the situation during the final years of the Japanese occupation. Song remembered that rice was always in short supply, and she had to drink gruel quite often.[16]

Print media promoted Xita as a symbol of the Koreans, although for different political purposes. In pro-Japanese media, we see Koreans in Xita mobilizing to celebrate the imperial enterprise of "Japan and Korea becoming one" (J. *naisen ittai*)[17], while in nationalist news outlets we read about the miserable lives of local Koreans. On March 8, 1937, the *Apkil* (Road ahead), a newspaper run by the provisional government of the Republic of Korea in China, published an in-depth report about unemployment among Korean youth in Fengtian. The article compares Xita with the Japanese quarter. "The Japanese neighborhoods are extremely extravagant, but the Korean neighborhoods of Xita and Shijianfang are extremely pathetic." Unemployed Koreans were frustrated, and they looked pale. "In this ghetto, when you open the door, a terrible smell stings your nose." Even though Koreans kept begging for better jobs, the Japanese seldom gave them official positions because they were Korean. "The only way out," the article concluded, "is to beat down the Japanese enemy and the Korean youth should gather under the banner of revolution."[18]

As a Korean enclave, Xita naturally attracted anti-Japanese activists. From time to time, there was an announcement in the news about the arrest of "unruly" Koreans in Xita. "Eighteen people, including Korean Communist leader Kim Rye-ch'ŏn, came to Shenyang from Andong," the *Shishi xinbao*, a Shanghai-based Chinese newspaper reported in 1931. "They were besieged and then arrested by the Japanese police in a Korean inn in Xita. Propaganda in Russian, English and German was found and [the suspects] escorted to the court in Lüshun [Port Author]."[19] In 1934, the *Chosŏn Chung'ang-ilbo* also reported that members of the Ŭiyŏltan (Society of Righteous Martyrs), a radical militia organization for Korean independence, were arrested on September 13 "near Xita in Fengtian."[20] It is quite obvious that the enclave, as a base for the anti-Japanese movement, also attracted Japanese police and spies, to the extent that the name Xita frequently appeared in their secret reports.

Two early intelligence reports deserve special attention. Both documents mention a Korean Christian church on Xita Street. In 1919, the military staff of the Kwantung Army were closely tracking Korean political trends after the famous March First Movement, a nationwide protest against Japanese rule. They reported in October that an American missionary (named Kunmaes) had gone to Fengtian from Pyongyang and given a speech to some 50 Koreans "at a Christian church" in Xita. The missionary prayed for those who had been arrested and imprisoned by Japanese authorities after the protest.[21] Then in 1921, another American came to Xita. E. M. Mohry, a teacher at Soongsil University in Pyongyang, spent two days in Fengtian with his Korean students. He too gave a speech at the Korean church, this time to an audience of about 250 people. Japanese agents reported to the commander of the military police that in his remarks, Mohry had expressed deep sympathy for the Koreans, who were insulted and deprived of their freedom. He said he would take necessary measures for his country and for Korea and hoped his audience wouldn't miss the opportunity to contribute to the revival of their motherland.[22] However, the Japanese reports provided no further detail about the church itself.

As in many East Asian cities, Christian missionaries from Europe or the US had established posts in Mukden/Shenyang as early as the nineteenth century. Most of the missionaries came from Inner China or directly from abroad (Ireland, Scotland, Canada, the US, and Denmark). In Mukden, Scottish missionary John Ross translated the New Testament into Korean while the first group of baptized Protestants in Korea was organized by missionaries who came from Manchuria.[23] But the Korean church in Xita was different—it was a reverse extension of the church nexus from Korea to Manchuria and, from the very beginning, composed entirely of Korean immigrants. During the Japanese colonization, Christian churches helped create a new type of social network for Koreans both within and beyond the peninsula.[24] Xita Church was no exception. Like many others, it acted not only as a social center for local believers but also as a lifeline connecting the immigrants with their homeland.

The early history of the church is not exactly clear. According to church materials, in 1913, about twenty believers began their religious practice in the area. The Female Missionary Society in Sinŭiju then dispatched Kim Dŏk-sŏn and four other pastors to set up Xita Church (K. Sŏt'ap gyohoe).[25] However, according to the 1940 *Yearbook of the Korean Presbyterian Church*, Xita Church was established on April 11, 1914.[26] In any case, 1917 was a more critical moment. That year, construction began on a tall, three-story chapel on the south side of Shijianfang Avenue with a beautiful bell tower at the top. Upon its completion in the 1920s, the brand-new house of worship could accommodate over two hundred people. Claiming to be the biggest of all the Korean churches in Manchuria at the time,[27] it was a new landmark in the Xita neighborhood (fig. 26).

It is one of three religious landmarks in Xita that remains today, along with the Tibetan Buddhist stupa and the small Orthodox chapel in the Russian cemetery. Interestingly, despite Xita Church being located only 340 meters (or 370 yards) east of the stupa and 200 meters (or 218 yards) south of the Russian chapel, local Koreans did not pay much attention to the other two places. "When I was a child," said Song, "the Buddhist tower was still there, and I remember I saw some lamas. But we did not really go to observe that tower since we were Christian." None of my interviewees ever mentioned the Russian clerics who tended the cemetery until the 1950s. One may also wonder how the lamas or the Orthodox priests viewed the Koreans and their church? Sadly, there is no record in any format that I am aware of. For that matter, aside from some experts, few even knew that there once also existed a small Shinto shrine (the Seitō Jinja) and a Japanese Buddhist temple (the Nishi Hongganji) in

堂 會 教 謀 耶 人 鮮 朝 天 奉

26. Xita Church (1932). Yi Hun-gu, *Manju wa Chosŏnin,* 224.

the neighborhood. It seems that different religious spheres rarely mingled in this multiethnic neighborhood, each functioning only within its
own georeligious network.

Xita Church belonged to the network of the Presbyterian Church
of Korea (PCK), which was based first in Pyongyang and then later
in Seoul. This meant all the pastors had to be assigned and sent by the
PCK. The situation was not unlike the royal Tibetan Buddhist temple
nexus in Qing Mukden, where the top lama leader had to be transferred
from Beijing rather than being promoted locally. In 1925, Pastor Paek

Yŏng-yŏp came to Xita Church. Born in Korea but educated in China, Paek graduated from the famous Jinling Theological Seminary in Nanjing. Before coming to Xita, he worked for several churches in Inner China and Manchuria.[28] In 1931, Chŏng Sang-in replaced him as the new pastor. Four years later, dozens of Korean churches in Manchuria organized the Presbyterian Church of Fengtian (Pongch'ŏnnohoe), with Chŏng serving first as vice president and then as president.[29] The Korean church network in Manchuria grew rapidly, establishing a theological seminary as well as several Bible schools, nurseries, and kindergartens. In 1940, besides Pastor Chŏng, Xita Church also had a minister and seven elders.[30] Despite these developments, Korean Presbyterians in Manchuria maintained close ties with the PCK. The *Kidokkyobo*, the PCK newspaper, regularly supplied church updates from Manchuria, including Xita. In November 1936, it published a short essay written by Pastor Chŏng. In the piece, called "Manchuria in Revival," Chŏng enthusiastically expressed his gratitude for progress in the general social environment in Manchuria as well as in the Korean communities, the gospel mission, and the church.[31]

Again, as in the case of the Tibetan Buddhist temples, the most challenging issue for the Korean church was how to merge with local society. The sole purpose of the church was to serve Korean believers. It never really attracted any Han Chinese, with language being the most obvious barrier. Sure, the number of churchgoers kept increasing, but that number remained a small fraction of the Korean population in the area, much less the entire population. This is not to suggest that the church did not want to root locally. Paek, who was pastor from 1925 to 1931, embraced the idea of localization. Facing the aggravated political tension between China and Japan over the governance of Koreans in Manchuria, he strongly suggested that Korean immigrants acclimatize to Chinese culture, study theology in China, and serve in Chinese communities. In so doing, he believed Korean and Chinese churches could collaboratively solve the governance problem.[32] Yet nothing seemed to get accomplished. In 1945, the year Japan was defeated and Korea resumed its independence, Pastor Paek Ri-ŏn was assigned to Xita. But many Korean immigrants began to leave. Just three years later, Pastor Paek left for South Korea, taking with him all twelve elders and around six hundred followers.[33] By the time Chinese Communist troops took over Shenyang, there were only twenty believers attending church activities regularly. They were led by elder Kim Sŏk-yun, who passed away in 1951. Once Paek left, there was no pastor at the Xita Church for the next thirty plus years.

Among the remaining twenty Christians was Wu Aien (K. O Aeŭn), who later became one of the most respected female pastors and a national Christian leader in China. Wu's father had worked at a hospital found by American missionaries in P'yŏng'anbuk-do. He had to escape Korea because he was sought by the Japanese police for his participation in the independence movement. Born in Manchuria, Wu moved to Fengtian/Shenyang from Changchun in 1940 and immediately joined the Xita Church at age fourteen. "For all my life," she once told a South Korean pastor, "I attended Xita Church only."[34] It was not an ordinary life, for sure.

From Korean Diaspora to Chinese Citizen

East Asia was in great turmoil from 1944 to the early 1950s, and the situation was especially gloomy for the Korean diaspora. They went through the last phase of Japanese rule (1944–45), the Division of Korea (1945), the Chinese Civil War (1946–49), and the Korean War (1950–53). Triggered mainly by the Japanese annexation of Korea in 1910, a great number of Koreans—poor peasants as well as educated elites—had been pushed out of the peninsula to places such as Manchuria, the Russian Far East, Japan, Southeast Asia, and America. Calling it "an unprecedented mobilization of a colonial population," historian Andre Schmid estimates that by 1944, somewhere between 13 to 20 percent of the Korean population were pulled outside the borders of their country.[35] Manchuria, particularly the Yanbian region in southeast Jilin Province, accommodated the largest of the Korean diasporas. By 1945, there were nearly two million Koreans in Manchuria. After World War II, however, every one of them had to make the ultimate decision: whether to stay or return. And if they opted to return, then the even more challenging question was: Where to? North or south of the thirty-eighth parallel—a randomly drawn dividing line made without Korean consent? Pastor Paek and his followers chose to return South, more likely than not, for religious reasons. Yet most of the Koreans in China came from the northern part of the country. Those in Fengtian/Shenyang, including the Xita enclave, were largely northerners, particularly from P'yŏng'anbuk-do and P'yŏng'annam-do. How would they choose?

The policies of the Chinese government had a great impact on their decision-making. When the nationalist government controlled Manchuria from 1945 to 1948, it viewed the Koreans as foreign expatriates who were eventually to be repatriated. Numerous Koreans returned for that reason. In 1948, the Chinese Communists (CCP) took over

Manchuria. Unlike the Nationalists, the CCP provided the Koreans there with flexible options: they could either return as Korean citizens or remain as Chinese citizens with an ethnic Korean identity.[36] Koreans in China, like other officially recognized ethnic minorities, established local autonomous administrations. Yanbian in Jilin Province, the largest Korean enclave, founded a Korean autonomous prefecture. Many other autonomous administrations were installed on the county or township levels. It was a more welcoming policy. In this situation, Koreans' choices were fluid. Some returned first and then moved back again; some, the opposite. In many families, some would decide that it was better for them to go back to Korea, while the rest preferred to stay. After all, the state boundary between China and North Korea was not strictly controlled at the time. In the years immediately following the founding of the People's Republic, transborder movements were relatively easy.

According to official statistics, in the early 1950s, the Korean population in Shenyang dropped remarkably. The first national census, completed in 1953, suggested that around 27,600 Koreans were living in urban and rural Shenyang. This was less than half the number in 1943 or 1944. However, it seems that the population loss occurred mainly in the suburban and rural areas, whereas the number of urban dwellers did not change dramatically. The same census demonstrates that a little over 13,900 Koreans in Shenyang were living in a few central districts. This was almost the same level as in 1936. Over the next three decades, the number of ethnic Koreans in central districts grew only modestly, to 21,850 in 1985, compared to a 3.7-times jump (or over 51,100) in the suburban population in the same period. In all the census reports taken by the PRC, the ethnic Koreans living downtown were largely concentrated in two adjacent districts: Heping (previously Yamato District, where Xita is located) and Huanggu.[37]

Che decided to stay because she got married in 1947. When she was living outside the city in Manrong, a neighbor introduced her to Li Bingxun (K. Yi P'yŏng-hun), a young Korean doctor. Born in Xita, Li was six years older than Che. His father worked at a rice factory and his mother ran an inn. Their hometown was near Pyongyang in P'yŏng'annam-do. He was the youngest child in the Li family, with two elder brothers and an elder sister. An excellent student, he attended Tokyo Medical College (the predecessor of Tokyo Medical University) in Japan. In March 1945, six months before his graduation, the US military bombed Tokyo and he was summoned home by his father. Upon returning, he opened a private clinic. "As long as you can survive," his father used to say, "it doesn't even matter if your income is low." After getting married, Che returned to Xita in 1949. "I think a large portion of the Xita people were Koreans," Che said, "at the time, I did not speak a single sentence of Chinese."[38]

Song stayed because her family stayed. While they were living in the rural area of Fushun, the Japanese seized their harvest. She remembered how the village head, a Han Chinese, tapped on their floor with a heavy stick to make sure there was no grain hidden underneath. "We had farmed for a year but could not eat rice in the end. Eating rice became a crime. Vegetables were also limited." The Japanese drafted Koreans into the army, including one of her uncles. Some girls were enlisted too. Many Korean families married their daughters in a hurry when the girls reached fifteen or sixteen. "Because once [a girl] gets married, she would not be drafted. I saw it myself that a family whose daughter was drafted cried so hard." Song's family decided they should not live in the countryside any longer. After several days riding on a horse-drawn cart delivering grain, they finally arrived in Shenyang in January 1946. "Life was better after the Japanese left." Song said. Although the family did not live in Xita, she took a bus to the enclave every day to attend a Korean middle school. Established in 1948, it was one of the first Korean middle schools in Shenyang. During the Korean War, her father bought many clothes for their relatives in P'yŏng'annam-do. "They were bombed by the US and lived pathetically." Throughout her life she only went to North Korea once, when she was six. The family gradually lost contact with their relatives there. Influenced by her Christian father, Song began to go to church.[39]

For Che, the 1950s were a better period in her life. After the socialist transformation campaigns,[40] all the private businesses in Xita, such as grocery stores, rice factories, or inns, became state-private cooperatives.[41] Her husband was assigned first to a Korean hospital and then transferred to a hospital for women and children in the Shenhe District. Being an experienced doctor was highly prestigious. Dr. Li Bingxun earned a monthly salary of 180 yuan, compared to 28 yuan for an entry-level (Class 1) factory worker or 80 yuan for a top-level (Class 8) worker. In addition, the state provided him with pork, cigarettes, rice noodles, and other privileged commodities. Aside from occasionally assisting the resident committee, Che did not have to find a job. But she was busy at home, like many housewives in China in the period. "I did all the housework," she pronounced with a sense of pride. "My husband was a nerd, he cared about nothing but studying. He didn't even know how to hammer a nail. He had a lot of books. But when we moved to a new home, all he said was 'Do not crease my books' and did not even lift a finger." He loved clean clothes and changed his shirts every other day.

She washed, starched, and ironed them. Their first three children were born, respectively, in 1948, 1950, and 1955, all daughters.[42]

Shenyang attracted ethnic Koreans from other places. In 1952, Jin Yukui (K. Kim Ok-kyu) lost his father. Originally from P'yŏng'anbuk-do, his father had hoped his son would be a peasant. But born and raised in Xinbin County, 170 kilometers (or 106 miles) east of Shenyang, Jin was unwilling to quit school. "I took classes in a Han middle school whenever I had time," he explained. "In this way, I learned my Chinese." Jin was fourteen when his father died and had only a vague memory of the Japanese. But he remembered how his family was threatened by the Nationalists because his father once delivered supplies for the Communists. After the land reform, his family got three mu of a water field and eight mu of a dry field,[43] along with a wardrobe, a house, and a small hill. After his father passed away, his mother sold the water field and the house, entrusted the hill and dry field to a relative, and took the children and the wardrobe to rural Fushun, where Jin's uncle was the leader of a Korean agricultural commune. On the journey, he saw a train for the first time. The best part of the move was that Jin could continue his studies. In 1956, representatives from a technical school in Shenyang came to his village to recruit workers. Jin passed the test. "The tuition was free. But I still needed to pay for my own trip and living costs. So, my mom and I picked *doraji* [balloon flower root] on the mountain, looking for purple flowers everywhere. Only one out of 10 jin of original doraji could be sold to the market, and the price was merely 0.5 yuan per jin.[44] That was how I got to Shenyang." Two years later, Jin graduated from the Shenyang Metal Production Plant technical school. He joined the plant as a Class 1 worker, with an initial salary of 28 yuan per month. A year later, his monthly income increased to 32 yuan. He did not live in Xita at first because the factory provided dormitories in the Tiexi District. But he would take a bus to Xita whenever he missed the taste of Korean rice cake. "There were also self-organized study groups in Xita, and I joined the Korean literature club."[45]

However, for Korean Christians the 1950s were the beginning of a period of suffering. Because Pastor Paek and the others had taken the real estate deed for the Xita Church to South Korea—an enemy state of the PRC—the remaining believers were unable to prove that the church had actually been funded collectively. Tagged by the authorities as "enemy property," the church building was confiscated and converted into a Korean Cultural Center. The ground floor was later renovated as a kindergarten and the second floor used as an activity hall. Wu, Song, and other Korean Christians had to go to a Han Chinese church, praying together—perhaps for the first time—with local Chinese Christians. "I did not understand [sermons in Chinese]," Song said, "so I just followed others to worship."[46] Xita Church had de facto cut off its ties with the PCK. So did all the churches in China—Protestant and Catholic alike—that had been part of foreign orders. In the heyday of the Korean War, Chinese Christian leaders launched the "Three-Self Patriotic Movement," declaring that all churches in China be self-governing, self-supporting, and self-propagating.[47] The movement eliminated foreign influences in Chinese Christianity while putting church affairs under the direct supervision of the state.

In 1953, Wu and Song went to Beijing to study at the newly founded Yanjing Union Theological Seminary, one of only two official seminaries in China.[48] Three years later, Wu graduated with a college degree and went back to Shenyang. Song, who was a high school student when she started the program, completed preparatory courses. Just as she was ready to begin college-level theological training, the program was shuttered and all the students sent to the Beijing Eastern-Suburb Farm. "Other than the teachers and students from the seminary, the farmworkers there were either 'right-wing' *[you pai]* or 'objects of transformation' *[gai zao dui xiang]*." The two terms, in Mao's period, referred to politically subaltern groups who needed to be "corrected" and "educated" through labor works. Song was assigned to a poultry team. In 1958, the state launched the Great Steelmaking Campaign, a core component of the Great Leap Forward. Song worked with furnaces in the evening after taking care of chickens and ducks during the day. "I had worked there for three years," she shared about her Beijing experience, "then I was the first among the farmworkers to leave because [the authorities] considered that I am an ethnic minority." Now fluent in Chinese, Song returned to Xita in 1959. The next year, she married another ethnic-Korean Christian. Upon returning, she found that Wu had reorganized the Korean Christians and resumed their activities. Without their own church, they borrowed some space from a nearby Baptist church to continue practicing.[49]

Every Chinese who lived through the late 1950s and early 1960s was deeply impacted by the Great Leap Forward. The radical socialist experiments of the campaign led to a series of disastrous socioeconomic failures, including the Great Famine from 1959 to 1961. How did Xita residents endure this period? Song remembered that the most pressing issue "was not that we didn't have grain but that we didn't have much nonstaple food. Each individual got only half jin [250 grams] of meat [per month], and I had to line up for a long time to purchase cabbage."[50] Official accounts freely admit that "during the GLF . . . the supply of nonstaple food shrank to the so-called 'six items': three liang [150 grams] of cooking oil, two liang [100 grams] of vinegar, one jin [500 grams] of soybean oil, a half jin [250 grams] of soy sauce, and a half jin of fish per

person per month, and two liang of vegetables per day. . . . In 1960, only a
small quantity of meat, eggs, and rice noodles were provided to residents
on the holidays." The quality of food also dropped significantly. In 1960,
an average Shenyang resident got merely 126.5 kcal from nonstaple food
per day, down from 262.7 kcal in 1956.[51] Song's first child was born in
1961, "the hardest year." It was not until her second kid was born in 1962
that "the situation got slightly better."

To my surprise, all the seniors I interviewed said that while it was
a "very difficult moment," they were "treated favorably" (zhao gu) as
an ethnic minority. Song told me, "[The state] treated our Chaoxianzu
favorably, providing us with two jin [one kilogram] of extra rice per
person per month."[52] Jin provided more background information on
the food rationing system. During the "difficult years," a nonworking
individual received only twenty-six to twenty-eight jin of grain every
month. A male worker got forty-four jin. Since Jin's job required heavy
labor, his monthly supply was fifty-five jin. After he got married in 1960,
he managed to transfer his wife, also a factory worker, from Fushun to
Shenyang. Normally, the allotment for a female worker was less than that
of a male. But considering her ethnicity, "[the state] set up her ration at
forty-four jin." In addition, the pair each received three jin of fine grains
every month. "So, in those years we did not really suffer from hunger."[53]
Mr. Li Yiming (alias), a teacher at Xita Korean Middle School, said
"our Chaoxianzu benefited from the state's ethnic policy. We had more
fine grain than ethnic-Han. In my impression, we rarely ate wowotou
[steamed corn bread]. The worst scenario was sorghum or wheat, but
we had more rice. During the difficult years, we cooked mixed grains."[54]
Other interviewees also recalled being given extra grain as Chaoxianzu,
although they remembered the exact amount differently. Bian Shihong
(K. Pyŏn Si-hong), the former head of the Korean Cultural Center,
suggested it was "probably two jin."[55] Jin Dayuan (K. Kim Dae-won), a
retired staffer from the Chaoxianzu Department Store, claimed that "the
state took care of us and gave us four to five jin of [extra] rice per person
per month."[56] Viewed today, that amount of rice seems trivial. But for
these seniors, it was a proud episode as an ethnic minority in socialist
China. It was also one of the rare moments that they highlighted their
Chaoxianzu identity during our conversations.

The Family and the Boundary

In 1958, Che went to work again. In the first decade of the People's Republic, the urban economy developed rapidly. Shenyang, at a core of
China's heavy industry, expanded its labor pool and mobilized as many

human resources as possible to build a new state and society. In this context, female laborers were regarded as a pillar of the grand movement. Socialist Dong Yige suggests that to the leaders of the early PRC, mobilizing women to join the Great Leap Forward meant two things. First, "a significant portion of the young women who had already been working outside the home should substitute for their male counterparts." Song's case fits this category. Second, for housewives like Che, who had no formal job "but made up the majority of the urban women's population, their tasks now were to join production or collectivized social reproduction."[57] Many family functions were collectivized so housewives or other dependents could serve in the newly created public space.

The Xita subdistrict, as a grassroots-level administration, also established many factories, restaurants, stores, and kindergartens. In 1957, the number of people with formal employment in Xita was double that of 1949.[58] Since the children were sent to nurseries or kindergartens, the housewives worked outside the homes. For Che, it was not compulsory but her own choice. "Even ladies in their fifties served as babysitters at nurseries," Che said. "I felt bored staying alone at home." She then found a job as a proofreader at a small printing house. Despite her limited oral skills, Che read Chinese. But she did not feel she was sufficiently prepared for her role. Two years later, with the help of her husband, she transferred to the Institute of Urban Design as a document keeper—the perfect job.

In 1963, however, a family crisis occurred. The year before, Che's mother-in-law had returned to Pyongyang to live with her sister-in-law, who had married a North Korean. She now requested that her son, Dr. Li, join them. "Because I gave birth to three girls, my mother-in-law did not like me anymore," Che explained. Her husband took their two oldest daughters with him to pay a visit, leaving the youngest one with Che. It was the first time he had been to Korea. Sometime later, the eldest daughter wrote a letter saying she wanted to return. Che decided to go to Pyongyang to check on them herself. She entrusted her youngest daughter to a friend and snuck into North Korea, without asking for leave from work. "I thought the trip would take me no more than a week. Therefore, I went to North Korea illegally."

In the 1960s, trespassing along the Sino-Korean boundary was risky because the border was under increasing scrutiny. But having been born and raised in a border town, it was what Che was familiar with. "I first arrived at Dandong [a new name for Andong] and followed the mountain road to the upper stream. It was summer, the Yalu River was narrow. The water on the Chinese side was also shallow, one could wade to an island that belonged to North Korea. The river was deep on the Korean side. There I took a boat [to the other side of the river bank]."

Only after arriving at Pyongyang did Che realize how serious the situation was. Her mother-in-law and sister-in-law were urging her husband to marry a twenty-nine-year-old North Korean girl. There was great tension in the family. "My mother-in-law provoked me," Che recalled. "After a while, I finally thought it all through. I said to my husband: 'OK, marry her if you want. I am going back.'" Because she had gone to Korea illegally, she had to return to China the same way. This time she found a helper in Sinŭiju, her hometown. On a dark night in November 1963, Che took a boat to the middle of the Yalu River, disembarked, and then waded through cold water into China under the Yalu River Bridge. "It was very hard. If you got caught, you would be severely punished. Not many people dared to do so. But I was young and I knew someone, so I was not afraid."

During her journey home, Che believed her husband would never come back. When she opened her front door, to her surprise she found him waiting for her. Dr. Li, too, had crossed the border illegally. But he had picked another route in Changbai County and arrived home even earlier. "My mother-in-law did not want me to return. She said my husband would follow me if I did." After all, a mother knows her son. Since then, members of Li's original family have lived separately in the two countries, and they have rarely crossed the Sino-Korean boundary again. In one way, the boundary divides the family; but in another, families and individuals were not passive receivers of the division. They also manipulated the boundaries, and in so doing, they kept redefining the meaning of a border.

The crisis was solved—but not without a price. Che lost her job because she had been absent for no reason for several months. At first, Dr. Li did not want her to work. Nevertheless, she took another position at a subdistrict-run factory once again as a document keeper. The next year, the couple's fourth child was born: this time a boy.[59]

Living in Mao's China

During the 1960s and '70s, the infrastructure in Xita remained generally shoddy. In industrial cities in the early PRC period, city planning served the sole purpose of developing industrial enterprises.[60] Thus, the Shenyang government prioritized infrastructure buildings in Tiexi District, where most of the state-owned factories were concentrated. Compared to the brand-new, Soviet-model "workers' villages" in Tiexi, where numerous three-story concrete apartment buildings were erected,[61] most of the houses in Xita were still single-story, brick-and-tile, low-quality structures. A family's living space was modest in size (some 30 square meters, or

322 square feet, according to one estimate), and the alleys were cramped. With limited funds, the municipal and subdistrict administrations had to prioritize basic projects related to food and hygiene—installing drinking water pipes and building grocery stores and public restrooms. The official records of the Real Estate Bureau in Heping District in the 1960s show that most years the bureau's main tasks were repairing and redistributing the existing residential buildings rather than adding new ones.[62] Take the year 1962 as an example: the bureau spent 1.02 million yuan (or 30 percent of the total investment) tearing down and rebuilding dilapidated houses (with a small community in Xita as the main project), 1.31 million (or 38.5 percent) on major repairment; 238,000 (or 7 percent) on maintenance, 663,000 (or 19.5 percent) on the heating system, 102,000 (or 3 percent) on the electric system, and 34,000 (1 percent) on the sewer system.[63]

By the 1960s, most families in Xita had installed running water in their houses, although they still had to share public restrooms. But the hardest part, it seems, was heating. While in some parts of the district there was heating system, in Xita, coal was the sole source of energy. Since coal blocks were expensive, most families could only afford crushed coal. A coal yard sat right beside the Buddhist tower, and every family purchased crushed coal from there. "On the weekend, all of us went to buy coal," recalled Song, "each time we bought 1,000 jin." Che said in her interview, "There was no delivery service, so I had to borrow a wheelbarrow, push it to the tower, and push back." But that was only the beginning. To make crushed coal usable, one had to mix it with sand and water, shape it into blocks, and dry it. The process is called *da meipizi*. "Every family had to da meipizi in the fall in order to have heat in the winter," Jin explained, "but it was difficult to burn." Both Song and Che remembered how they had to use blowers to dry the coal mixture. "Alas, don't even mention it," Che lamented. "I got a headache whenever I thought about the work. I had to purchase sand and da meipizi myself on Sunday. And it was so slow to get them actually burning."

That said, as an ethnic enclave, the neighborhood had some remarkable developments, for example in education and medical care. In the 1960s, Xita had both a Korean elementary school and a Korean middle school, separate from their Han Chinese counterparts. Korean was assigned as the teaching language. Teachers and students followed a curriculum designed by educators in the Yanbian Korean Autonomous Prefecture. Li Yiming, who attended the Xita Korean Elementary School in the 1960s, explained:

There were nearly 60 students in my class and every grade had about seven classes. The whole school accommodated two thousand kids, the overwhelming majority of whom were from local families. At the time, China had not yet established diplomatic relations with South Korea [so we did not have South Korean textbooks]. Nor did we use North Korean textbooks despite that it was also a socialist country. Instead, we used textbooks compiled in Yanbian. We studied Chinese too. But unlike your [Han Chinese] language textbook, which is called *Yuwen* [i.e., literal language], ours was called *Hanyu* [i.e., Han language]. The Hanyu course was half in Korean and half in Chinese. All other courses were in Korean.[64]

The Korean Middle School had branches in other districts and was later renamed Shenyang No. 1 Korean Middle School.[65] It was one of the most elite schools in the entire province. The state-owned Korean Xinhua Bookstore was also in Xita, the only bookseller in the city supplying textbooks and other reading materials to Korean students. In addition, a public health system covered the entire city, including the subdistrict. A Korean health center, which was later converted into an ethnic-Korean hospital, was established in Xita.[66]

But for the residents, Korean and Han alike, the most important institution in their daily lives was the Ethnic-Korean Store (Chaoxianzu shangdian), a state-run shopping center converted from a co-op. In 1959, the Ethnic-Korean Store was renamed the Xita Street Store, supplying groceries, nonstaple foods, clothes and shoes, daily necessities, and home appliances to the locals. In 1962, the municipal government erected a two-story building, with 1,200 square meters (more than 12,900 square feet) of shopping space, and transformed the Xita Street Store into the Shenyang Chaoxianzu Department Store.[67] Further, in 1964, the nonstaple food section was separated and became an independent food store.[68] Although the two shops featured Korean-style foods and daily supplies, attracting ethnic Koreans from all over Shenyang and even nearby cities, they were also regularly frequented by Han Chinese customers. According to Zhang Liming, a retired Shenyang Municipal Bureau of Commerce official, the reason was that government policy under the central-planning economy granted more importance to ethnic minority communities. That meant the materials supplied to the Shenyang Chaoxianzu Department Store were relatively more stable in terms of both quantity and variety. The store became one of the commercial hubs in the downtown area. "You see," Zhang said, "it was the only store in the entire city that was named after an ethnic minority. We do not have a store named Ethnic Hui or Mongol. This shows how unique the Chaoxianzu store was."[69] There were also several Korean-style restaurants in the neighborhood; Xita Cold Noodle (K. Sŏt'ap daenaengmyŏn) was the most popular one. Li's father was one of the first cooks at the restaurant. "He was quite famous in the neighborhood. Everyone knew him. Once a North Korean art troupe visited China and the Korean embassy invited my father to make *naengmyŏn* for them. At the time, over 90 percent of staff were ethnic Koreans, and the taste was also much better than it is now."[70]

Observers easily misunderstood the demographic composition of Xita. Even local Korean residents had the impression that ethnic Koreans made up a larger or equal share of the demography. For example, Li guessed that the local population was "probably half (Korean) and half (Han)."[71] But the government census shows that this was never the case. In 1964, the entire population of Xita totaled 16,322, with roughly a quarter or 4,400 ethnic Koreans.[72] The demographic ratio altered slightly over time. In 1982, the total number of registered residents was 21,041, with 15,866 (or 75.4 percent) Han Chinese and 4,676 (22.22 percent) Chaoxianzu. In other words, the Korean characteristics of the space were purposefully highlighted by the socialist policies of the early PRC. The reason many exaggerated the size of the Korean local population was probably because most Chaoxianzu families tended to stay together instead of mixing with Han Chinese families.

In the 1960s and 1970s, Chinese people's living conditions were largely lacking. Although life in urban areas was much better than in the countryside, material supplies were quite limited compared to later decades. Working people's salaries remained low, increasing only slowly. In addition, everyday commodities, such as pork, cooking oil, grain, and cloth could only be purchased with special coupons at a fixed amount. The pricing system remained relatively stable. For example, from 1952 to 1980, the price of soybean paste in Heping District was fixed at 0.08 yuan per jin, tofu stayed at 0.02 yuan per jin, locally produced cigarettes at 0.31 per pack, soy sauce went up a little from 0.10 to 0.11 yuan per jin. Other prices also changed only modestly. Over twenty-plus years from 1957 to 1978, pork went up only from 0.73 to 0.87; beef, from 0.62 to 0.73; eggs, from 0.76 to 0.92; white sugar, from 0.75 to 0.83; and apples, from around 0.33 to 0.35. The commodities experiencing the highest inflation were fish and liquor (*baijiu*), with fish increasing 25 percent, from 0.40 per jin in 1957 to around 0.50 in 1978, and liquor increasing from 0.95 to 1.25, a 32 percent jump.[73]

"There is nothing one cannot deal with," Song repeated when talking about her living standards in the 1960s, "it all depends on how you plan." Upon returning from the farm in Beijing, Song took a job at a local factory, with an initial salary of thirty-two yuan per month. She and her husband, also a worker, lived with her mother-in-law and brother-in-law, both of whom were homebound due to illness. Every morning, she got up at 5:00 a.m., cooked lunch for the whole family, and then left home to take the streetcar to her factory on the south side of the city. Both of her children attended the nursery run by the factory, so "I wrapped up my babies with a cloth and got on the streetcar. The car was extremely crowded during rush hour. I brought wowotou (steamed corn bread) for lunch, and sometimes it was stolen from me in the streetcar." On rainy days, she covered the kids with a raincoat and carried them through flood waters that reached as high as her calf. When she got off work, Song did all the housework; "nobody helped me." After dinner, she had to prepare meals for the next day. "I went to bed at 10:00 p.m. at the earliest."

"Our living standard was third class," Song said. "There were some families who were doing good. I had some neighbors who were Class 8 workers [top-ranked workers whose salary was eighty yuan per month]. But even they ran out of money and borrowed from others. I never did that." The key was planning. "I took charge of the house money. [When we got our paychecks], I saved a certain amount for the kids' medical cost, some for pocket money, I set aside money for treating guests, and gift money for relatives. Then I divided the rest into four amounts and spent one of them each week. A budget must be strictly kept. In so doing we saved enough money to buy a sewing machine and watches. I made all the clothes for my children. We saved fish coupons and meat coupons for the holidays and birthdays and did not eat meat on normal days." When there were guests visiting the house, she invited them to the cold noodle restaurant. "The whole of the 1960s were like that. One has to adjust with his time."[74]

When the Cultural Revolution began in 1966, Che's family situation suffered a free fall. Dr. Li was denounced by jealous colleagues for his experience studying in Japan. Refusing to admit his "crime," he was pushed down the stairs and left half paralyzed. Che took care of him for the next six years until he passed away in 1973. At the time, Che herself was transferred from an office to a workshop doing physical work. Their second and third daughters joined the "sent-down youth" and left home, with only their eldest daughter and son staying with them. The whole family lived on her twenty-six yuan monthly salary for several years. "My working hours were from 8:00 a.m. to 5:00 p.m. But oftentimes we had to do overtime work as volunteers. That was even harder than our daytime work. In that case, I went home at 9:00, even 10:00 p.m."[75]

Her husband's doctor tried to persuade her to give up on him since any effort was unnecessary and medicine too expensive. Che refused, saying her husband must be cured no matter the cost. "I got the prescription from the doctor, picked up the medicine from the drug store, and gave the injections myself." To pay the high medical bill, she sold the sewing machine and other items. But that was not enough. She ended up with a debt of 500 yuan and had to find more ways to earn money. On Sundays, she bought pollock from the urban market and went to the countryside to exchange them for rice. "I know [private trade] was not allowed, but it is better than stealing or robbing." The situation got slightly better when her eldest daughter started to work. "With two salaries and a five-yuan bonus for each person each month, the family income was 62 yuan. Every month, we took 20 yuan to pay our debt. I also did knitting and sewing work to earn some extra [but small] money. In those years, I slept only five hours a day."[76]

During the Cultural Revolution, all religions suffered under the hostile attitude of the state. Wu, as the only clergy for the Xita Church, was an "object of transformation" and forced to do work at a factory, together with thirty-plus Christian, Buddhist, Daoist, and Catholic clergy. "She was beaten by the Red Guards," Song said. "After that her health was never good." All Bibles were confiscated, along with other religious and even foreign language books. "Christians like us dared not get together. When we met, we did not talk much. All we could do was pray at home, silently."[77]

Being a Christian was a social burden for Song too, yet she had a good reputation at her factory. The secret to her success was that she matched if not outdid the efforts of her male counterparts in the workplace. "Ever since I returned from the seminary, I engaged in the hardest labor work, first in a subdistrict-run factory and then in a car steering wheel factory. I did whatever was assigned to me. During the Cultural Revolution, the trucks could not come into the city [to deliver the materials] due to the martial conflicts. We had to use wheelbarrows to deliver the materials ourselves. I learned how to push one by following what others did. Like all the other workers, I brought wowotou as lunch, drank tap water, and sat on the street curb to rest. There is nothing one cannot deal with." Once, the workshop director asked her to learn how to hammer from a skilled worker. "The master was from Shandong and he would scorn you if you did it wrong. So, I told him, 'Please teach me how to hammer since I never have.' The master taught me patiently, little by little." Later on, Song was promoted to workshop director. "Alas, that was not an easy job," she said. "Many lads had returned from the Send-Down Movement. They did not listen to you and were difficult to govern." Workers in her workshop took one of the two shifts in turn, but Song took both every day. In order to clean the furnaces, she wore thick cotton uniforms even in summer. "Because I set an example, young workers also worked hard. Therefore, our workshop always completed the tasks with extra productivity. When the factory elected 'March-Eighth Red-Banner Holders' [an honorific title for women who had extraordinary achievements], I won the first prize of course. But I never took the whole bonus home, only a portion of it. I bought candies for all the workers in my workshop to encourage them [with the rest of the money]."[78]

Holidays were the happiest moments during these hard years. For Koreans in Xita, the most memorable holidays were not the traditional, ethnic ones but the national ones. Li said the most celebrated holiday for the Chaoxianzu in Shenyang was International Children's Day on June 1 "The adults gathered in Beiling Park. They ate rice cakes and we children ate eggs and popsicles. That was fun. I even keep a photo of me holding an egg at the park."[79] I thought it was just his personal opinion until I read the *Shenyang Chaoxianzu zhi* (Gazetteer of Ethnic-Korean in Shenyang), which lists the "Spring Tour on June 1st" as one of the "traditional holidays," along with the Spring Festival, the Lantern Festival, the Mid-Autumn Festival, and others.[80] For Che, the most entertaining holiday was International Women's Day on March 8. "Once a year, the Korean female workers in my factory got together at someone's home. We ate and chatted overnight. Only women over forty were welcomed, and we did not invite young girls." Seeing from this perspective, state and daily life, again, infiltrated into each other and merged together. In addition to the national holidays, the Chaoxianzu in Xita also celebrated family holidays like *chanch'i* (the one-hundredth-day celebration of a newborn), *handol* (the one-year birthday), or *hwan'gap* (the sixtieth birthday). But these were limited to the private realm. Other traditional customs, such as ancestor worship, were practiced by non-Christians. Che's husband was not a Christian, but he did not worship his ancestors either.

Jin moved his family to Xita as late as 1970. During the Great Leap Forward, he brought his mother to Shenyang. His mother, like most Koreans in her generation, had only slept on a Korean bed-stove and was not accustomed to a normal bed. So, he moved several times trying to find a house with a bed-stove. But he eventually chose Xita due to another issue. "My biggest concern was that my children had almost forgotten how to speak our native language. [Korean] schools in Xita were famous for their studious environments." He and his wife raised four children. When they moved to Xita, their eldest son was six years old. Many Choaxianzu workers in the Tiexi District decided to live in Xita, rather than in workers' villages near their factories, for the same reason. Finding an empty house in the area was not difficult since many youths had been "sent down" to the countryside. Jin bought a single-story house with two rooms located right across the street from the Chaoxianzu

Department Store. Two years later, the government tore down the old houses in their area and replaced them with a new, three-story apartment building. The Jin family moved into one of the apartments, "it was sort of like the Pyongyang Buildings in the neighborhood."[81]

The so-called Pyongyang Buildings or P'yŏng'an Buildings was the nickname for the first apartment buildings in Xita. Many of my interviewees mentioned a few three- or four-story apartments erected in the early 1970s. Yet they do not agree on what exactly the nickname was: Pyongyang or P'yŏng an. What they do agree on was that these structures were the best residential houses at the time. The interiors were Korean in style and suited for Korean needs, probably taking after residential buildings in Pyongyang. The most striking feature was that every unit had a Korean-style bed-stove. Unfortunately, I do not know what the buildings looked like since they were all replaced by newer buildings in the late 1980s. I failed to find anyone who had lived there, nor did I find any photos of the buildings. But the Jin family provided a description close enough to the actual Pyongyang Buildings. The apartment they moved into was also in a concrete-and-brick building. A kitchen and a restroom had been installed in the apartment, although gas was not yet the source for fire and heat. The residents still burned coal.

Every family had a storage room on the first floor to preserve their kimchi in winter. Making kimchi was a major family project that required a collective effort. Jin's eldest son, Chunfeng (K. Ch'unbong), remembered the scene vividly. "Every family made their own kimchi for winter. Because we were a big family, we did 2,000 to 3,000 jin (1,000 to 1,500 kilograms) every year." The work had to begin before the start of winter. "My grandma made a list and my father did the shopping: a lot of white sugar, chili powder, garlic, salt, apples, and pears. Then my grandma commanded us to do this and do that. Every child took turns." In late autumn, the sound and smell of chopped garlic filled the entire building. Some families even ground their own chili powder. They carefully seasoned the cabbage and stored it in big vats. It was a lot of work and neighbors helped each other. Two or three days later, the kimchi was ready. "We gave some of our kimchi to other families and tasted that of others. Once, a Han Chinese from the neighborhood dropped by and I asked him to have a try. He took a bite and liked it a lot. When I asked him to take more, he waved his hands saying it was too spicy."[82] In summer when the kimchi was all consumed, the residents cleaned the vats immediately and thoroughly to avoid leaving a strong vinegar smell. Then they waited for autumn. "I had four children helping me do the kimchi," Jin said proudly. "My neighbors always praised them."

Jin's wife, Cui Jingshun (K. Ch'oe Kyŏng-sun), worried about her children's education too, but for another reason. Her original factory cut staff, and she became a "temporary worker" with a lower wage. "I took the night shift, going to work at 5:00 p.m. and returning home the following morning at 9:00 a.m. There was only one [night] bus to the Tiexi District, which was extremely crowded. Fortunately, I had my mother-in-law to take care of my children." With the decrease in the family income, "I made clothes for my kids myself. The eldest one passed them on to the second, then the third. The fourth, my daughter, always complained she had to wear the oldest clothes."[83]

Life in Post-Mao China

The year 1978 marked a new era for the Chinese. Deng Xiaoping, the new leader of the PRC, launched the Reform and Opening-Up (*gai ge kai fang*) policies that focused the country more intently on economic development. But for Wu and Song, the real beginning of the new era happened in 1979. Toward the end of that year, they were told that religious ceremonies were allowed again. "The Han Chinese chapel that we used to go to had been used by local residents as a garbage station during the Cultural Revolution. We cleaned it all up. Nobody had a Korean language Bible except one copy secretly hidden by a Christian." They immediately divided up the labor, hand-copying the Bible paragraph by paragraph, and mimeographing forty-plus hymns. Some engraved the stencil steel board, others oversaw printing, still others did bookbinding, and together they made dozens of copies. "On December 22, for the first time in thirty years, we finally worshiped again. Some forty-plus people participated in the event. Holding the mimeographed book, some of us cried."[84]

The next step was to petition for the return of the church building, which had been converted into a kindergarten and a cultural club. In 1980, during a ball with over two hundred guests, the southeast corner of the main hall on the second floor suddenly cracked. People fled. Determining that the building was hazardous, the local government planned to tear it down. "When we saw the scaffoldings," Song remembered, "some of us rushed into it [the former church] and occupied the place for more than ten days. We would not let it happen." Just as the two parties entered deadlock, an important document from the central government in Beijing was passed on to the provincial government. The document, codified as No. 188, requested all local governments to "return property rights to religious organizations." As a result, the entire church building was given back to the Christians of Xita Church. The kindergarten and club were moved out. "We soon asked a professional to check the building. Surprisingly, nothing was wrong. We simply did some internal renovation and the general structure of the building remained the same." Song believed "it was all God's arrangement."

In April 1981, Wu was ordained as the new pastor of Xita Church. Not only was she the first pastor in thirty-one years, but she was also the first female pastor. Within two months, she baptized sixty-two new members.[85] The next year, Minzu Press in Beijing published the first Korean language Bible since 1949. "The first edition had printed ten thousand printed copies," Song recalled, "because of the kind of paper [they used] was for printing newspapers, every copy was as heavy as three jin [1.5 kilograms]." The Bibles were mainly distributed in three Northeast provinces (Liaoning, Jilin, and Heilongjiang). On July 4, the Xita Church even held a ceremony to celebrate.[86]

Wu asked Song to retire and help her. Song initially hesitated. In China, the retirement age for a woman was fifty, and she was not yet forty-five in 1980. "I was a second-rank worker, and my salary was 40-plus yuan," Song said. "If I retired early, my pension would be minimal. After deducting living expenses, tuition, rent, water, and electricity bills, there was only 20 yuan left from my husband and my salaries. I wanted to send two children to college. Pastor Wu comforted me: 'The church needs you. God will arrange all.'" That year, Beijing issued a policy that any female worker who had engaged in heavy labor for more than thirteen years could apply for early retirement at forty-five and receive 60 percent of her salary as a pension. Furthermore, a new policy later regulated that one year of heavy labor counted as fifteen months of service for a worker. In that case, Song could retire with 75 percent of her salary as a pension. "I finally understood. God had arranged all for me: for all those years I had done hard and heavy work and now my age was exactly forty-five. These [new policies] were all prepared for me to return to the church. Do you think it was just a coincidence? No, it was not." At the time, some smaller village-and-town factories offered her 120 yuan a month if she would work half days as an advisor. "I thought about taking the offer. But I couldn't. God would not allow me. So be it—if we have to drink gruel [live a poor life], let's drink gruel."[87] She retired from the factory and worked full time for the church.

With the Xita Church congregation expanding quickly in the 1980s, there were plans to erect a new, six-story chapel next to the old one. This proved to be much more difficult than Song thought. The twelve ethnic Korean families living next door refused to move. She tried every method, including filing a lawsuit, but still failed to find a solution. It was not until the government started a "shanty area rebuilding" project in the neighborhood that the church-residents conflict was finally solved. The families received compensation from the government as part of the overall rebuilding project. In 1991, construction on the new chapel began and was completed two years later, costing four million yuan. "What I want to say is this: we were able to achieve this not because of our ability but because of God's ability and state policies," Song shared with me. "Pastor Wu used to say, 'I will always be on the right path as long as I do not betray my faith and I do not violate state policy.' She suffered a lot, but she did not complain because it was God's arrangement. For us Christians, faith and state do not contradict each other. Maybe it is hard for you to understand since you are not [a Christian]."

At its peak in the early 1990s, Xita Church had more than 1,700 members. Wu organized several theological courses at Northeastern Seminary for the Chaoxianzu clergy. Altogether 120 clergies graduated from these classes. To cope with the problem that younger generations of Chaoxinazu did not speak Korean that well, the church began to provide Chinese language services for them in 2003, which unexpectedly attracted Han Chinese worshippers. With more Han Chinese joining the congregation, a Chinese language department was established in 2013. In recent years, the number of Chinese members has surpassed that of ethnic-Korean members.

Due to her outstanding contribution to the church as well as the Christians in China, Wu was twice elected vice president of the China Christian Council, the organization representing all Protestant churches in China. From 1988 to 2003, she also served as a national member of the Chinese People's Political Consultative Conference, a political advisory body in the People's Republic. In 1990, under the invitation of the (North) Korean Christian Federation, Wu visited North Korea as a delegate of Chinese Christian. Thinking about Koreans like her parents who escaped Japanese prosecution and took refuge in China, she felt excited to set foot in the country.[88] Under her leadership, Xita Church developed into one of the most renowned churches in China. During our conversations, Song repeatedly expressed her admiration for Wu, her mentor and lifelong friend who passed away in 2016 at the age of ninety-one. "She was a noble person and a miracle of the church in Shenyang."[89]

Che retired in 1981 at fifty-three. When we first met in 2018, she was ninety-two and felt satisfied with her postretirement life. "Why? I worked [in the last factory] for only eighteen years but have received my pension for thirty-eight years. I did nothing but got paid." This, of course, was an optimistic assessment. At the time, with a pension of less than thirty yuan per month, it was still very hard to support the whole family. "My son needed to go to school, so I had to do something." A month after her retirement, she and three friends opened a restaurant called Chindallae (meaning "Korean rosebay"), which purported to be one of the first private restaurants in Xita since the Reform and Opening Up. Che was in charge of the accounting and also did some kitchen work. "It was not easy at all. We did it for one year and could not continue. We did not sign a contract and the landlord stopped leasing the house to us."

"Then I started to sell [Korean] side dishes," Che said. She got up at 3:00 a.m., preparing kimchi, doraji, and many other sides. After loading all the dishes on a tricycle, she left home at 7:00 a.m. and rode to her stall. Her stall was in an alley beside the former SMR train station, then called the Southern Train Station of Shenyang, the exact same station where she had disembarked some forty years before and started a new life. She normally worked for twelve or thirteen hours before going home. "Selling dishes was tiresome but profitable. I worked every day without taking a rest. I could earn 300 to 400 yuan [a month] at least, sometimes 500 to 600 in a good situation." In 1988, she thought she had earned enough. "My son graduated from college, so I quit. From then on I worked no more."[90]

That year, the "shanty area rebuilding" project began. The government replaced all the old houses with modern apartment buildings. While waiting for a new apartment, Che lived with her daughter for a time and visited South Korea for two months. "At the time [China and South Korea] had not yet established diplomatic relations. I got the visa through the British consulate in Hong Kong. I don't like the country. There were many rich people of course, but the poor people were even poorer than here." When the rebuilding project was completed, Che moved back to Xita. She switched apartments for a better one, lived there for several years, and then rented it out. When we met, she was living happily with her son's family, also in Xita. In our final conversation, she apologized for only talking about herself during the interviews. "If my son knew this, he would probably admonish me [for not being polite to a guest]."[91] Che passed away peacefully in 2020.

Jin never stopped studying. He completed a postsecondary degree in machine manufacturing in the 1960s. But because of the Cultural Revolution, he did not receive his diploma until 1986. "At the time I had two choices, either continue being a worker or go to work in an office. A worker got twenty-five yuan as a bonus per month, but office staff only received five yuan. My children were in school and they needed money, so I gave up my option to work in an office." Still, the salary was not that much. He retired early in 1988 at the age of fifty and ran a small restaurant near the train station, serving Korean cold noodles and barbecue. "When I worked in the factory, I did the night shift to earn more money. It was exhausting. But when I retired, I realized that running a restaurant was even more tiring than working in a factory. I got up at 5:00 a.m. to do the shopping at the market and returned home as late as 1:00 a.m. I had to deal with all the administrators, from the local police to the urban management staff and the tax collector. Some of them were hooligans, and I could not afford to disobey them."[92] But he believed it was all worthwhile because three out of his four children went to university. Jin passed away peacefully in 2024.

Being Chaoxianzu in Contemporary Xita

In the post-Mao era, and especially after the "shanty area rebuilding" project, living conditions in Xita improved significantly. In 1992, the PRC officially established diplomatic relations with South Korea, bringing tremendous investment and business opportunities to the ethnic Korean neighborhood, so it prospered further. But for the local Chaoxianzu residents, these changes were not all positive. For example, all my interviewees complained that neighborhood bonds are not as intimate as before. Che said, "Our living conditions are much better now. We all moved into apartment buildings. But I barely know my neighbors, and there is no communication between neighbors." With new immigrants flooding in, the social environment has been corrupted. "There are more liars, and some businessmen sell fake stuff to customers," Jin lamented. "And my old neighbors all scattered." A more serious issue is that many young Chaoxianzu had either departed or lost their Koreanness. Song said that ever since the mid-1990s, a lot of ethnic Koreans have left, seeking opportunities in South Korea, Japan, the US, or coastal cities, and church membership has dropped.[93] "Many food makers left their small businesses to the Han Chinese. The taste [of ethnic food] is not authentic anymore." Political scientist Shih Chih-Yu, in his research in 2000, also found that a great number of young teachers at Xita Elementary School had left. Some of them went abroad, and some took more profitable jobs, creating a challenging issue for Korean education.[94] Other studies reveal that most young Chaoxianzu in Shenyang tend to speak Chinese, instead of Korean, in public and in their daily life.[95]

   On the other hand, the "Koreanness" of the neighborhood was enthusiastically promoted, although in a highly symbolic way. From the late 1980s to the early 1990s, along with the rebuilding project, the local government introduced a new set of names for the streets, alleys, and communities in the Xita area. The names—Yanbian, Yanji, Hunchun, Antu, Dunhua (the streets), Longjing (an alley), Helong (a road), and

Tumen (a residential community)—came from the prefecture/city names of Yanbian, the largest Korean enclave in China.[96] The streets mapped out a Yanbian network in central Shenyang, and the implication could not be clearer. This practice is comparable to efforts in numerous cities in the PRC where streets were named after other provinces and cities to create a sense of national solidarity; for that matter, it is also similar to how Japanese names were once imposed on the streets of the SMR zone to remind people of the metropolitan state. Connecting the largest urban Korean enclave with that of the Korean autonomous prefecture demonstrates Chaoxianzu solidarity in a multiethnic Chinese state. In the newly renovated neighborhood, many shop signs are bilingual, and public street art propagates Korean customs and traditions. The space is undoubtedly Koreanized. But it is also a peculiar combination of two seemingly contradicting phenomena: the increasingly visual "Korean-ness" and its unavoidably degraded authenticity.

But let's not forget that the authenticity of ethnicity (or nationality) is itself an artificial invention in modern times.[97] Just like the meaning of Xita, the West Stupa, gradually lost its original Buddhist connotation over a prolonged history, the significance of being ethnic Korean in China also transformed over the period of a century, into ordinary yet unique daily existences. This kind of identity maintains organic links with its origin through language, culture, food, and customs while distinguishing itself from its origin in accordance with the diversity of human experiences. From a global perspective, this is a theme that is embodied in almost every Korean diaspora society, not only in China, but also in Japan, Central Asia, and the US.

Jin Changyong, whose poem appears at the beginning of this chapter, was born in 1967 in Jilin Province. After graduating from Yanbian University, he first worked as a teacher in his hometown of Ji'an and then quit that job and moved to Shenyang. He lived in several different places, all close to Xita.

He told me how he came up with the idea of writing *Sŏt'ap*, by far his magnum opus. "Once, I drank with a few Korean statesmen at Pyongyang Restaurant in Xita. I mentioned my two motherlands—China and Korea. I said I do not regard only South Korea as my motherland. The [South] Koreans were displeased and left. They had a different understanding of unification than mine. At that moment, I started to think about how to clearly interpret my identity as a Chinese Chaoxianzu in the form of poetry. When I tried to organize all the materials and thoughts, I found that *Sŏt'ap*, or Xita, was a perfect symbol." Jin began publishing this series of poems in the *Changbaeksan*, a Korean language literature magazine in China in 2004, which eventually led to the collected volume published in 2011. "Xita represents a unification that is harmonious," Jin said. "[You can hear] North Korean songs on one side, and South Korean songs on the other."[98]

In the second poem of *Sŏt'ap*, the poet describes the metamorphosis of the space in this way:

> Not many people know about the Life-Prolonging Temple
> It was not merely a Buddhist temple anymore
> On rainy days, the sound of a wooden clapper soaks in raindrops
> The chanting of the monks sounds beautiful under sunshine
> Now the Life-Prolonging Temple transfers to Sŏt'ap
> White doraji flowers boom in its heart
> When all the monks are leaving
> The soul of men-in-white penetrated the temple
> The Buddhist tower was erected in the hearts of passengers
> Now it lies down, turning into a street
> On the street where the West Stupa lies
> White doraji flowers replace the floating incense smoke
> And they give a bright smile[99]

The "doraji flower" and "men-in-white" are obvious references to Korea. The author imagines that Xita, originally a monument to Tibetan Buddhism, has changed into a spiritual monument to the ethnic Koreans. But I would argue that such a transformation was far from linear, nor was it a "replacement." The multilayered symbolism of Xita could not be monopolized by a single group of people. In an era when neither Buddhism, Christianity, nor ethnicity stands for a shared identity in the neighborhood space, the space reveals yet another layer of representation. The new representation is a ritual one, a rite of both contemporary consumerism and the political performances around it. The next chapter unfurls this layer.

CHAPTER 6

The Model

In 1968, the West Stupa was dismantled. The entire project took five months, lasting from May to October. According to the demolition report, the reason for the tear-down was that the ancient tower, after being exposed to heat, rain, and snow for nearly three and a quarter centuries, was "in such disrepair that bricks often fall off from the top," threatening the people and houses nearby.[1] Since the beginning of the century, when with the arrival of the railway a coal yard was set up right beside the tower, the structure had suffered more erosion than the other three stupas. Aside from the antique artifacts that were discovered inside, the only reusable part of the tower was the axial pillar that decorated the top of the stupa. The pillar, which was made of bronze, was removed in its entirety and put on the East Stupa.[2] At the time, it seems no one regarded the shabby building as a precious relic that deserved preservation. For local residents, demolishing the tower did not affect their daily lives in any significant way. Over the next thirty years, Xita was just the abstract name of an urban quarter. The stupa (*ta*) in a place called the West Stupa did not exist anymore, nor did the memory of it.

The year 1968 marked a historic moment in China, when everything in the past was under severe attack. The Great Proletarian Cultural Revolution had reached its zenith. The country's Maoist leaders launched a campaign to sweep away the "Four Olds"—Old Ideas, Old Culture, Old Customs, and Old Habits—categories that the Qing dynasty Buddhist stupa definitely fell into. I'm actually surprised that the stupa was carefully disassembled by professional archaeologists rather than simply destroyed by radical Red Guards. In May, when the project began, it was announced that provincial and municipal Revolutionary Committees would be established, taking over power from the Liaoning and Shenyang governments. In September, the municipal revolutionary committee decided that all middle and high school students in Shen-yang would be "sent down" to the countryside to engage in agricultural production, in accordance with Mao's instructions. More than 144,000 students left their urban families in just a month. In October, when the West Stupa was gone completely, during the twelfth plenary session of the Eighth Party Congress, Liu Shaoqi, the former state chairman, was condemned as an antirevolutionary enemy and deprived of all his titles and duties. People in Shenyang, a city where Liu had led a labor move-ment in the 1920s, also joined in the brutal verbal attack.

Beyond China, revolutions of all kinds were engulfing the globe—anticolonial and anti-imperial struggles against the suppressive world or-der of past centuries. Students in the US, Japan, Europe, Latin America, and other regions vibrantly protested the unjust Vietnam War. Waves and waves of social movements violently rocked the exploited social, political and cultural systems.[3] The old systems also strived for survival. It was the year of the Tet Offensive, the Prague Spring, the My Lai mas-sacre, the assassination of Martin Luther King Jr., the university protests in Japan, the Mai 68 in Paris, the police riot in Chicago, the election of Richard Nixon as US president, and much more. In such a year, the demolition of an old stupa in a small neighborhood in northeastern China would not arouse public interest. But the action, in a peculiar way, composed a tiny spray in the historical tsunami of the global 1960s.

Before and after 1968, Chinese society experienced drastic changes, not just once but at least twice. The first was a socialist transforma-tion that fundamentally reshaped the socioeconomic structure of the country. After the initial revolutionary passion faded, it was followed by an equally impactful market-oriented transformation that began in 1978 and is still ongoing. To what extent we can call it a neoliberal turn is debatable.[4] Yet some aspects of neoliberalism were exemplified in a local place like Shenyang or in Northeast China in general. The Xita neighborhood witnessed, experienced, and adapted to both transitions. In 1998, three decades after its dismantlement, a replica of the stupa was erected in the same location. Once again, the new overrode the old. The demolition and rebuilding of the West Stupa, two seemingly contradictory actions, demonstrated the entanglement of old and new in a constantly changing society.

Throughout the process, Xita and its vicinity have served as a "model" of various kinds in different times. What happened to this micro space and its people during the rise and fall of socialist industrialization? What were some of the gains and losses when neoliberalism and consumerism were introduced here? In chapter 6, Xita and its adjacent areas are used as a lens to probe into the plural transformations of northeastern China from a local perspective. The ethnographic narrative—based mainly on local gazetteers, news reports, personal experiences, and interviews—is more descriptive than conclusive. Since the second transformation is very much ongoing, the features and meanings of the newest layer of this historical space are yet too early to be defined.

A Socialist Space, 1950–78

In 1950, right after the founding of the PRC, the Shenyang municipal government set up a police station in Xita. With two staff, the station took care of civilian affairs in the region. In 1954, the Xita Subdistrict (*jie dao*) was established as one of 124 grassroots administrations in Shenyang. It was the first time that a basic governing body was installed in Xita. From 1959 onward, the "subdistrict" was temporarily renamed the "people's commune" (*ren min gong she*) until the title was changed back in 1978.[5] Although the exact area under its supervision kept adjusting, state power was now rooted deeply in neighborhood-level society.

The early PRC state launched a series of social reforms. One of the most prominent campaigns was the eradication of brothels.[6] According to statistics, in November 1948 Shenyang had 144 brothels, of which 102 (or 71 percent) were concentrated in the Beishi (Northern Market) area near Xita. Out of 660 prostitutes in the city, 407 plied their trade there. After the Communists took over, the government made prostitution illegal, and by 1952, the number of brothels in Beishi dropped to twelve. Then in October 1954, all the remaining brothels were shut down over the course of a night. The prostitutes, most of whom were addicted to drugs and had contracted venereal diseases, were sent to "education institutions" (*jiao yang yuan*) to receive rehabilitation and medical treatment. They also took thought-and-political courses as well as trained in various job skills. After one or two years, most of them found work through the civil affairs department of the municipal government. Many got married. Meanwhile, the state confiscated the wealth and property of the brothel owners.[7] The campaign happened not only in Shenyang, but in all the major cities like Beijing, Shanghai, Wuhan, and Tianjin.[8] It was one of the most highlighted trademarks of social reform in the early PRC.

In 1964, the local government tore down the old houses in Yongyili, where most of the former Beishi brothels were concentrated. The *Real Estate Gazette of the Heping District* recorded that the buildings in Yongyili, after being confiscated by the government, were repurposed as residential housing. But the structure of the buildings was not suitable for habitation: they were crowded, dark, and damp. Most of the rooms were too small and in disrepair. So, the government temporarily removed 170 households and demolished 88 buildings. Over the next eight months, one four-story commercial and residential building and three three-story apartment buildings, all with kitchens, toilets, bed-stoves, and sewer and garbage facilities, were constructed in the loca-tion. The living areas were nearly three times larger—5,813 square meters as opposed to 1,810 square meters. The real problem, however, was how to distribute the new quarters fairly. Since the residents were varied, including "families of military or revolutionary martyrs, staff, ethnic minorities, private house owners, self-employed businessmen, former brothel owners, and the unemployed," and each had their own interests and requirements, the local authority introduced a "democratic review" as an experiment. A committee was set up to first determine the basic principles (e.g., only former residents could move back in), and then ev-ery household participated in a series of meetings to negotiate a possible solution. After ten days and with no less than thirteen rounds of meet-ings, all the households reached a final agreement on the distribution.[9]

Shenyang was the cradle of Chinese industrialization. Connected to the Xita neighborhood by a set of railroad tracks (the former SMR line), the Tiexi District lay at the heart of Shengyang's industrialization. From the 1950s to the 1970s, Tiexi was no doubt the model of urban modernization in socialist China. Through a combination of the initial facilities left behind by the Japanese, systematic financial and technolog-ical support from the Soviet Union, and consistent investment by Bei-jing, Tiexi acquired the nickname the "Ruhr of the East," a comparison to the most advanced industrial region in Germany. It developed into not only the basis of Chinese heavy industry but also an exemplar of a socialist worker community. Within the community, major factories, or *danwei*, were the most critical components of local society. Public goods, such as education, medical care, housing, and a whole range of subsi-dies and social services were provided by the factories rather than local governments. Sociologists called it the "danwei system," or the system of the working unit.[10] As Lü and Perry pointed out, "the working unit was once so essential to daily life in urban China that people would say one could be without a job, but not without a *danwei*."[11]

Xita was not an industrial quarter. Yet the biggest danwei factory in the neighborhood was not an insignificant one—the Shenyang Cotton Mill (SCM) or the former Fengtian Cotton Mill, was established there in 1921 (see chapter 3). Supervised by the municipal government, it was the leading cotton mill enterprise in the province. In 1985, the SCM manufactured 46.1 percent of the cotton products in the city and con-tributed 31.8 percent of the tax revenue from the cotton spinning indus-try.[12] The medium-size, light industry enterprise employed 3,627 workers and staff by the end of that year. Among them was Ji Changjiang, who had lived near Xita for sixty years.

Ji's family story was a typical one among the working class in north-eastern China. His father, Ji Deming, joined the SCM at the age of nineteen in 1952 and spent most his life in the cotton industry. In 1958, the year Ji was born, his father managed to get his mother, who had previously lived in the countryside, a job at SCM.[13] The whole family, therefore, was attached to the danwei. "When I was a child, we lived in the family courtyard of the SCM, which was very close to the factory," Ji began. "There was a factory-run kindergarten and a primary school. I myself attended the SCM Children's Elementary school." Unlike some giant factories in Tiexi, the SCM did not have its own middle school, so Ji attended a public middle school nearby, which he called a "society-run"—as opposed to a "factory-run"—school.

Ji has two siblings, an elder brother and a younger sister. The family lived on the salaries of the two parents while the children were growing up. "At the time, the salary for light industry labor was less than that of heavy industry. For example, a class-two worker in cotton spinning earned thirty-one yuan per month, compared to thirty-eight in heavy industry." According to Ji, the seven-yuan gap was not trivial at all, it could support a family of five with two weeks of side dishes. For more than twenty years, salaries increased only modestly. But under the planned economy, the factory provided a great deal of other assistance. Aside from housing, education, medical care, and a pension, a seemingly small but practical benefit was the shower. Houses in the family courtyard did not have a private toilet in the room, let alone a shower. Yet the factory offered a daily shower service for employees since "the working environment of the cotton mill was quite dirty."[14] And it was open to family members on Sundays. At a time when most urban citizens in northern China had to pay to take showers in public bathrooms (normally once a week), this kind of benefit through the danwei made a real difference.

"Xita was a poor area," Ji commented. "No way the living conditions could compete with that in Tiexi." The giant enterprises in Tiexi provided dormitories in three-story apartment buildings, which were built with Soviet help, for their workers. Xita, in contrast, was merely a narrow street running from north to south. Most people crowded into one-story houses. "I had a Chaoxianzu classmate. His house had only a small space near the door for placing shoes, the rest was a stove bed. We did everything— eating and talking—on the stove bed." There were several shops on the street that Ji and his family often visited. One of the most famous was the Chaoxianzu Department Store. The railroad was an important part of his childhood memories. "We lived very close to the track and got quite used to the noise. A train would pass every other minute, but I fell asleep quickly at night. I was a naughty kid back then. Sometimes I didn't want to walk to school, so I climbed on a slow-moving train and jumped off near school." Asked about the West Stupa and the Xita Church, however, Ji responded that he had no particular memory of either.[15]

When Ji graduated from high school in 1976, he was not sent down to the countryside like his elder brother. The reason was quite unusual. Ji's father, a top-class electrician, was selected as a Chinese "foreign aid" worker to Syria. During Mao's era, workers and technicians in Shenyang were constantly transferred to other places to support local industrial projects. For example, numerous Shenyang workers participated in the Third Front, a defense-related industrialization campaign in the western hinterlands.[16] But the opportunity to go abroad to assist in another third-world nation was rare. Although Ji did not know any details of this mission, upon checking the records of PRC foreign aid, I found that Ji senior was very likely one of the Chinese workers who helped build a cotton mill in Hama in the late 1970s and early 1980s.[17] At a time when most Chinese had never even dreamed about visiting another country, this was considered extraordinarily good fortune and an honor. "For that reason," Ji said, "I took advantage of my father's situation and stayed in the city."

Urban China was experiencing a serious social crisis at the time. By 1978, the sent-down campaign had finally stopped. Millions of sent-down youth returned to the cities and searched for jobs. The unemployment rate skyrocketed. A privileged danwei position was extremely hard to acquire. Although in the danwei system, many young people got their jobs by inheriting their parents' positions, this situation was not guaranteed. Ji was first assigned to a small factory run by a middle school. Shortly thereafter, the Reform began, and the factory was separated from the school. Now responsible for its own finances, the small factory barely functioned. Luckily for Ji, his mother successfully persuaded the director of the SCM to recruit him. "Because my father was in Syria and the director, an old worker, had a good impression of my father, I joined the factory in 1981. But it was very hard." State-run enterprises assumed a great deal of responsibility for easing the job crisis and many second-generation workers, like Ji, were adopted by their parents' danwei. In the same way, Ji's sister, newly graduated from high school, was offered a cotton spinner's position later. "Consequently, four of the five members of my family were working in the same factory," Ji told me.[18]

The Painful Transformation of Shenyang, Post-1978

China's rapid industrialization from the 1950s to the 1980s was only possible under certain conditions. For one thing, the state reinvested as much of the profit generated by workers as possible to expand production while maintaining low labor costs. To compensate for long-stagnating

wages, the state determined the prices of commodities while providing basic public goods via the working units. This is exactly what we
saw with Ji's family. But by reversing the centrally planned economic
structure, the marketization reform created a series of problems in a
society that had been so accustomed to the former system. As a model
of the socialist planned economy, northeastern China in general, and
Shenyang in particular, endured a painful transformation during the
marketization process.

As some scholars have pointed out, when the market-oriented reform
began in the early 1980s, the old system was not replaced immediately.
Rather, many state-run enterprises benefited from both the new market
opportunities that came with reform and the resources provided by the
planned economy.[19] The SCM was such a case. Ji recalled that prior to the
1990s, the factory actually earned a profit every year. "Our factory was
the largest in the province, and the workers enjoyed high-quality benefits.
At one point, the factory even owned a farm and provided workers with
free lunch." Female workers at the factory were famous for their high self-
esteem. "Shenyang was a heavy-industry city and there were many more
male workers than female ones," Ji explained. "With their nice salaries
and benefits, the female spinners in our factory were at a great advantage
in finding a partner. Many wanted a boyfriend in the military because the
social status of a serviceman was even higher than a worker."[20]

The big downturn came in the 1990s. Losing secured resources and
orders, state-run enterprises outperformed in the market. Meanwhile,
the social obligations of the factories prevented them from adopting
more flexible strategies to increase efficiency. The state called for "building big ships," that is, letting larger factories annex smaller ones and, in
this way saving the latter from bankruptcy. Once again, state-run enterprises shouldered major social responsibilities. As a leading producer
in the cotton industry, the SCM annexed several smaller cotton mills in
the city while taking over all of their liabilities. Yet, other than dispatch-
ing some managerial personnel to the smaller mills, nothing changed
structurally. Ji called it "old wine in a new bottle." This, in the long run,
was not sustainable. To make matters worse, cotton sources, previously
guaranteed by the planned system, were no longer available. The factory
had to purchase raw cotton on the open market. Since northeastern
China was never a major cotton producer, the SCM was easily outbid
by its counterparts in the south. Gradually, the enterprise fell into in-
solvency. More and more workers were laid off. "My workshop used to
have more than two hundred workers," Ji lamented. "In the end, there
were fewer than one hundred."

Ji did not lose his job since he was a seasoned worker. But many of his
younger or less experienced colleagues were let go. The enterprise either

persuaded them to retire early (with a small pension) or be paid a lump sum to "buy out" years of service. He remained there until 2011, when the SCM was privatized. "I did not feel comfortable. But what could I do? The factory was not mine anymore and my feelings had changed. Before I felt like a master [of the factory] and now I was just an employee. I had to obey whatever the boss said. After the privatization, I got no benefits other than salary. Well, how could I request benefits when the enterprise had no money at all?" Ji eventually opted to be "bought out" and received 97,000 yuan (or 12,000 USD) for his thirty years of service. His sister had done the same thing a few years before. "For an electrician like me, it was not difficult to find a new job. But for a spinner, it was hard to say. My sister was working as a cleaning lady, like many of her coworkers."

The old system collapsed and countless workers were suddenly pushed out of the danwei. They lost their jobs, social benefits, security, and hope. Receiving onetime buyouts like Ji, many of them were deprived of the security and steady income from once promised pensions. Those who were young and talented left for good; those who remained endured. Xita was not the worst-effected area. Rather, Tiexi was. The so-called Ruhr in the East turned into the Chinese Rust Belt. As shown in the award-winning *Tie Xi Qu: West of the Tracks*, a nine-hour, three-part documentary, the former model community was plunged into poverty.[21] "The enterprises there were once so massive," Ji said to me, "yet they were just gone like that. Workers in Tiexi suffered much more than we did."[22] During the hardest years, the crime rate increased dramatically. In the media, the reputation of the laid-off workers was sometimes linked notoriously with that of the mafia. The "northeasterners" were simultaneously traumatized internally and demonized externally.

In the Chinese Industry Museum, Tiexi District of Shenyang, an exhibition board that cites a news report from *China Youth Daily* on February 6, 1996, describes the situation:

> After thirty years, Shenyang was left with 500,000 retired workers and a great number of redundant personnel. But there was no corresponding safety net. No pension fund, no unemployment insurance fund, and no social security system. All of these were exchanged for steel factories, railway, and oil fields. They turned into the early stage of the modern industrial system in our country. . . . The general direction of the reform was not wrong. But we lack institutional settlements to cope with the huge cost that is needed to pay for the reform. In the past decades, we neglected to build a social security system. This forced the workers to bear the huge cost of the reform and made it extremely difficult for state-run enterprises to reform themselves.[23]

Low-quality food exemplified the poor conditions. Hunger was not an issue, but nutritious meals were limited. In Tiexi and other places, a popular local dish was the "chicken carcass." With only a little amount of meat attached to the bones, it was an affordable meal for proletarians— and it honestly tastes not bad. In the 1990s, when state-run factory workers were laid off on a large scale, numerous small chicken carcass restaurants emerged in Tiexi. Run by laid-off workers and serving the same population, they spread all over the city in just a few years. Even in the 2010s when the economy got better, these restaurants were still popular with locals and tourists alike. A meal of chicken carcass, typically accompanied with a bottle of beer, cost no more than 10 yuan (or 1.50 USD); it was a nostalgic footnote for the hardship of the 1990s.

It took the government a long time to finally settle all the laid-off workers in Shenyang. Ji had mixed feelings about this huge transition. "Before, people had 'iron bowls' with steady incomes. They went to work on time, got paid no matter what, and did not have to be anxious about anything. But when they were pushed into society, they worried about where to work first thing in the morning." Having said that, Ji personally considered the reform a positive thing in general. "When you have an iron bowl, you lose the spirit of hard work and become lazy. Now, young people shift their jobs frequently, which seldom happened in the past, because they have a dynamic spirit. If you asked me, I would say that the present is much better than the past." During our conversation, Ji offered me fruit from a plate on the table, pointing to it saying, "In the past, you ate an orange when provided an orange. But you never knew that other than oranges, there were also pears and bananas. Am I right?"[24]

In 1997, the entire SCM was moved out of Xita. In January 2000, its original office building was blown up by a developer. In its place, several high-end, high-rise commercial and residential buildings were erected.[25]

A Consumerist Quarter in a Rust Belt City

While the situation in the socialist workers' community in Tiexi turned bleak, surprisingly Xita, though so close by, thrived. Shining under neon lights in the night, it prospered as a new "city that never sleeps" in metropolitan Shenyang.[26] The striking contrast between Tiexi and Xita easily fall into a modernization discourse in which Tiexi represents a socialist past and Xita a capitalist future. Yet the fact that two opposite phenomena occurred almost at the same time in the same city told a different story. Their relationship was synchronic rather than diachronic. In other words, they formed a reciprocal causation: one was the reason of the other, and both shared the same neoliberalist logic. Under this logic,

Xita benefited while Tiexi paid the cost. The imbalanced development in different parts of Shenyang very much mirrored the same developmental imbalance in China, or even in the world.

Since the 1980s, a business corridor had taken form in Xita. Private and public investment created a bustling zone of restaurants, street shops, vendors, boutiques, grocery stores, and supermarkets. In 1992, the municipal government passed a comprehensive city-planning project that aimed to fundamentally transform the downtown area. Xita was included in the plan. Three years later, old commercial and residential buildings on Xita Street were torn down. Replacing them were brand-new shopping malls, restaurants, hotels, office towers, and commercial apartments. The main street, now about seven hundred meters long, was widened to about twenty meters, with several new, paved branch roads. Two overpasses at the north and south ends of the main street further integrated the neighborhood into the increasingly sophisticated transportation network of the city.[27]

The urban renewal project was not intended merely to improve living conditions per se; it served a more urgent purpose. In the language of the government, the objective was to "create a friendly environment for commerce." From the mid-1990s to 2010, Communist cadres in every Chinese county, city, and province competed aggressively for one goal: "attracting investment and capital [zhao shang yin zi]." Specifically, "investment and capital" referred to that from developed capitalist countries. How to attract it? The socialist transformation in the Mao era created two advantageous conditions—a solid, primary industrial base and a massive quantity of high-quality, low-cost human labor. But it was still necessary to nourish a business-friendly environment. This meant several things in the context of neoliberalism in the post–Cold War era: a better urban infrastructure, a favorable taxation policy, a lower bar for labor rights, and, last but not least, loose governmental regulations relating to environmental protection, monetary mobility, financial supervision, and the like. In a word, the state must facilitate capital.

Compared to cities on the eastern and southern coasts, such as Shenzhen or Shanghai, Shenyang did not have a geographical advantage. It nevertheless attracted some foreign investment from East Asian countries, particularly South Korea.

The first South Korean company came to Shenyang in 1989, three years before the two countries established an official diplomatic relationship. In the 1990s and early 2000s, investment from South Korea steadily increased. By 2003, the number of Korean enterprises in the city topped that of all other countries, with 2,227 registered, accounting for investments of 660 million USD or about 10 percent of the total foreign direct investment that year.[28] A large portion of the money went to Tiexi. The reason, as then Mayor Chen Zhenggao said in a symposium, was that South Korea was upgrading its industrial structure and sought to move out some (low-end, labor-intensive) industries, which Shenyang was fully ready to take over.[29] A survey also confirmed that in 2003, more than 51 percent of South Korean enterprises were attracted to China by cheap labor costs and over 30 percent by the Chinese market.[30]

For obvious reasons, when South Korean investors, managers, staff, fortune-seekers, or visitors came to the city, many chose to live in Xita, the vibrant ethnic-Korean neighborhood. In 2003, the Korean citizens who stayed long-term in Shenyang numbered over five thousand, increasing to thirty thousand in 2008.[31] Another report estimated that Xita alone accommodated five thousand long-term residents from South Korea and other countries.[32] Their daily and business consumption, in turn, drew more investments in the service industry to the neighborhood. "Benefiting from tax cuts and free leases from the Chinese government," these Korean investors "began to construct large Korean restaurants and saunas" on Xita's newly paved main street.[33] With no local knowledge, most of them relied on natives to get through the paperwork and conduct business. Many Chaoxianzu, with their language skills and know-how, worked for them as brokers, middlemen, and employees. This kind of collaboration or even partnership, thus, drew more ethnic Koreans from outside Xita to the enclave.

The local government was keenly aware of the economic opportunity. In 2002, Shenyang initiated the "(South) Korean Week" (Hanguo zhou) festival to attract Korean investors and visitors. This coincided with the Korean government's strategy to elevate the nation's soft power by exporting its popular culture, or the "Korean wave" (K. Hallyu), around the world.[34] Starting in 2003, the annual festival was held in Xita. In the name of promoting Korean culture, merchandise and food, Shenyang's Korean Week soon became a most celebrated consumerist carnival. In the daytime, businessmen and bureaucrats signed various trade and investment agreements. In the evening, they celebrated in Xita, enjoying gourmet food, drinks, and the arts alongside locals and domestic and foreign visitors in the thousands. In 2003, more than 5,200 Korean entrepreneurs, artists, performers, professionals, journalists, mayors, and statesmen flew in from Seoul to participate in the festival. The former Prime Minister Lee Han-dong, who was among the group, appreciated the support the Chinese government gave to the Korean entrepreneurs. "I know these merchants," he said in an interview, "they won't develop a place where there is no profit."[35] According to local media, during the weeklong celebration, the occupancy rate at high-end hotels (four stars and above) in Shenyang reached 100 percent, of which 70 percent were Korean guests. Stores on the major commercial streets extended their hours until midnight. Xita was almost certainly the greatest beneficiary: its daily revenues jumped three to five times on average from that on normal days.[36]

The pursuit of neoliberal-style prosperity tied China and Korea together and stimulated Xita's economy remarkably in the early 2000s.[37] By 2005, over 290 domestic and 116 foreign (mostly South Korean) enterprises had set up office in the small neighborhood. This number does not include another 960 self-employed individual businesses.[38] Quite a few North Korean enterprises, mainly restaurants, were also established there, making Xita one of the few places on earth where North and South Korean signboards hung side by side.[39] By 2012, the total number of businesses in Xita climbed to 1,750, drawing a daily customer flow of approximately a hundred thousand people.[40] Many local residents also told me that in the heydays of its development, Xita Street was so jammed in the evening that the whole avenue was like a parking lot (fig. 27).[41]

In preparation for the eleventh annual Korean Week in 2013, the Xita subdistrict office circulated a comprehensive tourist guide.[42] The one-hundred-plus page pamphlet painstakingly listed all the retail, service, and entertainment facilities packed in the 1.2-square-kilometer area, each with a photo. Tourists or visitors were enticed to spend money in

27. Xita Street at night. Photo taken by the author, 2017.

140 restaurants
25 saunas, massages, bars, or KTVs
14 shopping malls or name-brand clothing stores
24 beauty salons
12 hotels or motels
176 grocery and specialty stores

The guide boldly claimed that "Xita has become famous worldwide as a paradise for shopping, gourmet food, and entertainment."[43] But even more striking was the pamphlet's new design. On the cover, the Korean word *Sŏtap*, in large print, occupies the center of the page. The Chinese title appears in much smaller print below. On the first page, directly above the same *Sŏtap* characters, a carefully crafted image informs readers of the meaning of the Xita space. The white Tibetan-style Buddhist stupa is placed between a traditional Korean-style house and the background of a tricolored *t'aegŭk* (or Samt'aegŭk, a popular Korean version of *taiji*), and surrounded by *mugunghwa*, South Korea's national flower. The old landmark of the space, the tower, is thus merged compatibly with the new cultural symbols of the Korean wave (fig. 28).

Indeed, the neighborhood was very much South Koreanized, literally and figuratively. "Any tourist who unintentionally came to Xita Street in the evening," a journalist claimed, "would have the exotic feeling that they were walking on a foreign street. Approaching late at night, the restaurants and KTVs with neon lights in the Korean alphabet were the most bustling. What you heard on the street at night were (people talking in) Korean."[44] It seemed that the local government did not see any inconvenience in rebranding a Chaoxianzu community with a South Korean trademark. Newspapers, social media, and tourist advertisements constantly described Xita as a "little Seoul" or the "world's second-largest Koreatown next only to that in the US."[45] This, of course, was a false assertion in multiple ways. Other than the fact that there is no singular form of Koreatown in the US, to portray Xita as a mini-Seoul ignored its unique history and identity as a Korean-Chinese space. Nonetheless, the phrase "little Seoul" was so catchy for marketing purposes that aside from a few local Chaoxianzu (e.g., the poet Jin Changyong in chapter 5), no one even questioned it. In contemporary China, where every locality was eager to find its selling points to attract consumers, this kind of "self-exoticism" was certainly not an isolated case found only in Xita.[46]

That said, in Xita the Chaoxianzu community did not remain unchanged either. One significant shift was in the local demography. This meant not only the incoming new residents from South Korea but also

28. Page one of the Xita tourist pamphlet. *Sŏtap, Xita lüyou quan gonglue,* author's collection.

the outflow of local Chaoxianzu as well as the influx of new domestic immigrants, Chaoxianzu and non-Chaoxianzu alike. In 2010, the registered population (Chinese citizens) in Xita reached 36,601, an increase of nearly 32 percent from ten years before. Yet the proportion of ethnic Koreans dropped from 23.3 percent in 2000 to less than 19 percent in 2010.[47] This echoed what I heard from many interviewees: that younger generations of Chaoxianzu had left for better opportunities, many to

South Korea.[48] One study shows that "nearly 700,000 Korean Chinese minorities of a total population of about 2.3 million lived in South Korea as of 2017, representing by far the largest group of 'foreigners' in the country."[49]

Li Yiming was one of them. Li's father, who had worked for the famous Xita Cold Noodle restaurant, was originally from P'yŏngan-do, while his mother was from Kyŏngsang-do in the south. It was not until Li attended Yanbian University, majoring in Korean literature, that he realized that his mother spoke a different dialect. At the invitation of relatives in South Korea, Li went abroad for the first time. That was before the Sino-South Korean diplomatic relationship was established. He felt quite shocked. "One earned more money as a laborer in Korea in a day than as a teacher in China in a month. The monthly salary in China could not even match what one spent in a KTV in a night. Therefore, I lost my perspective as a teacher. I wanted to go out and strive."

Upon returning to Shenyang, he quit his job, got divorced, and went back to South Korea to work. "If there had not been an economic wave, my wife and I probably would not have divorced but lived a normal life," Li said. "We separated in 1993. I left China that year and came back as late as 2009, staying in Korea for sixteen years."[50] Returning to where he grew up in his early fifties, he found there was nothing worth noting. "All of my old neighbors have scattered to other places. Xita is now an entertainment area. People just come here to have a meal or a bath." In his opinion, many old residents left Xita because houses in other parts of the city were of better quality. They would rather lease their Xita apartments to new migrants and live elsewhere. "Plus, more and more people own private cars, and they could come here anytime they want." The only thing that still bound local Chaoxianzu here, he believed, was the Korean primary and middle schools.[51]

Population outflow has occurred in almost every city in northeastern China since the 1990s. Shenyang had been a rare exception. The largest metropolis in Manchuria, it lost population to coastal regions but at the same time absorbed more emigrants from the Manchurian hinterlands, especially the Jilin and Heilongjiang Provinces. Xita exemplified this trend. Its superb business opportunities attracted ethnic Koreans and non-Koreans from relatively marginal places. To cope with the situation, Shenyang was also one of the first cities in China to abandon the outdated migrant population regulations. In 2003, it canceled the temporary residence permit, which aimed to prevent nonnatives from settling permanently in the populous city. Reporting on this story, a journalist came to Xita because, "it was a major enclave of Shenyang's migrant population." A young worker from Jilin, surnamed Ren, came to the police station to apply for a permit, where he was informed that there was no need to do so anymore. Instead, all that was required was a national identification card, just like the natives. The official news account sent a message—Shenyang was no longer a city belonging exclusively to the natives.[52]

Ethnic Koreans were one of the most mobile groups in China. In 2018, I met Piao Aigen (K. Pak Aegŭn), the owner of Fuweiting, a midsize restaurant serving Korean cuisine in Xita. Born in 1969, Piao and her family originally lived in the countryside outside Harbin, Heilongjiang Province. They moved to Shenyang as early as 1992. Like many Chaoxianzu at the time, Piao paid 50,000 yuan to an agent and went to South Korea illegally in 1995. Later, her husband joined her in Seoul, leaving their son with her parents. "My mom raised my son for me. This was quite normal in my generation." The couple worked diligently for ten years and accumulated some money. Their first few years in Korea were hard, and they experienced discrimination. "But later, things got better and we gradually adjusted to it." When their son reached middle school age, the couple decided to return and take care of him. Piao found a job as a manager in a Korean restaurant in the neighborhood. Her husband opened a small barbecue shop. "In Korea, we were foreigners and did hard work for someone else. Now we were getting old and couldn't work as migrant laborers for the rest of our lives. Therefore, we thought about opening a restaurant of our own."[53]

But being a boss was not easy either. "In the first three years, we felt even more exhausted than in Korea." When her son entered college, Piao went to South Korea again. This time, she got her permanent residency but did not stay there for long. In 2010, she returned to Shenyang and opened Fuweiting. According to Piao, the majority of the Chaoxianzu business owners in Xita shared a similar experience. "We went to South Korea in a good time. Some of us came here and started businesses directly, some started businesses after returning from Korea, and some failed (to earn money) and had to go to Korea again. On the other hand, the policies in South Korea are getting better and those who had worked there for a long time, like my aunt, chose not to return." Just as Li said about the local Chaoxianzu, Piao did not live in Xita despite the fact that she owned a two-bedroom apartment there. She rented out the apartment to young migrant workers, who had come to Shenyang just as she once had three and a half decades before.

We sat and talked in her restaurant one afternoon. Fewer guests came in at this point in the day. Piao said she worked seven days a week and was more tired than her employees. I asked how business was. She complained that it was getting worse and worse, unlike when she first opened. She believed the situation had a lot to do with the recent anticorruption campaign (which banned government officials from paying for dinners with public funds). She was thinking about investing in South Korea, but the economic situation there was not as good as before either. "Someone suggested that I run a restaurant in Canada. I am not sure about it. My parents are too old, and Canada is too far away." I was amazed she did not worry about the language barrier or cultural differences. "This year is slightly better than last year," she said. "Let's see [if things get better]. Maybe next year, or the year after that."[54]

Sex, Drugs, and Underground Banks

On a summer evening, leaving a restaurant after dinner, I found myself approached by a group of men and women in their twenties and thirties. "Hey, bro, come sing at our karaoke bar!" They wouldn't take no for an answer. One of them followed me still trying to get my attention. "We have over one hundred chicks you can pick up, all are very hot!" I shook my head and kept walking. "Just have a look," the pimp did not give up. "It costs nothing to take a look. Leave if you don't like it." I ignored her and sped up my pace, but her voice still called from behind, "Over one hundred chicks!"

In the first two years of my research, I got quite accustomed to this kind of scenario. Xita was famous for its sex industry. Every native knew that. Even local cadres openly admitted to the situation. In contemporary China, female sex workers are not called "prostitutes" but the euphemistic expression *xiaojie*, meaning "miss." "Xita has become so popular since the late 1990s," Jin Xizhen, a municipal government staffer, informed me, "many xiaojie came here and served in the bathhouses, karaoke clubs, hotels, and massage shops. The two main streets, Xita and Yanbian, formed a red-light district."[55] A former party secretary of the subdistrict was even more frank. "At the beginning, Xita xiaojie served mainly Korean clients because they had more money. In the late 1990s, for example, a Korean client paid 800 yuan for sex, whereas the normal price was only 30 to 50 yuan." Sex workers in Xita, roughly half ethnic Koreans and half Han, arrived mostly from other cities or provinces. "I was told that during the Korean Week festivals, an additional two thousand xiaojie would come to Xita."[56]

Prostitution, which was not tolerated in Mao's era, resurfaced in the new era. Although still illegal on paper, the sex industry became so widespread in every major Chinese city that most local governments turned a blind eye to, if not acquiesced or even encouraged, the business. From a certain perspective, this was probably considered part of the job of

creating "a friendly environment for commerce." Many of my interviewees mentioned a jingle about how to make a city prosper, which, they
claimed, was created by former mayor Mu Suixin. "Grow some flowers,
plant some grasses, and carefully protect the misses" (*yang yang hua,
zhong zhong cao, xiaojie baohu hao*). Of course, I have no way to verify
this anecdote.

As a historian, I was fascinated by the persistent social role the Xita
space played in the city in drastically different times. The fact that this
urban quarter was a famous red-light district in both pre-PRC and post-
Mao Shenyang demonstrates not so much the continuation of history:
the social context for prostitution thriving in the 1920s was not the same
as that of the 1990s. Remember that prostitution in SMR zone served
Japan's empire building and a large portion of the brothel customers in
Beishi were laborers.[57] But in the 1990s and 2000s, the clients in Xita
were mostly privileged Korean expatriates or Chinese middle class.
Prostitution reemerged from the newly thrived neoliberal economy. Yet
despite the shift in the social structure, the space presents a peculiar
kind of "stickiness," which somehow overcame the rupture of history.

The tolerance policy began to change in the 2010s. The government
repeatedly cracked down on the sex industry. Although far from being
eradicated completely—I still encountered those pimps on street—the
general atmosphere turned much "cleaner." What caused the shift? The
former party secretary of the subdistrict explained that the idea of municipal administration had been upgraded. "Before, we only thought
about how to attract investment. But later, a series of social problems
emerged: the degradation of public security, the drug issues, and the
problem of AIDS. It forced us to change our ideas."[58]

There is a dearth of comprehensive and accessible studies on the
sex industry in Xita, but one can certainly sense, from health studies
and media accounts, that it turned Xita into a prime area for AIDS.
For example, the *Chinese Journal of AIDS/STD* published a study on
AIDS intervention based on a survey in Xita from 2002 to 2003. The
researchers chose the neighborhood because "the entertainment facilities are concentrated, the sexually active population is dense, and the
sexual activity is intense." The survey also used the expression "sexual
activities beyond boyfriends or husbands (commercial sex)" to imply
prostitution.[59] *Liaoning Daily*, the most authoritative news outlet in the
province, reported in 2004 that there were three AIDS prevention programs operating in Shenyang simultaneously. All three programs (one
on the national level and the other two on the international level) were
in Heping District where Xita was. For the "National Models for AIDS
Prevention Program," Heping was one of the first of fifty-one models

selected, and it was the only one in an urban setting. Among the twenty testing communities for the "China-European Union Sex Disease/AIDS Prevention Program," Xita and Beishi were on the list. And Heping was also one of the five districts/counties in China to implement the "China–United Nations Population Fund AIDS Prevention Program."[60] The *Xinhua Daily Telegraph* reported a story in 2005 about a medical intervention team in Heping District, whose work included teaching basic AIDS knowledge and promoting the use of condoms. "Heping has 729 public entertainment facilities . . . the service persons there are the targeted high-risk population." Despite many efforts, however, the result was not entirely satisfactory. "The majority of the bosses in Xita, where the entertainment facilities are concentrated, understood and supported the work. However, the team still could not find a breakthrough in the facilities run by foreign owners."[61]

There is no evidence that the crime rate in Xita was higher than in other places. But since the space maintained tight personnel and business connections with the Korean Peninsula, the criminal activities occurring in Xita revealed a salient transboundary, even global, character. Two major problems exemplified this: illegal drugs and underground banks. Drugs did not become a serious issue in Shenyang until the early 2000s, coinciding with the arrival of the Korean wave.[62] But drugs spread to northeastern China via several routes, and South Korea was just one of them. News coverage on the antidrug campaign indicated that dealers from Korea, who came to Shenyang to distribute, would usually stay in Xita.[63] Perhaps the environment made it easy for the dealers to hide in a Korean-speaking crowd. Additionally, with its many entertainment facilities, the neighborhood naturally attracted potential buyers, turning it into a drug-consuming marketplace.[64]

Underground banks became prevalent in Xita due to huge demand for money transactions across the country. Not all the business was illegal. In fact, researchers found that because one could not directly exchange Korean and Chinese currencies without using US dollars as the intermediary currency and because both South Korea and China regulated the outflow of their US dollar reserves, normal money transactions from one country to another were largely limited. Since the volume of Sino-Korean trade and personnel exchanges had increased rapidly, the demand for money transactions surged. For merchants, Korean expatriates in China, Chinese laborers in Korea, international students, migrants, and even tourists, underground banks with much better services and exchange rates, were their first choice.[65] However, underground banks in Xita did provide an easy channel for criminal activities like gambling, the drug trade, illegal fundraising, and money laundering. Since the underground banks in Xita mainly served Koreans or Chaoxianzu, and most were operated through family networks, local police barely detected or investigated their activities. Based on a few special cases, a conservative estimate was that the money flow at Xita underground banks might be as high as 30 billion yuan (or 4.38 billion USD) each year.[66]

The most notorious financial crime associated with Xita was arguably the "Gao Shan" case in 2004. Gao was a subbranch manager at the Bank of China in Harbin, Heilongjiang Province. From 2000 to 2004, collaborating with his friends Li Dongzhe and Li Donghu, he secretly embezzled over 800 million yuan from the savings accounts of over twenty companies. Before the misappropriation was exposed, Gao and the Li brothers fled to Canada, leading to prolonged legal bargaining between Beijing and Ottawa since there was no bilateral extradition treaty. The public was shocked by the huge loophole uncovered in China's banking regulation and called the case "one of the biggest financial frauds in PRC history." Eventually, in 2007, Gao turned himself in and was sentenced to fifteen years in prison in 2014.[67] The key figures in this case were the Li brothers, who were ethnic Koreans. They transferred the illicit funds overseas through underground banks in Xita. In a news report on the problematic financial regulations, a high-ranking executive told journalists, "The largest underground banks in the three provinces of northeastern China are in Xita. Everyone in our circle knows that."[68]

In a neoliberalist era, a transnational and global criminal web relying on airlines, the internet, and bank wires was woven around Xita. Comparing to the railway system, they challenged state boundaries and state capacities in a more profound way, further complicating the nuanced meaning of the space.

A New Stupa, a New Xita

In 1998, the municipal government erected a new West Stupa in Xita along with a new Life-Prolonging Temple. The project was proposed by then-mayor Mu Suixin, who regretted the absence of one of the four ancient stupas in Shenyang. The most difficult part of the re-erection, according to the manager in charge, Mr. Liu Weimin, was the axial pillar. The pillar had to be cast in one pouring, yet the builders could not find a mold that was as tall as the original one anywhere. After failing a few times, the team got the authority's approval to temporarily remove the pillar from the North Stupa, which they then copied to create a mold three meters high (9.8 feet) and finally complete the job. The finished pillar weighed three tons.[69] The episode attested to the impressive technological achievements of craftsmen in the early seventeenth century. The rebuilding of the tower cost 4 million yuan,[70] and the entire Life-Prolonging Temple project cost 30 million.[71]

The stupa was not the only reproduced monument in Xita. When the SCM's original office building was destroyed by a real estate developer, it invited tremendous criticism. The opposition argued that the cotton mill building was not only historic architecture representing the development of Shenyang's national industry but also important revolutionary remains since Liu Shaoqi had worked there for a short time. In response to pressure, the developer built a replica on the same site: a three-story European-style building, with a bell tower in the middle. The "old site of the Fengtian Cotton Mill" was now registered as an "unremovable cultural heritage" on the municipal level.[72]

I see the two imitation monuments—the stupa and the cotton mill office building—as an effort to reinterpret the space's significance. People tried to reestablish a link with the past, associating the space with memories of dynastic history and modern revolution. Nonetheless, the

29. Bird's-eye view of the new West Stupa Temple in the neighborhood.
Photo taken by Zuozuodawang; copyright purchased by the author.

connection was largely superficial. Neither the stupa nor the cotton mill played an active role in the neighborhood. Rather, they were simply surrounded by it, so irrelevant that they were ignored if not forgotten. Like two dispensable appendixes, the two cultural heritage sites decorated a bustling, consumerist space consisting of commercial apartments, bars, karaoke clubs, restaurants, beauty salons, shopping malls, bathhouses, and supermarkets.

In 2001, Mu Suixin, the mayor who rebuilt the West Stupa, was sentenced to death-with-reprieve for corruption. He died of cancer a year later in prison.

Since the end of the first decade of the twenty-first century, capitalist fever in Xita gradually cooled down, as Korean capitalists found it more and more difficult to make a profit in the Chinese market. The number of South Koreans living in Xita, along with their investment, dropped significantly. In her study of the "precarious" South Korean emigrants in Xita, anthropologist Cho Mun Young suggests three major reasons for the shift. First, the 2008 global financial crisis severely weakened South Korea's currency, causing turmoil in the exchange markets. Many small businesses run by Korean citizens in Xita were forced to close. Second, the implementation of a new labor law in China aimed at easing the increasing social inequality in the country, significantly raised labor costs. Gone was the golden age of the neoliberal economic boom. Finally, the South Korean government changed its visa policy, allowing overseas Koreans (e.g., Chaoxianzu), who previously came there to work illegally, to acquire legal status in Korea. Since they could now go back and forth relatively freely, many Chaoxianzu returned to China. Combining skills learned in Korea with local knowledge, they gradually took over the businesses started by South Koreans in Xita.[73] (The story of restaurateur Piao Aigen, it seems, particularly proves the third point.) The social hierarchy in the neighborhood shifted subtly. Many South Korean small businessmen, who had once dreamed of earning a fortune in China because they were cornered by the financial-industrial conglomerates (*chaebol*) in their home country, fell into a socially and economically vulnerable group in the so-called Koreatown in China.

In addition, unstable political relations at the highest level affected economic collaboration at the grassroots level. Against Chinese protests, the Park Geun-hye government installed the Terminal High Altitude Area Defense, an antiballistic missile defense system, in 2016, which was seen by Beijing as a major security threat and a political provocation. China responded by curtailing many bilateral exchange programs, including banning Korean entertainment products. In this tense environment, Shenyang suspended Korean Week in 2016 and 2017. Even though the festival resumed in 2018, the scale of the celebration and the volume of trade and investment shrank remarkably. The long-term foreign residents in Xita, once numbering over 5,000 (including 1,200 North Koreans and more than 100 Japanese), decreased to fewer than 400 after 2016. On Shifu Avenue (previous Shijianfang Avenue), a planned shopping mall called Seoul Plaza has been left unfinished for nearly ten years. The ambitious project, which was meant to showcase the international attraction of the city, turned into nothing but an inconvenient embarrassment.

Even after the financial pinnacle of the early 2000s was over, Xita remained one of the most robust commercial districts in the city in the late 2010s. According to the former party secretary of the subdistrict, there was an "inward-looking transformation" after the South Koreans departed. "The South Koreans brought us not only funds and enterprises but, most importantly, innovative ideas about service and management. That said, local businesses cannot depend on Korean expats and serve them only. They must target local Chinese consumers."[74]

With the obvious ebbing of the Korean wave, the state promoted a new image of the Chinese nation, or Zhonghua minzu, in this small neighborhood. Xita, as one of the most dynamic ethnic enclaves in urban China, was seen by the government as a perfect place to showcase "ethnic solidarity," a core concept of the country's new nation-building project in the early twenty-first century. "We emphasized more the notion of national/ethnic rather than that of international," the former party secretary said to me. The neighborhood repeatedly received national-, provincial-, and municipal-level honors. In 2009, the State Council (the chief administrative authority) recognized the Antu residential community in Xita as a "model community for national ethnic solidarity and progress." Then in 2014, Beijing granted the subdistrict two more national awards for ethnic solidarity.[75] In 2016, the National Ethnic Affairs Commission named the Tumen residential community, another subneighborhood of Xita, one of the "national harmonious bilingual villages or communities," together with six others in the frontier provinces of Inner Mongolia, Guangxi, Sichuan, Guizhou, Tibet, and Gansu.[76] Walking in the neighborhood, visitors can't miss the street art in the intersections and alleys. All the sculptures, installations, and graffiti highlight the Chaoxianzu features of the space. On one tall apartment building, a giant Chinese slogan has been fixed on the exterior, so eye-catching against the blue sky that one can easily see it from a distance. The slogan, in red, reads, "All ethnic groups unite and strive together, [so that we] prosper and develop together."

A Final Tour of the Neighborhood

On a Sunday in 2019, I walked in the Xita neighborhood once again. For me, this was almost a ritual: I visited each time I was researching, either before or after my intense fieldwork. I started at about 9:00 a.m. at the Life-Prolonging Temple. Although the stupa was a precise copy, the temple compound was much smaller than the original. As I entered through the main gate, the stupa stood right in front of me, so tall that there was nowhere on the grounds where I could get a full view. One or two monks were on duty that day, but there were no other visitors. Nor was there any trace of Tibetan Buddhism in the temple besides the stupa. It is worth mentioning that Tibetan Buddhism did revive, to a certain degree, in Shenyang. In the early 2000s, the government invited a tulku (living buddha) from the Tibetan region in Sichuan to be the host at the North Stupa/Dharma-Wheel Temple. Within years, he and his followers had rebuilt the temple and turned it into a dynamic center for Buddhist and Tibetan studies, even creating a small Tibetan cultural space in the nearby neighborhood. Compared to it, the West Stupa/Life-Prolonging Temple looked deserted and lonely.

Crossing the intersection of Shifu Avenue and Xita Street, I walked farther east for a few minutes and arrived at the Xita Church. It was around 9:20 a.m., and many people were going inside. Six or seven volunteers wearing blue T-shirts stood to the side, opening their arms, bowing to every churchgoer, and greeting them loudly with "Jesus loves you!" A sermon in Chinese was slated to start in ten minutes on the fifth floor. There was an elevator inside the building, but I took the stairs to see the photos hanging in the stairwell, which recorded the recent history of the church. The chapel hall on the fifth floor had room enough to accommodate five hundred people, maybe more. The ceremony began with reading the Bible, and then the church musical group began to play, not traditional choir or gospel music, but pleasant pop music. Some of the songs, as I later found out, were written by Lin Wanrong (Seh Lin), a Taiwanese musician who specializes in worship songs. The crowd was enthusiastic and the energy in the chapel hall resembled a live concert. An hour later, Pastor Piao, one of the Chaoxianzu pastors of the church, began his sermon. When I took off after listening for a while, I noticed that not only was every seat taken in but there were also people crowding the doorway of the hall. Needless to say, the contrast between the temple and the church was striking.

Exiting the church, I turned left, to the west. Just a few steps away was the famous Xita Cold Noodle restaurant. It was not even 11:00 a.m., and there were already many customers eating there. I had tried to go several times before. But the two-floor restaurant was packed both times with lunch or dinner guests, and I hated to wait. The historic restaurant was nothing like its neat, cozy, middle-class counterparts on Xita Street. The environment was more like the dining hall for a socialist work unit: congested, untidy, and noisy, with a strong ever-present smell of meat, alcohol, and cigarettes (despite the no-smoking sign). There were no waiters or waitresses serving tables. Instead, patrons ordered and paid at one window, received different-colored metal cards, and lined up to pick up their food at another window. The final task was to find an empty seat to enjoy the meal and be prepared to share your table with other guests. The restaurant served noodles in two flavors. The sweet-and-sour version was favored by Han Chinese customers. But if you wanted an "authentic" northern Korean experience, you ordered the savory noodle dish. The price was incredibly affordable: 16 yuan (or $2.50) for the famous noodles and 10 yuan for a side dish. In that year, the restaurant accepted cash only—no WeChat pay or Alipay via phone (the app is now the most popular form of payment in China), not even a credit card. In a consumerist era, the restaurant stood fast to the old ways, tenaciously and stubbornly, maybe a little too much. Why it remains so extraordinarily popular is both fascinating and frustrating. The restaurant did, however, remind people of the 1970s and 1980s, a golden age of Shenyang for many older-generation natives. If ever I mentioned Xita to an older-generation interviewee, the most frequent response was, "Oh, Xita Cold Noodle!"

My favorite spot in the neighborhood was Zhuoru alley, opposite Xita Cold Noodle across Shifu Avenue. It was a small but lively alley that ran parallel to Xita Street with dozens of vendors and mom-and-pop stores selling kimchi, rice cakes, rice wine, doraji, chili powders, and numerous Korean prepared foods and ingredients. The stalls displayed their goods out front, and customers were welcomed to sample. It was an intimate space where everyone seemed to know everyone. The buyers and sellers greeted each other and had a little chat. Most businesses there, I was told, were run by emigrants; many of them were not Chaoxianzu, although all of them spoke some Korean. After interviewing many locals, I tended to believe that this small alley represented a source of energy for the neighborhood.

The alley connected to the Yuwen residential community, where the Russian Orthodox chapel was hidden. Seniors still remembered that there used to be a Russian cemetery. After the cemetery was removed in the 1990s, the chapel became the only trace of Russian existence in Xita. The chapel's story was associated with the coming of the railways in the early 1900s, which denoted the beginning of the modern history

30. Street shops in Zhuoru alley. Photo taken by the author, 2019.

of Shenyang. The best spot to see the railways was the Three-Arch Bridge (Sandongqiao), where the former SMR and PMR lines intersected. It took me about ten minutes to walk from Yuwen to the northern end of Xita Street; then I crossed the city's east–west expressway and set out on a narrow road toward the bridge. To get a better look, one must go through a dark, underground tunnel and stand on the northwest side of the bridge. A tall monument has been erected between the tracks, informing passengers that this was the spot where Zhang Zuolin was assassinated on June 4, 1928. The bridge was still in use, the only difference being that all the trains passing by now are super-fast bullet trains. The skyline was defined by the commercial skyscrapers in Xita.

In the evening, I returned to my hotel room. From my window on the fifth floor, I could watch Xita Street down below. When all the neon lit up and the traffic jammed, the street finally woke up and began another energetic day. Feeling tired, I decided not to go out for dinner. Instead, I picked up my cellphone, opened a popular app for food delivery, and placed an order. In China today, urban residents could not live without these super-convenient services. Once the seller received my order, a street map appeared on the screen, informing me of every step in the delivery process.

"Your order has been picked up by the rider; thirty minutes away."

A cartoon figure riding a motorcycle was heading to my hotel. Thanks to satellite positioning systems, the icon moved on the screen as the rider moved along the street. Here, space was measured by time. There was also an option to speed up the delivery if you chose to reward the rider a bonus. For a price, it seems, you could overcome both time and space.

"Twenty minutes away"

The map zoomed in, showing all the important landmarks along the way: the Shenyang train station, the neatly defined urban quarter of the central Heping District (the former SMR zone), and the giant shopping malls there.

"Five minutes away"

The map zoomed in further, and I saw all the sites I had visited earlier that day: Xita Cold Noodle, the church, and the Life-Prolonging Temple. All the landmarks were organized by the progress of my online order.

"One minute away"

The rider icon stopped at my hotel. "Knock, knock." I rose from my chair and opened the door. Usually, the delivery person leaves the food at the front desk, but this time, it was brought right to my room. I thanked the man, closed the door, and returned to my desk. The rider icon disappeared from the screen on my phone. The map, along with all the geographic signs and places, faded away. Lost was the connection between the people and the space. A new message appeared on the screen:

"Your order is now complete."

Epilogue and Conclusion

A place does not automatically acquire meaning. People, in one way or another, create its significance. Since a place can have different meanings for different people, the historical memory of a place varies. In the eyes of Shenyang residents who lived a distance from Xita—say in the former "old town," the former SMR zone, or the Tiexi industrial district—the neighborhood was rather marginal. Or at least it did not represent any of the fixed characteristics of the city. It was not as historic as the royal palace, as industrial as Tiexi, or as exotic as the former SMR zone. To Mia (Miao) Yu, an independent curator, artist, and researcher who was born and grew up in the core of the former SMR zone, Xita was a "frontier." "I knew there were several buses I could easily take to go to Xita or the Yellow Temple," she said. "But in my childhood memories, they were so far away."[1]

In 2021, Yu invited me to participate in her years-long art project about the entanglement between humans and the environment in northeastern China. Knowing she was a Shenyang native, naturally I asked her about Xita. Despite the fact that her home was not far from the neighborhood, she admitted that she had only a vague impression of it. Instead, our conversation focused more on her memories of her hometown experience, which surprisingly resonated with the theme of my research: a place where layers of time and symbolism are compressed. She preferred a rather dramatic term, *haunting*, to describe history's impact on her everyday life and feelings.

Yu's home was near Sun Yat-sen Park, which was originally built during the Japanese colonial period and called Chiyoda Park. Her father worked for the provincial government and so the family was provided with a small apartment in an old, Japanese-style building. The building was packed—approximately eight households, very common in the 1970s and 1980s. Her family had a room on the first floor on the north side of the building that received less sunshine than other rooms. "Our home was chilly and damp," Yu said. "And there were rats running under the wood floor. Therefore, I realized there was an empty space beneath the floor." An only child, Yu spent much of her time by herself. Staring at the ceiling, hearing the small noises within the house fueled her fantasy of a "haunting" house.

In the early 1990s, the family moved to a new apartment that was much larger and nicer. The family's old house, along with many other residential buildings from the colonial period, was torn down. Yu's father witnessed the dismantling process. There was indeed a layer of space, about one foot deep, between the flooring and the ground. This space was quite common in Japanese architecture designed in the 1930s and 1940s. "My father joked to me, 'I saw a leg of your missing doll (down there).' I thought it was so creepy." He also found many items that had fallen through cracks in the floor: a sock, toys, and crumpled papers, for example. Some of it, her father claimed, looked like it belonged to the Japanese in the old times. "For me, it was like my secret, imaginary garden was suddenly uncovered," Yu said. "But when the one foot space beneath the floor was uncovered, it in turn confirmed my fantasy and imagination." Yu did not go to the ruins to check herself. After all, it was her home that held so many of her childhood memories.

The long shadow of the past appeared at not only her home but also her school. The No. 20 high school near Sun Yat-sen Square that Yu had attended was the former Naniwa Girls' High School during the Japanese occupation. In the 1980s, the Sino-Japanese relationship continued to improve, and Japanese pop culture, in the form of TV dramas, cartoons, and music, significantly influenced the Chinese children in her generation. At the time, Japan was a role model for "modernization," the goal of China's state building. As a government official, Yu's father visited Japan several times and even studied Japanese in his spare time. Meanwhile, China had a large number of Japanese visitors. "Many Japanese visited our school," Yu remembered. "My teacher said that they had attended this school. It was rather confusing for me as a child to imagine Japanese people had actually lived in my city." Like many her age, Yu's mind was filled with terrifying images of the Japanese invasion from watching Chinese films and TV series. "So, I asked my teacher, 'How could the Japanese possibly live in my city peacefully? How could they possibly build beautiful modern buildings like my school? Weren't they violent invaders?' My teacher couldn't give me a good answer except to say that they came because they wanted our resources." At the time, Chinese youth learned a great deal about the Sino-Japanese War but not a lot about Japanese colonialization. A lack of awareness about historical colonialism and the decolonization efforts in China, ironically, led to the younger generation's contemporary fascination with the colonial period. "Partly in resistance to the loss of cultural pride in the context of economic decline since the 1990s," Yu claimed, "the remnants of colonial modernity were reappropriated" in present-day Northeast China as a new local identity.

In the early 2000s, Yu pursued graduate study in art history at McGill University. The past haunted her even in Canada. At McGill, she met her mentor, Professor Hajime Nakatani, a Japanese cultural anthropologist and art historian, who specialized in medieval Chinese arts. Yu appreciated him greatly, saying it was Nakatani who enlightened her about Chinese art, even leading her to her current career. They formed a strong friendship. "Hajime often borrowed Chinese films from me. I gave him many films on disk, which I bought during summer breaks. When he returned the disks, he would always make comments." But one time when she presented him with the film *Devils on the Doorstep*, a black comedy directed by Jiang Wen about the Counter-Japanese War, the professor became closed and squeamish. He tried to avoid a response, saying politely that he had not watched it yet. Another moment Yu remembered vividly was when she told her mentor that she was from Shenyang. "Hajime seemed quite excited and said spontaneously, 'My father was born in that city!' But suddenly the mood turned." Although she made several attempts to continue the subject, Yu clearly sensed his resistance. She never found out the possible connection between her dear teacher and her childhood experiences. "In fact," Yu recalled, "Hajime's evasion of, or rather, his refusal to respond reminded me of the lack of explanation about Japanese colonialization from my Chinese schoolteacher. History was denied from both sides for different reasons."

Professor Nakatani returned to Japan in 2010. Unfortunately, he passed away soon after at a young age. It was not until then that Yu learned more about his family background. Nakatani's grandfather was serving in the Japanese military in Manchuria when his father was born. Later, his grandfather was promoted and transferred to the Philippines and then returned to Japan when the war ended. The Nakatani family was a highly educated one. His grandfather was an aficionado in Chinese calligraphy and painting, which certainly influenced young Hajime.

∷

Space can effectively be understood through the lens of time and vice versa. For Mia Yu, history haunted her in different places, be it the crawl space under her floor, her high school, or her professor's office in Canada. Time and place are entangled together while history often unfolds itself in multiple layers of time. What connects these layers is human activity, experience, emotion, memory, and even imagination. Jorge Luis Borges, in his famous short story "The Garden of Forking Paths," provides a powerful metaphor for this. For the heroes in the story, time was not necessarily "uniform and absolute." Instead, there was "an infinite series of times, a growing, dizzying web of divergent, convergent, and parallel times. That fabric of times that approach one another, fork, are snipped off, or are simply unknown for centuries, contains all possibilities."[2]

By the same token, a space can also be "divergent, convergent, and parallel," containing many possibilities. Xita, the subject of this book, was one such "infinite series" of spaces, which approached one another through unique historical significance in different periods. In the Qing dynasty, it revealed the Tibetan Buddhism network and its religious bureaucratic institution. In the early twentieth century, it connected the webs of railway capitalism and urban construction. During the Japanese colonization period, it solidified a transregional tourist system that echoed the blueprint for a Pan-Asianist empire. From the early twentieth century to the early twenty-first century, the place witnessed the formation and evolution of an ethnic Korean society. It also embodied, from the 1950s onward, China's huge transformation from socialism to (quasi-)neoliberalism. The aforementioned did not exist on one spatial level but were strung together through diverse layers of space, including an urban neighborhood, a city, Manchuria, China, and East and Inner Asia.

With this book I hope to extend theoretical discussions in two directions. First, it further complexifies our understanding of the histories of Manchuria, China, and Asia by seeing them through the prism of a micro space. For each chapter, I spoke with experts in relevant fields, creating conversations about, for example, the Qing's Inner Asian politics, the state-church relationship, East Asian modernity brought by railway capitalism, Japan's tourist imperialism, the Korean diaspora in China, the transition in Chinese socialism, and the rise of global consumerism. Xita served as a local case study whereby to examine all these important epochs. Second, the book probes into the making of various modern spaces—community, urban, state, and transnational world—from the perspective of micro history. Here the book aims to respond to the human or humanistic geographers who inspired this project by pointing out the spatial elements in the making of the modern state, capitalism, and human society. Xita manifests multiple spaces: religious, imperial, capitalist, ethnic, gender, socialist, and neoliberalist. And these spaces overlapped rather than replaced one another. Therefore, space is not something static or stagnant. Time, or history, infills the space with energetic life. It was human activities that kept changing the meaning of the space.

What theme linked the multiple layers of Xita or connected its different spatial networks? One answer is the development of long-distance transportation. In the Qing dynasty, horses and camels served as the most important tools for geopolitical interaction and trade, making Mukden a meeting ground between East Asia and Inner Asia. In the twentieth century, the intrusion of the railway crushed the natural barriers separating different ecological systems in Manchuria, not only reshaping the political and economic gravity of urban Shenyang, but also stimulating large-scale population flows. It also tied the city into a much larger, global capitalist system. When I first came to Xita to do research, there was a branch of a travel agency at the start of the street with a giant board advertising airline tickets for sale. It was certainly not a coincidence that the travel agency chose that spot to open a branch. In the early twenty-first century, as demonstrated in chapter 6, Xita turned into a business hub with a commerce network spanning all of East Asia, if not more. Through these different vehicles, time and space are compressed with each other at different velocities.

Fluidity, therefore, was the key to understanding the meaning of this space. Despite the fact that Xita was and is a small neighborhood, people arrived there from all over the world and crossed all kinds of boundaries. The transborder flows that manifested, in the forms of religion, trade, ideas, and capital, were not confined by state, region, or even continent. Throughout Xita's nearly four-centuries-long history, the state was certainly a key player in making and remaking the place. But people—lamas, colonizers, city builders, tourists, emigrants, workers, prostitutes, and common residents—also had their own agency. Their power in shaping the place was no less remarkable. The daily activities of individuals, groups, families, and communities penetrated all layers of the history of the place, providing it with a humanistic meaning that continued to change.

From the perspective of human experience, history and space constructed and transformed one another. The book ends in the 2010s, which is also when I first encountered Xita. During the years I visited frequently, the community was constantly changing—sometimes positively, sometimes less so, depending on one's perspective. Even as an outsider, I could easily sense the changes; local residents were more than aware of them. Therefore, although the story of Xita in this book concludes at this point, we all know that Xita's story will never truly end here. Perhaps one day, someone will write about more exciting transformations.

ACKNOWLEDGMENTS

Numerous scholars and friends helped and aided my research. Without their generous assistance, this history would have been simply impossible to complete. Professor Li Qinpu not only provided invaluable documents and advice but also introduced me to a network of local scholars. Whenever I encountered difficulties, Li was the first person I consulted. It is only natural that I relied on his wisdom in my own studies. He Rongwei at the Liaoning Provincial Archive, Dong Baohou at the Liaoning Provincial Museum, and Liu Bing and Xue Ming at the Liaoning Provincial Library received me kindly and guided me through their abundant collections. The intellectual exchanges with these brilliant individuals enhanced my understanding of the city, its people, and the local history significantly.

During my field trips to Shenyang, I had the good fortune to talk with, and learn from, scholars at different local universities. I especially thank Professors Lü Haiping and Wang He at Shenyang Jianzhu University and Professors Nie Jiaxin, Wu Shixu, and Mao Wei at Shenyang Normal University, who shared their knowledge, field experience, and personal networks unreservedly. Their hospitality further motivated my research, making my prolonged academic journey not as lonely as it might appear.

My special gratitude goes to Jin Taibin and his family. Jin is a thoughtful, enthusiastic young man who introduced me to many elderly residents in Xita. Without his assistance and that of his parents I could not have collected some of the most precious memories in the book. Wu Xicheng was also a huge help, sacrificing his own time to accompany me to talk with his ethnic Korean friends. A volunteer group that protects local cultural relics lent a hand when I encountered problems finding detailed and underdocumented information. And the book benefited from my conversations with Yang Shu, He Xi, Yang Shuo, Wang Lian, Zhang Liming, and others. For any researcher, finding the right person to talk to at the right time and place is lucky and critical. Gu Mengfei and Zhao Meiqing at the China Christian Council offered generous help when I requested information about the Xita Church. Thank you to Mia Yu, who kindly shared personal memories of her hometown with me, which inspired my thoughts on temporal-spatial relationships a great deal.

Listing all my friends and colleagues who read and commented on my manuscript is mission impossible. My first and biggest thanks go to Leila Corcoran, an excellent editor, who put great effort into improving my expression, paragraph by paragraph and chapter by chapter. In the early stages of my research, I consulted with William Rowe, Kate Brown, Ruth Rogaski, Ding Yizhuang, Jun Yoo, Albert Park, Yu Zhou, and Sun Ge on various issues—all shared insightful opinions. The project was partially presented at several online conferences during the pandemic. Although we could not meet in person, Christopher Atwood, Evelyn Rawski, Zhang Ying, Loretta Kim, and Wu Lan encouraged me with their enlightened comments and responses. Kung Ling-wei, Qiu Yuanyuan, Chen Shuang, Wang Yuanchong, Xu Jin, Xie Wen, Zhang Ling, Yan Yuqian, Wang Chao, Zhan Yang, Dong Yige, Liu Dong, Chen Weifen, Loretta Kim, Li Ji, Dan Vukovich, Zhou Sicheng, Zhong Han, Hou Haoran, Li Limin, Gegeqi, Surina, Madeleine Yue Dong, and Hu Xiaobai read some of the chapters and provided discerning suggestions on revision. The research had sponsorship from my former employer, the University of Maryland–Baltimore County (UMBC). It was supported by many colleagues. Rachel Brubaker revised my grant applications several times, and I feel such relief that her tremendous help can finally be honored in some way. My former colleagues in the History and Asian Studies Departments—Constantine Vaporis, Amy Froide, Christy Ford Chapin, Marjoleine Kars, Meredith Oyen, Kyung-En Yoon, and Fan Yang, just to name a few—took great care of me and the project. My appreciation is beyond words.

In addition to the contribution from UMBC, the research benefited from smaller grants provided by the Northeast Asia Council of the Association for Asian Studies, the Harvard-Yenching Library, and the American Geographic Society Library. After I joined Tsinghua University in 2021, the research received funding from the university and the Chinese Ministry of Education. I thank the grant committees who acknowledged the value of this project.

Two reviewers of the manuscript provided great comments and revision suggestions, which were immensely helpful. Many thanks to James Millward, the chief editor of the Silk Road series, and Dylan Joseph

Montanari and Mary Al-Sayed, editors at the University of Chicago Press, for kindly guiding me through the publication process at different stages.

Whether I'm in the US or China, I am protected and supported by my family. My parents gave me all their love while rarely requesting anything in return. My wife, Zhao Yanling, who has devoted her time to looking after me and our children, is the true hero behind all my humble achievements. During my years of research and writing, our children, Chuhe and Charles, grew from babies to teenagers. They enrich my life in such an important way that I realize all my hard work has already been rewarded.

Last but not least, I have to express my deepest gratitude to a special friend who first introduced Xita to me. It was summer 2012 when I was doing fieldwork for another project in Shenyang. Quan Hexiu, a history professor at Liaoning University and my local liaison, suggested we meet at Xita. It was the first time I'd heard of the neighborhood. Quan explained that since my research project involved ethnic Koreans in China and Xita was the largest Korean enclave in the city, it made sense to take me there. That day, we ate supper in a North Korean restaurant and then walked across the street and enjoyed a coffee in a café run by a South Korean. There are only a few places on the planet where you can have this experience. Quan, an ethnic Korean (Chaoxianzu), placed our orders in his native tongue and talked to me in Chinese, switching between the two languages deftly. While chatting with him, I turned my head to look outside, amazed by the busy street full of shops, traffic, and bilingual neon signs. It was at that moment I started to wonder: Why was the place called the West Tower? It was a simple question that eventually led to this book. On September 10, 2017, I received the shocking news that Professor Quan, who thoroughly encouraged my research, had passed away at home from serious depression. He was only fifty-five. I have no other way to express my deepest sorrow than to present this book as a trivial comfort. May he rest in peace.

NOTES

Introduction

1. Piao and Zhou, *Xita: Shenyang shi aepingqu xita jiedao zhi*, 25.

2. The municipal government of Shenyang also governs a county-level city and two counties, which are not counted as urban Shenyang.

3. The government website of Shenyang, accessed July 24, 2024, https://www .shenyang.gov.cn/. The total does not include another fifty-three *xiang* (town) and sixteen *zhen* (township-level) divisions in the rural area.

4. Shao, *Remote Homeland, Recovered Borderland*.

5. Rogaski, *Knowing Manchuria*.

6. For a vivid account of the changes in rural Manchuria, see Meyer, *In Manchuria*. For a study on urban poverty in Heilongjiang, see Cho Mun Young, *Specter of "The People"*.

7. Allen, Massey, and Cochrane, *Rethinking the Region*.

8. Some recent works include L. Wu, *Common Ground*, and Oidtmann, *Forging the Golden Urn*. There are many more scholars, including David Farquhar, Mark Elliott, Evelyn Rawski, Pamela Crossley, Peter Perdue, Johan Elverskog, Ishihama Yumiko, Shen Weirong, and many others, who mention Qing Inner Asian politics and Tibetan Buddhism.

9. See Lattimore, *Manchuria*; Young, *Japan's Total Empire*; Matsusaka, *Making of Japanese Manchuria, 1904–1932*; and Hyun Ok Park, *Two Dreams in One Bed*.

10. Many works deal with these topics. See Mullaney, *Coming to Terms with the Nation*; Meisner, *Mao's China and After*; Yan, *Private Life Under Socialism*; X. Zhou, *State and Life Chances in Urban China*; and Chun, *Transformation of Chinese Socialism*.

11. Emmanuel Le Roy Ladurie, *Montaillou: Cathars and Catholics in a French Village, 1294–1324*, trans. Barbara Bray (London: Penguin Books, 1990); Natalie Zemon Davis, *The Return of Martin Guerre* (Cambridge, MA: Harvard University Press, 1983); Carlo Ginzburg, *The Cheese and the Worms: The Cosmos of a Sixteenth-Century Miller*, trans. John Tedeschi and Anne C. Tedeschi (Baltimore: Johns Hopkins University Press, 2013).

12. In recent years, many brilliant studies in the category of "micro-global history" have emerged that have largely expanded our understanding of the links between a micro-level subject and global trends. In the field of China studies, several works focusing on an individual are worth mentioning here: Harrison, *Missionary's Curse and Other Tales*

from a Chinese Catholic Village; Sachsenmaier, *Global Entanglements of a Man Who Never Traveled*; J. Li, *At the Frontier of God's Empire*; and Y. Liu, *Cheng Yunheng de shijiu shiji*.

13. Since the works that inspired my research are too many to list here, I will mention just a few representative works: Skinner, *City in Late Imperial China*; Naquin, *Beijing*; Rowe, *Hankow*; Meyer-Fong, *Building Culture in Early Qing Yangzhou*; D. Wang, *Street Culture in Chengdu*; D. Wang, *Teahouse*; Singaravélou, *Wanguo Tianjin*. J. Liu, *Modu Shanghai*. I respond to some of the studies of Manchurian cities in each chapter.

14. D. Harvey, *Paris, Capital of Modernity*.

15. M. Y. Dong, *Republican Beijing*, 17.

16. Lefebvre, *Space, State, World: Selected Essays*, 170–71.

Chapter 1

1. Zhongguo diyi lishi danganguan, *Qing chu nei guo shi yuan Man wen dang an yi bian*, vol. 2, 27–28. Zhao Zhiqiang corrected a mistranslation in the volume. See Zhao Zhiqiang, "Beita falunsi yu mengguzu manzu xibozu guanxi lunshu," 82. Also see Li Qinpu, "Xizang de fogou jingjie," 26–43.

2. Zhongguo diyi lishi danganguan, *Qingchu neiguoshiyuan*, 2:28.

3. For example, see Millward et al., *New Qing Imperial History*; Forét, *Mapping Chengde*; Whiteman, *Where Dragon Veins Meet*.

4. Oshibuchi, *Hōten to Ryōyō*, 1–17.

5. See Yi, Dong et al., *Shengjing tongzhi*, juan 1; Wang and Lü, *Jindai Shenyang Chengshi Xingtai Yanjiu*, 41–50.

6. Agui, *Qinding shengjing tongzhi*, juan 15.

7. Wang Maosheng, *Cong Shengjing dao Shenyang*, 57–61.

8. Wan Shubang, "Shenyang chengnei zui zao de mingcha, Chang'ansi," 11.

9. We are not clear about his monastic affiliation due to source limitations. However, Kam Tak Sing believes he was most likely from the Gelug sect. See Kam, "dGe-lugs-pa Breakthrough," 161–76; Oshibuchi, *Manshū hikikō*.

10. Primary sources about Orlog Darhan Langsu could be found on the two stelae in Liaoyang. The Han Chinese inscriptions, "Liaoyang dajin lama fashi baojibei" and "Liaoyang Da lama fen tabei," are recorded in Wang Jingchen, *Liaoning beizhi*, 44–46. As for the Manchu and Mongol inscriptions on the stelae and secondary studies, see Oshibuchi Hajime, "Ryō yō ramafun hiki" in *Manshū hikikō*, 50–130; Kam, "Manchu-Tibetan Relations in the Early Seventeenth Century: A Reappraisal"; Li Qinpu, "Wolu daerhan nangsu," 12–29, 12–23; Li Qinpu, "Manhanmeng hebi 'da lama fenta beiwen' yizhu," 3–12.

11. Li Qinpu, "Bailama yu Qingchao zangchuan fojiao de jianli," 65–100.

12. Zhongguo diyi lishi danganguan, *Qingchu neiguoshiyuan*, vol. 1, 74.

13. Zhongguo diyi lishi danganguan, 1:126–27; *Qingshilu, Taizongshilu*, juan 21, 282. See also Shinchō Manshūgo tō Shiryō no Sōgōteki Chīmu, *Naikokushiin tō: Tenchō hachinen*, 390.

14. Atwood, *Encyclopedia of Mongolia and the Mongol Empire*, 334–35. While the conventional story is that Ligdan died of smallpox, some scholars believe he was killed in a coup. See Munkh-Erdene, *Taiji Government and the Rise of the Warrior State*, 5.

15. See Hasibagen, *Qingchu manmeng guanxi yanbian yanjiu*.

16. Kam, "'Zhengtong' zhiyuan," 119–74.

17. Shen Weirong, *Dayuanshi yu Xinqingshi*, 122–35.

18. Atwood, "The First Mongol Contact with the Tibetans," 22.

19. Delege, *Neimenggu Lamajiao shi*, 80–84.

20. Contrary to popular belief, the Ming court largely promoted the unprecedented popularity of Tibetan Buddhism in China proper. See Shen Weirong, *Xiangxiang Xizang*, 118–54. Hu, "Mingchao zhengce yu 15 shiji zhongqi zangchuan fojiao zai hanzang zoulang de chuanbo jizhi saulun." Robinson, "The Ming Court and the Legacy of the Yuan Mongols," 365–423.

21. Elverskog, *Our Great Qing*, 54.

22. Elverskog, "Mongol Time Enters a Qing World," 142–78.

23. Wang Yao, "Cult of Mahakala and a Temple in Beijing," 117–26.

24. Li Qinpu, "Shengjing mahagala kaozheng," 95–120.

25. About the Imperial Jade Seal and the Yuan lineage, see Morikawa, "Daigen no kioku," 65–81.

26. *Qingshilu Taizongshilu*, juan 28, 360–63.

27. See Wang Yuanchong, *Remaking the Chinese Empire, Manchu-Korean Relations, 1616–1911*.

28. See Perdue, *China Marches West*.

29. Kawachi, *Naikokushiin manbun tōan yakuchū*, 533. See also: *Qingshilu, Taizongshilu*, juan 43, 565–66.

30. The full name is the Lotus Pure Land Essential-Victory Temple (C. Lianhua jingtu shisheng si; Ma. Šul ilgai soorin i yargiyan etehe soorin). Later, Emperor Qianlong retrospectively associated the name with Hong Taiji's military victory against the Ming troops at Songshan in 1641, which was obviously a mythmaking. See Qianlong, "Yuzhi shishengsi beiji," in *Qinding rixia jiuwen kao (juan 120)*, First Historical Archive of China. This book uses its most common name, the Essential-Victory Temple.

31. *Chongde san nian manwen dang'an yibian*, 183.

32. Itō, "Manshū no butsuji kenchiku," 1–76.

33. For the Chinese version of the text, see Wang Jingchen, *Liaoning beizhi*, 70–71. All four of the versions were recorded by Ishihama Yumiko. See Ishihama "Sei-hatsu chokuken Chibetto bukkyō jiin satoshi gōteki kenkyū," 1–39.

34. Kam, "Manchu-Tibetan Relations in the Early Seventeenth Century," 128–29.

35. Li Qinpu, "Bilitu lamasu, Qingchu zangchuan fojiao de xianyang zhe," 46–75; Ishihama, "Sei-hatsu chokuken Chibetto bukkyō," 22–23.

36. Japanese scholar Wakamatsu Hiroshi challenged a rare source that indicates that Sibja was the first envoy sent by both the Fifth Dalai Lama and the Fourth Panchen Lama to meet Hong Taiji. Chinese scholar Baoyindeligen, however, defended the accuracy of the source. See Wakamatsu, "Xiletu kulun lama zhuan huidian chutan," 17–23; Baoyindeligen, "Xiletu kuleng bandi da nuomenhan shiji kaoshu," 126–35. The rare source *tegüs čoγtu nom-un uqγaruγ-a-yin namtar-i sayidurnigenjüg-tü quriyangγuilaγsan toli*, originally written in Tibetan after the 1820s, was translated into Mongolian in 1959 and then translated into Chinese in 1989. See Qikeqi, "Xiletu kulun lama zhuan huidian," 129–48.

37. Zhongguo diyi lishi danganguan, *Qing chu nei guo shi yuan Man wen dang an yi bian*, 1:345.

38. While the emperor named it "the Xingyuan Temple," the Dalai Lama called it "dga' ldan chos gling."

39. For the Chinese version of the temple stelae, see Wang Jingchen, *Liaoning beizhi*, 72–73. For the complete list of builders, see Li Qinpu, "Shengjing sisi zangyu beiwen jiaoyi," 98–107.

40. The full names of the four temples were as follows:

TABLE 1

	Han Chinese names	Manchu names	Tibetan names
East	Chi-jian hu-guo Yongguang si	Unenggi eldembuhe fucihi soorin	rnam-par snang-mdzad kyis lha-khang
South	Chi-jian hu-guo Guangci si	Amba gosin i fucihi soorin	thugs-rje chen-povi lha-khang
West	Chi-jian hu-guo Yanshou si	Enteheme jalafun fucihi soorin	tshe-dpag med kyis lha-khang
North	Chi-jian hu-guo Falun si	Forgon be ejelehe soorin	dus kyi 'khor-lo'i lha-khang

Their full names in Chinese contained four characters of *chi jian hu guo*, meaning "found under the imperial edict to protect the state." Their corresponding Tibetan names contained *dam-pa mchog gi rgyal-po'i bka'-sa*, meaning "found under the imperial edict" (adapted from Li Qinpu, "Xizang de fogou jingjie" and "Shengjing sisi manyu beiwen jiaoyi," 90–100).

41. Qikeqi, "Xiletu kulun lama zhuan huidian," 138–39; Ikejiri, "Qingchu zhasake da-lama zhidu de xingcheng," 3–11.

42. The song "Let Us Sway Twin Oars" is the theme song of the film *Flowers of the Motherland*, which tells the story of a group of primary school students in Beijing. A line in the song goes, "The beautiful white stupa casts its shadow in the lake." Famous author Qiao Yu (1927–2022) wrote the lyrics.

43. Roth, "Symbolism of the Buddhist Stupa," 183–209.

44. P. Harvey, "Symbolism of the Early Stupa," 67–93.

45. See Liu Guoyong, "Yanshousita chaichu baogao," 186–89, and Ding Jun, "Shenyang yanshousita jiqi chutu wenwu kaolue," 122–29.

46. Tucci, *Stupa*, 54–55. Also see Berounsky and Sklenka, "Tibetan Tsha-Tsha," 60.

47. Zhou and Li, *Xueshan Zhong de mantuluo*, 50.

48. Fussman, "Symbolisms of the Buddhist Stupa," 37–53.

49. Li Qinpu, "Xizang de fogou jingjie," 38.

50. Grupper, "Manchu Imperial Cult of the Early Ch'ing Dynasty," 160.

51. Grupper, "Manchu Patronage and Tibetan Buddhism during the First Half of the Ch'ing Dynasty," 47–74.

52. For example, Liu Shiying, *Peidu jilue*; Miao Runfu, *Peijing zashu* (Shenyang: Shen-yang chubanshe, 2009).

53. Oshibuchi, *Hōten to Ryōyō*, 50.

54. Li Qinpu, "Xizang de fogou jingjie." Also see Angba, *Zangchuan fojiao mizong yu mantuluo yishu*, 48–50.

55. For example, see Wang Mingqi, *Liaohai wenwu kaobian* , 2–37. Also see Ishihama, "Sei-hatsu chokuken," 26.

56. Lü, Song, and Wang, *Shengjing tongzhi*, vol. 26, 2b.

57. Qianlong, *Yuzhishi siji*, juan 100, collected in *Jingyin wenyuange siku quanshu*, vol. 1308, 898–99. Also see Agui, *Qinding shengjing tongzhi*, Juan 15, also collected in *Jingyin wenyuange siku quanshu*, vol. 501 273–74. Taipei: Taiwan shangwu, 1986.

58. My analysis is based on Elliott, "Turning a Phrase," 12–41; Kam, "Manchu-Tibetan Relations in the Early Seventeenth Century"; Li Qinpu, "Shengjing sisi zangyu beiwen jiaoyi" and "Shengjing sisi manyu beiwen jiaoyi," 90–100.

59. Translated by Mark Elliott, my emphasis. I also made a few adjustments: I translate the word *shengwang* (圣王) as "holy king" instead of "divine ruler," and the word *guo* (国) as "state" instead of "nation."

60. Only when introducing the temple of the Wheel of Time in the north, the non-Chinese versions mention that the function of the temple is to "bring perpetual strength to the Imperial Throne." See Elliott, "Turning a Phrase," 35, 37, and 40. However, interestingly, the Chinese text here is completely different. The purpose of this temple became "for the promulgation of the True Law." And the deity (the Wheel of Time) is introduced as "the Wheel of Law." I address this issue later in the chapter.

61. Elliott, "Turning a Phrase," 21.

62. Wang Jingchen, *Liaoning beizhi*, 72.

63. For detailed discussion, see Elliott, "Turning a Phrase"; Li Qinpu, "Shengjing sisi zangyu beiwen"; Kam, Manchu-Tibetan Relations in the Early Seventeenth Century," 148–71; and Li Qinpu, "Shengjing sisi manyu beiwen jiaoyi."

64. I found two sources for this story. One was told by a local resident, An Jingshan. See Guan Fang, "Mahagala folou de chuanshuo," in Hepingqu "sanjicheng" bianwei-hui, *Heping ziliaoben*, 1:31–33. The other was told by Chang Haifeng, a late lama at the Essential-Victory Temple. See Li Fengmin, *Shenyang huangsi sanbainian* (Shenyang: Dongbei daxue chubanshe, 2012), 47.

65. See Min Jinwŏn, "Yŏnhang Ilgi," in Im, *Yŏnhaengnok chŏnjip*, vol. 34, 341; Han Dŏkhu, "Yŏnhang Illok," in Im, *Yŏnhaengnok chŏnjip*, vol. 50, 193.

66. Tong, *Qingdai peidu Shenyang*, 176–77.

67. Farquhar, "Emperor as Bodhisattva in the Governance of Ch'ing Empire," 5–34; Kam, "Zhengtong zhiyuan," 160.

68. Shen, *Dayuanshi he Xinqingshi*, 240.

69. Ishihama, "Notion of 'Buddhist Government' (chos srid) Shared by Tibet, Mongol and Manchu in the Early 17th Century," 15–31.

70. Shen, *Dayuanshi he Xinqingshi*, 244–49.

71. Evelyn Rawski, in *Last Emperors*, has a succinct yet comprehensive description of the Qing's policy toward Tibetan Buddhism. See chapter 7 of *Last Emperors*. However, she seems confused about the Essential-Victory Temple and the Mahākāla Pavilion, even wrongly suggesting that the Mahākāla statue was moved to Beijing in the early Qing.

72. Shi, *Mengzhang fojiaoshi*, 187; Zhao Yuntian, "Qingdai qianqi liyong lamajiao zhengce de xingcheng he yanbian," 63–76; Zhang Yuxin, *Qingzhengfu yu lamajiao*; Blo-bzang-chos-kyi-nyi-ma, *Zhangjia guo shi Ruobiduoji zhuan*; Wang Xiangyu, "Tibetan Buddhism at the Court of Qing."

73. Lai, *Qianlong Huangdi de Hebao*, 227 and 318.

74. *Qianlongchao neifuchaoben "Lifanyuan zeli"*, 117–37.

75. Kung, "Guofa yu jiaofa zhijian," 187–219.

76. For a comprehensive study of the institution in English, see Oidtmann, *Forging the Golden Urn*.

77. *Da Qing huidian*, compiled in Jiaqing's reign. See *Qianlongchao neifuchaoben "Lifanyuan zeli"*, 368.

78. *Fengtian Shengzhang gongshu dang*, JC010-01-004384, Liaoning Provincial Archive.

79. Sŏ Gyŏng-sun, "Monggyŏngtang ilsa" in Im, *Yŏnhaengnok chŏnjip*, vol. 94, 229.

80. Shi, *Mengzhang fojiaoshi*, 220–22.

81. Luo, *Longpao yu Jiasha*, 555.

82. Delege, *Neimenggu Lamajiao shi*, 253; Luo, *Longpao yu Jiasha*, 560–61.

83. Only the Da lama of the Long-lasting-Peace Temple was exempted for this duty. *Fengtian Shengzhang gongshu dang*, JC010-01-012622, Liaoning Provincial Archive.

84. Luo, *Longpao yu Jiasha*, 561; Li Fengmin, *Shenyang Huangsi*, 119–21.

85. Elliott, *Manchu Way*.

86. The entire Tibetan Buddhist canon was divided into two categories: Kangyur, or "Translated Words," refers to the word of Buddha and Tengyur, or "Translated Treatises," refers to the later commentaries.

87. Bingenheimer, "History of the Manchu Buddhist Canon and First Steps Towards Its Digitization," 203–17.

88. The First Historical Archive of China, no. 03-18-009-000043-0001.

89. Zhao Zhiqiang, "Beita falunsi," 79–86.

90. Walter Fuchs reported that he witnessed the Manchu canon in Mukden. A large part of it was destroyed in the Russo-Japanese War. Some remnants were taken to Japan by Naitō Konan but were destroyed in the Kantō earthquake. See Fuchs, "Early Manchurian Inscriptions in Manchuria" 5–9.

91. The First Historical Archives of China, no. 04-01-09-0005-013. The document shows that in 1901, the vacancy of the Da lama at the Dharma-Wheel Temple was filled by the vice Da lama and the role of vice Da lama which was further filled by the demchi of the same temple.

92. Qianlong. "Ti Falunsi," *Yuzhishi siji*, juan 100, 216.

93. Qianlong, "Falunsi," *Yuzhishi siji*, juan 100, 2–3, 898–99.

94. Elliott, "Turning a Phrase."

95. *Fengtian Beita Falunsi Jianshe Bing Shilun Jingang Yiwen Shuoming Beikao*, pamphlet. It clearly says that the deity in the Dharma-Wheel Temple was Shilun Jingang, Lord of the Wheel of Time.

96. Crossley, *Translucent Mirror*, 224.

97. Yan Zinan, "Kuilei youxi." 77–88.

98. Shenyangshi minwei minzuzhi bianzuan bangongshi, *Shenyang Xibozu zhi*.

99. Zhao Zhiqiang, "Beita falunsi," 86.

100. Elliott, *Manchu Way*, 408n175.

101. See Lü, Song, and Wang, *Shengjing tongzhi*, juan 26, 2. The story, of course, was a fiction. It said that Ligdan khan's mother, not the Mergen Lama, used the camel to deliver the statue, along with the golden sutra and the jade seal. The story contradicted the early Qing archives. Nor did the first edition of the *General Chronicle of Shengjing* (with 32 juan), compiled by Yi Bahan, Dong Bingzhong et al. in 1684, mention anything about the camel. See Yi, Dong et al., *Shengjing tongzhi*, vol. 20, 2.

102. Hepingqu "sanjicheng" bianweihui, *Heping ziliaoben*, 1:23–25.

103. For example, the Qing regulated that the annual tribute offered by the Khalkha tribes, including the Jebtsundamba Khutuktu, should be one white camel and eight white horses, known as the "Tribute of the Nine Whites."

104. Elliott, "Limits of Tartary," 603–46.

105. Shenyangshi minzu shiwu weiyuanhui, *Shenyang Mengguzu zhi*, 7–15.

106. Perdue, *China Marches West*, 110–11.

107. Sonoda, *Dattan hyōryūki*, 21–22.

108. Oshibuchi, *Hōten to Ryōyō*, 49.

109. Verbiest et al., *History of the Two Tartar Conquerors of China*, 106.

110. Verbiest et al., 125.

111. Ribeiro and O'Malley, *Jesuit Mapmaking in China*.

112. The first spelling is found in Ribeiro and O'Malley, *Jesuit Mapmaking in China*, 114. The second is found in another version of *Nouvelle Atlas De La Chine*, preserved by the American Geographical Society Library at the University of Wisconsin–Milwaukee.

113. See Elliott, "Limits of Tartary."

114. Chun, "Sino-Korean Tributary Relations in the Ch'ing Period," 99.

115. Yi Il-sang, "Yŏnhaengji," in Im, *Yŏnhaengnok chŏnjip*, vol. 21, 257.

116. Han Tae-dong, "Yangse Yŏnhaengnok," in Im, *Yŏnhaengnok chŏnjip*, vol. 29, 203.

117. Kim Ch'ang-ŏp, "Rogaja Yŏnhaeng ilgi," in Im, *Yŏnhaengnok chŏnjip*, vol. 32, 287.

118. Yi Ch'ŏl-pu, "Chŏnsa Yŏnhaeng ilgi," in Im, *Yŏnhaengnok chŏnjip*, vol. 37, 447.

119. Song, "'Those Ridiculous Monks'" 206–26.

120. [Author unidentified], "Yŏnhaeng illok," in Im, *Yŏnhaengnok chŏnjip*, vol. 61, 23.

121. About the Buddhist monasteries and local society in Tibet, see Ran, *Zhongguo zangchuan fojiao siyuan*.

Chapter 2

1. *Qianlongchao qinding daqing huidian zeli*, vol. 1, 139, Board of Rites in Mukden, First Historical Archive of China. The actual number of lamas living in a temple, as mentioned in chapter 1, was usually much higher. Besides the lamas, there were some banner soldiers guarding the temple.

2. "Fengtian xingsheng gongshu wei shishengsi lama chengqing fagei daily shiwu fu menggu xuanbu gonghe zhashi," Liaoning Provincial Archive, no. JC010-01-23493.

3. Story, *Campaign with Kuropatkin*, 94.

4. "Fengtian xingzhenggongshu wei changningsi Da lama deleke citui yique jianxuan zhengpei zaoce songbu zhuanzou bufangshi," Liaoning Provincial Archive, no. JC010-01-12622.

5. About monastery hierarchy in Mongolia, see Atwood, *Encyclopedia of Mongolia and the Mongol Empire*, 326–27.

6. "Xita yanshousi sha lama," in Hepingqu "sanjicheng" bianweihui, *Heping Ziliaoben*, 1:67–68.

7. This is a custom in both Han and Mongol traditions. It signals the beginning of the new year celebration.

8. "Tiwei tecan shu chengdexian dianli yankai deng shufang Da lama baladan beijushang shensi yian xianman xiongzei weihuoshi," First Historical Archive of China, no. 02-01-03-11440-031.

9. Sŏ U-jŭng, "Myŏngsan Yŏngsiryo," in Im, *Yŏnhaengnok chŏnjip*, vol. 69, 148–50. Notes are original.

10. *Qianlongchao qinding daqing huidian zeli*.

11. Li Fengmin, *Shenyang huangsi sanbainian*, 151.

12. It is not necessary to list all the archives. The first case was in 1755, no. 02-01-008-001900-0005-0000 The last one was in 1893, no. 04-01-037-000142-0015-0000.

13. The hypothetical narrative of the boy L is based on several sources: *Qinding Da Qing Huidian* (Kangxi, Yongzheng, Qianlong and Jiaqing versions) and *Shangyudang*, Jiaqing 16-L3-19, no. 9, First Historical Archive of China; Liaoning Provincial Archive,

no. JC010-01-12622 and no. JC010-01-012623; Li Fengmin, *Shenyang huangsi sanbainian*, 109–14.

14. Story, *Campaign with Kuropatkin*, 94.

15. Xu Hao, *18 shiji de zhongguo yu shijie: Nongmin juan* [China and the World in the Eighteenth Century, Peasants] (Shenyang: Liaohai chubanshe, 1999).

16. Li Fengmin, *Shenyang huangsi sanbainian*, 111. But according to Longdan Jiabu, the Jasak Da lama in the 1930s, the Qing government provided altogether 15,852 taels of silver per year as lamas' salary, which is at odds with other sources. If his account was more accurate, the individual income of a lama was much higher than what I describe here. See Longdan, *Fengtian shisheng qisi shuoming lama sengzhong jianshe dagang quanlu*, 4.

17. See Wu, Zhang, and Zhang, *Dongbeitudi guanxishi yanjiu*, 81.

18. The incident and trail reports could be found in the First Historical Archive of China, no. 04-01-27-0021-009 and no. 03-2287-027.

19. Here I use the term *banner farmland* to refer to the lands first occupied then redistributed by the Qing state. These lands were owned by neither the government, the royal family, nor banner soldiers.

20. About this topic, see Wu, Zhang, and Zhang, *Dongbeitudi guanxishi yanjiu*; Ding and Qiu, *Jinji wubaili, Qingdai jifudiqu de qidi yu zhuangtou*.

21. Qiu, "Tudi, Jicheng yu Jiazu," 17–52.

22. Isett, *State, Peasant, and Merchant in Qing Manchuria, 1644–1862*, 3–6.

23. Shangyudang, Jiaqing 16-01-07, no. 2, First Historical Archive of China.

24. The case is found in "Tiwei zouyi qianren shengjing hubu shilang dewen dengyuan wujiang youjun sichan duanwei lama xianghuodi shi," First Historical Archive of China, no. 02-01-03-08907-013.

25. About *zhuangding*, see Wu, Zhang, and Zhang, *Dongbeitudi guanxishi yanjiu*, 76–77.

26. *Shangyudang*, Jiaqing 16-01-07 (bu), First Archive of China.

27. *Shangyudang*, Jiaqing 16-L3-19, no. 9, First Historical Archive of China.

28. Wu, Zhang, and Zhang, *Dongbeitudi guanxishi yanjiu*, 78.

29. "Zouwei shengjing gesi lama yongdu jieju qing jiang zizhi sichan zhaodian quzushi," First Historical Archive of China, no. 04-01-35-0601-020.

30. "Zouwei changningsi Da lama zhi que benfu bubian bufangshi," First Historical Archive of China, no. 05-0037-029.

31. "Tiwei huishen shengjing chengdexian lamabandi baidanjin yin chihe taoqi xiachuoshangbi tusun duiyue yian," First Historical Archive of China, no. 02-01-007-023342-0002.

32. "Zouwei zunyi shengjing jiangjun yinglong de huitong shenming guansan lama xishi yapianyan leshu bijian funv an," First Historical Archive of China, no. 04-01-01-0856-063.

33. The first case is found in "Zouwei zunzhi yanshen jieren menggu zhushixian rongzhi jiaojie lama lvyou zhiguanzhuangpian dengqing'an," First Historical Archive of China, no. 04-01-01-0749-047. The second case is found in "Zouwei huitong shenming megu baijihu huoqie bing Da lama jieduan zhazang'an," First Historical Archive of China, no. 04-01-01-0743-027.

34. Han Tae-dong, "Yangse Yŏnhaengnok" in Im, *Yŏnhaengnok chŏnjip*, vol. 29, 203.

35. Yi Hap, "Yŏnhaenggisa," in Im, *Yŏnhaengnok chŏnjip*, vol. 52, 361.

36. Han Dok-hu, "Yŏnhaengillok," in Im, *Yŏnhaengnok chŏnjip*, vol. 50, 193.

37. Cho Ch'o-su, "Imjayŏnhaengilgi," in Im, *Yŏnhaengnok chŏnjip*, vol. 50, 387; Yi Gi-hyŏ, "Yŏnhaengilgi," in Im, *Yŏnhaengnok chŏnjip*, vol. 65, 63.

38. Hong Dae-yong, "Tamhyŏn Yŏngi," in Im, *Yŏnhaengnok chŏnjip*, vol. 49, 258. For another example, see Kwŏn Si-hyŏn, "Sŏktangyŏngi," Im, *Yŏnhaengnok chŏnjip*, vol. 90, 407.

39. About its various forms, see Delege, *Neimenggu Lamajiao shi*, 572–78; Chen, "Qingdai gongting lamajiao huodong," 65–69, and Fu, "Mingqing shiqi de 'tiaobuzha' xisu," 37–40.

40. See Jia, "Shishengsi lama tiaoda zanguanji," 76–79, and Guan Fang, "Shenyang de sita qisi ji qita," in Zhengxie shenyangshi weiyuanhui wenshiziliao yanjiu weiyuanhui, *Shenyang wenshi ziliao*, vol. 5, 105–36.

41. See Hou, "Zangchuan fojiao wenben de xingcheng jiqi lishi xushi chuantong de chuangjian," 84–188.

42. For example, Susan Naquin talks about "ghosting beating" rites in imperial Beijing. See Naquin, *Peking*, 589.

43. While most documents suggest it was performed twice a year, a local gazetteer compiled in 1910, *Chengdexian zhishu* records that it was presented three times a year. See *Chengdexian zhishu*, "zongjiao zhi," 1910, 21.

44. *Chengdexian zhishu*, "zongjiao zhi," 1910, 21.

45. Li Fengmin, *Shenyang huangsi sanbainian*, 168–80.

46. Story, *Campaign with Kuropatkin*, 96–97.

47. Shenyang tujing, "Wo jianguo huangsi lama tiaota."

48. About the south touring, see Chang, *Court on Horseback*.

49. The throne's patronage to Tibetan Buddhism declined everywhere, not just in Mukden. See Naquin, *Peking*, 591.

50. Liaoningsheng dang anguan, ed., *Zhongguo jindai shehui shenghuo dang'an (dongbei juan 1)*, vol. 15 (Guilin: Guangxi shifan daxue chubanshe, 2005), 451–58.

51. Guan, "Shenyang de sita qisi," 117 and 119.

52. Li Fengmin, *Shenyang huangsi sanbainian*, 220–23. Also see Liaoningsheng dang'anguan, ed. *Zhongguo jindai shehui shenghuo dang'an (dongbei juan 1)*, vol. 13 (Guilin: Guangxi shifan daxue chubanshe, 2005), 378–80.

53. Story, *Campaign with Kuropatkin*, 94.

54. "Zouqing jiang jieji lama yinyuan guiru shanghou jingfeikuan nei zuozheng kaixiao shi," First Historical Archive of China, no. 04-01-35-1060-020.

55. "Fengtian qiwuchu wei duzhisi zi shishengsi denggechu lama yingban bupi zhejia chizhi juling shi," Liaoning Provincial Archive, no. JC010-01-12630.

56. Liaoning Provincial Archive, no. JC010-01-023492 and no. JC010-01-012628.

57. "Fengtian xingzhenggongsu wei shishengsi lama chengqing fagei dailishiwu fu menggu xuanbu gonghe zhashi," Liaoning Provincial Archive, no. JC010-01-23493. Li Fengmin, *Shenyang huangsi sanbainian*, 240–42.

58. "Fengtian xunanshi wei shengyang gesi lama wei bianmai yangzhan dingdi qing ju fangzhang shi," Liaoning Provincial Archive, no. JC010-01-004384.

59. Wu, Zhang, and Zhang, *Dongbeitudi guanxishi yanjiu*, 145–53.

60. According to Li Fengmin, the Fengtian government first appointed Jin Rongting as the Jasak Da lama in 1929. But he died after just three months (*Shenyang huangsi sanbainian*, 259).

61. The sources for the narrative are from Liaoning Provincial Archive: no. JC010-01-16584, no. JC010-01-31349, no. JC010-01-17050, no. JC010-01-31349, and no. JC010-01-012625.

62. Liaoning Provincial Archive, no. JC010-01-16584.

63. Liaoning Provincial Archive, no. JC010-01-192905.

64. Liaoning Provincial Archive, no. JC010-01-31349.

65. Li Fengmin, *Shenyang huangsi sanbainian*, 244–45.

66. "Liaoningsheng wei shishengsi cheng beita Da lama yi'echang binggu yi gaisi fuDa lama shulishi," Liaoning Provincial Archive, no. JC010-01-12626.

67. "Liaoningsheng zhengfu wei xingzhengyuan xunling fa menggu lama simiao tiaoli shi," Liaoning Provincial Archive, no. JC010-01-001030.

68. Temole, "Weiman lamajiao zongtuan chengli shimo," 55–58.

69. "Liaoningsheng zhengfu wei lama baoshan chengkong lama zhaoxiling deng mengshang qixia tunkuan feiji shi," Liaoning Provincial Archive, JC010-01-17505.

70. Longdan, *Fengtian shisheng qisi shuoming lama sengzhong jianshe dagang quanlu*.

71. Li Fengmin, *Shenyang huangsi sanbainian*, 279–80.

72. Wang Shiyi, "Wo yu zangchuan fojiao," in Shenyangshi zongjiao shiwuju, *Shenyang Zongjiao*, 78.

73. About the social ecology of the temples in the Mongolian region, see Jagchid, "Mongolian Lamaist Quasi-Feudalism During the Period of Manchu Domination," 27–54; Li Qinpu, "Qingdai zhi minguo waifan menggu de simiao, minzhong yu guojia," 52–82; Tsai, "Ju guozhong yi biguo," 129–67.

74. The narrative is based on the published interviews with lamas witnesses. See "Jinfo beidao yi'an," in Zhongguo remin zhengzhi xieshang huiyi liaoningsheng weiyuanhui, wenshi ziliao yanjiu weiyuanhui, *Liaoning wenshi ziliao*, vol. 12, 145–53.

Chapter 3

1. Story, *Campaign with Kuropatkin*, 93.

2. Kōmoto, "Watashi ga Chō Sakurin o koroshita."

3. The narrative is based on several memoirs of witnesses. See Zhou Dawen, "Zhang Zuolin huanggutun beizha shijian qinliji," in Zhengxie Shenyangshi weiyuanhui wenshi ziliao yanjiu weiyuanhui, *Shenyang wenshi ziliao*, 12:209–15; Wen Shoushan, "Zhang Zuolin zhi si," in Liaoningsheng zhengxie wenshi ziliao weiyuanhui, *Liaoning wenshi ziliao*, vol. 22, 161–63.

4. Ienaga Saburo, *The Pacific War: 1931–1945* (New York: Pantheon, 1978). In recent years, more and more Chinese historians have also adopted 1931, as opposed to 1937, as the starting point of what they call the "Counter-Japanese War."

5. See Mitter, *Manchurian Myth*.

6. Christie, *Thirty Years in Moukden*, 72–73.

7. About the process of the debate and the contribution of Witte, see Wolmar, *To the Edge of the World*.

8. See Wolmar, *To the Edge of the World*.

9. Witte, *Memoirs*, 89–90.

10. Witte, in his memoir, firmly denied that he bribed Li at the time. But Russian government files indicate that it did pay Li later altogether 3 million rubles. It is still debatable whether Li received the bribe or to what extent it affected the outcome of their negotiations. See Ford, *Russian Far Eastern Diplomacy*, 142–43.

11. S. C. M. Paine, "The Chinese Eastern Railway from the First Sino-Japanese War until the Russo-Japanese War," in Elleman and Kotkin, *Manchurian Railways and the Opening of China*, 18.

12. Witte, *Memoirs*, 99–100. Italics are mine.

13. Ford, *Russian Far Easter Diplomacy*, 141–68.

14. Witte, *Memoirs*, 103–4.

15. Christie, *Thirty Years in Moukden*, 124.

16. Christie, 130.

17. Wang and Lü, *Jindai Shenyang chengshi xingtai yanjiu*, 90–92; Liaoningsheng dang'anju, *Fengwu Liaoning*, vol. 1:47–48.

18. Lü and Wang, *Shuangchong quanli tixi*, 60.

19. See Esherick, *Origins of the Boxer Uprising*.

20. Liaoningsheng dang'anju, *Fengwu Liaoning*, vol.1, 49.

21. Rosenbaum, "Chinese Railway Policy and the Response to Imperialism."

22. Xie Xueshi, *Manzhou jiaotong saigao*, vol. 1, 233–584.

23. Alan Trachtenberg, foreword to Schivelbusch, *Railway Journey*, xiii.

24. Christie, *Thirty Years in Moukden*, 64.

25. Gao, *Jindai zhongguo dongbei yimin yanjiu*, 69.

26. Yao, *Zhongguo jindai jingji dili*, 56; Gao, *Jindai zhongguo dongbei yimin yanjiu*, 68.

27. Calculated from *Chengde xian zhishu*, 45–46.

28. Fukuda, *Manshū Hōten Nihonjin shi*, 47–48.

29. Story, *Campaign with Kuropatkin*, 97.

30. Lattimore, "Origins of the Great Wall of China: A Frontier Concept in Theory and Practice," in *Studies of Frontier History*, 92.

31. Liaoning Provincial Archive, "Jun Du Bu Tang," no. JC010-01-012618.

32. Fukuda, *Manshū Hōten Nihonjin shi*, 50.

33. Patrikeeff and Shukman, *Railways and the Russo-Japanese War*.

34. Xie, *Mantie ziliao huibian*, vol. 4, 3–30.

35. Liaoningsheng dang'anju, *Fengwu Liaoning*, 1:43.

36. I use SMR to refer to the railway and Mantetsu to refer to the company thereafter.

37. Xie Xueshi, *Mantie dang'an ziliao huibian*, vol. 5, 118–30.

38. Xie Xueshi, *Manzhou jiaotong saigao*, vol. 4, 690–704.

39. N. Song, *Making Borders in Modern East Asia*, 196–201.

40. JACAR, "Manshū go anken ni kansuru kyōyaku," Ref. B13c90914400.

41. "To Department," no. 79, United States Consular Records for Mukden, China, National Archives at College Park, Maryland, NAID: 1330338.

42. D. Harvey, *Paris, Capital of Modernity*, 3.

43. There is a lot of literature about colonial modernity in other Manchurian cities, such as Harbin, Changchun, or Dalian. For English readers, see Carter, *Creating a Chinese Harbin*, for Harbin; O'Dwyer, *Significant Soil*, for Dalian; and Sewell, *Constructing Empire*, for Changchun.

44. I did not invent this kind of "dual" lens. The concept derives from the "dual power system" raised by Lü Haiping and Wang He, two architectural historians who study urban architecture in modern Shenyang. See Lü and Wang, *Shuangchong quanli tixi*.

45. Zhengxie shenyangshi heping cuweihui, *Heping lao jianzhu*, 81.

46. Sewell, "Reconsidering the Modern in Japanese History."

47. Lü and Wang, *Shuangchong quanli tixi*, 161.

48. Nishizawa, "Study of Japanese Colonial Architecture in East Asia"; Nishizawa, "Guanyu riben ren zai zhongguo dongbei diqu."

49. Sewell, *Constructing Empire*, 71

50. Tatsuno designed the Tokyo and Pusan stations. The Keijō Station was designed by Tsukamoto Yasushi, Dalian by Ōta Sōtarō, and Changchun by Ichida Kikujirō, all of whom were either Tōdai graduates or Mantetsu employees.

51. Metcalf, *Imperial Vision: Indian Architecture and Britain's Raj*.

52. Nishizawa, "Study of Japanese Colonial Architecture."

53. Sewell, *Constructing Empire*, 68.

54. Nishizawa, "Guanyu riben ren zai zhongguo dongbei diqu."

55. Cordes, *Das jüngste Kaiserreich. Schlafendes, wachendes Mandschukuo*, 116–17.

56. And the city of Fengtian was renamed as Shenyang. But right after the Japanese occupation in 1931, both names were changed back to Fengtian. For convenience, I kept the name Fengtian to address the history between 1929 and 1931.

57. Jeffrey W. Cody, introduction to Cody, Steinhardt, and Atkin, *Chinese Architecture and the Beaux-Arts*, xvi.

58. Xing Ruan, "Yang Tingbao, China's Modern Architect in the Twentieth Century," in Cody, Steinhardt, and Atkin, *Chinese Architecture and the Beaux-Arts*, 153–54.

59. Lü and Wang, *Shuangchong quanli tixi*, 281.

60. Nanjing gongxueyuan jianzhu yanjiusuo, *Yang Tingbao jianzhu zuopin ji*, 11.

61. Crush, *Imperial Railway of North China*.

62. Ruan, "Yang Tingbao," 157.

63. Liaoning Provincial Archive, Fengtian shengzhang gongshu dang, no. 23184.

64. Denison and Ren, *Ultra-Modernism*, 43–44.

65. Lü and Wang, *Shuangchong quanli tixi*, 124–27.

66. Osterhammel, *Transformation of the World*, 301.

67. Schivelbusch, *Railway Journey*, 179.

68. Manshikai. *Manshū kaihatsu 40-nenshi Hokan*, 46–47.

69. Elleman, Köll, and Matsusaka, *Manchurian Railways and the Opening of China*, 7.

70. Duus, Myers and Peattie, *Japanese Informal Empire in China*.

71. Qu, *Jindai dongbei chengshi de lishi bianqian*, 76.

72. Liu, *Dongsansheng jiaoshe jiyao*, 245–50.

73. "To Department," no. 168, United States Consular Records for Mukden, China, National Archives at College Park, Maryland, NAID: 1330334.

74. Fukuda, *Manshū Hōten Nihonjin shi*, 76. Also see Christie, *Thirty Years in Moukden*, 227.

75. Komuta, *Dariben diguo shiqi de haiwai tiedao*, 316.

76. Thomas Cook Ltd., *Cook's Handbook for Tourists to Peking, Tientsin, Shan-Hai-Kwan, Mukden, Dalny, Port Arthur, and Seoul*, 76.

77. Shenyangshi Hepingqu fangdichan ju difangzhi bangongshi, *Hepingqu fangdichan zhi*, 5.

78. Cordes, *Das jüngste kaiserreich*.

79. Xie Xueshi, *Mantie dang'an ziliao huibian*, vol. 2, 800.

80. Wang Maosheng, *Cong shengjing dao Shenyang*, 110.

81. Wang Maosheng, 796.

82. Fukuda, *Manshū Hōten Nihonjin shi*, 96; Shenyangshi Hepingqu fangdichan ju difangzhi bangongshi, *Hepingqu fangdichan zhi*, 4–6.

83. Zhengxie Shenyangshi Hepingqu weiyuanhui, *Heping laojianzhu*, 86.

84. Denison and Ren, *Ultra-Modernism*, 31.

85. Shenyangshi Hepingqu fangdichan ju difangzhi bangongshi, *Hepingqu fangdichan zhi*, 5.

86. Weisenfeld, *Imaging Disaster*, 86; Hein, "Shaping Tokyo," 449.

87. *Fengtian shengzhang gongshudang*, Liaoning Provincial Archive, no. 003707.

88. *Fengtian shengzhang gongshudang*, Liaoning Provincial Archive, no. 3748.

89. Liaoningsheng dang'anju, *Fengwu Liaoning*, 2:412–18; Sun Hongjin, *Jindai Shenyang chengshi fazhan yanjiu*, 175–214.

90. See, for example, "From Miscellaneous," United States Consular Records for Mukden, China. NAID: 1330293, National Archives at College Park, Maryland.

91. Zhengxie shenyangshi hepingqu weiyuanhui, *Laobeishi biannian jishi*, 241.

92. *Fengtian shengzhang gongshudang*, Liaoning Provincial Archive, no. JC010-01-012040.

93. Sun Hongjin, *Jindai Shenyang chengshi fazhan yanjiu*, 222–24. About the early history of the factory, also see Minamimanshū Tetsudō Kabushiki Gaisha Sōmubu, *Manshū no sen'i kōgyō*.

94. Zhonggong Hepingquwei dangshiban, *Heping Dashiji*, 10–15.

95. Liaoningsheng dang'anju, *Fengtian jishi*, 259.

96. Mitter, *Manchurian Myth*, 23.

97. Kikuchi and Nakajima, *Hōten Nijūnenshi*, 665.

98. Qu, *Jindai dongbei chengshi de lishi bianqian*, 106.

99. Yue, "Zabadier."

100. Zhongguo renmin zhengzhi xieshang huiyi Liaoningsheng weiyuanhui wenshi ziliao weiyuanhui, *Zabadi jiuyi*, 82.

101. "From Local Officials," No. 94(a) and No. 91, United States Consular Records for Mukden, China. National Archives Identifier: 1330311, National Archives at College Park, Maryland.

102. About this plague, see Summers, *Great Manchurian Plague of 1910–1911*.

103. Christie, *Thirty Years in Moukden*, 234–50.

104. Xie Xueshi, *Mantie dang'an ziliao huibian*, vol. 5, 40.

105. McDonald, "Asymmetrical Integration," 123.

106. Xie Xueshi, *Mantie dang'an ziliao huibian*, 5:41.

107. Minamimanshū Tetsudō Kabushiki Gaisha, *Manshū to mantetsu*, 108.

108. McDonald, "Asymmetrical Integration," 119.

109. McDonald, 130.

110. Xie Xueshi, *Mantie dang'an ziliao huibian*, 5:91–103.

111. H. Zhao, *Manchurian Atlas*, 71–75.

112. Denison and Ren, *Ultra-Modernism*, 41–42.

113. "Dayuanshuai jiejian rishi tanhua bilu," Liaoning Provincial Archive, photo taken in the archival exhibition in 2017.

114. "Shenhai tielu gongsi chewu guanggao," Liaoning Provincial Archive, photo taken in the archival exhibition in 2017. Italics mine.

115. H. Zhao, *Manchurian Atlas*, 78.

116. Xie Xueshi, *Mantie dang'an ziliao huibian*, 5:43–44.

117. Kadono Chokyuro, *Development of Railways in Manchoukuo*, 10, quoted in McDonald, "Asymmetrical Integration," 73.

118. Kōmoto, "Watashi ga Chō Sakurin o koroshita."

119. "Gong Beidaying zaoyou zhunbei," *Shi Bao*, September 23, 1931, 2.

120. See Duara, *Sovereignty and Authenticity*.

121. Geng, "Eluosi dongzhengjiao zai shenyang de lishi tanxi," 69–73.

122. "Xita sha'e dongzheng jiaotang," *Shenyang Ribao*, September 14, 2014.

123. Yosano, *Travels in Manchuria and Mongolia*, 119.

Chapter 4

1. Tokutomi, *Shina man'yūki*.

2. Pratt, *Imperial Eyes*.

3. There are quite a lot of studies on the topic of Japanese tourist literature in China, to which I am in great intellectual debt. For example, see Fogel, *Literature of Travel in the Japanese Rediscovery of China*; McDonald, *Placing Empire*; X. Wang, *"Bi bu dui" he qinhua zhanzheng*; S. Wang, *Wenhua zhimin yu dushi kongjian*, just to name a few.

4. About Naitō Konan, see Fogel, *Politics and Sinology*.

5. Naitō, *Naitō Konan Zenshū*, vol. 4, 177–78, cited in Qian Wanyue, "Neiteng hunan fengtian fangshu jiqi xueshu yiyi."

6. Naitō, *Naitō Konan Zenshū*, vol. 6, 370–73.

7. Naitō, *Naitō Konan Zenshū*, vol. 7, 427–34.

8. Naitō, *Naitō Konan Zenshū*, 6:384.

9. See "Manshū shashinchō," Naitō, *Naitō Konan Zenshū*, 6:625.

10. See "Yū Sei dai san-ki," Naitō, *Naitō Konan Zenshū*, 6:369–92.

11. The Tokyo University changed its title to the Tokyo Imperial University in 1886.

12. See Nagashima Satoshi, "Ichimura Sanjirō (1864-1947)," in Egami, *Jindai riben hanxuejia*, 21–28.

13. Conrad, "Greek in Their Own Way," 25.

14. Itō, *Nochō*, vols. 14 and 15, "Shinkoku Manshū," Architectural Institute of Japan.

15. Itō, "Manshū no butsuji kenchiku."

16. Shiratori Yoshirō, "Torii Ryūzō (1870–1953)," in Egami, *Jindai riben hanxuejia*, 79–86.

17. Askew, "Empire and the Anthropologist."

18. Xiao and Xu, "Riben ji xifang xuezhe guanyu riben minzu qiyuan de yanjiu"; Yang and Luo, "20 shiji chu niaoju longzang zai zhongguo xinan diqu de renleixue diaocha jiqi yingxiang."

19. Tabata, "Torii Ryūzō no manmō chōsa."

20. Naitō, *Naitō Konan Zenshū*, 6:388.

21. Ketelaar, *Of Heretics and Martyrs in Meiji Japan*.

22. Ueyama Daishun, "Ōtani Kōzui (1876–1948)," in Egami, *Jindai riben hanxuejia*, 129–36.

23. Boyd, "Undercover Acolytes"; Galambos and Kōichi, "Japanese Exploration of Central Asia."

24. About the oversea enterprises of the Nishi Hongan-ji, see Shibata, *Xingya yangfo*.

25. Jaffe, "Buddhist Material Culture."

26. Naitō, *Naitō Konan Zenshū*, 6:384.

27. About Watanabe Tesshin, see Shirasu, *Wasurerareta Meiji no tankenka Watanabe Tesshin*. About Honda Eryū, see Honda, *Ōtani Tankentai to Honda Eryū*. About Tasue Yoshinobu, see Wada, "Otani tankentai no ichisokumen."

28. It is worth mentioning that Naitō met with more important figures in his trip. One of the most prominent among them, for example, was Ariga Nagao (1860–1921), a pioneer scholar in the field of Japanese international law. Ariga, who was serving in the army at the time, was introduced to Naitō through Ōsato Buhachirō's classmate Shinoda Jisaku, another jurist serving in the army. Because Ariga did not involve himself in the field survey in Fengtian, I choose not to highlight him in the story.

29. N. Song, *Making Borders in Modern East Asia*.

30. Nawa, *Naitō Konan no Kokkyō Ryōdoron Saikō*.

31. Naitō, *Naitō Konan Zenshū*, 6:376.

32. Naitō, *Naitō Konan Zenshū*, 7:427–34.

33. Conrad, "Greek in Their Own Way."

34. Itō, *Zhongguo jixing*, 287.

35. Jaffe, "Buddhist Material Culture," 276–77.

36. Torii, *Man meng gu ji kao*, 7.

37. Tabata, "Torii Ryūzō no manmō chōsa."

38. JACAR Ref. B16080719400.

39. Askew, "Empire and the Anthropologist."

40. Galambos and Kitsudō, "Japanese Exploration of Central Asia."

41. Pratt, "Imperial Eyes," 3.

42. Thomas Cook Ltd., *Cook's Handbook for Tourists to Peking, Tientsin, Shan-Hai-Kwan, Mukden, Dalny, Port Arthur and Seoul*. The same passage also appeared in the 1917 edition of *Peking and the Overland Route*, and the 1920 edition of *Peking, North China, South Manchuria and Korea*.

43. Fogel, *Literature of Travel in the Japanese Rediscovery of China*, 297.

44. Kang and Hyun, *Dainihon manshu teikoku no isan*.

45. See Natsume, *Mankan tokoro dokoro*. The narrative in the following paragraphs is drawn from this source.

46. Tokutomi, *Shina man'yūki*.

47. Pierson, "Early Liberal Thought of Tokutomi Sohō"; Ye, *Gensui diguo de jiaobu*.

48. Quoted from Saaler and Szpilman, *Pan-Asianism*, 282–83.

49. Akutagawa, *Shina Yū-ki*, 162.

50. Huang, "Unsettled Rhetoric of Colour."

51. Akutagawa, *Shina Yū-ki*, 162.

52. See Rabson, "Yosano Akiko on War," and Zhang Xiaoning, "Yuxieye jingzi de zhanzheng guan."

53. Li Wei, "Cong 'fanzhan' dao 'zhuzhan.'"

54. Yosano, *Travels in Manchuria and Mongolia*, 129, with minor revisions.

55. McDonald, *Placing Empire*, 5–7.

56. Japan Tsūrisuto Byūrō Manshū Shibu, *Man-Shi ryokō nenkan*, 14–18.

57. Yamaguchi, "Daitōa sensō to kankō no shinninmu."

58. Komuta, *Dariben diguo shiqi de haiwai tiedao*, 345–47.

59. Tahara, *Manshū no tabi*, 147.

60. The only exception I saw was footage in a documentary film. The camera captures a streetcar on the Shijianfang Avenue with the West Stupa in the background. The documentary doesn't provide the source of the footage, but it was most likely taken by Mantetsu or the Japan Tourist Bureau.

61. Naitō, *Zhongguo fangshu ji*, 42.

62. Mantetsu Tōkyō Sen-Man Annaijo, *Sen-Man Shina ryotei to hiyō gaisan*, 4–11.

63. Japan Tsūrisuto Byūrō Manshū Shibu, *Man-Shi ryokō nenkan*, 99–100.

64. Japan Tsūrisuto Byūrō Manshū Shibu, 101–3.

65. Japan Tsūrisuto Byūrō Manshū Shibu, 94.

66. Komuta, *Dariben diguo shiqi de haiwai tiedao*, 280–90.

67. About the arrangement of the sightseeing in Japanese Manchuria and Korea, see Song Anning, "Chūtōkyōin no man sen shisatsu ryokō," and Ruoff, "Japanese Tourism."

68. Minamimanshū Tetsudō Kabushiki Gaisha, *Tsuzurikata manshū*.

69. Minamimanshū Tetsudō Kabushiki Gaisha, 59–60.

70. About the comparison of the two books, see Wei Chen, "Kōsaku suru manazashi, sogo suru manshū yume."

71. Tetsudōshō Kokusai Kankōkyoku and Mantetsu Tetsudō Sōkyoku, *Manshū gakudō no mita tsuzurikata Nihon*.

72. The South Manchuria Railway Company, *Mukden (Fengtien)*, 7

73. Minamimanshū Tetsudō Kabushiki Gaisha, *Minamimanshū tetsudō ryokō annai*, 70.

74. Cordes, *Das jüngste kaiserreich*, 162–63.

75. Smith, *Hosts and Guests*, 266.

76. Here, I use the term "sex industry" not in its modern, narrow sense, but rather in a broader sense, encompassing businesses aimed at entertaining male customers, whether or not sexual intercourse was involved. This broader definition reflects the context of early twentieth-century East Asia, where the boundaries between "entertainers" and "sex workers" were often blurred.

77. Caroll, "Place of Prostitution in Early Twentieth-Century Suzhou."

78. Driscoll, *Absolute Erotic, Absolute Grotesque*, 299.

79. Driscoll, 75.

80. Kikuchi and Nakajima, *Hōten nijūnenshi*, 708.

81. Kikuchi and Nakajima, 709.

82. Fukuda, *Manshū Hōten Nihonjin shi*, 61–66.

83. Shenyang shi hepingqu fangdichan ju difangzhi bangongshi, *Heping qu fangdichan zhi*, 9.

84. Shinoda, *Hōten meisho zue*.

85. Zhongguo bianjiang shidi yanjiu zhongxin, *Dongbei Bianjiang Dang'an Xuanji*, vol. 56, 286–88.

86. Zhongguo bianjiang shidi yanjiu zhongxin, vol. 57, 392–93.

87. Zhongguo bianjiang shidi yanjiu zhongxin, 57:394.

88. Usui, *Hirakeyuku manshū*, 149–150.

89. Tahara, *Manshū no tabi*, 175.

90. Zhongguo renmin zhengzhi xieshang huiyi Liaoningsheng weiyuanhui wenshi ziliao weiyuanhui, *Zabadi jiuyi*, 71–79.

91. Liaoning provincial archive, no. JC010-01-019920.

92. Zhongguo renmin zhengzhi xieshang huiyi Liaoningsheng weiyuanhui wenshi ziliao weiyuanhui, *Zabadi jiuyi*, 71–79.

93. Liaoning provincial archive, no. JC010-01-003643.

94. "Shenyang chun se," *Shengjing shibao*, October 10, 1906.

95. "Hua bang ti ming," *Shengjing shibao*, November 6, 1906.

96. Japan Tourist Bureau, *Touring Chosen & Manchoukuo*, 14.

97. Cordes, *Das jüngste kaiserreich*, 122–26.

98. Cordes, *Das jüngste kaiserreich*, 138–41.

99. Cordes, *Das jüngste kaiserreich*, 146–52.

100. Cordes, *Das jüngste kaiserreich*, 157.

101. Brook and Wakabayashi, *Opium Regimes*, 17.

102. M. Gao, "Competing for Opium Profits," 474.

103. Zhongguo renmin zhengzhi xieshang huiyi Liaoningsheng weiyuanhui wenshi ziliao weiyuanhui, *Zabadi jiuyi*, 73–74.

104. Zhongguo renmin zhengzhi xieshang huiyi Liaoningsheng weiyuanhui wenshi ziliao weiyuanhui, *Zabadi jiuyi*, 92–93.

105. Ning, *Xizheng jishi*, 3.

106. Ning, 64.

107. Cai, "Mu Mutian de shengping he zhuzuo."

108. Mu, *Liuwangzhe zhige*, 14–16.

109. Wang Yuanzhou, "1914 nian qianhou Beijing hanren huodong yu liuxue de xingqi."

110. Yi Sŭng-hŭi, "Ponch'ŏnsŏn," *Han'gye yugo*, vols. 7–26, no. 46.

111. An, "Hwahaeng ilgi," in Im, *Yŏnhaengnok chŏnjip*, vol. 99, 496.

112. Park Jin-sung, "An Hyo-jin ŭi 'Hwahaeng ilgi' yŏngu."

Chapter 5

1. Zhang Chunzhi, "Chaoxianzu minzu shenfen rentong de wenxue jiangou.".

2. Kim Ch'ang-yŏng (Jin Changyong), *Sŏt'ap.* 1.

3. Kim Kyŏng-il et al., *Tong Asia ŭi minjok isan kwa tosi*, 103.

4. Shenyangshi minwei minzuzhi bianzuan bangongshi, *Shenyang Chaoxianzu zhi*, 2.

5. Kim Kyŏng-il et al., *Tong Asia ŭi minjok isan kwa tosi*, 106–7.

6. Shenyangshi minwei minzuzhi bianzuan bangongshi, *Shenyang Chaoxianzu zhi*, 26.

7. Chŏng P'al-lyong, *Kohyang ttŏna 50-yŏn*, 6–13.

8. Kim Kyŏng-il et al., *Tong Asia ŭi minjok isan kwa tosi*, 116.

9. Wang Mingke, "Shui de lishi," 61–83.

10. Here I use the term *humanistic* in the sense of how Yi-fu Tuan brilliantly discussed "humanistic geography." See Tuan, "Humanistic Geography."

11. Che Renxi, interview by Nianshen Song, June 9, 2018.

12. Song Jishu, interview by Nianshen Song, July 14, 2017.

13. "Saitō Jitsukenbō no dōro kaishū kōsaku," *Chosŏn Shinbun*, April 8, 1936, 4.

14. Che Renxi, interview by Nianshen Song, July 9, 2019.

15. Cho Tong-wŏn, "Pongch'ŏn sŏt'ap ŭi ch'uŏk."

16. Song Jishu, interview by Nianshen Song, June 11, 2018.

17. For example, "Pongch'ŏn jaeryudongp'o ŭi ch'uk'adaehoe," 2–5.

18. "Pongch'ŏn shirŏp Chosŏn ch'ŏngnyŏn ŭi ch'amsang."

19. "Xian gongdang beibu," 2.

20. "Ŭiyŏltanwŏn chŏngmo tŭng Pongch'ŏn yŏnggyŏng ye p'ich'e," 3.

21. "Senjin sōjō jiken."

22. "Senjin gakudan no kyorai ni kansuru ken."

23. Rhodes, *History of the Korea Mission*, 367.

24. About the Christian network in Yanbian, Manchuria, see N. Song, *Making Borders in Modern East Asia*, 244–51. About the Christian activities in colonial Korea, see A. Park, *Building a Heaven on Earth*.

25. Sŏt'ap gyohoe, "Simyang sŏt'ap gyohoe yŏksa," pamphlet. Also see Hyung Shin Park, *Presbyterian Missionaries in Southern Manchuria*, 200.

26. Chŏng In-gua, *Yesugyo jangnohoe yŏn'gam*, 350.

27. Yi Hun-gu, *Manju wa Chosŏnin*, 224.

28. Hyung Shin Park, *Presbyterian Missionaries in Southern Manchuria*, 203–04.

29. Chŏng In-gua, *Yesugyo jangnohoe yŏn'gam*, 104.

30. Chŏng In-gua, 350.

31. Chŏng Sang-in, "Kaengsaeng ŭi manju."

32. Hyung Shin Park, *Presbyterian Missionaries in Southern Manchuria*, 204.

33. Song Jishu, interview by Nianshen Song, July 14, 2017.

34. Yi Yun-t'ae. "Chungguk che 1 ho yŏja moksa—O Aeŭn moksa."

35. Schmid, "Historicizing North Korea," 441–42.

36. N. Song, *Making Borders in Modern East Asia*, 260–64.

37. Shenyangshi minwei minzuzhi bianzuan bangongshi, *Shenyang Chaoxianzu zhi*, 26–34.

38. Che Renxi, interview by Nianshen Song, July 9, 2019.

39. Song Jishu, interview by Nianshen Song, June 11, 2018.

40. The campaigns include the Sanfan, Wufan, and socialist cooperation movements. For detail account, see Meisner, *Mao's China and After*, 75–89.

41. Piao and Zhou, *Xita*, 113.

42. Che Renxi, interview by Nianshen Song, June 9, 2018.

43. Approximately six mu is one acre.

44. One jin is five hundred grams.

45. Jin Yukui and Cui Jingshun, interview by Nianshen Song, June 15, 2018.

46. Song Jishu, interview by Nianshen Song, July 14, 2017.

47. Bays, *New History of Christianity in China*, 153–82.

48. The other was the Jinling Theological Seminary in Nanjing.

49. Song Jishu, interview by Nianshen Song, July 14, 2017; June 11, 2018; July 9, 2019.

50. Song, Jishu, interview by Nianshen Song, June 11, 2018.

51. *Shenyangshi hepingqu fushizhi*, 142–44.

52. Song Jishu, interview by Nianshen Song, June 11, 2018.

53. Jin Yukui, interview by Nianshen Song, June 15, 2018.

54. Li Yiming, interview by Nianshen Song, June 5, 2018. Upon the interviewee's request, his name is an alias.

55. Bian Shihong, interview by Nianshen Song, June 7, 2018.

56. Jin Dayuan, interview by Nianshen Song, June 8, 2018.

57. Dong, "'Red Housekeeping' in a Socialist Factory," 15.

58. Piao and Zhou, *Xita*, 34.

59. Che Renxi, interview by Nianshen Song, June 9, 2018; July 9, 2019.

60. Hirata, "Mao's Steeltown," 2.

61. Liu and Wang, "Shenyang: Gongren cun de bianqian."

62. Shenyangshi Hepingqu fangdichan ju difangzhi bangongshi, *Hepingqu fangdichan zhi*.

63. Shenyangshi Hepingqu fangdichan ju difangzhi bangongshi, 98–99.

64. Li Yiming, interview by Nianshen Song, June 5, 2018.

65. Liaoningsheng jiaoyuzhi bianzuan weiyuanhui bangongshi, *Zhongxiao xuexiao jiaoyu jiaoxue gaige jishi*, 313.

66. Shenyangshi minwei minzuzhi bianzuan bangongshi, *Shenyang Chaoxianzu zhi*, 264.

67. Piao and Zhou, *Xita*, 118.

68. *Shenyangshi hepingqu fushizhi*, 95.

69. Zhang Liming, interview by Nianshen Song, June 29, 2022.

70. Li Yiming, interview by Nianshen Song, June 5, 2018.

71. Li Yiming, interview by Nianshen Song, June 5, 2018.

72. Piao and Zhou, *Xita*, 25; Shenyangshi minwei minzuzhi bianzuan bangongshi, *Shenyang Chaoxianzu zhi*, 27.

73. *Shenyangshi hepingqu fushizhi*, 197.

74. Song Jishu, interview by Nianshen Song, June 11, 2018.

75. Che Renxi, interview by Nianshen Song, June 9, 2018.

76. Che Renxi, interview by Nianshen Song, June 9, 2018; July 9, 2019.

77. Song Jishu, interview by Nianshen Song, July 14, 2017; June 11, 2018.

78. Song Jishu, interview by Nianshen Song, June 11, 2018.

79. Li Yiming, interview by Nianshen Song, June 5, 2018.

80. Shenyangshi minwei minzuzhi bianzuan bangongshi, *Shenyang Chaoxianzu zhi*, 281–82.

81. Jin Yukui and Cui Jingshun, interview by Nianshen Song, June 15, 2018.

82. Jin Chunfeng, interview by Nianshen Song, July 2, 2022.

83. Jin Yukui and Cui Jingshun, interview by Nianshen Song, June 15, 2018.

84. Song Jishu, interview by Nianshen Song, July 14, 2017.

85. Han Shik Park, "Political Culture and Ideology of the Korean Minority in China," 19.

86. Liaoning sanzi, "Chaoxianwen shengjing chuban faxing," 29.

87. Song Jishu, interview by Nianshen Song, July 14, 2017.

88. Wu Aien, "Fang Chao ganshou," 17–8.

89. Song Jishu, interview by Nianshen Song, July 14, 2017.

90. Che Renxi, interview by Nianshen Song, June 9, 2018.

91. Che Renxi, interview by Nianshen Song, July 9, 2019.

92. Jin Yukui and Cui Jingshun, interview by Nianshen Song, June 15, 2018.

93. A personal anecdote testifies to the global dispersal of the Xita Chaoxianzu. A friend of mine, a native Shenyanger who is living in Baltimore, Maryland, sent me a message in 2021, sharing his encounter in a local H-Mart (a Korean supermarket chain in the US) where I also often did my shopping. He tried to place an order in the food court, but the Korean waiter spoke neither English nor Chinese. Another staff came out and helped with translation. After a brief small chat, they found out they were from the same city. The man was a Chaoxianzu of Xita.

94. Shih, "Assimilation Through Ethnicity," 203.

95. Jin and Ji, "Chaoxianzu jujuqu shequ chuanbo de xianzhuang yu duice yanjiu"; Xia, *Shenyang xita diqu chaohan shuangyu zhuangkuang de shehui yuyanxue kaocha.*

96. Shenyangshi diming bangongshi, *Shenyang shi jiexiang minglu,* 2.

97. See Duara: *Sovereignty and Authenticity.*

98. Jin Changyong, interview by Nianshen Song, July 8, 2019.

99. Kim Ch'ang-yŏng (Jin Changyong), *Sŏt'ap,* 2.

Chapter 6

1. Liu Guoyong, "Yanshousi ta chaichu baogao," 186.

2. Ding Jun, "Qingchu Shengjing sita kaolue," 162.

3. Katsiaficas, *Global Imagination of 1968.*

4. Some scholars (for example, David Harvey) conclude that China's economic growth in Deng Xiaoping's era was "neoliberalism with 'Chinese characteristics," while others argue that China's economic success in the post-Mao era had more to do with its socialist experiments during the Mao era. See D. Harvey, *Brief History of Neoliberalism,* and Lin, *Transformation of Chinese Socialism.*

5. Piao and Zhou, *Xita,* 12.

6. Walder, *China Under Mao,* 71–2,

7. *Zabadijiuyi,* 1992, 86–93.

8. One of the most vivid records of the brothel crackdown campaign was a film made in 1951, *Stand UP, Sister* (Zizi meimei zhan qilai), directed by Chen Xihe. The plot was based on true stories from Beijing brothels and many of the characters were played by former prostitutes.

9. Shenyangshi Hepingqu fangdichan ju difangzhi bangongshi, *Hepingqu fangdichan zhi,* 119–21.

10. Lu and Perry, *Danwei.* Andrew G. Walder, *Communist Neo-Traditionalism: Work and Authority in Chinese Industry* (Berkeley: University of California Press, 1986).

11. Lu and Perry, *Danwei,* 3.

12. Shenyangshi renmin zhengfu difangzhi bianzuan bangongshi, *Shenyang shizhi,* vol. 5, 1994, 362.

13. Ji Changjiang, interview by Nianshen Song, December 13, 2019.

14. Ji Changjiang, interview by Nianshen Song, June 5, 2018.

15. Ji Changjiang, interview by Nianshen Song, June 5, 2018.

16. About the industrialization campaign in the hinterlands, see Meyskens, *Mao's Third Front*.

17. Zhonghua renmin gongheguo guowuyuan xinwen bangongshi, "Zhongguo de dui wai yuanzhu (2001 njan 4 yue)," *Renmin Ribao*, April 22, 2011, 22.

18. Ji Changjiang, interview by Nianshen Song, December 13, 2019.

19. Xie Wen, "Lishi shehuixue shijiao xia de dongbei gongye danweizhi shehui de bianqian."

20. Ji Changjiang, interview by Nianshen Song, December 13, 2019.

21. The documentary by director Wang Bing was filmed from 1999 to 2001. It won several international awards and was praised by cinematic scholars as "the most significant example of the New Chinese Documentary Movement." See Ramos-Martínez, "Oxidation of the Documentary," 1–13.

22. Ji Changjiang, interview by Nianshen Song, December 13, 2019.

23. "Shenyang bu xiangxin yanlei," *Zhongguo qingnian bao*, February 6, 1996, quoted at Chinese Industry Museum, visited July 5, 2022.

24. Ji Changjiang, interview by Nianshen Song, December 13, 2019.

25. Piao and Zhou, *Xita*, 125; Xu Baojun and Mu Yunping, "Shoulou pai li ci butuo," *Huashang chenbao*, May 29, 2003, quoted "Shoulou pai li ci butuo," in Sina News, May 29, 2003, http://news.sina.com.cn/s/2003-05-29/08331110459.html.

26. Local media and tourist literature constantly use the phrase "the city that never sleeps" to describe Xita. See, for example, Xiao Chunping and Cong Banglin, "Hepingqu jiji fazhan quanguo kechixu fazhan shiyanqu," *Shenyang Ribao*, July 20, 2010, A03.

27. Piao and Zhou, *Xita*, 7.

28. Shen Shangming and Zhang Aiyang, "'Hanliu' gei Shenyang dailai le shenme," *Liaoning Ribao*, August 26, 2003, 1.

29. Sun Qiantong, "'Hanliu' gei Shenyang chuilai le shenme," *Jingji Ribao*, July 29, 2003.

30. Shen and Zhang, "'Hanliu' gei Shenyang dailai le shenme."

31. Liu Meijun, "Shenyang Xita: Zhong Han youyi de 'jianzheng zhe,'" *Guoji Shangbao*, May 14, 2008, 3.

32. Shenyang wanbao bianjibu, "Xita, ni de xiangyi nali lai," *Shenyang wanbao*, August 24, 2012.

33. M. Y. Cho, "Neoliberal Production of a 'Culture of Poverty' in a Korean Migrant Enclave in Northeast China," 525.

34. For more on the Korean wave, see Yoon and Jin, *Korean Wave*.

35. Shen and Zhang, "'Hanliu' gei Shenyang dailai le shenme."

36. Shen and Zhang.

37. A similar transnational enclave created by neoliberal forces can be found in the Wangjing area in Beijing. See S. J. Yoon, *Cost of Belonging*.

38. Bian Tiecai, "Hanguo zhou yinfa 'hanliu' yongdong," *Shenyang Ribao*, July 1, 2005, A3.

39. Hastings, *Most Enterprising Country*, 127–28.

40. Shenyang wanbao bianjibu, "Xita, ni de xiangyi nali lai."

41. There are also reports calling for improving the traffic issue. See Sun Quan, "Xita shangyejie jidai 'bianshen shengji,'" *Shenyang Ribao*, April 7, 2008, 9.

42. Xita jiedao banshichu, *Sŏtap, Xita lüyou quan gonglue*, tourist pamphlet.

43. Xita jiedao banshichu, 10.

44. Liu Meijun, "Shenyang Xita."

45. For example, see Wei Ping, "Shenyang xita jie: Zuori penghuqu, jintian 'beifang xiao hancheng," 76–77.

46. A more stunning example is when Zhongdian County in Yunnan was renamed Shangri-La in 2001. Shangri-La, unlike Seoul, is a purely fictional place that first appeared in an English novel, *The Lost Horizon*, by James Hilton. Since its publication in 1933, the novel has propagated an orientalist imagining of a mysterious valley called Shangri-La.

47. Piao and Zhou, *Xita*, 25–27.

48. Wu Xicheng, interview by Nianshen Song, June 6, 2018; Jin Shanshui, interview by Nianshen Song, June 6, 2018.

49. S. J. Yoon, *Cost of Belonging*, 8.

50. Li, interview by Nianshen Song, June 5, 2018.

51. Li, interview by Nianshen Song, June 5, 2018.

52. Wang Yan, "'Zanzhuzheng' shuo quxiao jiu quxiao le," *Liaoning Ribao*, July 23, 2003, 4.

53. Piao Aigen, interview by Nianshen Song, June 8, 2018.

54. Piao Aigen, interview by Nianshen Song, June 8, 2018.

55. Jin Xizhen, interview by Nianshen Song, June 7, 2018.

56. Anonymous interview by Nianshen Song, June 7, 2018. To protect my source, I would like to keep this interviewee anonymous.

57. Ji Changjiang also mentioned that according to the older generation of SCM workers, male laborers from the Fengtian Cotton Mill visited the brothels quite often before 1949 (Ji Changjiang, interview by Nianshen Song, December 13, 2019).

58. Anonymous interview by Nianshen Song, June 7, 2018.

59. Gu Yuan et al., "Shenyangshi xita diqu yule changsuo fuwuyuan yufang AIDS/STI xingwei ganyu yanjiu," 104–6.

60. Huang and Wang, "Wei aizibing zonghe fangzhi er gongzuo."

61. Jiang Min, "Shenyang: gaowei renqun ganyu dui shenru yuleichang," 4.

62. Qi Yuefeng, "Liaoshen jidu," *Liaowang dongfang zhoukan*, quoted in Zhongguo jidu wang, June 26, 2015, http://www.mncc626.com/2015-06/26/c_127954623.htm.

63. See "Liaoning pilu teda fandu anjian," Xinhua.com, November 28, 2005, quoted in Sohu News, November 28, 2005, http://news.sohu.com/20051128/n227615933.shtml; "Shenyang pohuo teda fandu'an, zhuabu 28 ming du fan," *Huashang chenbao*, December 6, 2006, quoted in Sina News, December 6, 2006, http://news.sina.com.cn/c/l/p/2006-12-06/052411710585.shtml.

64. Yu Lei, "Gaosan nusheng he 'buchaqian' de nanyou fandu," *Liaoshen wangbao*, December 9, 2009, quoted in CCTV News, December 9, 2009, http://news.cctv.com/law/20091209/101882.shtml.

65. Guo, *Shenyang xita dixia qianzhuang fazhan taishi yu renhang Shenyang fenhang yingdui fang'an yanjiu*, 21–32.

66. Tian and Li, "Chanzhu xiqian de wenchuang," 9.

67. Xinhua News Agency, "Zhonghang Gaoshan an xuanpan, beigaoren nuoyong gongkuai 8 yi bei pan 15 nian," *The Paper*, September 13, 2014, https://m.thepaper.cn/newsDetail_forward_1266672.

68. Tan and Bi, "Jianguan loudong: jinrong shuoshu de jile tiantang."

69. Liu Weimin, phone interviewed by Nianshen Song, December 12, 2019.

70. Liu Xiaoqian, "Shenyang you youle xin xita," *Zhongguo xin diming*, no. 3 (1999): 26.

71. Piao and Zhou, *Xita*, 193–94.

72. "Hongse zhuixun," *Jinri Liaoning*, no. 3 (2011): 94.

73. M. Y. Cho, "Neoliberal Production," 527–29.

74. Anonymous, "Interview with a former party secretary of Xita subdistrict." Date not specified.

75. Liang Xinyue and Ma Yinsong, "Xita jiedao: Zhulao minzu tuanjie jinbu shengmingxian," *Shenyang Ribao*, September 19, 2017, 2.

76. "Guanyu mingming shoupi quanguo shuangyu hexie xiangcun (shequ)de gongshi," National Ethnic Affairs Commission of the People's Republic of China, February 15, 2017. https://www.neac.gov.cn/seac/xxgk/201702/1072713.shtml.

Epilogue and Conclusion

1. Yu Miao, online interview by Nianshen Song, March 28, 2022.

2. Borges, *Collected Fictions*, trans. Hurley.

BIBLIOGRAPHY

Unpublished Primary Sources

First Historical Archives of China. 中国第一历史档案馆. Various items.

Japan Center for Asian Historical Record (JACAR). アジア歴史資料センター https://www.jacar.go.jp/.

Liaoning Provincial Archive. 辽宁省档案馆. Various items.

Oral Interviews with the Xita residents.

RG 84 Records of Foreign Service Posts Consular Posts, Mukden, Manchuria, China. National Archives in College Park, MD.

Published Primary Sources

Agui 阿桂 ed. *Qinding shengjing tongzhi* [欽定盛京通志, Chronicle of Mukden]. Collected in *Yingyin wenyuange siku quanshu, Vol.501.* Taipei: Taiwan shangwu yinshuguan, 1986.

Akutagawa Ryūnosuke. 芥川竜之介. *Shina Yū-ki* [支那游記 China Travelogue]. Translated by Qin Gang as *Zhongguo youji.* Beijing: Zhonghua shuju, 2007.

Asahi Shinbun Gaisha. 朝日新聞社. *Rosettamaru mankan jun'yū kinen shashinchō* [ろせった丸満韓巡遊紀念写真帖, Photo Collection of the Manchurian-Korean Tour with Rosettamaru]. Tōkyō Asahi Shinbun Gaisha, Tōkyō, 1906.

Chengde xian zhishu [承德县志书 Gazetteer of Chengde County]. 1910.

Cho Tong-wŏn 趙東源. "Pongch'ŏn sŏt'ap ŭi ch'uŏk" [奉天西塔의追憶, The Memory of Xita in Fengtian]. *Sahaegongnon,* July 1938, 89–90.

Chongde san nian manwen dang'an yibian [崇德三年满文档案译编, Edited Translation of the Manchu Archives in the Third Year of Chongde]. Translated and edited by Ji Yonghai and Liu Jingxian. Shenyang: Liaoshen shushe, 1998.

Chŏng In-gua 鄭仁果, ed. *Yesugyo jangnohoe yŏn'gam* [耶穌教長老会年鑑 昭和十五年1940年, The 1940 Yearbook of the Korean Presbyterian Church]. Kyŏngsŏng: Taedongch'ulp'ansa, 1941.

Chŏng Sang-in 鄭尚仁. "Kaengsaeng ŭi manju" [更生의满洲]. *Kidokkyobo,* November 10, 1936.

Christie, Dugald. *Thirty Years in Moukden, 1883–1913.* London: Constable, 1914.

Cordes, Ernst. *Das jüngste Kaiserreich. Schlafendes, wachendes Mandschukuo.* Frankfurt a. M: Societäts-verlag, 1936.

Fengtian Beita Falunsi Jianshe Bing Shilun Jingang Yiwen Shuoming Beikao [奉天北塔法輪寺建設並時輪金剛譯文說明備考, The Construction of the Fengtian North Stupa Falun Temple and the Translated Description of Lord of the Wheel of Time]. Pamphlet, n.p., 1937.

Hepingqu "sanjicheng" bianweihui [和平区 "三集成" 编委会], ed. *Heping ziliaoben* [和平资料本, Folk Tales of Heping District]. Vols. 1 and 2. Shenyang: n.p., 1986.

Im Ki-jung [林基中], ed. *Yŏnhaengnok chŏnjip* [燕行錄全集, Complete Collection of Travel Essay of Yanjing]. Seoul: Tongguk Taehakkyo Ch'ulp'anbu, 2001.

Itō Chūta [伊東忠太]. *Nochō (Itō Chūta Shiryō)* [野帳 (伊東忠太資料) Filed Note, The Itō Chūta Documents]. Architectural Institute of Japan. Accessed February 22, 2018. http://news-sv.aij.or.jp/da2/yachou/gallery_3_chuta2.htm.

Japan Tourist Bureau. *Touring Chosen & Manchoukuo*. 1937. Harvard-Yenching collection.

Japan Tsūrisuto Byūrō Manshū Shibu [ジャパン. ツーリスト. ビューロー 滿洲支部]. *Man-Shi ryokō nenkan* [滿支旅行年鑑, The Tourist Yearbook of Manchuria and China]. Hōten: Dō Shibu, 1939.

Kawachi Yoshihiro [河内良弘], ed. and trans. *Naikokushiin manbun tōan yakuchū: Chūgoku daiichi rekishi tōankan zō; Sūtoku ni sannenbun* [内国史院満文档案訳註: 中国第一歴史档案館蔵: 崇徳二 · 三年分, The Translation and Notes of the Manchu Archives in the Palace Historiographic Academy, the Second and Third Years of Chongde]. Kyōto: Shōkadō Shoten, 2010.

Kikuchi Akishirō [菊池秋四郎], Nakajima Ichirō [中島一郎]. *Hōten Nijūnenshi* [奉天二十年史, Twenty Years' History of Hōten]. Hōten: Hōten Nijūnenshi kankōkai, 1926.

Kim Ch'ang-yŏng [김창영.]. *Sŏt'ap: Kim Ch'ang-yŏng sijip* [서탑:김창영시집, Sŏt'ap: Poems of Kim Ch'ang-yŏng]. Shenyang: Liaoning minzu chubanshe, 2011.

Kobayashi Aiyū [小林愛雄]. *Shina inshōki* [支那印象記, The Impression of China]. Tōkyō: Keibunkan, 1911. Chinese translation, Li Wei, trans. *Zhongguo yin xiang ji.* Beijing: Zhonghua shuju, 2007.

Kōmoto Daisaku [河本大作]. "Watashi ga Chō Sakurin o koroshita" [私が張作霖を殺した I Killed Zhang Zuolin]. Aozora Bungo, https://www.aozora.gr.jp/cards/001797/files/56628_57514.html. Originally published in *Bungeishunjū*, no. 12 (1954).

Liu Ruilin [劉瑞霖], ed. *Dongsansheng jiaoshe jiyao* [東三省交涉輯要, The Collective Documents on the Diplomatic Negotiations Regarding the East Three Provinces]. Taipei: Wenhai chubanshe, 1968.

Longdan Jiabu [隆旦加卜]. *Fengtian shisheng qisi shuoming lama sengzhong jianshe dagang quanlu* [奉天實勝七寺說明喇嘛僧眾建設大綱全錄, The Introduction of the Seven Temples in Fengtian, and the Outlined Record of the Lamas and Constructions]. Pamphlet, 1936.

Lü Yaozeng [呂耀曾], Song Yun [宋筠], and Wang He [王河], eds. *Shengjing tongzhi* [盛京通志 Chronical of Shengjing], with 48 juan. Fengtianfu, 1736.

Manshikai [満史会], ed. *Manshū kaihastu yonjūnenshi* [滿州開発四十年史, Forty Years' Development of Manchuria]. Tōkyō: Manshū Kaihatsu Yonjūnenshi Kankōkai, 1965. Chinese translation, Dongbei lun xian shi si nian shi Liaoning bian xie zu, trans. *Manzhou kaifa sishinian shi.* Dongbei lun xian shi si nian shi Liaoning bian xie zu, 1988.

———. *Manshū kaihatsu 40-nenshi Hokan* [滿州開発40年史補卷, Additional Volume of Forty Years' Development of Manchuria]. Tōkyō: Manshū Kaihastu 40-nenshi Kankōkan, 1965.

Mantetsu Tōkyō Sen-Man Annaijo [滿鐵東京鮮滿案內所]. *Sen-Man Shina ryotei to hiyō gaisan* [鮮滿支那旅程と費用概算, Travels in Korea, Manchuria, and China and the General Calculated Costs]. N.p., 1924.

Miao Donglin [缪东霖]. *Peijing zashu* [陪京杂述 Miscellaneous remarks of the secondary capital]. Shenyang: Shenyang chubanshe, 2009.

Minamimanshū Tetsudō Kabushiki Gaisha [南滿洲鐵道株式會社]. *Manshū to mantetsu* [滿洲と滿鐵, Manchuria and Mantetsu]. Dairen: Minami Manshū Tetsudō Kabushiki Kaisha [Sōsaishitsu] Kōhōka, 1939.

———. *Minamimanshū tetsudō ryokō annai* [南滿洲鐵道旅行案内. 昭和5年版, The South Manchuria Railway Tourist Guide]. 1930 version. Harvard-Yenching collection.

———, et al. *Tsuzurikata manshū* [綴方滿洲, Composing Manchuria]. Ōsaka: Shūgakukan, 1940.

Minamimanshū Tetsudō Kabushiki Gaisha Sōmubu [南滿洲鉄道株式会社総務部]. *Manshū no sen'i kōgyō* [滿洲の繊維工業, Textile Industry in Manchuria]. Dairen: Minamimanshūtetsudō, 1931.

Mu Mutian [穆木天]. *Liuwangzhe zhige* [流亡者之歌, Songs of the Exiles]. Shanghai: Lehua tushu gongsi, 1937.

Naitō Konan [内藤湖南]. *Naitō Konan Zenshū* [内藤湖南全集, Complete Works of Naitō Konan]. Tōkyō: Chikuma Shobō, 1976.

———. Naitō Torajirō 内藤虎次郎. *Manshū shashinchō* [滿洲寫眞帖 Photo Album about Manchuria]. Tōkyō: Tōyōdō, 1908.

———. *Zhongguo fangshu ji* [中国访书记 Searching Books in China]. Translated by Qian Wanyue. Beijing: Jiuzhou chubanshe, 2020.

Natsume Sōseki [夏目漱石]. *Mankan tokoro dokoro* [満韓ところどころ, Travels in Manchuria and Korea]. Aozora Bungo, https://www.aozora.gr.jp/cards/000148/card781 .html. Chinese translation, *Zhongguo yinxiang ji; Manhan manyou*. Translated by Wang Cheng. Beijing: Zhonghua shuju, 2007.

Ning Xiewan [宁协万]. *Xizheng jishi* [西征纪事, Travel to the West]. Shanghai: Shangwu yinshuguan, 1914.

"Pongch'ŏn shirŏp Chosŏn ch'ŏngnyŏn ŭi ch'amsang" [奉天失業朝鮮青年의慘況]. *Apkil*, no. 2, March 8, 1937.

"Pongch'ŏn jaeryudongp'o ŭi ch'uk'adaehoe" [奉天在留同胞의祝賀大會]. *Hŭngahyŏp'oe*, April 1938, 2–5.

Qikeqi [齐克奇], trans. "Xiletu kulun kema zhuan huidian" [锡勒图库伦喇嘛传汇典, The Collective Bibliographies of the Lamas in Xiletu Hure]. In *Kulun Qizhi ziliao huibian, diyiji*, edited by Kulunqi zhi bangongshi, 129–48. Hure, 1989.

Qianlong [乾隆]. *Yuzhishi siji* [禦制詩四集, Poems by the Emperor,Volume Four]. In *Jingyin wenyuange siku quanshu*. Vol. 1308. Taipei: Taiwan shangwu yinshuguan, 1986.

Qianlongchao neifuchaoben "Lifanyuan zeli" [乾隆朝内府抄本《理藩院則例》, Transcript of The Code of Lifanyuan in the Qianlong Reign]. Beijing: Zhongguo zangxue chubanshe, 2006.

Qin Ding Da Qing Hui Dian [欽定大清會典, Compiled Codes of the Qing], 1787. *Qinding siku quanshu* (Wenyuange).

Qin Ding Shengjing Tong Zhi [欽定盛京通志, General Chronicle of Shengjing, the Royal Edition], 1778. Siku quan shu edition.

Qing Neimishuyuan mengguwen dangan huibian hanyi [清內秘书院蒙古文档案汇编汉译, The Translation of the Compiled Mongolian Archives in the Qing Palace Secretariat Academy]. Beijing: Shehuikexue wenxian chubanshe, 2015.

Qing Qianlong Neifu chaoben Shengjing Libu zeli [清乾隆內府抄本《盛京禮部則例》, Code of Board of Rite in Mukden, the Department of Imperial Affairs' Copy]. National Library of China, microfilm, #03609.

Qingshilu [清实录 *The Veritable Records of the Qing*]. Beijing: Zhonghua shuju, 1986.

"Senjin sōjō jiken" [鮮人騷擾事件, The Korean Harrasement Incidence.] In *Han'guktongnibundongsa charyo* [한국독립운동사 자료]. 41 kwŏn. Accessed on September 22, 2022. https://db.history.go.kr/modern/level.do?levelId=kd_041_0010_3650.

"Senjin gakudan no kyorai ni kansuru ken" [鮮人學生團ノ去來ニ關スル件, The Documents Related to the Korean Student Group's Activities]. In *Han'guktongnibundongsa charyo* [한국독립운동사 자료]. 38 kwŏn. Accessed September 22, 2022. https://db.history.go.kr/modern/level.do?levelId=kd_038_0010_1940.

Shengjing shibao [盛京時報, Shengjing Daily].

Shenyangshi caizhengju caizhengzhi bianzuan weiyuanhui [沈阳市财政局财政志编纂委员会], ed. *Shenyang Caizhengzhi* [沈阳财政志 Chronicle of Finance in Shenyang]. Shenyang: Shenyangshi caizhengju, 1988.

Shenyangshi diming bangongshi [沈阳市地名办公室], ed. *Shenyang shi jiexiang minglu* [沈阳市街巷名录, Records of the Street and Ally Names of Shenyang]. N.p., 1989.

Shenyangshi Hepingqu fangdichan ju difangzhi bangongshi [沈阳市和平区房地产局地方志办公室], ed. *Hepingqu fangdichan zhi* [和平区房地产志, The Real Estate Gazetteer of Heping District]. N.p., 1986.

Shenyangshi hepingqu fushizhi (1905–1984) [沈阳市和平区副食志, The Nonstaple Food Gazetteer of Heping District, Shenyang, 1905–85]. N.p., 1985.

Shenyangshi Hepingqu Renminzhengfu difangzhi bianzuan bangongshi [沈阳市和平区人民政府地方志编纂办公室] ed. *Hepingqu Zhi* [和平区志, Gazetteer of Heping District]. Shenyang: Shenyang chubanshe, 1989.

Shenyangshi minzu shiwu weiyuanhui [沈阳市民族委员会], ed. *Shenyang Mengguzu zhi* [沈阳蒙古族志, Ethnography of ethnic Mongol in Shenyang]. Shenyang: Liaoning minzu chubanshe, 2006.

Shenyangshi minwei minzuzhi bianzuan bangongshi [沈阳市民委民族志编纂办公室], ed. *Shenyang Xibozu zhi* [沈阳锡伯族志, Ethnography of ethnic Sibe in Shengyang]. Shenyang: Liaoning minzu chubanshe, 1988.

———, ed. *Shenyang Chaoxianzu zhi* [沈阳朝鲜族志, Ethnography of Ethnic Korean in Shengyang]. Shenyang: Liaoning minzu chubanshe, 1989. Shenyangshi renmin zhengfu difangzhi bangongshi [沈阳市人民政府地方志办公室], ed. *Shenyang jiedao xianzhen zhi, di 1 ji* [沈阳街道乡镇志 第一辑 Neighborhood and Township Gazetteers of Shenyang, Vol. 1]. Shenyang: Shenyang chubanshe, 2017.

Shenyangshi renmin zhengfu difangzhi bianzuan bangongshi [沈阳市人民政府地方志编纂办公室], ed. *Shenyang shizhi* [沈阳市志 Gazetteers of the City of Shenyang, Vol. 5]. Shenyang: Shenyang chubanshe, 1994.

Shinchō Manshūgo tō Shiryō no Sōgōteki Chīmu [清朝満州語档案史料の総合的研究チーム]. *Naikokushiin tō: Tenchō hachinen* [内国史院档: 天聡八年, The Palace Historiographic Academy Archive, the Second Year of Tiancong]. Tōkyō: Tōyō Bunko, 2009.

Shinoda Rokuzō. *Hōten meisho zue*. Osaka: Osaka Yagō Shoten, 1928.

South Manchuria Railway Company. *Mukden (Fengtien).* 1936. Harvard-Yenching collection.

Sŏt'ap gyohoe [서탑교회.], ed. "Simyang sŏt'ap gyohoe yŏksa" [심양서탑교회역사, History of the Xita Church in Shenyang]. Pamphlet.

Story, Douglas. *The Campaign with Kuropatkin.* T. Werner Laurie, Clifford's Inn, London, 1904.

Tetsudōshō Kokusai Kankōkyoku [鐵道省國際觀光局] and Mantetsu Tetsudō Sōkyoku [滿鐵鐵道總局]. *Manshū gakudō no mita tsuzurikata Nihon* [滿洲學童 の見た綴方日本, Composing Japan, Through the Eyes of Manchurian Students]. N.p., n.d.

Thomas Cook, Ltd. *Cook's Handbook for Tourists to Peking, Tientsin, Shan-Hai-Kwan, Mukden, Dalny, Port Arthur, and Seoul.* London: T. Cook & Son, 1910.

———. *Peking, North China, South Manchuria and Korea.* London: T. Cook & Son, 1920.

Tokutomi Iichirō (Sohō) [德富猪一郎]. *Shina man'yūki* [支那漫遊記, Journey in China]. Tōkyō: Min'yūsha, 1918.

Torii Ryūzō [鸟居龙藏]. *Man meng gu ji kao* [滿蒙古迹考, Investigation of Historical Relics in Manchuria and Mongolia]. Translated by Chen Nianben. Shanghai: Shangwu yinshu guan, 1935.

———. *Menggu lüxing* [蒙古旅行, A Trip to Mongolia]. Translated by Dai Yue and Zheng Chunying. Beijing: Shangwu yinshuguan, 2018.

———. *Manmeng de tancha* [满蒙的探查, Investigation of Manchuria and Mongolia]. Translated by Ma Fushan. Huhhot: Neimenggu renmin chubanshe, 2019.

"Ŭiyŏltanwŏn chŏngmo tŭng Pongch'ŏn yŏnggyŏng ye p'ich'e" [義烈團員鄭某等奉天 領警에被逮, Chŏng and Other Members of the Ŭiyŏltan Were Arrested by Japanese Police in Fengtian]. *Chosŏn Chungang-ilbo,* September 20, 1934, 3.

Verbiest, Ferdinand, et al., *History of the Two Tartar Conquerors of China: Including the Two Journeys into Tartary of Father Ferdinand Verbiest, in the Suite of the Emperor Kang-hi, from the French of Père Pierre Joseph d'Orléans, to Which Is Added Father Pereira's Journey into Tartary in the Suite of the Same Emperor, from the Dutch of Nicolaas Witsen.* London, 1854.

Wang Jingchen [王晶辰], ed. *Liaoning beizhi* [辽宁碑志, Stela Inscriptions in Liaoning]. Shenyang: Liaoning renmin chubanshe, 2002.

Wang Xiangfeng [王向峰]. ed. *Fengtian Tongzhi Shenyang Shilue* [奉天通志 · 沈阳事 略, Records about Shenyang in General Chronology of Fengtian]. Shenyang: Liaoning daxue chubanshe, 2012.

Witte, Sergei Yulievich. *The Memoirs of Count Witte, Translated from the Original Russian Manuscript and Edited by Abraham Yarmolinsky.* Garden City, NY: Doubleday Page, 1921.

Wu Aien [吴爱恩]. "Fang Chao ganshou" [访朝感受 Thoughts on Visiting North Korea]. *Tianfeng,* no. 12 (1990): 17–18.

"Xian gongdang beibu" [鲜共党被捕, Korean Communists Were Arrested]. *Shishi xinbao,* September 16, 1931, 2.

Xita jiedao banshichu [西塔街道办事处], ed. *Sŏt'ap Xita lüyou quan gonglüe* [서탑 西 塔 · 旅游全攻略, Complete Tourist Guides of Xita]. Tourist pamphlet, 2013.

Xie Xueshi [解学诗], ed. *Manzhou jiaotong shigao* [满洲交通史稿, Historical Materials about the Manchurian Transportation]. Beijing: Shehui kexue wenxian chubanshe, 2012.

————, ed. *Mantie dang'an ziliao huibian* [满铁档案资料汇编, Collected Volumes of the South Manchuria Railway Company Archives]. Beijing: Shehui kexue wenxian chubanshe, 2011.

Xu Ke [徐珂]. *Qing bai lei chao* [清稗类钞, Miscellaneous Histories of the Qing]. Vol. 1. Beijing: Zhonghua shuju, 1984.

Yamaguchi Jūji [山口重次]. "Daitōa sensō to kankō no shinninmu" [大東亜戦争と観光の新任務, The Great East Asia War and the New Mission of Tourism]. *Manchū Kankō* 6, no. 3 (1939): 5–6.

Yi Bahan [伊把汉], Dong Bingzhong [董秉忠], et al. *Shengjing tongzhi* [盛京通志, General Chronical of Shengjing]. 32 juan, 1684.

Yi Sŭng-hŭi [李承熙]. *Han'gye yugo* [韓溪遺稿 Works of the late Han'gye]. Seoul: Kuksa P'yonch'an Wiwonhoe, 1976.

Yosano Akiko [与謝野晶子]. *Manmō Yū-ki* [満蒙遊記, Travelogue of Manchuria and Mongolia]. Aozora Bunko. Accessed July 20, 2021. https://www.aozora.gr.jp/cards/000320/files/43481_60203.html.

————. *Travels in Manchuria and Mongolia: A Feminist Poet from Japan Encounters Prewar China*. Translated by Joshua Fogel. New York: Columbia University Press, 2001.

Yu Mingzhong [于敏中], Dou Guangnai [寶光鼐], and Zhu Yun [朱筠], eds. *Qinding Ri Xia Jiu Wen Kao* [欽定日下舊聞考, Investigations About Hearsay of Old Matters from Under the Sun]. First Historical Archive of China.

Zeng Youyi [曾有翼], ed. *Shenyang Xianzhi* [瀋陽縣誌, Gazetteer of Shenyang County]. In *Shenyangshi renmin zhengfu difangzhi bangongshi*, edited by Liaoning Jiufangzhi. Shenyang: Liaohai chubanshe, 2010.

Zhao Huanlin [赵焕林], ed. *Minguo Fengxi Junfa Dang'an* [民国奉系军阀档案, Archives of the Feng Clique Warlords in Republican China]. Beijing: Xianzhuang shuju, 2016.

Zhengxie Shenyangshi Hepingqu weiyuanhui [政协沈阳市和平区委员会], ed. *Heping Bainian Tuzhi* [和平百年图志, Photographic Gazetteer of Heping District in 100 Years]. Vols. 1 and 2. Zhengxie shenyangshi hepingqu weiyuanhui, 2013 and 2015.

Zhongguo bianjiang shidi yanjiu zhongxin [中國邊疆史地研究中心], ed. *Dongbei Bianjiang Dang'an Xuanji* [東北邊疆檔案選輯, Selected Archives of the Northeast Frontier]. Guilin: Guangxi shifan daxue chubanshe, 2007.

Zhongguo diyi lishi danganguan [中国第一历史档案馆]. *Qing chu nei guo shi yuan Man wen dang an yi bian* [清初内国史院满文档案译编, The Translation of the Manchu Archives of the Palace Historiographic Academy in the Early Qing]. Beijing: Guangming ribao chubanshe, 1989.

Zhongguo shehui kexueyuan zhongguo bianjiang shidi yanjiu zhongxin [中国社会科学院中国边疆史地研究中心], ed. *Qingdai Menggu gaoshengzhuan yiji* [清代蒙古高僧传译辑, Translation on the Biographies of Noble Mongol Monks in the Qing Dynasty]. Beijing: Quanguo tushuguan wenxian suowei fuzhi zhongxin, 1990.

Secondary Sources

Allen, John, Doreen Massey, and Allan Cochrane, eds. *Rethinking the Region*. London: Routledge, 1998.

Angba [昂巴]. *Zangchuan fojiao mizong yu mantuluo yishu* [藏传佛教密宗与曼陀罗艺术, Vajrayana of the Tibetan-Buddhism and the Art of Mandala]. Beijing: Remin chubanshe, 2011.

Askew, David. "Empire and the Anthropologist: Torii Ryūzō and Early Japanese Anthropology." *Japanese Review of Cultural Anthropology* 4 (2003): 133–54.

Atkin, Tony. "Chinese Architecture Students at the University of Pennsylvania in the 1920s: Tradition, Exchange, and the Search for Modernity." In *Chinese Architecture and the Beaux-Arts*, edited by Jeffrey W. Cody, Nancy S. Steinhardt, and Tony Atkin. Honolulu: University of Hawai'i Press, 2011.

Atwood, Christopher Pratt *Encyclopedia of Mongolia and the Mongol Empire*. New York: Facts on File, 2009.

———. "The First Mongol Contact with the Tibetans." In *Trails of the Tibetan Tradition: Papers for Elliot Sperling*, edited by Roberto Vitali, 21–45. Amnye Machen Institute, 2014.

Baoyindeligen [宝音德力根]. "Xiletu kuleng bandi da nuomenhan shiji kaoshu" [席勒图库棱班第大诺们汗事迹考述, Studies on the širegetü küregyen bandida nom un qayan]. *Qingshi yanjiu*, no. 5 (2020): 126–35.

Bays, Daniel H. *A New History of Christianity in China*. Wiley-Blackwell, 2011.

Berounsky, Daniel, and Lubomir Sklenka. "Tibetan Tsha-Tsha." *Annals of the Naprstek Museum* 26 (2005): 59–72.

Berger, Patricia Ann. *Empire of Emptiness: Buddhist Art and Political Authority in Qing China*. Honolulu: University of Hawai'i Press, 2003.

Bian Tiecai [边铁才]. "'Hanguo' zhou yinfa 'hanliu' yongdong" ["韩国周" 引发 "韩流" 涌动 The "Korean Week" Stimulates the "Korean Wave"]. *Shenyang Ribao*, July 1, 2005, A3.

Bingenheimer, Marcus. "History of the Manchu Buddhist Canon and First Steps Towards Its Digitization." *Central Asiatic Journal* 56 (2012/2013): 203–17.

Blo-bzang-chos-kyi-nyi-ma [土观 · 洛桑却吉尼玛]. *Zhangjia guo shi Ruobiduoji zhuan* [章嘉国师若必多吉传, The Biography of Changkya Rölpé Dorjé, the State Preceptor]. Translated by Chen Qingying and Ma Lianlong. Beijing: Zhongguo zangxue chubanshe, 2007.

Borges, Jorge Luis. *Collected Fictions*, trans. Andrew Hurley. Penguin Books, 1999.

Boyd, James. "Undercover Acolytes: Honganji, the Japanese Army, and Intelligence-Gathering Operations." *Journal of Religious History* 37, no. 2 (2013): 185–205.

Brook, Timothy, and Bob Tadashi Wakabayashi. *Opium Regimes: China, Britain, and Japan, 1839–1952*. University of California Press, 2000.

Cai Qingfu [蔡清富]. "Mu Mutian de shengping he zhuzuo" [穆木天的生平和著作, Biography and Works of Mu Mutian]. *Beijing shifan daxue xuebao*, no. 6 (1990): 79–83.

Caroll, Peter. "The Place of Prostitution in Early Twentieth-Century Suzhou." *Urban History* 38 no. 3 (2011): 413–36.

Carter, James H. *Creating a Chinese Harbin: Nationalism in an International City, 1916–1932*. Ithaca, NY: Cornell University Press, 2002.

Chang, Michael G. *A Court on Horseback: Imperial Touring and the Construction of Qing Rule, 1680–1785*. Cambridge, MA: Harvard University Press, 2007.

Chen Xiaomin [陈晓敏]. "Qingdai gongting lamajiao huodong: tiaobuzha" [清代宫廷喇嘛教活动：跳布扎. Tiaobuzha: A Lamaism Activity at the Qing Palace]. *Manzu yanjiu*, no. 4 (2005): 65–69.

———. "Qingdai zhujing lama zhidu de xingcheng yu yange" [清代驻京喇嘛制度的形成与沿革, The Formation and Evolution of the Institution of Capital Lama in the Qing Dynasty]. *Manzu Yanjiu*, no 4 (2007): 111–21.

Cho, Mun Young. "The Neoliberal Production of a 'Culture of Poverty' in a Korean Migrant Enclave in Northeast China." *Positions* 26, no. 3 (2018): 516–46.

———. *The Specter of "the People": Urban Poverty in Northeast China*. Ithaca, NY: Cornell University Press, 2013.

Chǒng P'al-lyong [정판룡.]. *Kohyang ttǒna 50-yǒn* [고향 떠나 50년, 50 Years of Leaving Home]. Pukkyǒng: Minjok Ch'ulp'ansa, 1997.

Chun Hae-jong. "Sino-Korean Tributary Relations in the Ch'ing Period." In *The Chinese World Order: Traditional China's Foreign Relations*, edited by John King Fairbank. Cambridge, MA: Harvard University Press, 1968.

Cody, Jeffrey W., Nancy Shatzman Steinhardt, and Tony Atkin, eds. *Chinese Architecture and the Beaux-Arts*. Honolulu: University of Hawai'i Press, 2011.

Conrad, Sebastian. "Greek in Their Own Way: Writing India and Japan into the World History of Architecture at the Turn of the Twentieth Century." *American Historical Review* 125, no. 1 (2020): 19–53.

Crossley, Pamela Kyle. *A Translucent Mirror: History and Identity in Qing Imperial Ideology*. Berkeley: University of California Press, 2002.

Crush, Peter. *Imperial Railawys of North China*. Beijing: Xinhua Publishing House, 2013.

Davis, Natalie Zemon. *The Return of Martin Guerre*. Cambridge, MA: Harvard University Press, 1983.

Delege [德勒格], ed. *Neimenggu Lamajiao shi* [内蒙古喇嘛教史, History of Lamaism in Inner Mongolia]. Hohhot: Neimenggu renmin chubanshe, 1998.

Denison, Edward, and Guangyu Ren. *Ultra-Modernism: Architecture and Modernity in Manchuria*. Hong Kong: Hong Kong University Press, 2017.

Ding Jun [丁军]. "Qingchu Shengjing sita kaolue" [清初盛京四塔考略, Studies on the Four Stupas of Mukden in Early Qing]. In *Shenyang wenshi ziliao*, vol. 17, edited by Zhengxie Shenyangshi weiyuanhui wenshi ziliao yanjiu weiyuanhui. N.p., 1990.

———. "Shenyang yanshousita jiqi chutu wenwu kaolue" [沈阳延寿寺塔出土文物考略, Studies on the Unearthed Artifacts from Shenyang Yanshou Temple]. In *Shenyang gugong bowuguan wenji, 1983–1985*, 122–129. Shenyang: Shenyang gugong bowuguan yanjiushi, 1985.

Ding Yizhuang [定宜庄]. *Qingdai Baqi Zhufang Yanjiu* [清代驻防八旗研究, Research on Qing's Eight-Banner Garrisons]. Shenyang: Liaoning minzu chubanshe, 2003.

Ding Yizhuang [定宜庄] and Qiu Yuanyuan [邱源媛]. *Jinji wubaili, Qingdai jifudiqu de qidi yu zhuangtou* [近畿五百里: 清代畿辅地区的旗地与庄头, Five Hundred Li around the Capital, the Banner Farm and Manor Head in Qing Dynasty's Capital Region]. Beijing: Zhongguo shehui kexue chubanshe, 2016.

Dong, Madeleine Yue. *Republican Beijing: The City and Its Histories*. Berkeley: University of California Press, 2003.

Dong, Yige. "'Red Housekeeping' in a Socialist Factory: Jiashu and Transforming Reproductive Labor in Urban China (1949–1962)." *International Review of Social History* 69, no. 1 (2024): 1–24.

Driscoll, Marc. *Absolute Erotic, Absolute Grotesque: The Living, Dead, and Undead in Japan's Imperialism, 1895–1945*. Duke University Press, 2010.

Duara, Prasenjit. *Sovereignty and Authenticity: Manchukuo and the East Asian Modern*. Lanham, MD: Rowman & Littlefield, 2004.

———. *The Global and Regional in China's Nation-Formation*. London: Routledge, 2008.

Duus, Peter, Ramon H. Myers, and Mark R. Peattie, eds. *The Japanese Informal Empire in China, 1895–1937*. Princeton, NJ: Princeton University Press, 1991.

Egami Namio [江上波夫]. *Jindai riben hanxuejia* [近代日本汉学家, Modern Japanese Sinologists]. Translated by Lin Qingzhang. Taipei: Wanjuanlou, 2015.

Elliott, Mark. "The Limits of Tartary: Manchuria in Imperial and National Geographies." *Journal of Asian Studies* 59, no. 3 (2000): 603–46.

———. *The Manchu Way: The Eight Banners and Ethnic Identity in Late Imperial China.* Stanford: Stanford University Press, 2011.

———. "Turning a Phrase: Translation in the Early Qing Through a Temple Inscription of 1645." In *Historische und bibliographische Studien zur Mandschuforschung*, edited by Martin Gimm, Giovanni Stary, and Michael Weiers, 12–41. O. Harrassowitz, 1992.

Elleman, Bruce, and Stephen Kotkin, eds. *Manchurian Railways and the Opening of China: An International History.* London: Routledge, 2015.

Elverskog, Johan. "Mongol Time Enters a Qing World." In *Time, Temporality, and Imperial Transition, East Asian from Ming to Qing*, edited by Lynn A. Struve, 142–78. Honolulu: University of Hawai'i Press 2005.

———. *Our Great Qing: The Mongols, Buddhism, and the State in Late Imperial China.* Honolulu, University of Hawai'i Press, 2008.

Esherick, Joseph W. *The Origins of the Boxer Uprising.* Berkeley: University of California Press, 1988.

Farquhar, David M. "Emperor as Bodhisattva in the Governance of Ch'ing Empire." *Harvard Journal of Asiatic Studies* 38, no. 1 (1978): 5–34.

———. "The Origin of the Manchu's Mongolian Policy." In *The Chinese World Order: Traditional China's Foreign Relations*, edited by John King Fairbank, 198–205. Cambridge, MA: Harvard University Press, 1968.

Fogel, Joshua *Politics and Sinology: The Case of Naito Konan, 1866–1934.* Cambridge: Harvard University Asia Center, 1984.

———. *The Literature of Travel in the Japanese Rediscovery of China 1862–1945.* Stanford: Stanford University Press, 1996.

Ford, Harold P. *Russian Far Eastern Diplomacy: Count Witte and the Penetration of China, 1895–1904.* PhD diss., University of Chicago, 1950.

Forêt, Philippe. *Mapping Chengde: The Qing Landscape Enterprise.* Honolulu: University of Hawai'i Press, 2000.

Fu Fenkui [付奋奎]. "Mingqing shiqi de 'tiaobuzha' xisu" [明清时期的 "跳布扎" 习俗, The Custom of "Tiaobuzha" in the Ming-Qing Period]. *Xizang minzu xueyuan xuebao (zhexue shehuikexue ban)* 33, no. 2 (2012): 37–40.

Fuchs, Walter. "Early Manchurian Inscriptions in Manchuria." *China Journal of Science & Arts* 5, no.1 (1931): 5–9.

Fukuda, Minoru [福田実]. *Manshū Hōten Nihonjin shi: Dōran no tairiku ni ikita hitobito* [満洲奉天日本人史：動乱の大陸に生きた人々, History of the Japanese in Fengtian of Manchuria]. Tōkyō: Kenkōsha, 1933.

Fussman, Gerard. "Symbolisms of the Buddhist Stupa." *Journal of International Association of Buddhist Studies* 9, no. 2 (1986): 37–53.

Galambos, Imre, and Kitsudō Kōichi. "Japanese Exploration of Central Asia: The Ōtani Expeditions and Their British Connections." *Bulletin of the School of Oriental and African Studies* 75, no. 1 (2012): 113–34.

Gao Lecai [高乐才]. *Jindai zhongguo dongbei yimin yanjiu* [近代中国东北移民研究, Studies on the Migration in Modern Northeast China]. Beijing: Shangwu yinshuguan, 2010.

Gao, Ming. "Competing for Opium Profits: The Japanese Empire and Imperial Subjects in Manchukuo, 1932–1937." *Critical Asian Studies*, July 3, 2022.

Geng Haitian [耿海天]. "Eluosi dongzhengjiao zai shenyang de lishi tanxi" [俄罗斯东正教在沈阳的历史探析, Historical Studies on the Russian Orthodox Church in Shenyang]. *Shijie zongjiao wenhua*, no. 5 (2015): 69–73.

Ginzburg, Carlo. *The Cheese and the Worms: The Cosmos of a Sixteenth-Century Miller*, trans. John Tedeschi and Anne C. Tedeschi. Baltimore: Johns Hopkins University Press, 2013.

Grupper, Samuel Martin. "The Manchu Imperial Cult of the Early Ch'ing Dynasty." PhD diss., Indiana University, 1979.

———. "Manchu Patronage and Tibetan Buddhism during the First Half of the Ch'ing Dynasty." *Journal of the Tibetan Society* 4 (1984): 47–74.

Gu Yuan [谷渊 等], et al. "Shenyangshi xita diqu yule changsuo fuwuyuan yufang AIDS/STI xingwei ganyu yanjiu" [沈阳市西塔地区娱乐场所服务员预防AIDS/STI行为干预研究, Study on the AIDS/STI prevention intervention among the service persons in the entertainment business in the Xita area of Shenyang]. *Zhongguo aizibing xingbing* 10, no. 2 (2004): 104–6.

Guo Hongjun [郭鸿军]. *Shenyang xita dixia qianzhuang fazhan taishi yu renhang Shenyang fenhang yingdui fang'an yanjiu* [沈阳西塔地下钱庄发展态势与人行沈阳分行应对方案研究, Study on the Development of the Underground Banks in Xita, Shenyang, and the Responses of the Shenyang Branch of the People's Bank of China]. Master thesis, Xi'an University of Technology, 2007.

Hamashita Takeshi. *China, East Asia and the Global Economy: Regional and Historical Perspectives*. London: Routledge, 2008.

Harrison, Henrietta. *The Missionary's Curse and Other Tales from a Chinese Catholic Village*. Berkeley: University of California Press, 2003.

Hasibagen [哈斯巴根]. *Qingchu manmeng guanxi yanbian yanjiu* [清初满蒙关系演变研究, Research on the Evolution of the Manchu-Mongol Relationship in Early Qing]. Beijing: Beijing daxue chubanshe, 2016.

Hastings, Justin V. *A Most Enterprising Country: North Korea in the Global Economy*. Ithaca, NY: Cornell University Press, 2016.

Harvey, David. *A Brief History of Neoliberalism*. London: Oxford University Press, 2007.

———. *Paris, Capital of Modernity*. London: Routledge, 2005.

Harvey, Peter. "The Symbolism of the Early Stupa." *Journal of International Association of Buddhist Studies* 7, no. 2 (1984): 67–93.

Hein, Carola. "Shaping Tokyo: Land Development and Planning Practice in the Early Modern Japanese Metropolis." *Journal of Urban History* 36, no. 4 (2010): 447–84.

Henry, Todd A. *Assimilating Seoul: Japanese Rule and the Politics of Public Space in Colonial Korea, 1910–1945*. Berkeley: University of California Press, 2014.

Hershatter, Gail. *The Gender of Memory: Rural Women and China's Collective Past*. Berkeley: University of California Press, 2011.

Hevia, James. "Lamas, Emperors, and Rituals: Political Implications in Qing Imperial Ceremonies." *Journal of the International Association of Buddhist Studies* 16, no. 2 (1993): 243–78.

———. "A Multitude of Lords: Qing Court Ritual and the Macartney Embassy of 1793." *Late Imperial China* 10, no. 2 (1989): 72–105.

Hirata Koji. "Mao's Steeltown: Industrial City, Colonial Legacies, and Local Political Economy in Early Communist China." *Journal of Urban History*, (2021): 1–26.

Hou Haoran [侯浩然]. "Zangchuan fojiao wenben de xingcheng jiqi lishi xunshi chuan-tong de chuangjian" [藏传佛教文本的形成及其历史叙事传统的创建, The Formation of Tibetan Buddhist Texts and the Construction of Its Historical Narrative Tradition]. In *Wenben yu Lishi* [文本与历史, Text and History], by Shen Weirong and Hou Haoran, 84–188. Beijing: Beijing daxue chubanshe, 2016.

Honda Takashige [本多隆成]. *Ōtani Tankentai to Honda Eryū* [大谷探検隊と本多恵隆, The Ōtani Expeditions and Honda Eryū]. Tōkyō: Heibonsha, 1994.

"Hongse zhuixun" [红色追寻 In search for red]. *Jinri Liaoning*, no. 4 (2011): 94.

Hu Xiaobai [胡箫白]. "Mingchao zhengce yu 15 shiji zhongqi zangchuan fojiao zai han-zang zoulang de chuanbo jizhi shulun" [明朝政策与15世纪中期藏传佛教在汉藏走廊的传播机制述论, On the Ming Policy and the Spread of Tibetan Buddhism along the Sino-Tibetan Corridor in the Fiftheenth Century], *Zhongguo zangxue* [中国藏学], no. 3 (2021): 43–52.

Huang, Junliang. "The Unsettled Rhetoric of Colour: Race in Akutagawa Ryūnosuke's Travels Across China in the 1920s." *Interventions* 21, no. 8 (2019): 1188–206.

Huang Le [黄乐] and Wang Yan [王研]. "Wei aizibing zonghe fangzhi er gongzuo" [为艾滋病综合防治而工作, Works for the Comprehensive Prevention of AIDS]. *Liaoning Ribao*, October 29, 2004.

Hung Ho-fung, ed. *China and the Transformation of Global Capitalism*. Baltimore: Johns Hopkins University Press, 2009.

Ienaga Saburo, *The Pacific War: 1931–1945*. New York: Pantheon, 1978.

Ikebe Hitoshi [池部鈞] et al. *Manga no Manshū* [漫画の満州, Manchuria in Cartoon]. Tōkyō: Hamai Matsunosuke, 1927.

Ikejiri Yoko [池尻阳子]. "Qingchu zhasake dalama zhidu de xingcheng" [清初扎萨克喇嘛制度的形成, Formation and Implementation of the Jasak Lama System in the Early Qing Period]. *Kansaidaigaku tōzai gakujutsu kenkyūjo kiyō* [関西大学東西学術研究所紀要] 53 (2020): 3–11.

Isett, Christopher Mills. *State, Peasant, and Merchant in Qing Manchuria, 1644–1862*. Stanford: Stanford University Press, 2007.

Ishihama Yumiko [石濱裕美子]. "The Notion of 'Buddhist Government' (chos srid) Shared by Tibet, Mongol and Manchu in the Early 17th Century." In *Relationship Between Religion and State (chos srid zung 'brel) in Traditional Tibet*, proceedings of a seminar held in Lunbini, Nepal, March 2000, edited by Christoph Cueppers, 15–31. Lumbini: Lumbini International Research Institute, 2004.

———. "Sei-hatsu chokuken Chibetto bukkyō jiin satoshi gōteki kenkyū" [清代敕建チベット仏教の総和的研究, A Comprehensive Study on the Tibetan Buddhist Temples Built Under Imperial Order in Early Qing]. *Manzokushi kenkyū*, no. 6 (2007): 1–39.

———. *Shinchō to chibetto bukkyō: Bosatsuō to natta kenryūtei* [清朝とチベット仏教: 菩薩王となった乾隆帝, The Qing Dynasty and Tibetan Buddhism: Emperor Qianlong as a Bodhisattva King]. Tōkyō: Waseda daigaku shuppanbu, 2011.

Itō Chūta [伊東忠太]. "Manshū no butsuji kenchiku" [滿洲の佛寺建築, Buddhist Temple Architecture in Manchuria]. In *Toyokyokai Chosabu Gakujutuhoukoku*, edited by Tōyō Kyōkai Chōsabu, vol. 1, no. 1 (1909): 1–76.

———. *Zhongguo jixing* [中国纪行, Travels in China]. Translatd by Xue Yaming and Wang Tiejun. Beijing: zhongguo huabao chubanshe, 2017.

Jacobs, Jane. *The Death and Life of Great American Cities*. New York: Vintage Books, 1961.

Jaffe, Richard M. "Buddhist Material Culture, 'Indianism,' and the Construction of Pan-Asian Buddhism in Prewar Japan." *Material Religion* 2, no. 3 (2006): 266–93.

Jeong Jong-Ho. "Ethnoscapes, Mediascapes, and Ideoscapes: Socio-Cultural Relations Between South Korea and China." *Journal of International and Area Studies* 19, no. 2 (2012): 77–95

Jagchid, Sechin. "Mongolian Lamaist Quasi-Feudalism During the Period of Manchu Domination." *Mongolian Studies* 1 (1974): 27–54.

Jia Dan'an [贾淡安]. "Shishengsi lama tiaoda canguanji" [实胜寺跳跶参观记, Visiting Tiaoda at the Shengshi Temple]. *Xinmanzhou* 1, no. 6 (1939): 76–79.

Jiang Min [姜敏]. "Shenyang: Gaowei renqun ganyu dui shenru yuleichang" [沈阳: 高危人群干预队深入娱乐场, Shenyang: High-Risk Population Intervention Team Went to the Entertainment Facilities]. *Xinhua meiri dianxun*, November 17, 2005, 4.

Jiang Niansi [姜念思]. "Qingdai shengjingcheng guihua linian tanxi" [清代盛京城规划理念探析, Analysis on Qing's Idea of the Urban Planinng of Shengjing]. *Zhongguo Mingcheng*, no. 3 (2011): 45–50.

———. *Shenyang Shihua* [沈阳史话 History of Shenyang]. Shenyang: Shenyang chubanshe, 2008.

Jin Xianhua [金仙花] and Ji Wei [季伟]. "Chaoxianzu jujuqu shequ chuanbo de xianzhuang yu duice yanjiu" [朝鲜族聚居区社区传播的现状与对策研究, A Study on the Current Situation and Response of Community Communication in an Ethnic Korean Enclave]. *Dazhong wenyi*, no. 16 (2014): 272–73.

Johnson, Linda, ed. *Cities of Jiangnan in Late Imperial China*. Albany: State University of New York Press, 1993.

Kaviraj, Sudipta. "Filth and the Public Sphere: Concepts and Practices About Space in Calcutta." *Public Culture* 10 (1997): 83–113.

Kam, Tak Sing. "Manchu-Tibetan Relations in the Early Seventeenth Century: A Reappraisal." PhD diss., Harvard University, 1994.

———. "The dGe-lugs-pa Breakthrough: The Uluk Darxan Nangsu Lama's Mission to the Manchus." *Central Asiatic Journal* 44, no. 2 (2000): 161–76.

——— [甘德星]. "'Zhengtong' zhiyuan: Manzhou ruguan qianhou wangquan sixiang zhi fazhan yu mengzang zhuanlunwang guannian zhi guanxi kaobian" ["正统"之源: 满洲入关前后王权与蒙藏转轮王观念之关系考辨, The Origin of Orthodoxy: A Study of the Relationship Between the Manchu View of the Imperial Power and the Mongolian-Tibetan Idea of Cakravartin Around the Manchu Conquest of China]. In *Minzu Rentong yu Wenhua Jiaorong*, edited by Wang Rongzu and Lin Guanqun, 119–174. Jiayi: Guoli zhongzheng daxue Taiwan renwen yanjiu zhongxin, 2006.

Kang San-jung [姜尚中] and Hyun Mu-an [玄武岩]. *Dainihon manshu teikoku no isan* [大日本・満州帝国の遺産, The Heritage of the Great Japan / Manchurian Empire]. Tōkyō: Kōdansha, 2010.

Katsiaficas, George. *Global Imagination of 1968: Revolution and Counterrevolution*. Oakland, CA: PM Press, 2018.

Ketelaar, James E. *Of Heretics and Martyrs in Meiji Japan*. Princeton, NJ: Princeton University Press, 1993.

Kikuchi Akishirō [菊池秋四郎] and Nakajima Ichirō [中島一郎]. *Hōten nijūnenshi* [奉天二十年史, Twenty Years' History of Fengtian]. Hōten: Hōten nijūnenshi kankō-kai, 1926.

Kim Doo-Sub and Jung Min Kim. "Endangered Korean Minority Society in China: Recent Socio-Demographic Changes in the Yanbian Korean Autonomous Prefecture." *Journal of International and Area Studies* 12, no. 1 (2005): 81–98.

Kim Joo-Yong [김주용]. "Simyang kŭndae tosihwaŭi Yangmyŏnsŏn" [심양(봉천) 근대도시화의 양면성, Dualism of Shenyang's Modern Urbanization]. *Sahak Yŏnggu*, no. 85 (2007): 159–96.

Kim Kyŏng-il [김경일], et al. *Tong Asia ŭi minjok isan kwa tosi: 20-segi chŏnban Manju ŭi Chosŏnin* [동 아시아 의 민족 이산 과 도시: 20세기 전반 만주 의 조선인, Korean Diaspora in Manchurian Cities in the Early Twentieth Century]. Sŏul: Yŏksa Pip'yŏngsa, 2004.

Kim, S. Hun, and Wonsuk Ma, eds., *Korean Diaspora and Christian Mission*. Eugene, OR: Wipf & Stock, 2011.

Komuta Tetsuhiko [小牟田哲彦]. *Dariben diguo shiqi de haiwai tiedao* [大日本帝国时期的海外铁道, The Overseas Railways of the Imperial Japan]. Translated by Li Yanhua, Taibei: Taiwan shangwu yin shu guan, 2020.

Kung Ling-Wei [孔令伟]. "Guofa yu jiaofa zhijian: Qingchao qianqi dui menggu sengren de jinxian ji chengchu" [国法与教法之间: 清朝前期对蒙古僧人的禁限及惩处, Between Statutes and Dharma, the Regulation and the Punishment of Mongolian Monks in the Early Qing Period]. *Lishirenleixue xuekan* 15, no. 2 (2017): 187–219.

Ladurie, Emmanuel Le Roy. *Montaillou: Cathars and Catholics in a French Village, 1294–1324*, trans. Barbara Bray. London: Penguin Books, 1990.

Lattimore, Owen. *Manchuria: Cradle of Conflict*. New York: Macmillan, 1932.

———. *Studies in Frontier History: Collected Papers 1928–1958*. London: Oxford University Press, 1962.

Lai Huimin [赖惠敏]. *Qianlong Huangdi de Hebao* [乾隆皇帝的荷包, The Wallet of Emperor Qianlong]. Beijing: Zhonghua shuju, 2016.

Lefebvre, Henri. *The Production of Space*. Translated by Donald Nicholson-Smith. Oxford: Blackwell, 1991.

———. *State, Space, World. Selected Essays*. Minneapolis: University of Minnesota Press, 2009.

———. *The Urban Revolution*. Minneapolis: University of Minnesota Press, 2003.

Lee, Ching Kwan, ed. *Working in China: Ethnographies of Labor and Workplace Transformation*. London: Routledge, 2006.

Li Fengmin [李凤民]. *Shenyang Huangsi sanbai nian* [沈阳皇寺三百年, Three Hundred Years History of the Imperial Temple in Shenyang]. Shenyang: Dongbei daxue chubanshe, 2012.

Li, Gertraude Roth. "State Building before 1644." In *Cambridge History of China*, vol. 9, part 1, *The Ch'ing Dynasty to 1800*, edited by Willard J. Peterson, 9–72. Cambridge: Cambridge University Press, 2002.

Li, Ji. *At the Frontier of God's Empire: A Missionary Odyssey in Modern China*. New York: Oxford University Press, 2023.

Li Qinpu [李勤璞]. "Bailama yu Qingchao zangchuan fojiao de jianli" [白喇嘛与清朝藏传佛教的建立, Be Lama and the Establishment of Buddhism from Tibet in the Ch'ing Dynasty]. *Jindaishi yanjiusuo jikan* 30 (1999): 65–100.

———. "Bilitu langsu, Qingchu zangchuan fojiao de xianyang zhe" [毕力兔朗苏: 清初藏传佛教的显扬者 Biliktu Nangsu: The Man Who Flourished the Tibetan Buddhism in Early Qing]. *Shenyang Gugong bowuyuan yuankan*, no. 1 (2005): 46–75.

———. "Manhanmeng hebi 'da lama fenta beiwen' yizhu" [满汉蒙合璧《大喇嘛坟塔碑文》译注, Annotated Translation of the "Great Lama's Tomb and Stupa Stela" Inscribed in Manchu, Chinese, and Mongolian]. *Xibu menggu luntan*, no. 1 (2020): 3–12.

———. *Menggu zhidao: Xizang fojiao he taizong shidai de Qingchao guojia* [蒙古之道: 西藏佛教和太宗時代的清朝國家, The Mongol Path (mongyo-un törü yosu),

Tibetan Buddhism and the State Building of the Qing, 1627–1645]. PhD dissertation, Inner Mongolian University, 2007.

———. "Qingdai zhi minguo waifan menggu de simiao, minzhong yu guojia: Ruiyingsi de ge'an" [清代至民国外藩蒙古的寺庙、民众与国家——瑞应寺的个案, Monastery, Mass, and State in Qing's Outer Subordinate Mongolia: The Case of the Ruiying Temple]. In *Zhongguo bianjiangxue*, vol. 6, 52–82. Beijing: Shehuikexue wenxian chubanshe, 2006.

———. "Shengjing mahagala kaozheng." [盛京嘛哈噶喇考证, Research on the Mahākāla statue in Shengjing]. *Zangxue yanjiu luncong* 7 (1994): 95–120.

———. "Shengjing sisi manyu beiwen jiaoyi" [盛京四寺满语碑文校译, Translation of the Manchu Scripts of the Four Temples in Shengjing]. *Manyu yanjiu* 27, no. 2 (1998): 90–100.

———. "Shengjing sisi zangyu beiwen jiaoyi" [盛京四寺藏语碑文校译, Translation of the Tibetan Scripts of the Four Temples in Shengjing]. *Liaohai wenwu xuekan* 23, no. 1 (1997): 98–107.

———. "Wolu daerhan nangsu: Qingchao zangchuan fojiao kaishan kao" [斡禄打儿罕囊素：清朝藏传佛教开山考, Örlüg darhan Langsu: A Study of the Beginning of the Tibetan Buddhism in Qing dynasty]. *Mengguxue xinxi*, no. 3 (2002): 12–29; no. 4 (2002): 12–23.

———. "Xizang de fogou jingjie: Shengjing si jiao lama si ta de chijian" [西藏的佛国世界：盛京四郊喇嘛寺塔的敕建, A Tibetan Buddhist World: The Imperial Construction of the Lama Temples and Pagodas in Shengjing's Four Suburbs]. *Meishu Xuebao*, no. 2 (2012): 26–43.

Li Wei [李炜]. "Cong 'fanzhan' dao 'zhuzhan': Yi Yuyexie jingzi de 'manmeng zhi lv' wei zhongxin" [从"反战"到"主战"：以与野谢晶子的"满蒙之旅"为中心, From "Antiwar" to "Prowar": With a focus on Yasano Akiko's "Travelogue of Manchuria and Mongolia"]. *Waiguo wenxue pinglun*, no. 3 (2017): 49–65.

Liaoning sanzi [辽宁三自]. "Chaoxianwen shengjing chuban faxing" [朝鲜文圣经出版发行 The Korean Language Bible Published and Circulated], *Tianfeng*, no. 5 (1982): 29.

Liaoningsheng dang'anju [辽宁省档案局], ed. *Fengwu Liaoning*. [风物辽宁, Liaoning Sceneries]. Vols. 1, 2, and 3. Shenyang: Liaoning renmin chubanshe, 2012 and 2014.

———. *Fengtian jishi* [奉天纪事, Chronicle of Fengtian]. Shenyang: Liaoning renmin chubanshe, 2009.

Liaoningsheng dang'anguan [辽宁省档案馆] ed., *Zhongguo jindai shehui shenghuo dang'an (dongbei juan 1)* [中国近代社会生活档案（东北卷1）Archives of Modern Chinese Society and Life (Northeast China)]. Guilin: Guangxi shifan daxue chubanshe, 2005.

Liaoningsheng jiaoyuzhi bianzuan weiyuanhui bangongshi [辽宁省教育志编纂委员会办公室], ed. *Zhongxiao xuexiao jiaoyu jiaoxue gaige jishi* [中小学教育教学改革纪实, The Reforms of Elementary and Middle Schools]. Shenyang: Liaoning daxue chubanshe, 1988.

Liaoningsheng zhengxie wenshi ziliao weiyuanhui [辽宁省政协文史资料委员会], ed. *Liaoning wenshi ziliao* [辽宁文史资料, Historical Materials About Liaoning]. Vol. 22. Shenyang: Liaoning renmin chubanshe, 1988.

Liu Fang [刘放] and Wang Jian [王健]. "Shenyang: Gongren cun de bianqian" [沈阳：工人村的变迁, Shenyang: The Transformation of the Workers' Village]. *Zhongguo dangan*, no. 1 (2008): 57–59.

Liu Guoyong [刘国镛]. "Yanshousita chaichu baogao" [延寿寺拆除报告, Archaeological Report on Yanshou Temple's Dismantlement]. *Shenyang gugong bowuguan wenji, 1983–1985*, 186–89. Shenyang: Shenyang gugong bowuguan yanjiushi, 1985.

Liu Jianhui [刘建辉]. *Modu Shanghai: riben zhishiren de "jindai" tiyan* [魔都上海: 日本知识人的"近代"体验, Shanghai the Capital of Magic: The "Modern" Experiences of Japanese Intellectuals]. Translated by Gan Huijie. Nanjing: Fenghuang chubanshe, 2023.

Liu Meijun [刘玫君]. "Shenyang Xita: Zhong Han youyi de 'jianzheng zhe'" [沈阳西塔: 中韩友谊的"见证者" Shenyang Xita: The "Witness" of the Sino-Korean Friendship]. *Guoji Shangbao*, May 14, 2008, 3.

Liu Shiying [刘士英]. *Peidu jilue* [陪都纪略, An Account of the Auxiliary Capital]. Shenyang: Shenyang chubanshe, 2009.

Liu Xiaoqian [刘晓谦]. "Shenyang you youle xin xita" [沈阳又有了新西塔 Shenyang Now Has a New West Stupa], *Zhongguo xin diming*, no. 3 (1999): 26.

Liu Yonghua [刘永华]. *Cheng Yunheng de shijiu shiji: yige huizhou xiangmin de shenghuo shijie jiqi bianqian* [程允亨的十九世纪: 一个徽州乡民的生活世界及其变迁 Mr. Cheng Yongheng's Nineteenth Century: Living World of a Countryman in Huizhou and Its Transformations]. Beijing: Shenghuo, dushu, xinzhi sanlian shudian, 2024.

Lin Chun. *The Transformation of Chinese Socialism*. Durham, NC: Duke University Press, 2006.

Lu Xiaobo and Elizabeth J. Perry, eds. *Danwei: The Changing Chinese Workplace in Historical and Comparative Perspective*. Me Sharpe, 1997.

Luo Wenhua [罗文华]. *Longpao yu Jiasha* [龙袍与袈裟, The Dragon Robe and the Kasaya]. Beijing: Zijincheng chubanshe, 2005.

Lü Haiping [吕海平] and Wang He [王鹤]. *Shuangchong Quanli tixi zhiyue xia de Shenyang Jindai Jianzhu zhidu Yanjiu, 1861–1945 nian* [双重权力体系制约下的沈阳近代建筑制度研究, 1861–1945年, Studies on the Modern Architectural Institution in Shenyang Under the Regulation of the Dual-Power System]. Beijing: Zhongguo jianzhu gongye chubanshe, 2016.

Matsusaka, Yoshihisa Tak. *The Making of Japanese Manchuria, 1904–1932*. Cambridge, MA: Harvard East Asia Center, 2003.

McDonald, Kate. "Asymmetrical Integration: Lessons from a Railway Empire." *Technology and Culture* 56, no. 1 (2015): 115–49.

———. *Placing Empire: Travel and the Social Imagination in Imperial Japan*. Oakland: University of California Press, 2017.

Meisner, Maurice. *Mao's China and After: A History of the People's Republic*. 3rd ed. New York: Free Press, 1999.

Metcalf, Thomas R. *An Imperial Vision: Indian Architecture and Britain's Raj*. Berkeley: University of California Press, 1989.

Meyer, Michael. *In Manchuria: A Village Called Wasteland and the Transformation of Rural China*. New York: Bloomsbury Press, 2015.

Meyer-Fong, Tobie. *Building Culture in Early Qing Yangzhou*. Stanford: Stanford University Press, 2003.

Meyers, Jeffrey F. *The Dragon of Tiananmen: Beijing as a Sacred City*. Columbia: University of South Carolina Press, 1991.

Meyskens, Covell F. *Mao's Third Front: The Militarization of Cold War China*. Cambridge: Cambridge University Press, 2020.

Millward, James, Ruth W. Dunnell, Mark C. Elliott, and Philippe Forêt, eds. *New Qing Imperial History: The Making of Inner Asian Empire at Qing Chengde*. London: Routledge, 2004.

Mitter, Rana. *The Manchurian Myth: Nationalism, Resistance, and Collaboration in Modern China*. Berkeley: University of California Press, 2000.

Morikawa Tetsuo [森川哲雄]. "Daigen no kioku" [大元の記憶, The Memory of the Great Yuan]. *Hikaku shakai bunka* 14 (2008): 65–81.

Mullaney, Thomas. *Coming to Terms with the Nation: Ethnic Classification in Modern China*. Berkeley: University of California Press, 2011.

Munkh-Erdene, Lhamsuren. *The Taiji Government and the Rise of the Warrior State: The Formation of the Qing Imperial Constitution*. Leiden, Netherlands: Brill, 2022.

Nanjing gongxueyuan jianzhu yanjiusuo [南京工学院建筑研究所], ed. *Yang Tingbao Jianzhu Sheji Zuopin ji* [杨廷宝建筑设计作品集, Collection of Architectural Designs of Yang Tingbao]. Beijing: Jianzhu gongye chubanshe, 1983.

Naquin, Susan. *Peking: Temples and City Life, 1400–1900*. Berkeley: University of California Press, 2001.

Narangoa, Li. "The Power of Imagination: Whose Northeast and Whose Manchuria?" In "Travelling Cultures and Histories: Nation-Building and Frontier Politics in Twentieth Century China," special issue, *Inner Asia* 4, no. 1 (2002): 3–25.

Nawa Etuko [名和悦子]. *Naitō Konan no Kokkyō Ryōdoron Saikō: 20-Seiki Shotō no Shin-Kan Kokkyō Mondai "Kantō Mondai" o tōshite* [内藤湖南の国境領土論再考: 二〇世紀初頭の清韓国境問題「間島問題」を通して, Further Investigation on Naitō Konan's Theory on National Border and Territory: Through the Issue of Qing-Korean Kantō Issue in the Early 20th Century]. Tōkyō: Kyūko Shoin, 2012.

Nishizawa Yasuhiko. 西泽泰彦. "A Study of Japanese Colonial Architecture in East Asia." In *Constructing the Colonized Land: Entwined Perspectives of East Asia Around WWII*, edited by Kuroishi Izumi, 11–41. London: Routledge, 2014.

———. "Guanyu riben ren zai zhongguo dongbei diqu jianzhu huodong zhi yanjiu" [关于日本人在中国东北地区建筑活动之研究, Studies on the Japanese Architect Activities in Northeast China]. *Huazhong jianzhu*, no. 2 (1987): 90–96.

O'Dwyer, Emer. *Significant Soil: Settler Colonialism and Japan's Urban Empire in Manchuria*. Cambridge, MA: Harvard University Press, 2015.

Oidtmann, Max. *Forging the Golden Urn: The Qing Empire and the Politics of Reincarnation in Tibet*. New York: Columbia University Press, 2018.

Ōsaka Sangyō Daigaku Sangyō Kenkyūjo [大阪産業大学産業研究所]. *Kairaku to kisei: Kindai ni okeru goraku no yukue* [快楽と規制: 近代における娯楽の行方, Pleasure and Regulation: The Course of Entertainment in Modern Time]. Daitō: Ōsaka Sangyō Daigaku Sangyō Kenkyūjo, 1998.

Oshibuchi Hajime [鴛淵一]. *Manshū hikikō* [満洲碑記考, A Study of the Stelae and Inscriptions in Manchuria]. Tōkyō: Meguroshoten, 1943.

———. *Hōten to Ryōyō* [奉天と遼陽 Fengtian and Liaoyang]. Tōkyō: Fuzanbō, 1940.

Osterhammel, Jürgen. *The Transformation of the World: A Global History of the Nineteenth Century*. Translated by Patrick Camiller. Princeton, NJ: Princeton University Press, 2014.

Park, Albert L. *Building a Heaven on Earth: Religion, Activism, and Protest in Japanese Occupied Korea*. Honolulu: University of Hawai'i Press, 2015.

Park Jin-sung [박진성]. "An Hyo-jin ŭi 'Hwahaeng ilgi' yŏngu" [安孝鎮의 『華行日記』연구 A Study on Hwahaeng ilgi of An Hyo-jin]. *Changsŏgak*, no. 35 (2016): 178–210.

Park, Han Shik. "Political Culture and Ideology of the Korean Minority in China." *Korean Studies* 11 (1987): 13–32.

Park, Hyun Ok. *Two Dreams in One Bed: Empire, Social Life, and the Origins of the North Korean Revolution in Manchuria*. Durham, NC: Duke University Press, 2005.

Park, Hyung Shin. *Presbyterian Missionaries in Southern Manchuria, 1867–1931: Religion, Society, and Politics*. PhD diss., Graduate Theological Union, 2008.

Patrikeeff, Felix, and Harold Shukman. *Railways and the Russo-Japanese War: Transporting War*. London: Routledge, 2007.

Perdue, Peter C. *China Marches West: The Qing Conquest of Central Eurasia*. Cambridge, MA: Belknap Press of Harvard University Press, 2005.

Piao Meihua [朴梅花] and Zhou Yu [周宇], eds. *Xita: Shenyangshi Hepingqu Xita Jiedaozhi* [西塔: 沈阳市和平区西塔街道志, Xita: Gazetteer of Xita Subdistrict, Heping District of Shenyang]. Shenyang: Liaoning minzu chubanshe, 2014.

Pierson, John D. "The Early Liberal Thought of Tokutomi Sohō: Some Problems of Western Social Theory in Meiji Japan." *Monumenta Nipponica* 29, no. 2 (1974): 199–224.

Pratt, Mary Louise. *Imperial Eyes: Travel Writing and Transculturation*. 2nd edition. London: Routledge, 2008.

Qian Wanyue [钱婉约]. "Neiteng hunan fengtian fangshu jiqi xueshu yiyi" [内藤湖南奉天访书及其学术意义, Naitō Konan's Book Investigation in Fengtian and Its Scholarly Significance]. *Shenyang gugong bowuyuan yuankan* 6 (2008): 41–52.

Qiu Yuanyuan [邱源媛]. "Tudi, Jicheng yu Jiazu: Baqi zhidu yingxiang xia de huabei difang shehui" [土地, 继承与家族: 八旗制度影响下的华北地方社会, Land, Inheritance, and Clan: Local Society in North China under the Influence of the Eight-Banner System]. *Lishi renleixue xuekan* 15, no. 2 (2017): 17–52.

Qu Xiaofan [曲晓范]. *Jindai dongbei chengshi de lishi bianqian* [近代东北城市的历史变迁 Historical Developments of the Cities in Modern Northeast China]. Changchun: Dongbei shifan daxue chubanshe, 2001.

Rabson, Steve. "Yosano Akiko on War: To Give One's Life or Not: A Question of Which War." *Journal of the Association of Teachers of Japanese* 25, no.1 (1991): 45–74.

Ramos-Martínez, Manuel. "The Oxidation of the Documentary: The Politics of Rust in Wang Bing's Tie Xi Qu: West of the Tracks." *Third Text* 29, no. 1–2 (2015): 1–13.

Ran Guangrong [冉光荣]. *Zhongguo zangchuan fojiao siyuan* [中国藏专佛教寺院, The Tibetan Buddhist Monasteries in China]. Beijing: Zhongguo zangxue chubanshe, 1994.

Rawski, Evelyn S. *The Last Emperors: A Social History of Qing Imperial Institutions*. Berkeley: University of California Press, 1998.

Rhodes, Harry A. *History of the Korea Mission, Presbyterian Church U. S. A.* Seoul: Chosen Mission Presbyterian Church USA, 1934.

Ribeiro, Roberto M., and John W. O'Malley, eds. *Jesuit Mapmaking in China: D'anville's Nouvelle Atlas De La Chine (1737)*. Philadelphia: St. Joseph's University Press, 2014.

Robinson, David M. "The Ming Court and the Legacy of the Yuan Mongols." In David Robinson ed., *Culture, Courtiers, and Competition: The Ming Court (1368–1644)*, 365–423. Cambridge, MA: Harvard University Asia Center, 2008.

Rogaski, Ruth. *Knowing Manchuria: Environments, the Senses, and Natural Knowledge on an Asian Borderland*. Chicago: University of Chicago Press, 2022.

Rosenbaum, Arthur Lewis. "Chinese Railway Policy and the Response to Imperialism: The Peking-Mukden Railway, 1895–1911." *Ch'ing-shih wen-t'i* 2, no.1 (1969): 38–70.

Roth, Gustav. "Symbolism of the Buddhist Stupa." In *The Stupa, Its Religious, Historical and Architectural Significance*, edited by Anna Libera Dahmen-Dallapiccola, Stephanie Zingel-Avé Lallemant, 183–209. Wiesbaden, Germany: Franz Steiner, 1980.

Rowe, William T. *Crimson Rain: Seven Centuries of Violence in a Chinese County*. Stanford: Stanford University Press, 2006.

———. "China: 1300–1900." In *The Oxford Handbook of Cities in World History*, edited by Peter Clark, 310–27. Oxford: Oxford University Press, 2016.

———. *Hankow: Conflict and Community in a Chinese City, 1796–1895*. Stanford: Stanford University Press, 1989.

Ruoff, Kenneth. "Japanese Tourism to Mukden, Nanjing, and Qufu, 1938–1943." *Japan Review*, no. 27 (2014): 171–200.

Saaler, Sven, and Christopher W. A. Szpilman, eds. *Pan-Asianism: A Documentary History*. Vol. 1, *1850–1920*. Lanham, MD: Rowman & Littelfield, 2011.

Sachsenmaier, Dominic. *Global Entanglements of a Man Who Never Traveled: A Seventeenth-Century Chinese Christian and His Conflicted Worlds*. New York: Columbia University Press, 2018.

Schmid, Andre. "Historicizing North Korea: State Socialism, Population Mobility, and Cold War Historiography." *American Historical Review* 123, no. 2 (2018): 439–62.

Shibata Mikio [柴田幹夫]. *Xingya yangfo: Dagu guangrui yu xi benyuansi de haiwai shiye* [興亞揚佛: 大谷光瑞與西本願寺的海外事業, A Study of Ōtani Kōzui: Activities in Asia]. Translated by Wang Ding et al. Xinbei: Boyang wenhua, 2017.

Schivelbusch, Wolfgang. *The Railway Journey: The Industrialization of Time and Space in the Nineteenth Century*. Oakland: University of California Press, 2014.

Schorkowitz, Dittmar, and Ning Chia eds., *Managing Frontiers in Qing China, The Lifanyuan and Libu Revisited*. Leiden, Netherlands: Brill, 2017.

Schwieger, Peter. *The Dalai Lama and the Emperor of China: A Political History of the Tibetan Institution of Reincarnation*. New York: Columbia University Press, 2015.

Sewell, Bill. *Constructing Empire: The Japanese in Changchun, 1905–45*. Vancouver: University of British Columbia Press, 2019.

———. "Reconsidering the Modern in Japanese History: Modernity in the Service of the Prewar Japanese Empire." *Japan Review*, no. 16 (2004): 213–58.

Shao, Dan. *Remote Homeland, Recovered Borderland: Manchus, Manchoukuo, and Manchuria, 1907-1985*, University of Hawaii Press, 2011.

Shen Shangming [沈尚明] and Zhang Aiyang [张艾阳]. "'Hanliu' gei Shenyang dailai le shenme" ["韩流"给沈阳带来了什么, What Did the "Korean Wave" Bring to Shenyang]. *Liaoning Ribao*, August 26, 2003, 1.

Shen Weirong [沈卫荣]. *Xiangxiang Xizang: Kuawenhua shiye zhongde heshang, huofo, lama he mijiao* [想象西藏: 跨文化视野中的和尚、活佛、喇嘛和密教, Imaging Tibet: monk, tulku, lama and Tantric Buddhism from a cross-cultural perspective]. Beijing: Beijing shifan daxue chubanshe, 2015.

———. *Dayuanshi he Xinqingshi: Yi yuandai he qingdai xizang he zangchuanfojiao yanjiu wei zhongxin* [大元史和新清史: 以元代和清代西藏和藏传佛教研究为中心, "The Great Yuan History" and "The New Qing History": Studies on Tibet and Tibetan Buddhism During the Yuan and Qing Dynasties]. Shanghai: Shanghai guji chubanshe, 2019.

Shenyang tujing [沈阳图景]. "Wo jianguo huangsi lama tiaota" [我见过皇寺喇嘛跳塔, I Have Seen Tiaota by the Lamas at the Imperial Temple]. *The Paper*, August 20, 2018. https://www.thepaper.cn/newsDetail_forward_2363503.

Shenyang wanbao bianjibu [沈阳晚报编辑部]. "Xita, ni de xiangyi nali lai" [西塔，你的香意哪里来, Xita, Where Does Your Fragrant Come From]. *Shenyang wanbao*, August 24, 2012.

Shenyangshi zongjiao shiwuju [沈阳市宗教事务局], ed. *Shenyang Zongjiao* [沈阳宗教 Religions in Shenyang]. Shenyang: Shenyang chubanshe, 2004.

Shi Miaozhou [释妙舟]. *Mengzhang fojiaoshi* [蒙藏佛教史, History of Mongolian-Tibetan Buddhism]. Yangzhou: Guangling Shushe, 2009.

Shih Chih-Yu. "Assimilation Through Ethnicity: China's Ethnic Language Policy in Yunnan and Shenyang." *International Journal on Minority and Group Rights* 7, no. 3 (2000): 189–206.

———. *Negotiating Ethnicity in China: Citizenship as a Response to the State*. Routledge, 2002.

Shirasu Jōshin [白須淨眞]. *Wasurerareta Meiji no tankenka Watanabe Tesshin* [忘れられた明治の探険家渡辺哲信, Watanabe Tesshin: A Forgotten Explorer in the Meiji Period]. Tōkyō: Chūō Kōronsha, 1992.

Sin Ch'un-ho [신춘호]. "Simyang K'oriataun 'Sŏt'ap' kwa Hangoku munhwa" [심양 코리아타운 '서탑' 과 한국문화, Shenyang Korean-town 'Xita' and Korean Culture in China]. *Chaeoe Hanin Yŏngu* 21 (2011): 173–233.

Singaravélou, Pierre. *Wanguo Tianjin: Quanqiuhua lishi de linglei shijiao* [万国天津： 全球化历史的另类视角, Tianjin Cosmopolis: Une autre histoire de la mondialisation]. Translated by Guo Ke. Beijing: Shangwu yinshuguan, 2021.

Skinner, G. William, ed. *The City in Late Imperial China*. Stanford: Stanford University Press, 1977.

Smith, Valene L., ed. *Hosts and Guests: The Anthropology of Tourism*. Philadelphia: University of Pennsylvania Press, 2012.

Song Anning [宋安宁]. "Chūtōkyōin no man sen shisatsu ryokō" [中等教員の満鮮視察旅行, Secondary School Teachers' Observatory Travels to Manchuria and Korea]. *Shakai shisutemu kenkyū*, no. 30 (2015): 55–80.

Song, Nianshen [宋念申]. *Making Borders in Modern East Asia: The Tumen River Demarcation, 1881–1919*. Cambridge: Cambridge University Press, 2018.

———. "Diejia de dongya bianjiang jingshenshi" [叠加的东亚边疆精神史, The Overlapped Spiritual History of an East Asian Frontier]. In *Xinshixue*, vol. 13,115–36. Beijing: Shehuikexue wenxian chubanshe, 2020.

———. "'Those Ridiculous Monks': The Failed Encounter Between Korea and Tibetan Buddhism in Qing Mukden." *Inner Asia* 25 (2023): 206–26.

Sonoda Kazuki [園田一龜]. *Dattar hyōryūki* [韃靼漂流記, Record of Castaways in Tartary]. Tōkyō: Heibonsha, 1991.

Summers, William C. *The Great Manchurian Plague of 1910–1911. The Geopolitics of an Epidemic Disease*. New Haven, CT: Yale University Press, 2012.

Sun Hongjin [孙鸿金]. *Jindai Shenyang Chengshi Fazhan Yanjiu, 1898–1945* [近代沈阳城市发展研究, The Research on the Urban Development of Modern Shenyang, 1898–1945]. Changchun: Jilin daxue chubanshe, 2015.

Sun Qiantong [孙潜彤]. "'Hanliu' gei Shenyang chuilai le shenme" ["韩流"给沈阳吹来了什么 What Did the "Korean Wave" Blow to Shenyang]. *Jingji Ribao*, July 29, 2003.

Sun Quan [孙全]. "Xita shangyejie jidai 'bianshen shengji' [西塔商业街亟待"变身升级," The Xita Commerical Street Needs to Be "Transformed and Upgrated"]. *Shenyang Ribao*, April 7, 2008, 9.

Tabata, Hisao [田畑久夫]. "Torii Ryūzō no manmō chōsa: Chōsa kiroku no bunseki kara" [鳥居龍蔵の満蒙調査: 調査記録の分析から, An Analytic Study on Torii Ryūzō's Expedition Reports of Manchuria and Mongolia]. *Hikaku minzoku kenkyū* 12 (1995): 63–89.

Tahara Kaname [太原要]. *Manshū no tabi* [満洲の旅, Traveling Manchuria]. Shin Kyō: Manchiyuriyadērīniyūsu, 1940.

Tan Lixin [谭力新] and Bi Shichun [毕诗春]. "Jianguan loudong: Jinrong shuoshu de jile tiantang" [监管漏洞: 金融硕鼠的极乐天堂, Regulation Loopholes: The Paradise for Financial Criminals]. *Zhonghua gongshang shibao*, March 23, 2005.

Tao, Demin [陶德民]. "Neiteng hunan 1905nian fengtian de wenxian diaocha" [内藤湖南1905年奉天的文献调查, The Document Investigation in 1905 Fengtian by Naitō Konan]. In *Jindai riben xuezhe duihua xueshu diaocha yu yanjiu*, edited by Zhang Mingjie, 233–45. Shanghai: Shanghai jiaotong daxue chubanshe, 2022.

Temole [忒莫勒]. "Weiman lamajiao zongtuan chengli shimo" [伪满喇嘛教宗团成立始末, Context of the Founding of the Order of Lamaism in the Puppet Manchukuo]. *Neimenggu shehuikexue (wenshizhe ban)*, no. 10 (1995): 55–58.

Tian Zhi [田治] and Li Gang [李刚]. "Chanchu xiqian de wenchuang" [铲除洗钱的温床 Eradicating the Hotbed for Money Laundering]. *Jinrong shibao*, January 17, 2006, 9.

Tong Yue [佟悦]. *Qingdai peidu Shenyang* [清代陪都沈阳, Shenyang: The Auxiliary Capital of the Qing Dynasty]. Shenyang: Wanjuan chuban gongsi, 2010.

Tsai Wei-chieh [蔡伟杰]. "Ju guozhong yi biguo: Dashabi yu qingdai yimin waimenggu zhi hanren jiqi houyi de mengguhua, 1768–1830" [居国中以避国: 大沙毕与清代移民外蒙古之汉人及其后裔的蒙古化, Evading the State within the State: The Great Shabi and Mongolization of Han Chinese Settlers and Their Descendants in Qing Outer Mongolia, 1768–1830]. *Lishirenleixue xuekan* 15, no. 2 (2017): 129–67.

Tuan, Yi-Fu. "Humanistic Geography." *Annals of the Association of American Geographers* 66, no. 2 (1976): 266–76.

Tucci, Giuseppe. *Stupa: Art, Architectonics and Symbolism*. New Delhi: Aditya Prakashan, 1988.

Tuttle, Gray. *Tibetan Buddhists in the Making of Modern China*. New York: Columbia University Press, 2005.

Usui Kameo [臼井亀雄]. *Hirakeyuku manshū* [開けゆく満洲, Manchuria Opened Up]. Tōkyō: Nittō Shoin, 1933.

Wada Hidetoshi [和田秀寿]. "Otani tankentai no ichisokumen: Nan'yo shoto o chosa shita Yoshinobu Tatsue no jiseki o chushin to shite" [大谷探検隊の一側面: 南洋諸島を調査した龍江義信の事績を中心として, A Study on an Aspect of Kōzui OTANI's Expeditions: Mainly on the Achievement of Yoshinobu Tatsue Who Investigated the South Sea Islands]. *Bukkyōgaku kenkyū*, no. 70 (2014): 37–71.

Walder, Andrew G. *China Under Mao: A Revolution Derailed*. Cambridge, MA: Harvard University Press, 2015.

———. *Communist Neo-Traditionalism: Work and Authority in Chinese Industry*. Berkeley: University of California Press, 1986.

Wakamatsu Hiroshi [若松宽]. "Xiletu kulun lama zhuan huidian chutan" [《锡勒图库伦喇嘛传汇典》初探, An Initial Investigation of the "Collective Bibliographies of the Lamas in Xiletu Hure"]. *Mengguxue xinxi*, no. 4 (1999): 17–23.

Wang, Di. *Street Culture in Chengdu: Public Space, Urban Commoners, and Local Politics, 1870–1930*. Stanford University Press, 2018.

———. *The Teahouse: Small Business, Everyday Culture, and Public Politics in Chengdu, 1900–1950*. Stanford: Stanford University Press, 2008.

Wang He [王鹤] and Lü Haiping [吕海平]. *Jindai Shenyang Chengshi Xingtai Yanjiu* [近代沈阳城市形态研究, A Research on Urban Morphological Transformation of Shenyang in Modern Times]. Beijing: Zhongguo jianzhu gongye chubanshe, 2015.

Wang Jiechun [王洁纯], ed. *Shenyang Zongjiao* [沈阳宗教 Religions in Shenyang]. Shenyang: Shenyang chubanshe, 2004,

Wang Mingke [王明珂]. "Shui de lishi: Zizhuan, zhuanji yu koushu lishi de shehui jiyi benzhi" [谁的历史：自传、传记与口述历史的社会记忆本质, Who's History: The Essence of Social Memory of Autobiography, Biography, and Oral History]. In *Koushushi duben*, edited by Ding Yizhuang and Wang Run, 61–83. Beijing: Beijing daxue chubanshe, 2011.

Wang Mingqi. [王明琦]. *Liaohai Wenwu Kaobian* [辽海文物考辨, Studies on Ancient Relics in Liaoning]. Shenyang: Liaoning daxue chubanshe, 2000.

Wang Maosheng [王茂生]. *Cong Shengjing dao Shenyang: Chengshi fazhan yu kongjian xingtai yanjiu* [从盛京到沈阳——城市发展与空间形态研究, From Mukden to Shenyang: A Study on Urban Development and Spacial Forms]. Beijing: Zhongguo jianzhu gongye chubanshe, 2010.

Wang, Shengyuan [王升远]. *Wenhua zhimin yu dushi kongjian: Qinhua zhanzheng shiqi riben wenhuaren de beijing tiyan* [文化殖民与都市空间：侵华战争时期日本文化人的"北京体验," Cultural Colonialism and Urban Space: The Beijing Experience of Japanese Intellectuals During the War of Invading China]. Beijing: Shenghuo, dushu, xinzhi sanlian shudian, 2017.

Wang Xiangyu [王湘云]. "Qingchao huangshi, zhangjia huofo yu lama simiao" [清朝皇室，章嘉活佛与喇嘛寺庙, The Qing royal family, the Changkya Khutuktu, and the Lama Temples]. *Xizang Yanjiu*, no. 2 (1995): 114–19.

———. "Tibetan Buddhism at the Court of Qing: The Life and Work of ICang-skya Rol-pa'i-rdo-rje (1717–86)." PhD diss., Harvard University, 1995.

Wang, Xiangyuan [王向远]. "Bi bu dui he qin hua zhan zheng: Dui ri ben qin hua wen xue de yan jiu yu pi pan" ["笔部队"和侵华战争：对日本侵华文学的研究与批判, "Pen Troops" and the War of Invading China: Studies and Criticism of Japanese Literature on Invading China]. Beijing: Kunlun chubanshe, 2015.

Wang Yao. "The Cult of Mahākāla and a Temple in Beijing." *Journal of Chinese Religions* 22, no. 1 (1994): 117–26.

Wang Yan [王研]. "'Zanzhuzheng' shuo quxiao jiu quxiao le" ["暂住证"说取消就取消了, The Temporary Resident Permit Was Canceled]. *Liaoning Ribao*, July 23, 2003, 4.

Wang Yuanchong. *Remaking the Chinese Empire: Manchu-Korean Relations, 1616–1911*. Ithaca, NY: Cornell University Press, 2018.

Wang Yuanzhou [王元周]. "1914 nian qianhou Beijing hanren huodong yu liuxue de xingqi." [1914年前后北京韩人活动与留学的兴起, The Activities of the Korean in Beijing and the Rise of Oversea Studies around 1914]. *Xuzhou gongcheng xueyuan xuebao (shehui kexue ban)* 13, no. 4 (2016): 28–34.

Wei Chen [魏晨]. "Kōsaku suru manazashi, sogo suru manshū yume" [交錯するまなざし、齟齬する満洲夢—『綴方日本』と『綴方満洲』の比較から見る日満関係のポリティクス, Discrepancy of Manchuria Dream Between Japan and Manchukuo: A Comparative Study of *Tsudurikata Japan* and *Tsudurikata Manchu*]. *Nagoyadaigaku Jinbungaku fōramu*, no. 1 (2018): 121-34.

Wei Ping [伟萍]. "Shenyang xita jie: Zuori penghuqu, jintian 'beifang xiao hancheng" [沈阳西塔街: 昨日棚户区, 今天"北方小汉城," The Xita Street of Shengyang: A Ghetto Area Yesterday, a "Little Seoul in the North" Today]. *Chengxiang jianshe*, no. 7 (2007): 76–77.

Weisenfeld, Gennifer. *Imaging Disaster: Tokyo and the Visual Culture of Japan's Great Earthquake of 1923*. Berkeley: University of California Press, 2012.

Whiteman, Steven. *Where Dragon Veins Meet: The Kangxi Emperor and His Estate at Rehe*. Seattle: University of Washington Press, 2020.

Wolmar, Christian. *To the Edge of the World: The Story of the Trans-Siberian Express, the World's Greatest Railroad*. New York: PublicAffairs, 2016.

Wu, Lan. *Common Ground: Tibetan Buddhist Expansion and Qing China's Inner Asia*. New York: Columbia University Press, 2022

Wu Tingyu [乌廷玉], Zhang Yunqiao [张云樵], and Zhang Zhanbin [张占斌]. *Dong-beitudi guanxishi yanjiu* [东北土地关系史研究, The Study on the History of Land Relations in Northeast China]. Jilin: Jilin wenshi chubanshe, 1990.

Xia Ying [夏莹]. *Shenyang Xita Diqu Chaohan Shuangyu Zhuangkuang de Shehui Yuy-anxue Kaocha* [沈阳西塔地区朝汉双语状况的社会语言学考察, Sociolinguistic Research of Xita District of Shenyang Korean and Chinese Bilingual Phenomenon]. Master's thesis, Shenyang Normal University, 2011.

Xiao Chunping [肖春苹] and Cong Banglin [丛邦林]. "Hepingqu jiji fazhan quanguo kechixu fazhan shiyanqu" [和平区积极发展全国可持续发展实验区, The Heping District Proactively Develops a Test Ground for National Sustainable Development]. *Shenyang Ribao*, July 20, 2010, A03.

Xiao Ping [肖平] and Xu Bing [徐冰]. "Riben ji xifang xuezhe guanyu riben minzu qi-yuan de yanjiu" [日本及西方学者关于日本民族起源的研究, The Studies about the Origin of Japanese Nation by Japanese and Western Scholars]. *Waiguo wenti yanjiu* 1 (1994): 46–90.

Xie Wen [谢雯]. "Lishi shehuixue shijiao xia de dongbei gongye danweizhi shehui de bi-anqian" [历史社会学视角下的东北工业单位制社会的变迁, The Industrial Work-Unit Society in Northeast China and Its Transformation: A Historical Sociological Examination]. *Kai Fang Shi Dai*, no. 6 (2019): 25–44.

Xu Hao [徐浩]. *18 shiji de zhongguo yu shijie: Nongmin juan* [18世纪的中国与世界: 农民卷China and the World in the Eighteenth Century: Peasants]. Shenyang: Liaohai chubanshe, 1999.

Yan, Yunxiang. *Private Life under Socialism: Love, Intimacy, and Family Change in a Chi-nese Village, 1949–1999*. Stanford: Stanford University Press, 2003.

Yan Zinan [颜子楠]. "Kunlei youxi: wenxue jizhi yu Qianlong yuzhishi de shengcheng" [傀儡游戏:文学机制与乾隆御制诗的生成 The Game of Puppetry: The Literary Mechanisms and the Poetry Production of Emperor Qianlong]. *Qinghua Daxue Xue-bao (zhexue shehui kexue ban)*, vol. 39, no. 6 (2024): 77–88.

Yang Zhiqiang [杨志强] and Luo Ting [罗婷]. "20 shiji chu niaoju longzang zai zhong-guo xinan diqu de renleixue diaocha jiqi yingxiang" [20世纪初鸟居龙藏在中国西南地区的人类学调查及其影响, The Anthropological Survey of Torii Ryūzō in Early Twentieth Century Southwest China and Its Influence]. *Minzu yanjiu*, no. 6 (2016): 51–60.

Yao Yongchao [姚永超]. *Zhongguo jindai jingji dili*. Vol. 9, *Dongbei jindai jingji dili* [中国近代经济地理 第九卷 东北近代经济地理, Modern Economic Geography of China. Vol. 9, Modern Economic Geography of Northeast]. Shanghai: Huadong shifan daxue chubanshe, 2015.

Ye Honglin [叶紘麟]. *Gensui diguo de jiaobu: defu sufeng renshi zhongguo de shijiao* [跟随帝国的脚步: 德富苏峰认识中国的视角, Following the Footsteps of Empire: Tokutomi Sohō's Perspective of China]. Taipei: Guoli Taiwan daxue zhengzhi xuexi Zhongguo dalu ji liang'an guanxi jiaoxue yu yanjiu zhongxin, 2009.

Yi Hun-gu [李勲求]. *Manju wa Chosŏnin* [滿洲와朝鮮人, Manchuria and the Korean People]. P'yŏngyang: Sungsil Chŏnmun Hakkyo Kyŏngjehak Yŏn'gusil, 1932.

Yi Yun-t'ae [이윤태]. "Chungguk che 1 ho yŏja moksa—O Aeŭn moksa" [중국 제1호 여자 목사—오애은 목사, The No.1 Female Pastor in China—Pastor Wu Aien]. Chemi kosin ch'onghoe. Accessed September 28, 2022. http://kosinusa.org/_chboard/bbs/board.php?bo_table=m2_5&wr_id=46385&page=4.

Yoon, Sharon J. *The Cost of Belonging: An Ethnography of Solidarity and Mobility in Beijing's Koreatown.* Oxford: Oxford University Press, 2021.

Yoon, Tae-Jin, and Dal Yong Jin, eds. *The Korean Wave: Evolution, Fandom, and Transnationality.* Lanham, MD: Lexington Books, 2017.

Young, Louise. *Japan's Total Empire: Manchuria and the Culture of Wartime Imperialism.* Berkeley: University of California Press, 1999.

Yue Yongyi [岳永逸]. "Zabadier, zhongguo dushi minsuxue de yizhong fangfa" ["杂巴地儿": 中国都市民俗学的一种方法, Zabadir, As a Method of Urban Folklore in China]. *Minsu yanjiu* 3, no. 145 (2019): 18–30.

Zhang Chunzhi [张春植]. "Chaoxianzu minzu shenfen rentong de wenxue jiangou" [朝鲜族民族身份认同的文学建构, The Construction of Ethnic Identity of the Korean-Chinese Through Literature]. *Yanbian daxue xuebao (shehui kexue ban)* 49, no. 3 (2016): 64–71.

Zhang Xiaoning [张晓宁]. "Yuxieye jingzi de zhanzheng guan" [与谢野晶子的战争观, Yosano Akiko's War Attitude]. *Waiguo wenxue yanjiu*, no. 3 (2009) 13–18.

Zhang Yuxin [张羽新]. *Qingzhengfu yu lamajiao* [清政府与喇嘛教, The Qing Government and Lamaism]. Lhasa: Xizang remin chubanshe, 1988.

Zhao, Hai. "Manchurian Atlas: Competitive Geopolitics, Planned Industrialization, and the Rise of Heavy Industrial State in Northeast China, 1918–1954." PhD diss., University of Chicago, 2015.

Zhao Yuntian [赵云田]. "Qingdai qianqi liyong lamajiao zhengce de xingcheng he yanbian" [清代前期利用喇嘛教的形成和演变, The Formation and Development of the Early Qing's Policy to Utilize Lamaism]. *Xizang Minzu Xueyuan Xuebao*, no. 1 (1984): 63–76.

Zhao Zhiqiang [赵志强]. "Beita falunsi yu mengguzu manzu xibozu guanxi shulun" [北塔法轮寺与蒙古族满族锡伯族关系述论, On the Relations between North Pagoda Falun Temple and Ethnic Manchu, Mongol, and Sibe]. *Manzu yanjiu*, no. 3 (1991): 79–86.

Zhengxie Shenyangshi weiyuanhui wenshi ziliao yanjiu weiyuanhui [政协沈阳市委员会文史资料研究委员会], ed. *Shenyang wenshi ziliao* [沈阳文史资料, Historical Materials About Shenyang]. Vols. 5 and 12. Shenyang: Zhengxie Shenyangshi weiyuanhui wenshi ziliao yanjiu weiyuanhui, 1984, 1986.

Zhengxie Shenyangshi Hepingqu weiyuanhui. [政协沈阳市和平区委员会], ed. *Laobeishi biannian jishi* [老北市编年记事, A Chronicle of Old Northern Market]. Shenyang: Liaoning daxue chubanshe, 2014.

———. *Heping de lisheng* [和平的历程, The Journey of Heping District]. Vols. 1, 2, and 3. Shenyang: Zhengxie Hepingqu weiyuanhui, 2005, 2007, and 2009.

———. *Hepingqu diming gailan* [和平区地名概览, Review of the Place Names in Heping District]. Hohhot: Yuanfang chubanshe, 2013.

———. *Heping lao jianzhu* [和平老建筑, Old Buildings in Heping District]. Shenyang: Zhengxie Shenyangshi Hepingqu weiyuanhui, 2015.

———. *Heping laozihao* [和平老字号, Old Brands in Heping District]. Shenyang: Zhengxie Shenyangshi Hepingqu weiyuanhui, 2016.

Zhonggong Hepingquwei dangshiban [中共和平区委党史办], ed. *Heping Dashiji* [和平大事记, Chronicle of Heping District]. Zhonggong Shenyangshi Hepingquwei dangshi ziliao zhengji bangongshi, 1996.

Zhongguo renmin zhengzhi xieshang huiyi Liaoningsheng weiyuanhui wenshi ziliao weiyuanhui [中国人民政治协商会议辽宁省委员会文史资料委员会], ed. *Zabadi jiuyi* [杂巴地旧忆, Memory of the "Zabadi"]. Shenyang: Liaoning remin chubanshe, 1992.

———. *Liaoning wenshi ziliao* [辽宁文史资料 第十二辑, Historical Materials of Liaoning]. Vol. 12. Shenyang: Liaoning renmin chubanshe, 1985.

Zhou Jing [周晶] and Li Tian [李天]. *Xueshan Zhong de mantuluo: Zangchuan fojiao daxing fota yanjiu* [雪山中的曼荼罗：藏传佛教大型佛塔研究, Mandala in the Snowy Mountains: Studies on the Giant Stupas of Tibetan Buddhism]. Beijing: Zhongguo jianzhu gongye chubanshe, 2016.

Zhou Yue [周悦]. "Neiteng hunan yu manmeng wenshi" [内藤湖南与满蒙文史, Naitō Konan and Histories of Manchuria and Mongolia]. In *Jindai riben xuezhe duihua xueshu diaocha yu yanjiu*, edited by Zhang Mingjie, 246–55. Shanghai: Shanghai jiaotong daxue chubanshe, 2022.

Zhou, Xueguang. *The State and Life Chances in Urban China: Redistribution and Stratification, 1949–1994*. Cambridge: Cambridge University Press, 2004.

INDEX

www.ingramcontent.com/pod-product-compliance
Lightning Source LLC
Chambersburg PA
CBHW051342280526
45784CB00007B/2782